THE NON-WESTERN JESUS

Cross Cultural Theologies

Series Editors: Jione Havea and Clive Pearson, both at United Theological College, Sydney, and Charles Sturt University, Australia, and Anthony G. Reddie, Queen's Foundation for Ecumenical Theological Education, Birmingham

It looks at the public nature of faith in complex, multicultural, multireligious societies, and compares how diverse.

It moves beyond the crossing of cultures in a narrow diasporic sense. It entertains perspectives that arise out of generational criticism, gender, sexual orientation, and the relationship of film to theology. It explores the sometimes competing rhetoric of multiculturalism and cross-culturalism and demonstrates a concern for the intersection of globalization and how those global flows of peoples and ideas are received and interpreted in localized settings. The series seeks to make use of a range of disciplines including the study of cross-cultural liturgy, travel, the practice of ministry and worship in multi-ethnic locations and how theologies that have arisen in one part of the world have migrated to a new location. It looks at the public nature of faith in complex, multicultural, multireligious societies, and compares how diverse faiths and their theologies have responded to the same issues.

The series welcomes contributions by scholars from around the world. It will include both single authored and multi-authored volumes.

Published

Global Civilization
Leonardo Boff

Dramatizing Theologies: A Participative Approach to Black God-Talk
Anthony G. Reddie

Art as Theology: The Religious Transformation of Art from the Postmodern to the Medieval
Andreas Andreopoulos

Black Theology in Britain: A Reader
Edited by Michael N. Jagessar and Anthony G. Reddie

Bibles and Baedekers: Tourism, Travel, Exile and God
Michael Grimshaw

Home Away from Home: The Caribbean Diasporan Church in the Black Atlantic Tradition
Delroy A. Reid-Salmon

Working Against the Grain: Black Theology in the 21st Century
Anthony G. Reddie

Forthcoming

Another World is Possible: Spiritualities and Religions of Global Darker Peoples
Edited by Dwight N. Hopkins and Marjorie Lewis

THE NON-WESTERN JESUS

Jesus as *Bodhisattva, Avatara, Guru,*
Prophet, Ancestor or Healer?

Martien E. Brinkman
Translated by Henry and Lucy Jansen

Routledge
Taylor & Francis Group

ONDON AND NEW YORK

First published in Dutch as *De niet-Westerse Jezus: Jezus als bodhisattva, avatara, goeroe, profeet, voorouder of genezer?* by Uitgeverij Meinema 2007.

This edition first published in English 2009 by Equinox Publishing Ltd, an imprint of Acumen

Published 2014 by Routledge
2 Park Square, Milton Park, Abingdon, Oxon OX14 4RN
711 Third Avenue, New York, NY 10017, USA

Routledge is an imprint of the Taylor & Francis Group, an informa business

© Uitgeverij Meinema 2007
This translation © Equinox Publishing Ltd 2009

The translation of this book was sponsored by the Stichting Van Eijkfonds, the C.J. de Vogelstichting, the Stichting Zonneweelde, the Maatschappij van Welstand and the Van Coeverden Adriani Stichting.

British Library Cataloguing-in-Publication Data

A catalogue record for this book is available from the British Library.
Library of Congress Cataloging-in-Publication Data
Brinkman, M. E., 1950-
 [Niet-Westerse Jezus. English]
 The non-western Jesus : Jesus as Bodhisattva, Avatara, Guru, Prophet, Ancestor, or Healer / Martien E. Brinkman ; translated by Henry and Lucy Jansen.
  p. cm.
 Includes bibliographical references and index.
 ISBN 978-1-84553-397-7 (hb) — ISBN 978-1-84553-398-4 (pbk.) 1.
Jesus Christ—Miscellanea. I. Title.
 BT304.94.B7513 2009
 232.09—dc22
                                   2008008692
ISBN-13   978 1 84553 397 7 (hardback)
          978 1 84553 398 4 (paperback)

Typeset by S.J.I. Services, New Delhi

Contents

Acknowledgments

This study was written during a sabbatical in the academic year 2005–2006. For six weeks, as of 1 September 2005, I was able to use the office of the collection specialist Mr. Peter van Rijn of the Utrecht Institute, now called the Centre for Intercultural Theology (Non-Western Theology, Interreligious Dialogue, Missiology and Ecumenics) (Centre IIMO), where I was a staff member from 1987 to 2000. In that period I saw with my own eyes what a wonderful collection had been built up there in the area of non-Western theology. With Peter van Rijn's frequent help I was able to make optimal use of this collection.

From mid-October to mid-December 2005 I was a guest at Ormond College, part of the University of Melbourne (Australia). I am grateful to my colleague there, Prof. C. Mostert, for his help, the director of the theological faculty, Prof. Randall Prior, and the professor of ecumenical theology, Robert Gribben, for the warm hospitality they showed me. Because of the excellent accommodations and library material (especially in the area of Asian theology), I could live there like a monk whose only concern was to read continually.

From mid-January to mid-April 2006 I was a guest at the Beijers Naudé Centre, associated with the theological faculty of the University of Stellenbosch (South Africa). This validated the contacts built up in the past decade through the International Reformed Theological Institute (IRTI) at the VU University within the SAVUSA project (Cooperation between the VU and South Africa). I would like to thank the head of the department of systematic theology, Prof. Niko Koopman, for his warm reception, the splendid accommodations for working within the institute and the opportunity to present the presuppositions of my manuscript to the staff and a wide, now mainly black, student audience in a number of lectures. I am grateful to Prof. Ernst Conradie of the University of the Western Cape (Capetown) for the same opportunity. In comparison with a previous visit to this university in 1988, it was a pleasant experience to see how the theologians have been able to expand their activities in a university setting that I consider one of the most exciting in South Africa.

The broad geographical terrain that this study covers makes it impossible to describe each area in detail and expertly. For that reason I asked various experts on site and in those areas to read the text critically. For Africa, this was the anthropologist and theologian Dr. G. van 't Spijker, assistant professor for years in Rwanda. The Islamologist and theologian Prof. Dr.

K. Steenbrink, who has worked for many years as an assistant professor in Yogyakarta, read the section on Indonesia. Prof. Dr. H. M. Vroom, who is closely involved in Buddhist–Christian dialogue as a philosopher of religion, read the section on Japanese Buddhism especially. My former fellow student and friend, Dr. J. P. Schouten, a scholar in religious studies, who because of his dissertation and later publications can be considered an expert in Bhakti Hinduism, read the section on India. I am grateful to all four for the time they were willing to devote to my manuscript and for their fruitful suggestions for improvement or supplementation.

I dedicate this book to my spouse, Hannie Dorr, who in recent years especially was often prepared in the most literal sense to be my travelling companion. Our mutual exchange of experiences has made that travel not only more meaningful but also considerably more pleasant.

Preface

When I asked an Indian student some years ago why he wanted to write a paper on the "Indian Jesus," he answered: "Because I'm afraid." When I inquired further, he told me that he lived in an area in which Muslims and Christians had suffered a great deal at the hands of the so-called *Hindutva* movement, a nationalistic Hindu movement whose motto is: "India for the Hindus." He recounted bloody attacks on Christians and Muslims. He wanted to equip himself for dialogue with Hindus by means of his paper and show that there was also room for Jesus within Hinduism. Thus, he wanted to indicate, in the most literal sense, that there should also be room for him and his fellow Christians.

It cannot be made any clearer than this example that something is at stake in the question of *inculturation*, in the question of how a religion is related to a certain culture. The issue here is not only the very concrete question of living space; it is also a matter of *identity*, of the self-image, of non-Western Christians. And then the question becomes very important. I can still hear a Korean doctoral student saying: "Western theologians used to have us study primarily their own theology. Now the same theologians are telling us that we should not study their own theology in particular (any more). They are still telling us what we should do." The *inculturation* question is therefore also a *power* question.

From 1993 to 1998, during my (part-time) position as professor of "ecumenism" at the theological faculty of the Catholic University of Louvain in Belgium, for the first time I was confronted directly with the questions of African and Asian students in the English-speaking department. At that time I began studying non-Western theology systematically and have been gathering material for this book since 1999. In the years 2000–2002, my former student assistant, Friso Mout, made a primary inventory of the material available in the Netherlands. My inaugural lecture at the Vrije Universiteit (VU University), Amsterdam in 2000 on *Verandering van geloofsinzicht: Oecumenische ontwikkelingen in Noord en Zuid* (Change in the Insight of Faith: Ecumenical Developments in North and South) was a first, methodological finger exercise.[1]

The topic of this study built on the content of the above-mentioned lecture but takes more explicitly into account the fact that contemporary non-Western theology can no longer be imagined without interreligious dialogue. For many Christians, especially in Asia, it is literally a matter of a dialogue on the faith of their neighbours and that dialogue also leaves its traces on their own faith. Contemporary Asian Christian theology cannot be understood without a fundamental knowledge of Asian religions. That is an insight that I became aware of especially since 2000 within the research group "Encounters of Traditions" at the VU University under the guidance of my colleague Henk Vroom.

I cannot, of course, jump over my own Western shadow. Therefore, it is a *Western study* on *non-Western theology*, written primarily for a *Western readership*. If the effect of this study is that Western readers discover how *Western* their own theology is, I will be more than satisfied. That is, in any case, one of the most important experiences that I myself have had while writing this book. I have become aware more than ever that the Christian images and concepts through which I myself have been formed are not self-evident to the majority of Christians living in the southern hemisphere. For them, other images with which I am not familiar are often more meaningful.

In the last three decades there has been a strong missiological tradition in Dutch theology that sought to pay attention to the great changes that are occurring in world Christianity. On the Roman Catholic side, this tradition was represented by – if I limit myself to full professors – A. Camps, R. G. van Rossum, J. van Nieuwenhove and K. Steenbrink, and on the Protestant side by L. A. Hoedemaker, T. Witvliet, J. A. P. Jongeneel, A. Wessels, P. Holtrop and M. R. Spindler. Because of them, Dutch missiology has gained a certain reputation worldwide through their English publications and involvement in international, ecumenical and missiological networks, symposia, journals and monograph series. Two of them have explored the non-Western Jesus specifically: Witvliet in his *A Place in the Sun: Liberation Theology in the Third World* (1985), and even more explicitly Wessels in his *Images of Jesus: How Jesus is Perceived and Portrayed in Non-European Cultures* (1990). Both studies acquired a broad international readership and can be found in university libraries the world over. A younger generation, now often occupying chairs of intercultural theology rather than those of missiology, is continuing their work. Next to Frans Wijsen, the missiologist at Radboud University in Nijmegen, there is also the German missiologist, V. Küster, who teaches at the Kampen campus of the Protestant Theological University. He has published *Die viele Gesichter Jesu* (1999), translated into English as *The Many Faces of Jesus Christ* (1999).

I include myself in this Dutch tradition of hermeneutical reflection on the shifts occurring in world Christianity, even though my background is not so much in missiology as it is in systematic and ecumenical theology. It may even be seen as characteristic of Dutch theology to want to mediate between East and West, North and South. That probably has something to do with our history in commerce, which opens channels of communication and creates possibilities of exchange. In particular, the two international journals edited in the Netherlands, *Exchange* and *Studies in Interreligious Dialogue*, make an important contribution to this exchange.

This study is also intended to contribute a frame of reference within which the current processes of change in world Christianity can be understood.

This frame of reference is unfolded in Part I, where I summarize thirty years (1976–2006) of academic reflection on questions in the area of tradition hermeneutics. I am still immensely fascinated by what exactly is transmitted by a tradition through the centuries and in different cultures. The other parts of this book are attempts to give content to the frame of reference discussed in Part I. They are intended to provide Western readers with a framework that will allow them to understand non-Western theology. That framework has been derived as much as possible from the reasons given by non-Western theology itself. It is therefore expressly not intended as a Procrustean bed. Such a framework is intended to provide a (small) contribution to bridging the visibly growing gulf particularly between North and South. A few simple examples will serve to clarify this.

Non-Western theology is much less of a theology based on books than Western theology is. Western book wisdom quickly encounters limits here. With respect to this, the Western conceptual approach is very different from the more narrative and often strongly rhetorically embedded non-Western approach. Non-Western theology does not have centres ("schools" of thinking) to the extent that Western theology does. That is undoubtedly due to the language problem: the variety of languages in Africa and Asia is so great that fruitful communication at conferences of African and Asian theologians can often only be done in a non-African, non-Asian language. Usually, that is English; sometimes it is French.

The publications cited most often on non-Western theology are also for the most part published in the West – even though that is changing quickly – and thus pre-sorted for a Western audience. Seldom are they published in the "first" language of the authors in question. That means that the width of the bridge that can be built by these studies should not be overestimated: they reveal only a narrow trail. They can illuminate a corner of the veil but cannot claim to show the soul of non-Western theology.

In addition to all these differences, we can point to another striking phenomenon. Western theologians still have the inclination to "cuddle" their non-Western colleagues "to death." Motivated by guilt over Western theological imperialism, non-Western theologians are frequently invited, as a kind of compensation, to guest lectures, contributions to symposia, sabbaticals, and sometimes also to temporarily occupy academic chairs. In itself this is good, but there is also a flipside. Some of these theologians have become true globetrotters. They travel here and there and sometimes spend more time at foreign universities in a year than they do at their own institution. Because of that, a process of alienation inevitably takes place. After some time, the non-Western theology that they have developed in the West is no longer representative of their home situation. Sometimes, as will be seen in Chapter 7 with respect to the Japanese theologian K. Koyama, they are hardly mentioned in their own country.

Their theology can be understood best as an "in-between" theology: not Western but also not really non-Western. Rather, it is something in between. This does not detract from the importance as such of an in-between theology; it is merely a restriction on their representativeness. Theologically, this "in-between" theology fills an important function between North and South, and for the theologians in question their international reputation sometimes also creates latitude that would not be granted by politicians or church leaders in their home situation. A number of non-Western theologians therefore stayed (or still stay), clearly involuntarily, abroad for years. The Cameroon Roman Catholic theologian Jean-Marc Ela and the Congolese bishop Emmanuel Milingo are clear examples of this. We will see in Chapter 8 how the American Korean theologian Jung Young Lee has actually made a theological virtue of this necessity of the "in-between" situation.

This study will probably introduce many names and concepts new to many readers. Despite all the limits that I have imposed upon myself, it remains a book with a considerably high level of information content. The introductory sections in italics at the beginning of each chapter and the conclusions at the end of each part will probably help readers not schooled in theology or interreligious dialogue to follow the line of the argument. The extensive index makes it easy to find unfamiliar names and concepts quickly. For the rest, each "world traveller" will be aware that real interest for the unknown and other things begins with the willingness to learn new concepts and terms, how to spell them and to remember them.

We have chosen in this book to keep quotations to a minimum for the sake of readability. The bibliography is arranged according to studies of a biblical-theological nature, those in the history of doctrine and modern overviews on the many images of Jesus, Western and non-Western inculturation studies and, subsequently, Asian and African studies on Jesus. The sections on Asia and Africa begin with background studies that have been selected on the basis of their relation to reflection on the meaning of Jesus. The Asian literature is further divided into literature from Buddhist, Hindu and Islamic contexts. A short overview of the interreligious dialogue between Christianity and Buddhism, Hinduism and Islam has been added. The literature that is explicitly engaged with non-Western interpreters of these four religions is cited here. This classification entails that the publications of one author can be divided over several categories. Thus, the works of the American-Korean theologian Jung Young Lee can be found under "Studies on Inculturation," "Background Studies," and "Asian Studies on Jesus."

Part I: Where is Jesus "at Home"?

This book is about the meaning that is ascribed to Jesus in contemporary, non-Western contexts. Our guideline for assessing those strongly divergent meanings will be the term double transformation. This term entails that when a concept is transferred from one context to another, both the giver as well as the receiver are changed. In another context, the concept in question (the giver) receives a somewhat different meaning, whereas that concept also gives something new to, or changes, the new context (the receiver). In Jesus' case, this transference event (inculturation process) is more complicated, because the meaning attributed to him is always passed on in a community of transmission that wants to preserve unity with the past as well as with as many fellow believers as possible in the present. The methodological justification of an argument for a way of dealing with the many complications of this process that preserves this unity finally ends in the proposition that genuine transfer always presupposes solidarity with the new context. This solidarity will also include a critical element, however, because the Gospel-culture relationship is never a one-to-one relationship. There is always critical space between culture and the Gospel.

1 The Cultural Embedding of the Gospel

Must Jesus Always Remain Greek?

In what culture would Jesus best feel at home? That seems, at first glance, a strange question to ask – as if that were up to us or Jesus! Cultural influences are too complex to be simply shoved aside. We can define culture as a *comprehensive system of meanings, norms and values by which people give form (meaning) to their material existence in a certain time and context*. This concept of culture keeps the notions of "superstructure" and "substructure" together. The act of giving form and meaning always presupposes a certain, concrete, material existence. In using the word culture, we are not speaking exclusively of something lofty but of the broad complex process of giving meaning and form to all aspects of human existence. Both the way we think and the way we act are part of our "culture." Cultures are subject to change just as much as how we think and act is. It is people who make or break a culture, but a (collective) culture can also be a power factor over against the individual. That is why we can also state that culture stamps the individual.

As a rule, an individual is more of a bearer than a maker of the culture in which he or she lives. But one can, nevertheless, be critical of his or her own culture. Religion can play a role here, because religion is not only a final grounding and thus a confirmation of a culture but often a critical factor as well. Religion always wants to "exalt" the current pattern of norms and values or make them more profound. This can lead to a sharp critique of culture, which is why culture and religion seldom display a one-to-one relationship. Religion has often been used in the service of the reigning powers, but it has also often stood in the way of the powerful, whereby it has a cleansing, purifying role with respect to the existing culture.

To put this in terms of a model, it could be said that the relationship between culture and religion has never been simply that of a combination of the *king* who creates norms and the *priest* who sanctions them. There has also always been the *prophet* who criticizes any decline in norms. The role of religion can therefore change constantly, and the history of religion is full of changes with respect to its role. Because of those changing roles we are opting in this study for a rather broad *threefold definition of religion.* We understand religion as referring to *the existentially experienced presence of a field of force (either personal or impersonal) that (1) transcends human existence, (2) influences thinking and acting, and (3) is expressed in shared symbols, rites and myths.*

By appealing to that which transcends tangible human existence but influences thinking and acting, religion acquires the character of something intangible. Neither those in power nor its adherents can control it. Religion always represents something transcendent, something that hints at that which is "greater than." That explains why religion and culture are never completely identical, and it is for that reason that critical questions can always be asked about the nature of the relationship. Those questions do not concern the cultural embedding of religion as such – religion never arises in isolation and there is no single religion without any cultural attire. Rather, these questions explore the latitude between religion and culture. This also expresses the paradox that is always present in the culture-religion relationship: on the one hand, religion is part of an existing culture and more or less supports it, but, on the other, it also always claims to be in a position to criticize the existing culture. The relationship is therefore always characterized by both integration and segregation (separation).

This specific cultural attire does not constitute a straitjacket; religion and culture are not riveted to each other for good. Each religion – just like each culture, incidentally – has a certain dynamic (vitality) that allows change as a result of internal development or outside events. (Cultural) clothing can be changed. That is why the question arises: "Must God (or Jesus) remain Greek?" In 1990 the Afro-American Protestant theologian Robert Hood published a book by that title in which he asked if the Greco-Roman concepts in which the early church articulated the meaning of God and Jesus should also be normative for other cultures in other times. For believers in the non-Western world, he argues, those concepts hinder faith more than they help it. They make it harder rather than easier to pass on the faith.[1] Thus, the intentional *rooting* of the faith in a non-Greco-Roman culture also always requires a certain *uprooting* from that Greco-Roman culture.

In contemporary non-Western theology, this point regarding the transmission of faith and thus also the relevance of faith is one of the most important arguments for a different conceptual apparatus for the proclamation of the Gospel. Non-Western theologians see a form of Western imperialism in the Western stress on the continuing validity of the terminology used by the early church. One specific inculturation – namely, that of the Greco-Roman culture that the West has appropriated – is absolutized. Other inculturations, such as those in contemporary Africa and Asia, are considered second-class right from the start.

In fact, the criticism of Western theology often comes down to three things. At first glance, the first and second appear to be paradoxically related. But if we look at them more closely – taking the time factor into account – they are not necessarily mutually exclusive:

1. Western theology is also contextual and therefore cannot simply be transmitted to other contexts.
2. Western theology has lost touch with the concrete life situation of Western people and has become an abstract, academic activity.
3. Western theology is modelled entirely on the requirements that obtain for Western science, which is still completely oriented to the demands of the Enlightenment.[2]

Hood's question has become even more urgent now that the heart of Christianity has shifted to the southern hemisphere. Usually based on the information contained in David Barrett's *World Christian Encyclopedia*,[3] it is estimated that there are now about 2 billion Christians in the world, i.e. one-third of the world population. Of this number, 480 million live in Latin America, 360 million in Africa, 313 million in Asia, 480 million in Europe, and 260 million in North America. Given current demographic expectations, it is thought that in twenty years, of the total 2.6 billion Christians in the world, 633 million will live in Africa, 640 million in Latin America and 460 million in Asia. That is considerably more than half of all Christians. Europe is expected to have 555 million Christians and North America 312 million. This will make the latter the least Christian continent, as P. Jenkins indicates.[4]

Even if one holds that the estimations made by Jenkins and Barrett are somewhat high for Asia (they are very dependent on population growth figures and the growth – which is difficult to substantiate – of evangelical and Pentecostal churches), they are still probably indicative of a shift in global Christianity's centre of gravity. It would then mean a doubling of the percentage of Christians in Asia in the next twenty years from three to six per cent. This would be an increase of a few hundred million but, with a population of at least two and a half billion, it would still be a small minority.

Asian Christians often clearly constitute a minority over against Buddhist, Hindu or Muslim majorities. This is the case, for example, in countries like Japan, India and Indonesia. How can the dialogue on vital questions be maintained in the immediate environment under such conditions? What requirements should there be for an Asian theological language and Asian theological concepts? How much room is there for new concepts? What is the common reference point with Christians in other parts of the world? These questions can also be asked, of course, in relation to African Christianity. It is these questions with which this book is concerned.

The concept of inculturation is central. This concept and that of contextualization are sometimes used as synonyms, but we prefer the term inculturation. Contextualization often refers to the political, socio-economic context and is viewed as a more critical concept than that of inculturation, which allegedly refers only to "cultural" phenomena such as language, symbols and rites. But such a concept of culture is too narrow, ignoring the influence of the "substructure," the conditions for material existence. At the start of this chapter we used a broader concept of culture, which included the so-called substructure. If it is clear that the conditions for material existence are also inalienably part of the concept of culture, then there is no objection to the concept of inculturation. To the contrary, it is even to be preferred, for this concept can express the *normative element* better, i.e. the point regarding the norms and values unique to each culture. The phrase religious process of inculturation refers to *the transmission of a religious conceptual apparatus and pattern of values formed in a specific culture to another culture with its own religious conceptual apparatus and pattern of values*. The appropriation of new concepts and values that is then necessary will always be accompanied by a process of change. In this study we will direct ourselves primarily *to the nature of that process of change*.

The most essential problem with respect to the inculturation of the meaning of Jesus in cultures other than the Greco-Roman one is the fact that decisive religious experiences are always bound to both time and place and also always transcend them in the case of Jesus. In the Greco-Roman world, Jesus was never presented purely as a local hero (of faith) who was associated completely with his immediate environment. If that were so, one could never introduce him into other cultures. He made an impression on the people around him in a historical situation that can be described with reasonable accuracy. On the basis of that impression, a number of terms and titles have been ascribed to him that have certain meanings. These meanings, in turn, have to do with the role that people ascribe to others or things in their lives. In Jesus' case, it always concerns a role that transcends one's own specific experience. The particular is always connected with the universal.

For example, Jesus' disciples had the experience that he displayed the nearness of the divine in a unique way. On the basis of that experience, they subsequently ascribed to him a meaning that, in principle, he should have for everyone everywhere and at all times. Could that simply be done? Here we encounter the classic problem with which every religion with universal claims is confronted. At the foundation of such religions are very specific experiences, often more or less historically placeable, that also prove to be of great value for later generations in circumstances other than those of the specific original context of the experience. Later generations can realize that value only if they can make the experiences of the first witnesses their own; these experiences can apparently be broadened into universal experiences. True universality does not arise through abstraction but through the apparently unlimited possibility of connecting particular experiences with other more or less similar experiences and experiencing their authenticity in that way. Authentic universality always concerns a particularity – to cite the African Roman Catholic theologian Fabien Eboussi-Boulaga – that transcends its own limits.[5]

The well-known story of Martin Luther King's "I Have a Dream" speech at the end of the march on Washington in 1963 illustrates this nicely. At a specific place and at a specific time, King articulated his dream of the end of racial segregation between black and white. This particular, historically placeable experience by King has since then been recognized by millions of people all over the world because they have had similar experiences of racial segregation and longed passionately for the end of such. Thus, a bridge could be built between King's dream and the dreams of millions of others and could acquire universal significance.

When something is accorded universal significance, there are two specific experiences involved here: the *original* experience and the experience of *recognition*. Even though the latter can be experienced by millions of other people, it nevertheless remains very specific for the one involved and thus also unique. One could think here of the many millions who, down through the centuries and everywhere in the world, could identify with the original experience of the disciples concerning Jesus. Those (conversion) experiences are often unique markers in their lives.

The transmission of the meaning of Jesus concerns three such experiences. (1) First are *the experiences of the disciples* close to him: we find the expression of those experiences primarily in the four gospels in the New Testament. (2) Then there is *the discovery* of people in the Greco-Roman world around the Mediterranean Sea that they could recognize and articulate these experiences in their intellectual categories. (3) Next, there are the experiences of recognition by contemporary believers who can see the same divine nearness in Jesus through the Greco-Roman conceptual apparatus.

This process of recognition is anything but smooth, and sometimes it occurred only after a great deal of effort. One can think here of Paul's assertion that the Gospel was "a stumbling block to Jews and foolishness to Gentiles" (1 Cor. 1:23). The blood of the early martyrs of the church testifies to the tensions that this process of transmission evoked in the Mediterranean area. It is still an ongoing discussion today among New Testament scholars and experts in the history of the early church as to what was lost in this transformation process and what was added from the Greco-Roman world.

The threefold transmission or bridging process just mentioned is usually viewed in church history as a mediation process that was guided by the Holy Spirit, who is also called *pontifex maximus*, the bridge-builder *par excellence*, the mediator between past and present. This mediation process is faltering, however: the old mediation strategies, based primarily on historical exegesis, no longer appear to be adequate.

Thus, we are back at the problem with which we began: *Must God Remain Greek?* It seems more difficult to transmit the language in which the writers of the Bible and the theologians of the early church spoke about the meaning of Jesus to cultures that have been less formed by the Greeks and Romans than the West. The possibilities of identification sometimes fall short. Incidentally, that is also becoming increasingly true for the West. At first glance, the quickly growing Latin American and African Pentecostal churches seem to be an exception to the rule. They do not reflect very much at all on the cultural attire in which Jesus comes to them. Leaving the Western development of doctrine aside without any qualms, they draw directly, as it were, from the source of living water that the New Testament Jesus has remained, unchanged, for millions of people. Does that relativize the current question of a contextual Jesus or does it illustrate the fact that the New Testament Jesus is very contextual in Latin America and Africa? And does it also illustrate perhaps the fact that these churches with their charismatic leadership, their own experiences, songs, stories, healings and dances are closer to the (spiritual) context of the average Latin American or African than the Western missionary churches?

In any case, this example makes it clear that the question of the non-Western Jesus does not have any standard answer. Churches sometimes turn out to be more contextual than they themselves are aware, and sometimes the historical Jesus is closer to them than they ever dreamed. The converse, however, is sometimes also true. Many Asian and African mission churches have a great deal of difficulty with forms of transmitting the faith that are oriented to acquiring more members. They seem to be "foreign" entities in their own culture and do not succeed in translating Jesus' message into appealing images. For many of them, Jesus remains a "stranger." With respect to this, it must be stated in all seriousness that Western missions have been far from successful. The impression often arises that the church is growing most where the Western missionaries have been absent in recent decades (Latin America, Korea and certain parts of Africa).

The above implies that we do not subscribe to the well-known thesis of the English anthropologist, Robin Horton, regarding the conversion of Africans to Christianity and Islam. Rather, we claim the complete opposite. To explain the "African conversion" to universal religions such as Christianity and Islam, Horton argues that the old tribal religions were inadequate.

Those religions provide answers to questions of meaning on the level of the village, the tribe and the family, but they have no further significance beyond that. The world religions thus offer consolation, for they have a macrocosmic view that extends to both the ends of the earth and the end of time. The conversion to Christianity and Islam is thus part of the "modernization" of the African worldview and can be replaced in time, with further modernization, by secularism.[6] Horton is, to be sure, clearly indebted here to the Western intellectual climate of the 1960s in which secularization was seen as logically following modernization. These expectations did not materialize. Horton's thesis would imply that one should speak of decontextualization rather than contextualization. The presupposition is then that the further one is removed from one's own small world (microcosmos), the more one becomes a citizen of the larger world (macrocosmos).

In fact, the developments in Christianity (and in a certain sense also in Islam) have gone precisely in the opposite direction. As was shown above, religious universalization occurs no longer through the abstraction from the local but precisely through concentration on the local. It is on the basis of that concentration that recognition outside one's own context is sought. Universal religion helps here in that, because aspects of a universal religion are recognized in the local situation, the universal religion functions more as an eye-opener *in* the local situation than as a springboard *out* of it.

The Remembered Jesus

Let us return once more to the very beginnings of the Christian tradition. The Jew Jesus of Nazareth was born in a specific place and time in the Palestine of that time. When he lived is placed at the beginning (the first thirty years) of the Christian era. He was a contemporary and compatriot of people who derived their ideas from what was known in their environment and times. The religious climate was strongly stamped by a mixture of Jewish-Greek-Hellenistic thinking, sometimes supplemented by influences from Rome, Egypt and the Mesopotamian (Persian) world. It is difficult to establish and thus discuss what was typically Jewish or Greek at that time. Much depends on the question of the particular Jewish or Greek (sub)culture one has in mind. Jesus lived, in fact, in a religious melting pot.

Everything we know about Jesus, we know via his contemporaries and compatriots, people who were deeply impressed by him and therefore passed on their impressions. After some time, these impressions were written down and, still later – in a process that lasted two centuries (from the second to the fourth) – the early church collected the written sources and accepted a number of them as canonical. There is still discussion in Christianity as to the precise extent of the canon. The Jesus that we know from the New Testament is thus a Jesus who is remembered by his contemporaries and the generations immediately following.[7]

Jesus is presented in the New Testament just as he was remembered. Therefore, every distinction between the historical Jesus and the Christ of proclamation is artificial – as if his disciples wanted to communicate something historical about him apart from their intention to proclaim him. We have to resign ourselves to the fact that we have no other source for the historical Jesus than the Jesus who was remembered by his disciples and, in the New Testament, that is the Christ of proclamation. That is how he has been passed on to us.

Therefore, if we use the term "Jesus' throughout this book as consistently as possible, we do not at all intend thereby to indicate that there is a significant distinction between Jesus and the Christ. It is more of a technical question. The attribution of meaning already began in the Greek world when he was given the title Christ. The name Jesus, of course, already points to a form of (Jewish) attribution of meaning, but, technically speaking, one cannot go further back than that name, whereas one can go further back than the title Christ. That is why we always start with the name Jesus.

By taking *the remembered Jesus* as our starting point, we are also taking into account the starting point – which is as such applicable outside the Bible – that there is *no text without a context* and *no context without a text*. Each text is always the result of experiences that are bound to time and place (the context) and experiences bound to time and place can be verified only if they have been put down in writing. At the present time we can supplement what has been written down with recorded images and sound.

All the terms that are used in the New Testament concerning Jesus – Lord (*kyrios*), teacher (rabbi), prophet, royal Messiah (king of the Jews, the Anointed, Christ), healer, exorcist, Son of God, Son of Man, high priest, redeemer, Word (Logos), light of the world, truth, miracle worker, etc. – were well-known religious terms in the Palestine of his time and have a Jewish or Greek background. The creative application of existing religious terms to what people remembered of Jesus thus lies at the foundation of how he is presented in the New Testament.

It is by means of these terms that he is proclaimed as the Messiah, as the one anointed by God, the Son of God and the Son of Man. Those who heard about Jesus during the period of oral transmission and later those who read about him could "place" him because of these well-known terms.[8] There were already those in Jesus' time who disputed whether those terms should be applied to Jesus. The titles "Messiah" and "Son of God" especially were the subject of constant dispute (Matt. 16:13–20; John 4:1–41). The terms mentioned above were often used so specifically with regard to Jesus that their meanings often shifted considerably.[9] We will return to this transformation process later in this chapter.

Although many theologians are well aware that there were a number of religious influences from elsewhere that played a role in the transmission of Jesus' message, at the same time they deny that such a process of inculturation can be repeated. For them, this process was a one-time event under the guidance of the Holy Spirit, who guided this process of inculturation once, and since then this process has been fixed once and for all in the Bible.

We do not subscribe to such a view, because it is simply arbitrary. Did an inculturation that was at least just as important not occur immediately after the extent of the New Testament canon had been determined in the formulation of the first doctrines about Jesus at the Councils of Nicea (325) and Chalcedon (451)? If one admits – and that is often the case – that the first doctrinal statements occurred under the guidance of the Holy Spirit, then one also recognizes that the inculturation under the guidance of the Holy Spirit did not cease when the New Testament canon was fixed. Thus, also given the continuing development of doctrine after Nicea and Chalcedon, there is no reason to stop the process of inculturation with these councils – all the more so because they cannot be seen immediately as high points of "spiritual" decision-making. Pope Leo I and the emperor Marcian interfered too forcefully in the ecclesiastical process during the Council of Chalcedon for one to make that claim.[10]

For that matter, the sometimes not very exalted course of affairs during this council led to a (modest) formula that has continually proved its usefulness in Western church history. In the East, however, the council brought only discord. We will return to that briefly in Chapter 4 in the section on "The Interwovenness of the Divine and the Human" and in Chapter 5 in the section "The Image of Jesus among the First Christians in China." The famous statement that Jesus' human and divine natures exist "inconfusedly, unchangeably, indivisibly, inseparably" in relation to each other has done away with any form of simplism in the West.

The council does emphasize that Jesus cannot be divided neatly into a divine half and a human half. Nor is the human in him absorbed into the divine or the divine into the human. The di-unity that Jesus personifies cannot be reduced to a simple duality or to a simple unity either. The mystery of the divine nearness in his person is more complex, and one of the merits of this conciliar decision is that it has preserved this mystery. Thus, there is always the possibility of new specifications of this mystery.

Instead of considering Chalcedon to be the end, we are more inclined to see it, with the Roman Catholic historian of doctrine Alois Grillmeier, as a beginning,[11] as a starting point of the reflection on the meaning of Jesus that has continued since then throughout all ages. The di-unity (to be confessed in Christ) of his divine and human natures articulated by Chalcedon in an appropriately tensive way is especially suitable as a starting point because it leaves open the way in which we deal with these tensions.

It does not therefore seem to be necessary to limit the work of the Holy Spirit to the first councils primarily. People were inclined to do so in the history of Christianity for two reasons, both of which are diametrically opposed to each other. Eastern Orthodoxy is inclined to see the statements of the great councils of the early church more or less as acts of origin, whether or not connected with a romantic view of the "undivided" early church. As constitutive acts of the one church, they can be accorded greater weight than later conciliar decisions. They are well aware of the influence of the Greek context but view the context as more or less sanctioned by the doctrine.

The opposite approach that leads to the same result can be found sometimes in Protestant theologians. For them, the development of doctrine in the early Christian period is proof that the content of the New Testament contains such a powerful witness that it can stand up to the influence of the Greek culture and survive more in spite of than because of that culture. The early Christian doctrines derive their value then not primarily – as in Eastern Orthodoxy – from their fundamentally historical character but from the fact that they have passed on the New Testament message so purely.

Neither approach, however, poses the question of the *limiting* role Greek culture may perhaps have played with respect to the proclamation of the Gospel. That obtains also for the New Testament – something that should be pointed out to those who hold to the Protestant approach cited above. The "opposite" that religion always represents with respect to a culture must be viewed as legitimate since Jesus' appearance and thus also obtains for the way in which the New Testament writers worded Jesus' message and for the way in which church fathers set down the meaning of Jesus in the earliest doctrines. Jesus' message was "strange" for them as well and could only with difficulty be fit into the cultural (linguistic) means at their disposal.

Therefore, what should be investigated is not only what was passed on but also what was lost, i.e. what was lost through the (cultural) limitations to which the New Testament writers were also subject. *Traduire est trahir* ("to translate is to betray") was true then as well.[12] No single culture can be declared to be the bearer of the Gospel hands down, and it should also be stated that every culture can stand in the way of the spread of the Gospel.

That is why we must also ask if the inculturation in the Hellenistic, Greco-Roman culture was not a straitjacket – one that closed our eyes to certain aspects of Jesus' meaning that can be discovered only now. At the very least, one should be able to pose this question legitimately in all openness with respect to the councils of the early church. An unimpeachable witness like Grillmeier, author of five hefty volumes on the continuing significance of this council, places it high on his list of questions that each contemporary evaluation of Chalcedon must answer.[13]

Who Decides?

Does the New Testament itself display a form of syncretism? The term syncretism (= mingling of religions) is often used in a negative sense and means in that case: *improper mingling*. The titles "Messiah" and "Son of God" were declared to be "improper" by the leaders of the Jewish religion from which the terms were taken. This "improper" was later voiced repeatedly in the often painful relationship between Jews and Christians.

From the first centuries of our era, we see in the early church that something can be declared improper not only by those whose religion is the source from which someone else, an outsider, takes something. It can also be declared improper by those who are considered to be the ones appropriating new concepts. Thus, after the necessary internal struggle, the early church finally refused to approve Gnostic thinking with its rejection of the material, physical world and thus also of God as creator.[14]

But the application of new terms was and is not always disputed. Sometimes, a relatively quiet borrowing occurs, with or without purification of certain aspects. Referring to Jesus by the Old Testament image of "sun of righteousness" (Mal. 4:2) is an example of a critical appropriation of the worship of the invincible sun (*sol invictus*). The striking parallels between Jesus and central figures of Greek mythology are often pointed out: Odysseus (his descent into the underworld to liberate those who were there), Orpheus (who also descends into the realm of the dead and who personifies the "good shepherd"), Asclepius (the doctor, saviour of people).[15] The tendency indicated by some thinkers toward monotheism in the Greek world in the first three centuries of our era make speaking of possible mutual influencing somewhat more attractive, without there being much undisputed evidence of direct dependence.[16]

In this study we will not use the concept syncretism in an inherently negative way. After all, there has also been a fruitful integration of new concepts that are better able to express the meaning of Jesus in a certain place and time than the concepts that were thus far known. Therefore, we will employ a rather neutral definition of syncretism and define it as *the accepted or contested taking over of elements from one religion into another.*[17]

The question of the criteria for such a process arises immediately. Who decides? The criteria cannot be indicated without reference to the role of the holy book in a religious community, because the content of a holy book always functions as a gauge for the identity of a religious tradition. This can be well illustrated by the role of the Bible in the church. Therefore we will now take a brief look at that.

The New Testament came into existence in a process that lasted some centuries. In those centuries a (to be sure, never undisputed) collection of texts took shape that now forms the canon of the New Testament.

This long process was seen by the early church as guided by the Holy Spirit. The churches of the Reformation always emphasized that the final collection arose through the persuasive power of the writings in question. In other words, the text speaks for itself. The Spirit of God was seen to be active in that internal persuasive power that belongs to the text. The Roman Catholic tradition has always emphasized more the decisions of the church in the process of forming the canon. The work of the Spirit of God was also seen in that ecclesiastical factor.

Of course, neither emphasis excludes the other. In the ecumenical discussions in the second half of the previous century on the authority of the Bible, reference was always made both to the internal persuasive power of the texts and to the synodical decisions of the early church. One could say: church and Bible presuppose each other. The "reading" church is the body that transmits the Bible and thus the "remembered Jesus" down through the centuries.

But the same Jesus who is the object of transmission is at the same time the Lord of the church, the subject of the transmission, the actual motor of the transmission process. He is, after all, the one who ultimately interprets the Scriptures, administers the sacraments, appoints office-bearers, etc. The church is thus not an independent, self-authorized owner of the tradition but only the body that represents Jesus. In its own, always inadequate way, the church can thus present Jesus as present in (a) its proclamation, (b) the administration of the sacraments and (c) its exemplary conduct.

Only if the Jesus transmitted in the Bible is also the criterion for his own transmission can the church and the Bible be closely connected with each other. If the church is indeed seen as an institute that is always to be reformed in light of Jesus' message, it does not, in its role as interpreter of the Bible, constitute a threat to the *sola scriptura*, to the Protestant slogan "Scripture alone." Rather, it is its presupposition. To prevent all arbitrary use of the Scripture, the interpretation of the Bible must, after all, always have a communal – and in this case that means: church – aspect.

That obtains also for the meanings that can be attributed to Jesus. In the concrete situation of the transmission of Jesus' message in a new cultural situation, the above-mentioned di-unity of church and Bible can never simply be left up to individual believers. The individual attribution of meaning must always be embedded in the way in which the church of all ages has understood the Bible.

The above discussion thus yields an important criterion for assessment that we could, using a classic term, call the criterion of the historical and contemporary *catholicity of the church*. By this we understand the *historical and current Christian community of transmission* in which (a) the interpretation and proclamation of the Bible has an authoritative role, (b) the essence of church history (the decisions of the great councils) is seen, despite everything, as the result of God's leading – church history has, after all, not been a mistake – and (c) the gathered community concentrates the believers around the Christian feasts and the principal sacraments at the heart of the transmission. In this formulation, the Bible, church history and liturgy form the soil and foundation for the meanings that can be attributed to Jesus.

The three components mentioned above belong closely together. If there is no active reading of the Bible, the study of the history of the church degenerates into unbridled speculation and liturgy becomes routine. Without any basic knowledge of the decisions regarding faith that have been taken in the history of the church, the understanding of the Bible quickly becomes naïve and the liturgy has no centre. And without the Sunday liturgy with its fixed readings on feast days and the reference to Bible stories in the administration of the sacraments, the Bible quickly becomes a maze. Then we forget that only that which is of lasting value in the history of the church is what can be sung in praise (*gloria*) or lament (*kyrie*) in the liturgy.

Does the di-unity of church and Bible now hinder or help the transmission of the faith in new circumstances? It must be admitted that each process of transmission always entails some ossification. Something that is constantly in movement cannot be transmitted very well. To that extent, the church's transmission is always conservative (conserving) and curbs renewal. Each process of transmission, however, has its own dynamic. Passing something on to new generations in other circumstances is also a creative process. Thus, the church's transmission is both a restraint as well as an engine for renewal. Wise church leaders will therefore always aim at a certain balance between both poles and challenge innovators to account for their viewpoints over against the common heritage.

The concrete community of readers thus forms an important aspect of the history of transmission of a holy book. With an eye to our topic, the non-Western Jesus, this means that the life situation of the reading community determines to a large extent the way in which the Bible will be understood. Its common cultural horizon of understanding colours the interpretation of the Bible. To the extent that the cultural differences between reading communities spread out over the globe are more recognized, the differences in interpretation will be greater.[18]

This means that, after two thousand years, the history of the interpretation of the Bible is not yet anywhere close to being concluded. New dimensions can still be discovered, dimensions that have perhaps been hidden until now because of the Western domination of the transmission but are now coming to light. Is it then more than merely a matter of revealing what has remained hidden until now? Could it also involve truly new aspects of which no trace can be found in Scripture or in tradition but which are seen as a continuation of the Christian transmission by the community in question?[19] We will show later in this study that such a question arises in the discussion of the role that ancestors can play for Christians. It then concerns new aspects that are introduced by the intense experience with – also inspiring for Christians – aspects from other religions (tribal religions or other world religions). The South African Protestant black theologian Tinyiko Sam Maluleke speaks candidly and provocatively in this context of African Christianity as a "new religion." Keeping in mind the process of *double transformation* that we will discuss in the following chapter, he calls it a new religion with respect to the Christian tradition that has existed until now and is new with respect to the African religions.[20]

2   Something New about Jesus?

Double Transformation

Christianity was never viewed as a faith that was bound to a certain territory. It was never viewed as the faith of a certain people who lived in a certain area. From the beginning it has always moved across borders and was universally inclined. That is even one of the most prominent features of the transmission of Jesus' message, enabling Paul to say: "There is neither Jew nor Greek, slave nor free, male nor female, for you are all one in Christ Jesus" (Gal. 3:28).

Moving across borders also implies moving across cultures. Wherever people live, a specific language arises, different customs (rites) develop and, in the course of time, a unique whole of norms and values forms. As stated above, we call that whole of meanings, expressed in language, rites, norms and values, culture. The more specific certain expressions of culture are the more limited usually is their range, leaving special, deeply human experiences of authenticity aside. These can be very specifically individual and very much bound to place and time and nonetheless recognizable across the world. Examples of this are Anne Frank's diary and Bonhoeffer's letters from prison. Generally, however, cultural transfer can occur only with a certain measure of collectivity; it mostly concerns group experiences on both the "giving" and the "receiving" end.

If the religion of a culture appears capable of being transmitted within the terms of the religion of the other culture, that indicates that the recognition of common features that move across boundaries or the recognition that the "other" of a certain culture nevertheless exerts an attraction in one way or another on one's own culture and can be experienced as an enrichment. If that *process of infiltration* is evaluated positively we can then speak of a *successful syncretism*.

This syncretism is completely different from Christianization, Islamization or Hinduization. In all those cases, what is at issue is a conversion (whether it is forced or not) from one religion to another. In that event it is always a matter of one-way traffic. But that is not the case here. The intention is not to convert from the one faith to another or to win adherents from the one religion to the other. Rather, it concerns the inevitable need for, e.g., millions of Christians in India and Indonesia to articulate important aspects of their own faith by means of the possibilities of expression in another faith.

The need emerges for many Christians in Asia in particular, because of the fact that Christianity is a religious minority there, and everything that is thought to be important in that society is already "occupied" religiously. The dominant majority religion usually takes a central place in social life and puts its stamp on all important facets of life. Religious interpretations have already been given to birth, marriage and death and to views about happiness, suffering, justice, hope for the future, etc. that lie at the foundation of such interpretations. Participation in such a culture cannot occur without some form of adopting the common central concepts in that culture. We can cite three examples of that inevitable process: a biblical one, an African one, and an Asian one.

The first example is a very classic biblical one. It concerns the change that the name of God underwent when Israel settled in the land of Canaan. It was thought necessary to connect the experiences that the Israelites had had with Yahweh, the God of Abraham, Isaac and Jacob, with El, the God of the Canaanites. That led in the Old Testament to a creative synthesis that enriched rather than impoverished the Israelites' belief in God. The extent to which one speaks of adoption here and the extent to which adoption led to adaptation is a fertile topic for discussion among Old Testament scholars, of course. In any case, it is clear that belief in God underwent a certain broadening: from that point on, a wider and thereby more universal belief in creation was associated with God. In addition, the socio-ethical implications of God's roles as king and judge were worked out more elaborately.[1] In the midst of all bad examples of syncretism condemned by the Old Testament, this appears to be an example of successful syncretism. The term "syncretic monotheism" has been used for this.[2] The South African Old Testament scholar Louis Jonker calls this phenomenon – which can be seen elsewhere in the Old Testament – one of the driving forces behind the writing of the different books of the Old Testament. New situations occasioned continually the need to formulate new applications of old concepts.[3]

The second example is the change the name is undergoing in Asia and Africa. These continents cannot be described as religiously uncultivated terrain any more than Canaan could be described as such at the time of the Israelites' settlement of that land. Christianity does not find any prospective believers here to be blank pages (*tabula rasa*). Via the questions that are encountered in translating the Bible into an African language, the African theologian Lamin Sanneh has spoken in this connection of the "irony of mission." People come to a strange country assuming that the people have never heard of the God of the Bible but then use names for God present in those cultures in their Bible translations to make clear who the God of the Bible is.[4]

At first glance, this seems to be merely a technical translation question: does one choose to think up new terms (neologisms) for the names of God or does one use existing, familiar names? As soon as one does the latter – and this is common practice nowadays – one should not be surprised if many conclude that God was thus already in Africa, Asia and Latin America before the missionaries arrived.[5]

The third example concerns the translation of the name of God into Korean. The name of God is translated as *Hananim* in Korean translations of the Bible. In Korean shamanism, *Hananim* means the one heavenly Spirit that was seen as the personification of *Han*, the one great entity that gives light and is exalted. As an aside, this divinity, *Han*, is to be distinguished from the concept *han* that we encounter in Korean Minjung theology. There it is a term for the misery *and* energy of the poorest of all.[6]

Han is considered to be the supreme ruler of the universe and is distinguished from the many spirits (gods) and demons that are manifest in nature. *Hananim* is never captured in a physical representation and never worshipped via rites. Although Koreans often speak the name of *Hananim*, especially in times of mortal danger, and associate him with the fertility of the rain and the fruit of the harvest, he is not worshipped at harvest time. The people mainly worship the nearer gods of the mountain and the hearth. *Hananim* is actually both close by and far away.

This shamanite monotheism has no perception of history and also does not assume any specific moral order to life. The shamanite concept of *Hananim* is ahistorical and amoral. That explains why Korean Christians who have absorbed only this shamanite background of the *Hananim* concept into their belief in God are so little inclined to connect their concept of God to the concrete history of their people and their own moral acts. Only the integration of Confucian rules for conduct creates the conditions for that.[7]

The examples of syncretism described above are, of course, not without risk. Later in this study we will discuss the necessary examples of derailments or risks of derailment that also appear. For many, this will raise the slippery slope question: Where will the process end? How far can adoption go? Where does adoption stop? Even where every form of adoption is vigorously resisted, there is some explicit or implicit talk of a certain influence from the non-Christian religious context.

The way in which, for example, the Korean church has given a place in church memorial services to shamanite ancestor worship is a good illustration of this. The same process can be observed in Korea (and elsewhere in Asia and Africa) concerning the phenomenon of exorcisms. In both cases it always concerns an adoption that always includes adaptation and change.

Here we encounter one of the most striking features of the syncretic process. Changes always appear *on two sides*: on the side of the concept used in a different context and on the side of its new context. This is always two-way traffic. The concept detached from its original religious context becomes a different concept in another religious context. After all, the context in which a concept is used determines its meaning to a great extent. The new context is subsequently changed in turn by the new concept that is used in its midst. For example, calling Jesus our exemplary ancestor changes both the known concept of ancestor and the known image of Jesus. We will return to this in Chapter 16 in detail in the section "Jesus as Ancestor." A *double transformation* thus takes place. A creative process occurs that does not leave either side – the adopted concept and the new context – untouched. It is precisely this objective process that is the object of this study.

The principle of *double transformation* used here is to be distinguished explicitly from the concept of "Christ the Transformer of Culture" that Richard Niebuhr discusses in his famous study on *Christ and Culture*.[8] There Niebuhr had explicitly one-way traffic in mind, just as in the opposite "model" of "Christ of Culture." In the former, culture is approached exclusively from the perspective of Jesus and in the latter Jesus is approached exclusively from the perspective of culture. In neither of the models is there any kind of exchange. This is also not the case with the other models that Niebuhr discusses: "Christ against Culture," "Christ above Culture" and "Christ and Culture in Paradox."

Although the working out of the principle of double transformation in this study claims to add new insights to the inculturation event and in that sense to be original – otherwise this book would not have needed to be written – the principle of double transformation is not at all original. It is found explicitly and implicitly repeatedly in the literature consulted, even though it is often applied less consistently and less explicitly in a bilateral way than this study does. An exemplary use can be found, e.g., in the two-part article by the Indian Jesuit, Noel Sheth, in the Indian Roman Catholic journal *Vidyajyoti* called "Hindu Avatara and Christian Incarnation: A Comparison" (I) and (II). He remarks in his final paragraph: "In this encounter of the two traditions there is also the further possibility that when one tradition tries to assimilate elements from the other tradition, these original elements may themselves undergo transformation and acquire new meanings and significance. Perhaps this is the path that future interreligious dialogue between the two traditions may take."[9] It is evident from the way in which Sheth provides some examples of mutual influence shortly before this passage how seriously he takes account of a transformation of both the "giving" and the "receiving" sides.

The process of transformation that accompanies every form of syncretism on both sides is one of the most important reasons to discuss syncretism in a more nuanced way than is usual in systematic theology. It is not for nothing that almost all Old and New Testament scholars who describe forms of syncretism in the Old or New Testaments emphasize this bilateralness.

"Pure" syncretism in the sense of unchanged merging is then also per definition impossible. For that, too much has been shoved aside on both sides. Syncretism always entails change. In a famous article from 1959 with the typically German long title, "The Appropriation of the Philosophical Concept of God as a Dogmatic Problem of Early Christian Theology,"[10] the German theologian Wolfhart Pannenberg characterizes the fusion process he describes as a "critical assimilation." But if "assimilation" is emphasized too much, then the bilateralness of the process just sketched above would be destroyed. Then it would be suggested that the "receiving" party stands ready, with fireproof gloves on, to begin the assimilation, whereas the whole point is that the assimilation process also affects the receiving party itself. Pannenberg argues, in fact, for a critical "theological appropriation,"[11] and that is a somewhat more adequate term. In the appropriation process, after all, something always happens to that which belongs to the side that does the appropriating. The addition of "critical" makes it clear that there is something at stake. One can also lose oneself in the appropriation process – then a Trojan horse has been pulled in. It is for that reason that it is worthwhile delineating precisely what changes in such a process and on which side.

We will limit ourselves here to a *theological analysis*, keeping in mind that this is only one side of the coin. After all, as soon as certain differences in the extent of the religions are broached, the *power factor* also begins to play a role.[12] With respect to the minority religion – and in Asia that is always Christianity (among others) – there is also the *psychological factor*, through which one either marks oneself off clearly from one's context or blatantly adapts to it. In the first case, one is constantly legitimizing one's own conversion and, in the second, trivializing it. These two divergent reactions sometimes occur simultaneously in different groups of Christians in the same context. That can be seen in Korea, for example. Some Korean theologians give the impression that they live in a religious vacuum from which they (can) borrow nothing. But others let the content of their theology be determined so much by the religious concepts around them that they give themselves hardly any latitude as Christians. Neither attitude seems to be fruitful. Sometimes it seems that people – even in Indonesia – shift from one attitude to the other. From an antagonistic attitude towards Islam people sometimes shift suddenly to the other extreme, namely to an attitude in which Islam, for example, seems to determine the latitude for views about Jesus. In this study we prefer to study those non-Western theologians who themselves have found a kind of balance in their attitude to their non-Christian context. They do not constantly justify their own conversion to Christianity by severely condemning their own religious background. Rather, they often display a remarkable, internal freedom that enables them to assess their religious environment fairly on its own merits on the basis of their own experience of the Gospel.

A well-known example of syncretism as *double transformation* occurred in early medieval Western Europe when the concept *heliand* from the ninth-century anonymous, Old Saxon epic poem of that name was applied to Jesus.[13] The transfer Christianized the concept and also changed the conception of Jesus. The kingly characteristics of the medieval *heliand* left its stamp on the image of Jesus as Saviour in Western Europe, but the *heliand* became a different kind of king than what people knew previously. The concept *heliand* now appears to be applicable to a Messianic king and the latter wages war in a much different way than the original *heliand*.

Theologically, such a process of adoption can be justified only if the view of the relationship among the religions requires that attention be paid not only to the differences but also to the similarities. Speaking of similarities is currently a tricky matter: Can one speak of similarities when dealing with strongly diverging belief systems in entirely different contexts? The question is already relevant with respect to ecumenical similarities within the Christian tradition, not to mention interreligious convergences. In this context one can also speak of "family resemblances," but one cannot make the family relationships too "close."

All great religions have strongly divergent traditions. Often the adherents of the one group do not want to be confused with the other at any price. One can think here of the differences between Roman Catholics, Eastern Orthodox and Protestants within Christianity, the adherents of Mahayana and Theravada Buddhism, the Islamic Shi'ites and Sunnis intent on killing each other in Iraq and elsewhere, the differences between liberal and orthodox Jews, and the Vaishnava and Shaiva Hindus. Each group has often also gone through radical changes in the course of its historical development. Thus, when indicating similarities, one also always needs to ask: What form of Buddhism, Islam, Christianity, etc. and from which period?

Neither ecumenical nor interreligious dialogue can be called naïve. The participants are usually very aware of how complex the matter of observing similarities and differences can be. At present, people would rather speak more carefully of partial "overlapping" on some points. The philosopher of religion Hendrik M. Vroom uses the image of the moving Olympic circles for this in his study *Religions and the Truth*. Thus, one cannot speak of one shared centre, e.g., the same God. The different circles (religions) do overlap one another at different and continually other points. This overlap has to do with the fact that, however divergent the interpretations in the different religions are, one can speak worldwide of common *basic insights* that articulate the experiences of joy and gratitude, admiration, dread and finitude.[14] They express existential feelings of trust, desire, resistance and forgiveness.[15] Only when it is shown that such common basic experiences are acknowledged is there room for partial or not partial identifications that always – as stated – entail adaptations (changes).

The idea of "overlap" mentioned above and, as part of that, of (partial) identifications can be made more precise by referring to the concept of analogy. In the classical discussions of the Middle Ages, the concept of analogy is always defined as a *similarity in the midst of a still greater dissimilarity*.[16] One can thus speak of a certain similarity (analogy) without glossing over differences. The concept of analogy has proven its worth primarily in the epistemological discussion of the possibility of using the same terms with respect to God and human beings – e.g. "father." In this study we will refer to the concept of analogy to justify the use of core concepts from other religions for specifying the significance of Jesus. By referring to a similarity in the midst of still greater differences, it can be made clear that the transposition (on the basis of a certain similarity) of a concept from one context to another also brings about a double transformation. The concept is changed and also changes its (new) context.

It is apparent from the above paragraphs that the theme of this book also touches on a number of central questions in interreligious dialogue. Nevertheless, this study is not, in the first place, to be viewed as a contribution to interreligious dialogue but primarily as a contribution to what is currently called *intercultural theology*. It concerns that branch of theology that integrates what used to be called oecumenics and missiology through the dynamic that characterizes the relation of the Christian tradition to different cultures, making it an object of study.[17]

In relation to interreligious dialogue, it can in any case be remarked that the current Indian, Japanese, Korean, Chinese and Indonesian theology cannot be studied without some basic knowledge of the content of the sacred books of Hinduism, Buddhism, Confucianism, Taoism and Islam. Similarly, non-Western theologians will say that the history of the early Christian development of doctrine cannot be understood without knowledge of Plato and Greek mythology, and contemporary Western theology cannot be understood without knowledge of nineteenth-century Western European Enlightenment thought.

Methodology

In Western overviews of the "non-Western Jesus' there is still a great tendency to begin or end such an overview with a biblical theological reflection. Such reflections then actually function as the criterion. There are objections to such a way of working. The impression arises quickly that the process of inculturation is a post-biblical phenomenon. That is not the case and most authors in question are aware of that. But when looking for a criterion, a Protestant author sooner or later always comes back to the Bible. There is nothing to be said against such an approach, if some complicating factors are taken into account.

In addition to the inculturation process that already occurs in the Bible, the denominational and cultural determination of each interpretation of the Bible should be honoured. The denominational background of the writer is expressed quite clearly primarily in exegetical studies on the church offices. It is indeed the custom at large, international conferences of the World Council of Churches to ask at the start of Bible study groups what one of central biblical texts are for each of those present. Subsequently, it is asked in a second round about everybody's church background. The combination of the two details then often leads to a great deal of recognition. The importance that is attributed to certain sections of the Bible often remains strongly influenced by the confessional tradition.

Moreover, not only does our contemporary culture influence our way of reading the Bible, but the history of our culture also influences it. The history of (our) culture has left its traces in the history of the interpretation of the Bible. Thus, the Greco-Roman culture, to which we owe our most important Christological doctrines, has deeply influenced not only our theology but also our way of reading the New Testament.

Therefore, we must also state that, when interpreting the Bible, we are always confronted with (a) internal biblical, (b) historical (early Christian, medieval, sixteenth- and nineteenth- to twentieth-century), and (c) contemporary inculturations of the Bible. We can always peel these away, like the layers of an onion, but that will not ultimately yield the "naked biblical facts" – because we can never step completely outside of all those contexts.

In the non-Western world as well, we see repeatedly that the appeal to the Bible, either directly or via biblical studies, is used to introduce a voice more or less "from outside" into the inculturation debate. We have been arguing up to now that that will not succeed, even though the Bible, as the book of the Christian community of transmission, will always have an authoritative voice, as we stated earlier and will also emphasize in the final chapter.

A fine example of processing what we have argued thus far is found in the Chinese theologian Chen Yongtao. He articulates precisely what the English Presbyterian New Testament scholar J. Dunn meant by the "remembered Jesus." Yongtao is fully aware that the "biblical Jesus' is also a theological "historical Jesus." There is a considerable amount of theology in the biblical witness about Jesus in the four evangelists and the Jesus of Paul. These writings are already theological answers to Jesus.[18] If we are aware of that and embed those theological answers in the whole of the history of transmission in the church, we can take into account both their continuing validity as well as their cultural limitedness.

The above is not an argument to omit biblical theological reflections from the inculturation debate. We ourselves refer to the biblical witness, primarily in the section on *"Tawhid* and Jesus' Divine Sonship" in Chapter 12, and the section on "Contextual Theology as Interreligious Dialogue" in Chapter 13, where we are concerned with the relationship of the Son to the Father and, among other things, the meaning of the New Testament use of the word "prophet" with respect to Jesus. Such considerations are not intended to formulate a final truth but to indicate how we justify our Christian position over against certain Islamic interpretations. The Christian position does not escape the above threefold interpretations, but it does occur within the complete consciousness of those inculturations.

Of course, we cannot discuss all recent non-Western inculturations in detail. We will direct ourselves here primarily to the inculturations of the Gospel in Asia and Africa in the last four decades (1965–2005). We cannot always avoid historical digressions, but the focus will remain on more or less *contemporary non-Western theology.* We have deliberately decided not to discuss Latin America after familiarizing ourselves with a great deal of literature from and discussions with Latin American theologians and Western experts. The shifts that are occurring there within Christianity itself – (a) the sometimes spectacular growth of the Pentecostal churches, (b) the still only fragmentary description of a Latin American popular religiosity and (c) the process of reorientation within Latin American liberation theology – make it difficult for the time being to apply the approach (of *double transformation*) described in this chapter to this part of the world. In due course we would like to write on Latin America from the perspective of an approach developed especially for this part of the world. For the moment, the law of the handicap of a head start could apply to Latin American liberation theology: ahead with respect to the struggle against social injustice but behind with respect to the integration of that struggle into the broad *popular religion.* At this time, the concept of inculturation, as we have used it so far, cannot be applied straightwardly to this part of the world.

The criteria regarding new inculturations always have to do with the tension between continuity and discontinuity. To that end, the following starting points will serve:

1. *Inculturation* is something that already occurred *in the Bible* and is always *twofold*: the appropriated concepts undergo a certain metamorphosis in a new context but also change their new context. It is therefore certainly a *double transformation*.

2. Jesus was never seen exclusively as a *local hero of the faith*. All the concepts that were applied to him, derived from a specific context, always claimed to articulate his meaning in a wider context. In other words, *the contextual Jesus* is always also – in principle or potentially – considered to be *the universal* Jesus.

3. *The recognition of new aspects in the interpretation of Jesus can refer to two phenomena: the exposure of aspects of the biblical or early Christian transmission that have until now remained hidden or underexposed or the discovery of new meanings that had been truly unknown until then and therefore not yet been formulated.* With respect to the former, one can point to the wealth of images in the biblical and early Christian traditions that are often not anywhere near to being exhausted. With respect to the latter, all kinds of questions concerning the progress of the work of the Spirit of God arise.

4. *The idea of mediation is inseparably attached to the person of Jesus.* We see that the idea is receiving different emphases in *three directions* worldwide. Jesus is then seen as the one who:
    (a) restores the *right relationship* between God and human beings;
    (b) opens the way for the *deification* of the human being;
    (c) opens the way for the *humanization* of God.

The first three points more or less summarize what has been argued thus far. The fourth point adds another dimension, namely, that of the purpose of Jesus' mediation between God and human beings.

This mediation can have in view *the restoration of the proper relationship* between God and human beings, as, for example, characterized by Karl Barth in the second, completely revised edition of his commentary on Paul's letter to the Romans (1922) by a reference to the book of Ecclesiastes (5:2) as "God is in heaven and you are on earth." The question then is whether Jesus is able to restore this relationship primarily because he is God or primarily because he is human. The discussion thus concerns his divine and human natures. That was the question in the classical Christological debate, but it was also a major part of the debate with Muslims. In African theology too, finding the right relationship between God and human beings is central. The ancestors play an important role in finding that relationship.

This mediation can also be intended to *take up* the human being, as it were, *into the divine existence* as the final end of a transformation process. The discussion then focuses on the question of how close a human being can get to God and the extent to which he can leave his humanity behind him. To what extent – a central question goes – can and must the difference between God and human beings continue to be used in this *deification process?* This is a debate that occurred in church history with the Greek church fathers and is now taking place in ecumenical discussions concerning the Eastern Orthodox concept of *theosis* (deification). A key text here is the famous statement by Athanasius in *De Incarnatione* 54: "He, indeed, assumed humanity that we might become God."[19] We will return to this in the section on the nature of this mediation in Chapter 17, also in relation to the Hindu and Buddhist images of Jesus.

One can also point to the *humanization* of God as a third intention. Here the question is whether the true humanity that Jesus reveals can also be seen as the true destiny of God. And the question that follows is of course what the humanization process precisely means. This question is central for the Protestant Taiwanese theologian Choan Seng Song and the Roman Catholic Sri Lankan theologian Alois Pieris. We will discuss it in the last two sections of Chapter 3. In Western theology, it was primarily Bonhoeffer who made this question his own and answered it in phrases like: "The cradle shows the man who is God."[20] The theological term used here is God's self-emptying, his *kenosis*. Philippians 2:6–7 is the chief witness for that view; the text states that Christ, "being in very nature God, did not consider equality with God something to be grasped, but made himself nothing, taking the very nature of a servant, being made in human likeness."

No one can jump over his own shadow, and in this study that means that the question of the meaning of Jesus cannot be posed in a vacuum but only against the background of my own theological development. This has been influenced by my Calvinistic background in which God is conceived of in a strong Trinitarian way. From the relationship with God the Creator that was disrupted by sin, salvation is sought via a mediator, Jesus, to whom one attempts to get as close as possible through the Holy Spirit. The threefold arrangement is not necessarily a limitation or a straitjacket.

The North American Roman Catholic theologian Dave Burrel pointed out in his study *Freedom and Creation in Three Traditions*[21] that this threefold speaking of God is a part of all three so-called Abrahamic religions: Judaism, Christianity and Islam. It is thus a *source experience* – in this case a disrupted source experience – a *liberation experience* and an *experience of inspiration* of a restored relationship. The (disturbed or not) source experience has everything to do with God, the Father of Jesus, with Yahweh and with

Allah. The liberation experience has to do with the way in which the words of Jesus (the Word), of the Torah and of the Qur'an offer a way out. And the Holy Spirit, the Covenant, and the *Umma* (the worldwide community of Muslims) offer the prospect of a new relationship.

Pieris even goes a step further. In all the major religions he sees salvation being unfolded in three forms: as internal connectedness with another existence, as mediation between us and that existence, bringing salvation, and as increased receptivity after acceptance of the mediation.[22]

But such broad and quite vague parallels put us on the path of abstraction, and that is not the path we want to follow in this study. We will therefore now leave that path. We referred to Burrel and Pieris only to show that the professed Trinitarian way of thinking is not necessarily a straitjacket.

Until now, however, the tenor of our discussion has been that we want to seek the worldwide recognition of insights of faith in the recognition of the authenticity of more specific faith experiences. We will stick to this position in order to prevent recognitions that are too quick and thus annex other experiences. In such a process, the social circumstances in which faith experiences arise all too often wrongfully disappear immediately into the background.

A certain abstraction of the confessional (denominational) background is inevitable in non-Western theology. Non-Western theology is becoming characterized increasingly less by its denominational background. That obtains most for the Protestant churches. The Roman Catholic Church still manages to maintain some confessional standards through its central authority and universal extent and attempts to do everything – however contrived it may be sometimes – to attribute an important place to old and new standards. The preparation and widespread distribution in many languages of a *Catechism of the Catholic Church* in 1992 fit that policy entirely. It is apparent that Roman Catholic theologians worldwide still appeal to Thomas Aquinas and the texts of the Second Vatican Council (1962–1965). They form common reference points.

Within the Protestant churches there is much less of such an appeal to common reference points – simply because there are none. The Calvinist tradition has no confession that enjoys unchallenged universal recognition. It does have confessions that have found acceptance far outside their historical context – the *Heidelberg Catechism* of 1563 and the Westminster Confession of 1646 are the most widespread – but their distribution is ultimately rather limited. The Lutherans do have a fixed reference point in the so-called *Book of Concord* (1578) in which their most important confessions are collected, but only a few works in it – particularly Luther's *Large* and *Small Catechisms* and the *Augsburg Confession* – actually function as reference points, and do so only in the Western world.

For Protestants, from the beginning it was always the appeal to Scripture, the *sola scriptura*, that obtained as the highest norm. Previously and now not at all, given the current appeal to a contextual reading of the Bible, that appeal could not be reduced to one common denominator. No one would want that. This confronts Protestant theology with a towering hermeneutical (exegetical) problem. In that connection we referred to the perspectives that could lie in the creative reflection on the concept *transmission community* as a modern description of the classical concept of the *catholicity of the church*.

If, in addition to the appeal to Scripture, one also appeals to one's own written sources of the history of the religion on the continent in question, the whole affair becomes even more complicated. We can see that in the Protestant Indian theologian Stanley Samartha.[23] We then land via the inculturation debate in the midst of an extensive discussion on the place of the Bible in a complete, millennia-old Asian library of holy books. We will discuss the questions that attend this phenomenon in the first section ("The Bible and Other Asian Holy Books") of Chapter 3 and the first section ("Too Western?") of Chapter 17.

There is no single African or Asian Lutheran, Anglican or Reformed theology. One does find increasing mention of a non-Western contribution to theological publications of, for example, the Lutheran World Federation, the World Alliance of Reformed Churches and the Anglican Church, but this contribution is usually not interpreted as an important contribution to African or Asian Lutheranism or Asian Calvinism. Rather, it is seen as a contribution that illustrates the variegated nature of the church traditions.

In this study we will cite as much as possible the church background of the writers we will be quoting. But this is often not a relevant detail (any longer). At most, it is sometimes informative regarding their frame of reference, primarily as far as older, non-Western theologians are concerned, whose thinking has been heavily stamped by the Western, confessional institution where they received their doctorate.

It is often said that, just as there is no European or North American theology, so there is no African or Asian theology. After all, there is such a great religious and, consequently, theological variety per country, linguistic area and region that such general labels are far too crude. That variety leads us to conclude in this study that we can in no way strive for completeness, not even for representativeness. Rather, we will present *illustrations*, i.e. illustrations of the deep theological questions with which contemporary inculturation confronts Christianity. The questions thus have to do with the position of the Bible, the interest of the early Christian development of doctrine and the position of Christianity with respect to the other world religions.

We will return once more to the question with which we began: *In what culture would Jesus feel most at home?* Posed abstractly in this way, it is of course a rather strange question. We can, after all, not escape the fact that Jesus lived in a concrete culture and that the first and strongly influential meanings were attributed to him from a very specific culture. Nevertheless, that does not settle the question. For who says that that culture is/was not a Procrustean bed for Jesus?

Why would aspects that have not yet been articulated in the history of doctrine that we know not emerge in other cultures? We cannot determine definitively the meaning of past events on the basis of our existing, always limited knowledge, can we? In essence, we should then – stated paradoxically – attempt to predict the future from the past. If the past is to have a future, however, then it must also be given the chance for that.

From the wealth of the history of doctrine, we uncover again and again experiences and insights that have been covered by later layers. Thus, we are always discovering forgotten truths behind and beneath doctrines. They do not take anything away from the doctrines but sometimes place them in a new perspective. For, indeed, the future of the dogmatic past of the church cannot be predicted. The question of the changeableness of language alone already makes that impossible.

The great affinity that the church in India especially has with the gospel of John should, in this context, make us think. Can the gospel of John be said to come fully into its own only in India? Could the meaning of Jesus' "descent into hell" only be grasped in those cultures where they still hold that future generations can hope for a final liberation from their ancestors?[24] There are dozens of questions to ask – enough to show that the question with which we began is not as strange as it may seem.

But good questions do not allow easy answers. The most specific follow-up question ("Must God remain Greek?") could include the suggestion that we are searching for an alternative to a Greek God. If God can no longer be Greek, what must he be then? What cap would fit him best? The Chinese have an apropos expression for offering someone something that does not really fit him: "placing Mr. Chang's hat on Mr. Li's head." That it does not fit is obvious.[25] But what is the alternative? Must Li just go around the whole time with his own hat? And does it mean that God, instead of remaining Greek, must now become Korean, Chinese, Indian, South African, Kenyan, Ghanian or Rwandan?

Whoever has clearly understood the essence of what has been argued in this chapter thus far will not give a simple affirmative answer. The tenor of the argument was, after all, that Christians feel both at home and not at home in their own culture. Or, to use the words from the famous *Epistle to Diognetus* (5,1) from the second century: "For them, any foreign country is a motherland, and any motherland is a foreign country."[26] A

Christian will feel at home everywhere and nowhere. With Augustine, we can say that on earth Christians are inhabitants of two kingdoms: an earthly and a heavenly kingdom.

The debate that the Jewish Polish-French philosopher Emmanuel Levinas conducted with the German philosopher Martin Heidegger after the first space flight by the Russian cosmonaut Yuri Gagarin in 1960 is a good example of this tension. In his now classic essay "Building, Dwelling, Thinking," Heidegger gave the anthropological meaning of what it means to have a familiar and safe place to live and worked that out convincingly – as far we are concerned.[27] But for Levinas, Gagarin's space flight made it clear that, in an age of space travel, no one could and would want to be bound to a fixed place on earth. He worked out that position in his now famous short article, "Heidegger, Gagarin and us."[28]

Heidegger indicates correctly that a person needs to be at home somewhere and cannot always be on the road like an eternal drifter. Without critical nuancing, however, his argument runs the danger of having no defence against a nationalism associated with a certain territory that is hostile to those who come from elsewhere.

Levinas indicates correctly that a person is not – like most animals – bound to a fixed place. But Levinas' position here comes awfully close to the literary image of the human being as the eternally "wandering Jew," the "flying Dutchman" or "wandering Odysseus." That is not an attractive perspective either. After all, it is only the poorest or the wealthiest who are always travelling – the former compelled by their stomach and the latter by boredom.

The two positions cited here are good illustrations of the two extremes between which a Christian will always seek a path. This way is formulated, briefly and to the point, in the New Testament in the classic Christian saying of being "in but not of the world" (John 18:36; Rom. 12:2). Nowhere did we ever come across a contribution during the preparation of this study in which this Pauline starting point was questioned. But reference was made to it even in the most divergent contexts. Here we see a confirmation of what is argued in the first section of Chapter 1, namely that the relationship between religion and culture is seldom a one-to-one relationship. There is always space for distance between them.

A, by no means, minor complication in the inculturation debate constitutes the simple but often overlooked fact that we never have a clear image of the subject and object of the inculturation event. Who inculturates what?

With respect to the "what," the object, the meaning attributed to Jesus by believers, we keep searching and groping for the most adequate words and concepts to imagine this mystery of divine nearness. We never grasp that revelation event completely in language and in concepts. It is not for nothing that Paul writes: "Now we see but a poor reflection as in a mirror.... Now I know in part" (1 Cor. 13:12). And in Romans 11:33–34, he sighs: "Oh, the depth of the riches of the wisdom and knowledge of God! How unsearchable his judgments, and his paths beyond tracing out! 'Who has known the mind of the Lord? Or who has been his counselor?'" The inability to come to complete understanding affects not only Paul but everyone who attempts to articulate the meaning of Jesus in his own language and culture. There is no cut and dried recipe for expressing the meaning of the divine nearness in one's own situation.

Also with respect to the "who," the subject, the culture in which meaning is attributed to Jesus, we are still unable to trace theoretically what happens precisely in the interplay between faith as a "belief system" and a culture as a "value system." How does a culture leave traces as a pattern of norms and values in someone's belief? And how precisely do the conceptions of our faith influence our norms and values? Even if there is usually no one-to-one relationship – a complete identification – between faith and culture, they do influence each other. No one can say how that interchange occurs precisely. A secular government does not as such make a country more secular and a Christian government does not as such make a country more Christian. No single study seems to have been able to capture this difficult phenomenon of the interaction between faith and culture in broad terms that can be used straightforwardly. The differences vary too much from situation to situation for that, and such an interaction has to go through too many channels. And if a plausible explanation is offered in a creative study, that explanation is usually valid for only a short time. Within a few years the religion-culture relationship can change worldwide, as can be seen by the attack on the twin towers in New York on September 11, 2001.

It becomes still more complicated when elements from one culture are transferred to another. In connection with this we spoke earlier of *mutual* or *double transformation*. The dynamic of such a twofold process appears to elude constantly any pattern to which researchers call our attention. Theologically, with respect to the subject, here the work of the Holy Spirit will always be indicated as the driving force between each inculturation and a parallel will often be made with the incarnation.

No Transmission without Solidarity

Always crucial in each form of transmission is the feeling of urgency and involvement. The transmission will be successful only if it is needed and if it expresses courtesy (involvement). The reproach of a lack of true solidarity with the needs of the continent is heard repeatedly from Asia especially, the continent where transmission of the Gospel failed for the most part. In Asia, Christianity remained a "strange" religion for too long, intended only for those who wanted to become alienated from their own situation. This situation has changed drastically. Christianity in Asia has received an unmistakable Asian face. And that is also why solidarity with the Asian context has also become priority number 1. Our first thesis is thus: *no transmission without solidarity* (I).

That solidarity can, of course, take many forms. In the case of the *dalits*, the casteless untouchables in India, many of whom are Christians, solidarity can assume the form of resistance to the caste system. One can thus speak of *cultural resistance* in connection with the inculturation of the Gospel. We see that in Korea as well in the circles of so-called Minjung theology.[29]

In a situation of social reconstruction, as in South Africa after apartheid, there was a strong appropriation of old (African) values in order to help restore dignity to tens of millions of former "second-class citizens."[30]

Solidarity can sometimes also consist to a large degree of *agreeing on what* is considered suitable *in the dominant culture*. The position of Christians as a religious minority can be so weak and threatened that a large degree of agreement regarding the dominant (religious) culture is essential for their survival.[31] Stronger or weaker examples of this form of solidarity have appeared in recent decades and sometimes still do in China, India and Indonesia. It has to do with situations in which millions of Asian Christians live – thus not a marginal occurrence! Outside the context in question, this form of solidarity in particular quite often meets with scepticism by Christians who live in a comfortable majority situation. That is too easy and quick a judgement; a certain reservation is required here. In some situations, it can, after all, also be a command by the Gospel to walk two miles with someone when forced to walk one (Matt. 5:41). We also see sometimes how – for example with respect to ancestor worship in Korea – the discussion on the degree of adaptation takes shape internally over time in a way that is satisfying to many.

Inculturation: Between Confirmation and Denial

Our second thesis is that, theologically speaking, *inculturation always takes place between two poles: the incarnation on the one hand and the cross and resurrection on the other* (II). The incarnation of the Word (John 1:14) implies that God wants to dwell among people. That means that the divine wants to take on cultural garb. While the incarnation represents the *fact* of the assumption, the cross and resurrection represent the *nature* of the assumption and, in fact, its *critical* character. The cross and resurrection are a model for dying and rising with Christ, an event that is symbolized in baptism. That is a critical event of dying and rising. We die to our old Adam and rise up as people reborn with Christ, our second Adam. It is not for nothing that Jesus says that only those who are prepared to lose themselves will find themselves (Mark 8:35; John 12:24). Believers are expected to make this experience their own not only at the moment of their baptism but throughout their whole lives. Baptism thus always refers to a critical *process of purification*, a catharsis. Whereas incarnation stands for confirmation, affirmation, the cross and resurrection stand for denial, negation and finding oneself through losing oneself.

If we then consider the incarnation and cross to be characteristic of a theologically adequate approach to the inculturation process, we refer to the same phenomenon described above as *double transformation*. That is why the incarnation can never be described without the experience of cross and resurrection. *Indwelling* never occurs without change on the entering and receiving sides, and *change* never occurs without solidarity (identification). No single culture can reveal anything (new) about Jesus apart from this interaction. Account should always be taken *in* this event, however, of new, creative syntheses.

How Do They Help Us?

Finally, we must ask the critical question of what precisely we can expect from the new inculturations of the meaning of Jesus in non-Western cultures. How do they help us? Are they a kind of panacea for church growth? Sometimes it seems that that is the undertone in many expositions by both Western and non-Western theologians on the inculturation of the Gospel in the non-Western world. The tenor of many arguments seems to be that, had Christianity simply adapted to Asian culture, for example, it would have become more rooted in Asia.

As we will show in our discussion of the "Korean" and "Japanese" Jesus, the correctness of this reasoning cannot always be demonstrated. A unique Japanese theology developed comparatively early in the twentieth century (immediately after the Second World War) in Japan, but this theology does not hold any special attraction. Only one per cent of the Japanese population is Christian. In Korea, Christian theology – despite the earlier cited example of assumption of the Korean name of God *Hananim* – has taken on a strongly Western character, primarily in the large churches. It is for that reason that the Korean Presbyterian theologian

Heup Young Kim can say somewhat bluntly: "There is Christianity in Korea, but no Korean Christianity!"[32] Nevertheless, after the Second World War, more than twenty-five per cent of the population became Christian. Thus, other factors played a role as well (on the differences between Japanese and Korean Christians see the section on the attitude of Japanese Christians to the state in Chapter 7).

If church growth is not the direct result of a successful inculturation, and therefore cannot be the immediate goal either, what then is? A better form of Christianity? A different Asia, Africa and Latin America? The Congolese Roman Catholic theologian Metena M'nteba raises this question in an article aptly titled "Inculturation in the 'Third Church': God's Pentecost or Cultural Revenge?"[33] By the "Third Church" he means the African Church that is emerging from the original Oriental Church (the "First Church") and largely formed by the Western Church as the "Second Church." Is the forming of a truly African church to be seen as a late fruit of Pentecost or are the old African cultures now grabbing their chance to bend the strange intruder to their will as the "revenge of the cultures"?

Has – he asks critically – the Western inculturation of Jesus' meaning in the last 2000 years made the West more Christian in the sense of more social, peace-loving? Has it drastically changed Western society? There has been an intense debate for decades in Europe and North America on how Christian or non-Christian Western culture is. Has the culture wrested free, thanks to the Enlightenment, from the grip of the church and Christianity or is the Enlightenment also partly a fruit of Christianity? That is an endless discussion that deteriorates into the trivial question of whether we can connect the joys and burdens of our cultural achievements with Christianity.

In any case, that debate does make clear that the fruit of the inculturation of the Gospel in the West is disputed.[34] Given this (bad) example, is there any reason to have higher expectations with respect to other continents? Modesty seems to be the wise choice here – a modesty that also has everything to do with the question of the extent to which religions truly function to improve the world. The opposite can always be argued: governments are supposed to improve the world and religions should point people to the limits of their own desperation or hope as a result of their own deeds.

With respect to new inculturations, therefore, it seems more meaningful to concentrate, with M'nteba, on the question of the existential experience of the Gospel in Africa and Asia, and not on the question of, for example, an Africanization or Asianization of Christianity. Then it will be clear that the question of the inculturation of the Gospel is not exclusively a question that has to do with *the present* of non-Western Christianity and with *the past* of Western Christianity. It also affects *the present* of Western Christianity.

It concerns the place the cross and resurrection can occupy in an individual human life and in human society as a whole. It is only too much apparent from Jesus' own life that a life that is characterized by cross and resurrection cannot be calculated in terms of profit and loss. The di-unity of affirmation (incarnation) and negation (cross and resurrection) has too much to do with *revelation* for that to be the case: with the surprising revelation of that which was unknown until now and never thought of previously.

Part II: The Asian Religious Context

In distinction from Africa or Latin America, Christianity encountered a context in Asia that was stamped religiously by the holy books of other religions. It is obvious, therefore, that the meaning of Jesus in Asia was related implicitly or explicitly to these other religions (Samartha). The sources for this included not only the study of the literature but also the life stories of Asian Christians, which often reflect the central stories of more than one religion (Song). Given the current Asian situation of overwhelming poverty, the connection should be sought preferably in stories of suffering (Pieris). In the second part of this chapter, we will look at the "critical Asian principle" that a large number of theological institutions in Asia have drawn up, on the basis of the above sketch of the Asian religious and social situation, as a guide for doing theology. What emerges clearly here is how the interweaving of the divine and human is viewed as one of the most prominent features of doing theology in Asia.

3   Sources of Asian Theology

The Bible and Other Asian Holy Books (Samartha)

The question of the "Asian Jesus" confronts us immediately with the question of how contemporary Asian Christians understand their own religious tradition. What, in their view, are the most important theological notions? Asian Christianity cannot be understood apart from its relation to the other great Asian world religions (Hinduism, Buddhism, Islam, Taoism and Confucianism) and *to the immense masses of the hopelessly poor.*

To illustrate this starting point, we will look at three Asian theologians (Samartha, Song and Pieris) in this first chapter of Part II. All three have given a close accounting of the above starting point from their own context, each with his own emphasis. Samartha and Song are concerned primarily with the *sources* of Asian theology, whereas Pieris' concern is the current situation in Asia. All three have left abundant traces in Asia and have acquired an authoritative position both within and outside of Asia, which can be seen in the honorary doctorates, visiting professorships and executive positions in Asian theological institutions and organizations. They can certainly be considered representative for the 1980s and 1990s.

Who Jesus is in Asia is coloured not only by the biblical tradition but also by familiarity with the written sources of other religions. These sources also contain stories of divine or human figures who travelled the path between the divine and the human in a special way and to whom believers preferably turn. To get a good view of the Asian Jesus, we have to reflect first on how Asian Christians relate to those sources.

A small book by the Protestant Indian theologian, Stanley Samartha (1920–2001), can serve as an introduction to this issue. The book, *The Search for New Hermeneutics in Asian Christian Theology*, which was published in 1987, was written under the auspices of Serampore College in West Bengal.

The basic starting point is that the holy books of a certain religion cannot be viewed as the exclusive possession of the members of that religion; rather, the holy books of the great world religions belong to the spiritual heritage of all of humankind.[1] A second starting point is that the Bible is not a Western book and that the revelation to which it witnesses did not occur in a Western historical context and was not written down in a Western language. The Christians in the West gave their own Western interpretation to the witness later. That also gives Asian theologians latitude to search for an Asian interpretation of the Bible. That interpretation will differ fundamentally from that in the West, because the West has only one holy book and has been influenced strongly by that book, whereas Asia has been influenced by the holy books of a great number of other religions for centuries before the Bible arrived.

The Asian interpretation of existence has been coloured for some millennia by the holy writings of Hinduism, Buddhism, Confucianism and Taoism. In comparison to them, Christianity – and thus also the Bible – is certainly a latecomer to East Asia. The Hindus had their Upanishads, Brahmasutras and the Bhagavadgita much earlier. The Buddhists had their Tripitaka (Sutra, Vinaya and Abhidharma) of the Pali canon, and the Confucians had their Analectica of Confucius and the Taoists their Tao Te Ching by Lao Tse.

In India, the books of the threefold canon of Hinduism have been the subject of continuous commentary and contemporizing throughout the centuries in various strong revival movements. During the Indian struggle for independence against the English in the second half of the 1940s, almost every political leader of significance wrote his own commentary on the Bhagavadgita. Thus, this work had direct significance for the Indian people's experience of freedom, and the content thus belongs to the Indian existential faith experience.

The same obtains for the Qur'an in the Muslim areas of Asia (Pakistan, Bangladesh and Indonesia), even though there is also an important difference between the way in which people treat a holy book within Islam, as one of the three Semitic religions from the Middle East, and the way in which people do that in the ancient religions of India and China. Judaism, Christianity and Islam are typical religions of the book, and the other Asian religions are much less so, even though the importance of being able to recite texts in Hinduism and Buddhism should not be underestimated.

Certainly as far as the East Asians are concerned, the Bible and the Qur'an can be called "foreign" books, which originated in another way of thinking than theirs. That is why it is such a long and difficult process for Asian translations of the Bible to become part of the living property of the culture in whose language they have been translated. Up to now, not a single Bible translation has been able to fulfil the role that, for example, the Luther Bible filled for the Germans, the King James Bible for the English and the Dutch Authorized Version (*Statenbijbel*) for the Dutch. It is exclusively Hindu texts that play a comparable role in India. Bible texts would probably receive that significance only if Christian authors succeed in translating central biblical themes into poems and stories and thus also into daily Asian life. It would then also be clear that the great themes are not the exclusive property of the Bible but are also found in Buddhist and Hindu writings.[2]

The important role that the tradition of interpretation in Hinduism, Buddhism, Confucianism and Taoism plays right up until the present makes Asian Christians realize that their non-Christian neighbours have their own religious tradition of interpretation that has developed independently for some millennia without any outside influence. The essence of their own tradition of interpretation lies in a view of reality in which they attempt to bridge the gulf (dichotomy) between subject and object, between the knower and the known. The knower is transformed by true knowledge. No single form of interpretation (*exegesis*) leads to the truth on its own. Truth always has to do with the purification of the human spirit, with the transformation of the heart and discipline with respect to the physical aspect of being human.[3]

Religious texts are always intended to bring us to existential truth. That truth breaks through at the moment that two-way traffic arises and our existential questions come into contact with the ultimate divine concern for us. Truth thus arises where an encounter occurs. The concern that one experiences as coming from God is not purely a matter of human knowledge. Rather, this concern is the basis of our questions. It is thus object and subject at the same time. That is precisely the experience of the mystics of all times, places and religions: it is the fusion of subject and object, of I and not-I.[4] In the following chapters we will see how this fusion returns continually as a central motif in Hinduism and Buddhism. The difference between Hinduism and Buddhism has to do primarily with the question of the extent to which there is still room in this fusion for the divine that transcends the human. This is less explicitly the case in Buddhism than in Hinduism.

We agree with Samartha's argument on the intention of religious texts. They presuppose indeed a form of knowledge that breaks through the conception of knowledge formed by the modern sciences. Religious knowledge is not concerned with empirical knowledge, the knowledge of the sciences based on verifiable facts, and also not on the discursive knowledge of the humanities based on consensus. It is, indeed, a form of knowledge that presupposes a certain unity between subject and object, the knower and the known. We also subscribe to Samartha's argument for taking account of the other, non-Christian Asian religious sources. It confirms completely our own experience with our work on this study. Indeed, it proved to be impossible to study contemporary Indian, Chinese, Japanese and Indonesian Christian theology without becoming acquainted with the Upanishads, the Bhagavadgita, the Analectica, the Qur'an and the Tao Te Ching. Asian theology contains far too many references to these texts to ignore them. But in the meantime, there is still the question of the specific role of the Bible in the Christian community of transmission. We looked briefly at this question in Chapter 2, in the section on "Methodology" and we will return to this in the conclusions in the section on "Too Western?" in Chapter 17.

From Israel to Asia: A Theological Leap (Song)

More than ten years earlier than Samartha, in 1976, the Taiwanese theologian Choan Seng Song, also a Protestant, raised the question of the role of the biblical tradition in the transmission of faith in Asia as well. He did so in a programmatic article called "From Israel to Asia: A Theological Leap." In this article on the "theological leap" between Israel and Asia, Song calls his Asian fellow believers to dare to leap directly from the biblical stories to Asia and vice versa, and to separate themselves from the compartmentalization that two millennia of Western tradition had produced.

Whereas we saw Samartha arguing for the rediscovery of the hidden treasures in the holy books of Asia in order to answer the question of what Jesus can mean for Asian Christians, we see Song – not in contrast to but rather parallel to Samartha's argument – argue for an Asian access of its own to the Bible, separate from the (Western) tradition until that point. The Western tradition is inextricably bound up with the history of Western imperialism. It was only colonialism that created the conditions for mission and that background gave Christianity in Asia a bad name. That is why Asian Christianity needs to look for its own access to the Bible. Only in that way can it become clear that the history of God's revelation – the way God wants to relate to people – is different from the history of the Western church and missions.

Israel needs to be seen as the symbol of how God wants to reveal himself to individuals and to peoples. Every other people can mirror itself in this history. Here, the actual history of a people such as, for example, that of China or Indonesia is just as important as that of Israel. The significance of Israel is that its history can be transferred symbolically to every other context. Song sees it as the task of Asian theology to complete this leap from Israel to Asia and to tell the story of, for example, the Chinese, Indonesian or Korean exodus, exile and destruction of the temple, and to look for a Chinese, Indonesian or Korean Joseph, Job, David, Amos, Ruth and Rachel.[5]

In this way Israel gets itself back again from the other peoples, as it were, and a leap back from Asia to Israel occurs. Song speaks here of a blessing in the opposite direction. As all peoples will be blessed in Abraham's people according to the Abrahamic blessing (Gen. 12:2–3), the reverse can also happen.

In this context Song cites a number of concrete examples from the Old Testament that show how other people bless Israel: Melchizedek who comes and blesses Abraham (Gen. 14:17–20), Nebuchadnezzar who is rewarded for the fact that he taught Tyre a lesson on behalf of Israel (Ezek. 29:1–3) and the well-known example from Isaiah 44:28 in which God says via his prophet that Cyrus, the king of Persia, "is my shepherd and will accomplish all that I please." And he does so while also stating explicitly that Cyrus, who can be called "God's anointed," did not acknowledge God (Isa. 45:1–4).

The above examples make it clear to Song that a Christian interpretation of history can never be complete if other non-Christian peoples cannot play their own role in it. Christians share in their lot; their cares are also Christian cares.[6] Thus, in addition to calling Asian Christians to become "Israel" themselves, Song arrives at the same point that we just discussed in connection with Samartha's work, i.e. taking account of central Asian religious motifs in the transmission of the meaning of Jesus.

In his later theological development, Song applied this integration process not so much to the major theological concepts from the different Asian religions but rather to the ordinary stories on the often terrible living conditions of millions in Asia. An *Asian incarnation* of the Gospel occurs by means of those stories – an incarnation that can be understood as a direct implication of Jesus' becoming flesh. It is apparent from this that God wanted to assume the form of a human being. That shows the solidarity between God and human beings. There is no limit to that solidarity.

Every Christian view of revelation and of salvation should be related to those that are not included within Christianity. It can be said, therefore, that the divine Word has also taken on "Asian flesh": the incarnation also occurs in Asia. This Asian flesh is also crucified.[7] Song is thinking here primarily of the hundred million poor in China, India, Indonesia, Indochina and the Philippines. Jesus identifies with them. The title, *Jesus, the Crucified People*, of the first part of his trilogy "The Cross in the Lotus World of Asia," is thus also intended, indeed, as identification: Jesus *is* the crucified people.

In this identification, the question is not so much *who* Jesus is, how the divine is related to the human in him, etc. but rather *where* Jesus is. Just as God can be called the story of Jesus and Jesus the story of God, so Jesus can be called the story of people and people the story of Jesus.[8] In an article, "The Decisiveness of Christ" in a volume published in the same year as the article "From Israel to Asia," Song emphasizes the same conclusion. If the incarnation does indeed mean that God shares human existence, then everything we say about the human being can be considered to be an integral part of what we say about God as well. This becomes a central theme in Song's later work.[9]

In his view, *theology* should always also be a form of *anthrop*ology: *human* theology. The *logos* of God (*theos*) is the same as the *logos* of the human being (*anthropos*): both find their ultimate destiny in each other.[10] With this accent on the interwovenness of the knowledge of God and human beings, Song, as a Presbyterian, is in good Calvinist company. Calvin begins his *Institutes* immediately with the same kind of thesis: "Nearly all the wisdom we possess, that is to say, true and sound wisdom, consists of two parts: the knowledge of God and of ourselves."[11]

Song sees the unlimited solidarity between God and human beings expressed already in the confession of God as creator. Christians have too often made creation a "Christian colony."[12] As the "second Adam," Jesus is also a model for the way in which God is connected to human beings. God cannot be conceived in Jesus without the human being. The "decisive" moment that Jesus reveals is that he reveals what must be evoked in human beings so that they can respond to the love of God shown in Jesus.[13] Song calls this the protomodel on the basis of which a Christian searches for recognition and acknowledgement in submodels outside of the Christian tradition.[14] Thus, he states in so many words that Jesus is a model for the way in which God and human beings are related to each other. That model, however, is not an exclusive model but an inclusive one. It can also be filled in more precisely and thus finds its fulfilment in other religious models.

Essentially, Song's intention can be summarized in the sentence: Christians in Asia must restore their *solidarity with their neighbours* in Asia.[15] At certain times, one could also say of the other religions in Asia: "I have not found anyone in Israel with such great faith" (Matt. 8:10). Song can speak in this context of "dialogical conversion" between the religions. People can learn, from one another's religious concepts, what the real issue is: "human theology."[16]

This solidarity arises primarily through listening. Song speaks in this context – using a Buddhist saying – of the "third" eye, i.e. the eye that sees things that cannot be seen with the other two. Using that third eye, Song looks at the situation in which many millions of Asians actually live. That is also why he calls his theology "Third-Eye Theology": this is a theology that listens to the popular stories in all great religions and thus attempts to trace what emerges in the daily struggle for existence regarding spirituality. It is only in this way, on the basis of such a "people hermeneutic," that we can be on Jesus' track, because people are the "clues" to the real Jesus.[17] Theology is thus given a human face. Let us tell one another our names and our accompanying stories – then we will again know who we are. That is what he also argues in *Tell Us Our Names: Story Theology from an Asian Perspective*.[18]

Song does not mean here at all that Christians can adopt all kinds of things from other religions uncritically. In his *Jesus, the Crucified People*, he criticizes sharply the way in which Hindus treat the untouchable, casteless *dalits* and condemns the caste system. He also criticizes the paralyzing effect of the Buddhist understanding of human destiny (*karma*).[19] Nor does he at all intend to arrive at a universal, syncretistic religion that is the same for everyone everywhere. Rather, through "popular storytelling" he wants to come close to what truly touches the hearts of Asians. That is the biggest problem he encounters as an Asian Christian – the Christian inability to touch the heart of the Asian multitudes. He sees that the other Asian religions do not do that (any longer). But who looks after the multitudes, then? Do they have someone who does so, a comforter, a saviour?

Song asks that we in any case listen to them, hear their stories, ask what their names are. Then it will appear that a certain language is also connected with the articulation of experiences and that that language is strongly influenced by the Asian religious context.[20] Within the language to be newly discovered by Christians, a new dialogue with one's Asian neighbours can be started. Then, perhaps, a common basis will also arise for thinking critically, for example, about an alternative to the, in many ways harsh, notion of the imputation that lies at the foundation of the Hindu and Buddhist eternal cycle of rebirth. And, perhaps, there can also be discussions on the critical limit that must be set to the idea of perfection that dominates the Confucian and Taoist view of the human being.[21]

The critical reader will see that we have looked at Song's work over a period of more than twenty years, during which a certain development is noticeable. Song has gradually begun to think less in terms of traditional Western theology. His attention has clearly shifted over the years, being directed more towards the religious dimension of concrete life stories, in which he sees many images that have been borrowed from the existing Asian religions. Since the 1990s he has been constructing his own theology on the basis of those images.

Those images illustrate that proximity to life can be effective only if it is placed against the background of religious symbols, actions and words (writings). The emphasis on stories' proximity to life can break through the fossilization process in a constructive way, a process that always appears in every religion whenever the distance to the original experiences increases. It cannot, however, replace theological reflection.[22] Then we would easily forget that views are always expressed in images and that one view is not another. Religious views can both subjugate and liberate people. Song pointed to that difference many times primarily at the beginning of his theological career. We are again consciously citing those "early" statements here at the end of our discussion of his case for an Asian Jesus because they show that there can be no emphasis on stories at the expense of the concern for the *moral of the story*. Narrative theology is, after all, not narrative itself. The "narrative" does not refer to the character of this form of theology but to the material that it studies. One should also be able to analyse that material critically, if only to break through its enchantment – the epic illusion – and its possibly manipulative character.

Overwhelming Poverty as a Theological Source (Pieris)

Next to Song, it is primarily the Jesuit, Alois Pieris, from the predominantly Buddhist Sri Lanka who, among Asian theologians, has worked out in a penetrating way the inseparable connection between the Asian religious context and Asian poverty and has made reflection on an Asian Jesus fruitful.

Pieris' starting point is a sober approach from the perspective of the history of religion. He divides the history of religion into two categories: *tribal and clan religions*, which are strongly oriented to proximate nature, and *universal religions*, which assume that a transcendent power impacts on our existence. Knowledge of that power can be acquired. It also constitutes an incentive for acting in a committed way. He calls the first category *cosmic religions* and the second *metacosmic*. The first category is regional and the second can – in Pieris' words – land anywhere, like a helicopter. The cosmic religions then constitute, as it were, the landing area that the helicopter can use. Preferably, however, only one helicopter should land on a spot. If several land quickly one after another, then religious conflicts quickly develop. If, however, only one lands and then another much later, then haste is the order of the day: first come, first served. It has happened sometimes that the one helicopter pushed the other out, as Islam pushed Christianity out in the Middle East and North Africa, but such cases are exceptions.

According to this perspective, metacosmic religions can spread only in areas where cosmic religions predominate or where a metacosmic religion was dominant – as, for example, Buddhism in Korea or Islam in certain areas in East Indonesia – but where, apparently, the regional, cosmic religion had retained a stronger grip on the masses than Buddhism or Islam had acquired afterwards.

Applied concretely to Christianity, this means that in those areas where another helicopter has already landed in the form of Islam, Buddhism or Hinduism, there is no more room for Christianity, unless in the sense of inreligionization or interreligionization, instead of inculturation.[23] Pieris reserves the latter term for the one-time entry of a metacosmic religion into a cosmic one.

With this word "interreligionization," Pieris wants to indicate that in these areas where a metacosmic religion that determines the culture already exists, a second metacosmic religion now penetrates the first. The latter, however, does not allow itself to be forced out by a new one, and this causes friction because the present religion is too much interwoven with the culture for that to happen. The whole of human existence in Asia is, after all, *theologically coded*, as Pieris could say in line with Song.[24] He characterizes this trait of being nonetheless intent on inculturation – and for Pieris this is the same as appropriating that culture – as *theological vandalism*. It tears too many concepts and customs irreparably from their context.[25]

It is clear, in light of Part I, that we do not share Pieris' critique of the term inculturation. For Pieris, inculturation is something that occurs only once and should occur flawlessly. It seems to presuppose a certain harmony between the cosmic and the metacosmic religions and has nothing of the dynamic and tension that the concept of double transformation we introduced contains. The concept of interreligionization that Pieris introduces does not seem very fruitful either. Indeed, enough examples can be cited from the history of missions in Asia of a forced and sometimes also violent penetration in cultures that were already occupied religiously. But to declare on that basis that a whole continent is occupied religiously goes a bit far. That would exclude any interaction, whereas Samartha argues for that precisely with his remark that the religious sources of a religion are not the exclusive property of the adherents of that religion. For that matter, that view is certainly not undisputed in Islam.[26]

Nonetheless, Pieris' "occupation theory" does confront us with penetrating questions on the compatibility of several, metacosmic religions in the same region. Can both religions ever have the same cultural impact? Or does religious plurality always require a secular society in which religion is not considered to have any impact?

It is clear that in Asia the world religions do not stand over against one another today like closed entities. That that is not an insight derived exclusively from the study of the literature can be confirmed by everyone who has talked about religion with a cabdriver in any city in Asia. It can be long ride – certainly if one lets drop in an unguarded moment that he is a theologian. It will quickly be clear that people like to talk about religion and readily talk about religion *across religious borders*. Such a simple empirical fact runs parallel to such examples of the inescapability of a certain interaction in the theological literature. We can no longer go back to a situation before that interaction.

Pieris is being completely faithful to his own approach, when he argues that Christianity has a place in a culture formed by Hinduism or Buddhism only if it fills an open spot, a lacuna. He sees such a lacuna in the underdeveloped social religious understanding in both of these religions. In his view, a strong social understanding in Buddhism is preserved, in fact, only in the rare phenomenon of the poor Buddhist monk living in small monastic communities.[27] The spirituality here – a di-unity of wisdom (knowledge) and love (action) – comes closest to that of Jesus.

Pieris also prefers to use the image of the poor monk for Jesus.[28] Both literally and figuratively, he speaks in this context of the *poverty of piety*, using this expression as a critical concept. He is all too familiar with the rich, Buddhist monasteries. It is only the poor, Buddhist monk who is supported by the spirituality of his monastic community (*sangha*) whom he finds credible.[29]

Even more so than Song, Pieris has worked out closely the way in which religion and poverty are bound together in Christianity and related this to his view of Jesus. For him, religion and poverty have two poles – liberation and bondage – and two dimensions – psychological and sociological. A one-sided internalization or externalization of poverty and religion can be prevented and the positive and negative aspects of both concepts be seen clearly only if all four aspects are taken into account. Only then can the conclusion be drawn that *religion without poverty* and *poverty without religion* are amputated concepts, i.e. without concern or perspective, respectively.[30] Because of this connection between religion and poverty, which comes to expression in an exemplary way in the life of Jesus, Pieris is not concerned so much with the *Asian aspect of this Jesus* but with the *Jesus aspect of all those Asians who live in bitter poverty*.[31] He is not concerned so much with the question of who Jesus is as with what Jesus brings about.

Using images borrowed from biblical geography, he speaks of a twofold baptism of Jesus in the Asian reality: first in the Asian religious reality by means of his baptism in the Jordan as an image of the Asian rivers of life, and subsequently his baptism in the Asian harsh reality of poverty by means of his journey to the cross at Calvary as an image of all the hills with crosses that dot Asia. Jesus does not baptize John the Baptist in the Jordan but *is baptized* by John in the Jordan. In the same way, Asian Christianity must be baptized, immersed, in the Asian rivers of life.[32]

A good theology of baptism always emphasizes that the person being baptized is immersed in the dying of Jesus, in his suffering. That is why Pieris can say that only in a double baptism in the Asian Jordan and in the

Asian Calvary do Jesus and Asia meet each other. Without the "second baptism" there is no true solidarity. Only in this double immersion will the gates of Asian spirituality be opened so that the words and symbols can be found for the situation in which millions of Asians live.[33]

Pieris makes it clear that the contemporary inculturation debate is not about "giving Jesus a place in Asia" but about Jesus "who is not allowed to have a place in Asia" – i.e. the poor who are not allowed to be seen. In this context Pieris also speaks of the "non-Christian Christ" who reveals his face in all the millions of poverty-stricken Hindus, Buddhists and Muslims. For him, the central issue is that all these Asian poor are Jesus: like Jesus they have no decent place to be born (Luke 2:7), no room to live and to work (John 1:46), no safe place in their country to hide from their own leaders (Matt. 12:13ff.), no respectable place to die (Luke 23:23) and no place of their own to be buried (Matt. 27:59). In short, it has to do with creating a place for the "displaced" Jesus. Church and theology need to make an all-out attempt to destroy this "placelessness" of Jesus in Asian societies.[34]

Like Song, Pieris also identifies the suffering of Jesus with the suffering of the poor. It is an identification that has been made in the history of Christianity for two millennia and ultimately goes back to Jesus' own words: "Whatever you did for one of the least of these brothers of mine, you did for me" (Matt. 25:40), followed by the reverse in verse 45: "whatever you did not do for one of the least of these, you did not do for me." For them, it is primarily the poor who, as "crucified people," show the true face of Jesus.[35]

As stated above, Pieris has placed his hope primarily on small monastic-like communities, because it is there that he finds the most inspiring examples in Buddhism of the di-unity of *orare et laborare*, of praying and working, of social analysis and action and introspection. It is from this circle that he also expects the most appropriate images for speaking of Jesus' presence in Asia.[36] According to Pieris, true Asian spirituality must always be grafted onto the *wealth* of the poor, onto their spirituality, and the *poverty* of the believers, their relativization of material goods. In the first di-unity, spirituality will never become a form of escapism but will always be a source of strength for resistance; in the second di-unity, the social struggle always remains embedded in a broader palette of religious desire and trust.[37] Here the distinction between "forced poverty" and "voluntary poverty" is crucial. "Forced poverty" is a stultifying power, but "voluntary poverty" is a vitalizing power, a source of inspiration. The point is that it is often not the rich who are able to free themselves of material concerns and live in spiritual wealth but only the poorest of all. The stultifying power of forced poverty does not then have the last word; it is not able to dominate them.[38]

It is clear from the above that Christian faith in Asia can never be experienced in isolation from the other Asian religions. The current understanding will also leave its traces in increasing measure in the conceptualization of Jesus. Buddhist, Hindu and Islamic motifs as well will inevitably play a role in this. We will show in Chapter 5 that this was already the case in the earliest proclamation of Jesus in seventh-century China.

In addition, the conceptualization of Jesus in Asia will always be coloured by the concrete situation of poverty in which so many – despite Asia's booming economies – still live. Certainly, in comparison with Hinduism and Buddhism, Christianity in Asia will be characterized in a prominent way by its connection with this issue.

4   The Unique *Nature* of Asian Theology

The "Critical Asian Principle"

The way in which the Indian Samartha and the Taiwanese Song formulate their position within the Christian tradition is characteristic of what is now the central starting point in contemporary Asian theology. This starting point is called the "critical Asian principle" and represents a contextual approach to Asian theology. This principle was accepted in 1972 as a starting point by the Southeast Asia Graduate School of Theology (SEAGST) and by the Association for Theological Education in Southeast Asia (ATESEA). This principle formulates what is characteristically Asian and how it can be effective in church and theology.[1] There are seven characteristics to be distinguished:

1. *Plurality* and difference in races, peoples, cultures, social institutions, religions, ideologies, etc. are characteristic of this area.
2. Most of the countries in this area have a *colonial past*.
3. Most of the countries are now involved in a process of *nation-building, development* and *modernization*.
4. The peoples in this region are looking for *authentic self-identity* and for *cultural integrity in a modern context*.
5. Asia is *the birthplace of the great, living world religions*. These religions (primarily the non-Christian) have determined the culture and consciousness of the great majority of the Asian people. They represent (with respect to the West) an alternative lifestyle and experience of reality.
6. The people in Asia are looking for *a social order that transcends the existing alternatives*. A few examples of attempts at this are well-known, but they are often accompanied by authoritarian forms of government that can be justified only as temporary emergency measures.
7. The Christian community is a small minority in the midst of the sizeable Asian population.

It is the intention of the Asian theological institutions that have accepted this principle as their starting point to have these seven characteristics function as a kind of framework for their theologizing. It is clear that this does not present a definitive blueprint but focuses on *method*. It is in that

way that this "critical Asian principle" must become a *situational,
hermeneutical, missiological* and *educative* starting point:

> It is *situational* in the sense that it is determinative for us with respect to the context
> in which we do theology;
> It is *hermeneutical* in the sense that the Gospel and the Christian tradition must be
> applied creatively to this context;
> It is *missiological* in the sense that not only must the Asian context be confronted by
> the Gospel as something from outside but it must also be shown how the Gospel can
> contribute to solving typical Asian problems.
> It is *educative* in the sense that the above starting points will also have to determine
> in a real sense the education in the theological institutions in question.[2]

The formulation of a separate "critical Asian principle" makes clear
how specific and exceptional the Asian situation is,[3] a situation that certainly
has to do not least of all with its enormous number of inhabitants. India,
the country that will probably soon have the highest population in the
world, and China alone already have more than two billion inhabitants.
According to official government figures, approximately 3 per cent of the
Indian population are Christian; that these figures are probably intentionally
kept low means that that there are still more than 25 million Christians in
India. Barrett's *World Christian Encyclopedia* even indicates six per cent
(more than 50 million). In any case, it is several times the number of
Dutch Christians, for example. The majority of Indian Christians belong
to the poorest inhabitants of India. They share that lot – if we also include
the poor from elsewhere in Asia – with two billion others. That is poverty
on a scale that transcends the ability of a rich Westerner to imagine and is
therefore something that a rich Westerner can never take account of in
the same way that an Asian can.

This leads us to a first characteristic of Asian theology: the confrontation
with and theological reflection on *wholesale degrading poverty*. If Asian
theology makes one thing clear, it is this: *poverty without religion is hopeless
and religion without attention for poverty is merciless*. These are two sides
of the same coin, however much this connection is criticized by both the
poor as well as by the religions. Religion can, after all, easily become a
sop – opium was the term Marx used – in the midst of overwhelming
poverty. For that reason, vehement protests are often made against religion
on behalf of the poor. And religion can also become merely an instrument
in the battle against poverty. Even though considerably worse
instrumentalizations are conceivable, no religion wants to be limited
exclusively to the fight against poverty. The transcendent aspect that is
characteristic of every religion in one way or another is denied, and
believers will sooner or later always protest against such an exclusive
instrumentalization.[4]

A second characteristic of the Asian situation is that about half of the Asian population (Vietnam, China and North Korea) still lives under a *communist dictatorship* that does everything it can to reduce the influence of religion. Even though China is slowly moving towards a market economy, it is still a country ruled by a dictatorship. How can such anti-religious, dictatorial regimes hold their own so long in religious Asia? Does that also say something about the way in which religion in Asia, leaving aside the Muslim countries, functions with respect to politics and society?[5]

A third characteristic that goes with the population size is the enormous increase in *environmental pollution* that increased affluence brings, a painful dilemma that has probably kept many Asian political leaders awake at night. If the Chinese act as irresponsibly as North Americans with respect to the environment, the future of the planet looks bleak indeed. Theologically, there is a great fascination in India as well as in China with the "cosmic" Christ, a Christ who can function, as it were, as a life principle for the whole earth (cosmos), thus for the whole creation.[6] Will this argument for a "cosmic" Christ also be related critically to the ecological disasters for which Asia is headed at full speed?[7]

A fourth characteristic is the *quickly changing position of women in Asia*. Asian society, including the religious part of it, is a typically masculine society. It is often the women in rural areas who have a double task: (assisting in) acquiring income for the family through heavy physical labour and looking after the family, often including aged parents. And this double task has been retained in urban areas: a job outside the home and a full-time job taking care of the family.[8] However, we are seeing more and more women expressing their own voice in Asian theology, precisely also in relation to the meaning of Jesus.[9]

Asian Theology in the Whole of World Christianity

It is obvious that the above characteristics of the current Asian situation do not leave theology unaffected and are also increasingly impacting reflection on Jesus. The "Asianization" of reflection on Jesus is no longer to be stemmed, it seems. There is also no reason to do so.

It seems to be beyond dispute that if the New Testament had been written in Asia, concepts like *avatar*, *guru* and *bodhisattva* would have been used to clarify the meaning of Jesus. This would again be accompanied, of course, by all the problems of understanding the exact meaning of these Asian religious concepts on other continents and determining what they add or subtract from the meanings known elsewhere.

As far as this is concerned, we will never escape the paradox that, as soon as Jesus receives a new meaning somewhere in the world within a specific context, that term will not be very recognizable outside that specific context. Wanting to prevent that is the same as searching for a Christological Esperanto – and we all know what happened to Esperanto. In fact, the policy practised in the previous century to present the Asian Christians primarily with the Western understanding of Jesus evokes the memory of the failed introduction of Esperanto – with this difference: Esperanto was a strange, artificial language for *everyone*.

Even when the qualifications applied to Jesus are kept as closely as possible to the concrete content of his message and one speaks of him, for example, as shepherd or healer (doctor), these terms will not necessarily be more recognizable. How many people are still familiar with the phenomenon of shepherd in a time when the world population is converging at a fierce pace in urban conglomerations of millions of inhabitants? And will the phenomenon of doctor not continue to evoke for a long time the associations of "never seen one" and "can't afford one" among the millions of poor?

All these considerations are an indication of the fact that we can take up our responsibility for the worldwide recognizability of the Christian expressions of faith – in theology we call that the *catholicity* of the church – in a meaningful way only if we continually reflect anew on the criteria to be used for that. Part I was an attempt to do so and is, in fact, the result of thirty years (1976–2006) of my own personal and academic reflection on the way in which the transmission of the faith *across borders* is justified in theology.

The concepts *community of transmission* and *double transformation* are thus the core concepts. There can be no transmission without a community that finds it important to transmit something. That importance is usually expressed by (1) the canonizing of central texts in which the essence of the transmission is written, (2) by a tradition of the transmission in which there are warnings of going off track, and (3) by feasts and symbols (sacraments) that contain the existential experience of the essence of the transmission. The transmission, which consists of three components – book, tradition (of teaching) and celebrating community – continually undergoes, as was shown in Chapter 1, "Who Decides?," a process of *double transformation*. Changes always occur on both sides in a process of appropriation.

Apart from these questions of understanding, we also have to ask if words and concepts are always the most penetrating representations of Jesus' significance in every culture. Would it not, for those who are starving, first be actual food? And for Africans would it not primarily be song and dance? Some relativization of the meaning of the words and concepts of theology is thus justified.

In the Asian context, each clarification of the meaning of Jesus by an Asian term (concept) always implies that the life world of a whole other world religion comes with it. For all words that relate in one way or another to "salvation" are simply – as Pieris has stated correctly – already "occupied" religiously. The problem is thus not the religious content of the concepts to be used – that is inevitable in Asia. The problem – or better, the challenge – is to give a careful account of the many "accompanying" associations. The Asians themselves are competent to be the first to judge this.

They themselves will also constantly have to provide the difference between the meaning they now ascribe to Jesus and the religious meanings long familiar to them from their context. The degree to which they (can) indicate that difference will probably also be determinative for the way in which they want to "encounter" and follow Jesus. Here they have a wide variety of possibilities available, which was also the case in New Testament times. Then discipleship also took a wide variety of forms. Not everyone, after all, belonged to the twelve or, later, seventy-two disciples. There were also women who followed him, touched him, asked him questions, cared for him or mourned for him in their own way; there were people who visited him only at night (Nicodemus, John 3:1–13) and those who waited to see which way the wind would blow (Zacheus, Luke 19:1–10), etc. In short, following Jesus took several different, very divergent forms.[10]

Certainly in India, one could perhaps subscribe to the statement made by Felix Wilfred that more people have come into contact with Jesus through "spectators" than through the proclamation of a comparatively small Indian Christian community.[11] He refers here to the many Hindu scholars who, since the nineteenth century, have given Jesus a place in their own Hindu theology. A whole library has in the meantime appeared on that subject – the Jesus reception among Hindu theologians (Clarke, Livermore, Rayan, Schouten, Sharma and Thomas). We will return to that in Part VI.

The Interwovenness of the Divine and the Human

Wilfred also points out that Western theologians will understand something of the "Asian Jesus" if they begin to see how the divine and human are interwoven in Asia. That also explains, perhaps, why the Eastern Asian theologians in the fifth century could not do anything with the statement of the Council of Chalcedon on how Jesus' human nature was related to his divine nature, however neatly Chalcedon left the precise nature of that connection open via negations (inconfusedly, unchangeably, indivisibly, inseparably). The terminology presupposes, however, that there were groups that taught either that the two merged radically into each other or that there was a radical separation of the divine and the human in Jesus. That was not the case, as the detailed research by Grillmeier, among others, in the history of doctrine incontrovertibly showed. It is for that reason that this council, which is usually considered in the West to be one of the most important pillars of the truth about Jesus, only caused confusion in the East and led to an unfruitful division. Both those who emphasized the importance of a clear distinction between Jesus' human nature and his divine nature as well as those who stressed that his human nature was absorbed by his divine nature felt they had been given short shrift. We will see how this point – *the relationship of the divine and the human* – will be the central theme around which everything turns with respect to understanding the "Asian Jesus."[12]

Part III: The Chinese Jesus

With respect to religion, China is viewed as a melting pot of Confucianism, Taoism and Buddhism. Since the seventh century Christianity has also played a small role here and Christians appear to have seen parallels with Jesus in the Buddhist bodhisattvas especially. Now that China is opening up religiously, there is a tendency to link Christianity with religious motifs that have always played a role in China. One can think here of the story about the emperor who, according to a famous passage in Confucius' Analectica, takes the place of his people before the god, Heaven, because of their sins. Or one could think of the way in which "word" and "path," which remind us of John's gospel, can mean the same in Taoism and represent the connection between ethics and mysticism. The same practical slant that characterizes Confucianism and Taoism can be detected in the Chinese variant of Buddhism, Ch'an Buddhism, which is strikingly similar to Japanese Zen Buddhism. In China, religion appears to have to do with very common everyday things, and it is only with difficulty that it displays the detachment so strongly present in Buddhism elsewhere. With the exception of a few forms of Tao Christology, up until now China has not really developed a contextual theology in which new meanings of Jesus are sought candidly against the background of its own rich religious tradition.

5 The Chinese Context

The Image of Jesus among the First Christians in China

It has often been argued that all the great religions come from Asia: Judaism, Christianity and Islam come from West Asia, and Hinduism, Buddhism, Confucianism, Taoism and Shamanism from East Asia. Of all these religions, Buddhism is the most widespread in Asia. It is the dominant religion in Sri Lanka, Thailand, Burma, Cambodia, Vietnam, Laos and Japan, and has left a strong imprint on the Chinese and Korean cultures.

Barrett's *World Christian Encyclopedia* estimates the number of Christians in China at 90 million, twice as much as the official figure. Whatever the exact figure may be, even as a small religious minority in China, Chinese Christianity is becoming an increasingly important factor in world Christianity.

Christianity is usually viewed as a latecomer in East Asia. Its arrival is linked to the missionary work of the Jesuits Robert de Nobili in the seventeenth century in India and Matteo Ricci at the end of the sixteenth century in China. This is incorrect. A well-known historical work like the first part of Moffett's *A History of Christianity in Asia* devotes hundreds of pages to the fact that, from the very beginning of our calendar, not only was there a Roman and a Byzantine Christianity but also a Persian one extending east of the Euphrates into China.

Although we are concerned particularly with new – in the sense of recent – inculturations of the Gospel, to be able to understand those new forms of giving meaning to Jesus, especially in the case of China, we must also look at the history of the Christian inculturations. Because of the discovery in 1623–25 of a three-metre-high, black monumental tablet with Chinese and Syrian inscriptions (the so-called *Sian-Fu* tablet, now preserved in Xian), we have known for almost four centuries that Christianity had reached China at the beginning of the seventh century and acquired an entirely unique form there.

The inscription, erected by a certain Yazedbouzid, informs us that in 635 Bishop Alopen (= Abraham) of Syria brought Christian writings to China that the emperor Tang Tai Zung included in his imperial library for translation from Syrian into Chinese. In 638 the emperor also issued an edict permitting the spread of Christianity. Moreover, he financed the first Christian monastery in China.

The tablet was erected at the very latest in 781 during the Tang dynasty and appears to prove the presence of a specific form of Christianity.[1] The crucifixion is not mentioned, although Jesus' death is. The resurrection is referred to only in vague terms, and prayer for the dead is emphasized.

Early Christianity in China is usually called "Nestorian." The Nestorians were Christians in the Middle East who followed Nestorius in laying strong emphasis on the distinction between the two natures of Jesus: his divine and human natures. For that reason, they are called Dyophysites (*physis* = nature). The Nestorians were condemned at the Council of Chalcedon, because the opponents of their view (or what was considered to be their view) thought it threatened the unity of the divine–human person of Jesus. But contemporary Christians in China still call themselves Nestorians and carry their specific Nestorian crosses (a cross with four arms, often above the base of a lotus leaf) on a chain around their necks, as a lapel pin or as a picture on their tie. A large part of Eastern Christianity proudly decorates itself in this way, bearing the name of someone who was and still is regarded in the West as a heretic. This also holds for Eutyches who held the opposite view to Nestorius' at that time. His disciples, who believed that the human nature of Jesus was absorbed into his divine nature, called themselves Monophysites and bore that name with honour.

Of the written sources that have survived from the seventh century, the so-called *Jesus Messiah Sutra* from 635 is one of the oldest and most well-known. Here Buddhist, Taoist and Confucian terminology is used in connection with the most important events in Jesus' life and to explain his message. As far as content is concerned, Manichaean influences can also be seen.[2]

Manichaeism was a dualist, non-Christian, Gnostic movement founded by Mani (216–276) that arose in Persia and appealed to Christians very much.[3] It held to a sharp opposition between good and evil, light and darkness, flesh and spirit. In the East it displayed a surprising power of integration with respect to Buddhism[4] and continued to exist as a religion in the East until the sixteenth century.

The discovery as such of this tablet does not indicate a broad and massive spread of Christianity in China, even though one could speak, to a certain extent, of a period of blossoming that lasted from 635 to 845. Christianity was probably the faith particularly of the merchants who travelled back and forth between Baghdad and Beijing along the silk routes. Most of the traces of Nestorian churches have been found along those routes. In 845 Christianity, together with Buddhism, was officially banned from China by the Taoist emperor Wu Zung, who viewed both as alien religions.[5]

That the Christian faith should receive the same treatment as Buddhism (or vice versa) should not surprise us if we see the candour with which

Yazedbouzid, who erected the *Sian-Fu* tablet, and later his son, the monk Adam (Chinese: Ching Ching), as well as Alopen, made use of the Buddhist body of thought in their own writings that have been preserved. One can either blame the Buddhist aid they received in the translations of their writings for this or, alternatively, be thankful for it. The Buddhists' moral conduct, wisdom and compassion for the suffering of fellow human beings appealed to the Nestorians. And that is not that strange if we consider, for example, how closely the depiction of the *bodhisattva Avalokitesvara* approaches the New Testament depiction of Jesus. In *Mahayana* Buddhism, the *bodhisattva* is the primary mediator between humans and *nirvana*. There are many *bodhisattvas*, but *Avalokitesvara* has been given a particular significance. He is regarded as the embodiment of compassion (*karuna*) *par excellence*. He appears wherever the cries of the suffering are heard. This *bodhisattva* can also be seen in the female form of *Kuan-Yin* (= the one who hears the cries of the poor). The terminology used for Jesus' concern for the poor on the *Sian-Fu* tablet gives rise, according to D. Scott, to the suspicion that Nestorian circles were aware of the Buddhist conception of *Kuan-Yin*.[6]

The reason for mentioning this historical fact of the discovery of the *Sian-Fu* tablet and other early traces of Christian presence in a study on current inculturations of the meaning of Jesus lies precisely in this substantive connection between the *bodhisattva* figure and Jesus. In Part IV we will see that that has been a central motif up to the present for Christians living in a Buddhist context.

A second central motif is the role that is attributed to Jesus with regard to ancestors. The worship of ancestors plays an important and apparently ineradicable role. This became apparent a thousand years later in 1724.

In 1724 Christianity was banned from China for a second time. This time it occurred under a Confucian emperor, which was remarkable because, following Ricci's example, at that time Chinese Christianity had adopted a number of rituals from Confucianism. Paul Rule even speaks of "Confucian Christians" in seventeenth-century China.[7] Particularly striking was the adoption of Confucian rites with regard to the veneration of the dead. In the end, Ricci's openness in this issue led to the lingering so-called "battle of rites" between the Franciscans and Dominicans supported by Rome on one hand and Ricci and his brothers in the order who enjoyed the sympathy of the emperor on the other.[8]

The Jesuits, who remained predominantly in Beijing, interpreted the worship of ancestors from the point of view of the Confucianism that dominated the Chinese court. This was indeed pre-eminently *veneration*, honouring one's ancestors. The Franciscans and Dominicans, however, worked mainly in the country and there they saw how the old Chinese folk religion invoked the spirits of the ancestors through numerous rituals.

This was not simply a matter of honouring but of manipulative interaction. Based on this experience, the Dominicans put together a seventeen-point charge against the Jesuit policy regarding the Confucian worship of ancestors. In their view this policy was far too lenient.[9]

In this conflict, Rome supported the Franciscans and Dominicans. The struggle ultimately resulted in the emperor accepting as of 1724 only missionaries who were willing to continue the by then accepted practice of worshipping ancestors. In 1742 the pope officially forbade these ancestor rituals in his decree *Ex quo singulari*. This decree meant the end of the Roman Catholic presence in China for a long time. It was not until December 18, 1939 that a papal decree was issued that declared that Confucian ancestral worship could be viewed as a Chinese cultural tradition in which Christians were also permitted to take part.[10] If we take Ricci's arrival in China as the starting point of this struggle, this "battle of rites" lasted almost three centuries. It may have been crucial to the way in which Christianity took (or did not take) root in China. That would confirm the position defended in this book that the meaning of Jesus in Asia (and in Africa as well) can never be made truly clear and therefore will never be widely adopted without taking into account a clearly beneficial relationship with the ancestors.

The historical account above deals with three other religions in addition to Christianity: Confucianism, Taoism and Buddhism. Up to the present, these three religions have determined the religious context of China. Despite their differences, which will be discussed later, they are not mutually exclusive. On the contrary, at times they overlap and display hybrid forms. All three religions also seem to attain their own practical Chinese composition in China. The Chinese spoke of the "unity of the three teachings" already at the time of the first Jesuit missionaries. It was not the dissimilarities among them that they saw in the first instance but rather that which was common to them or supplementary. This continues to be true today.[11]

Christianity has also found a (small) place in China in the midst of these three great traditions. At times, the fact that the Chinese language has no word for "religion" has led Western observers to express the suspicion that the Chinese have no real antenna for religion. Subsequently, they refer often to the "humanism" of the Chinese, but the Chinese have no word for that either![12] The scepticism with regard to the depth of the Chinese religious nature is sometimes also linked to the fact that Christianity has disappeared again from China.[13] But that is disputable. If the disappearance of Christianity is a criterion for having or not having religious antennae, then the religiosity of the Middle East and North Africa is also in poor shape. Moreover, after the banishment from China in 845,

Buddhism did return to China *en masse*. Apparently, the Chinese found something in Buddhism that they did not find in Christianity.

In order to get a somewhat clearer idea of China's religiosity, we will be guided very much in the following sections by the interpretations of the Chinese professor of religious studies Julia Ching. Because of her professorship at numerous famous Western universities, including the Sorbonne in Paris – until her death in 2001 – she is capable like no other of explaining the religious context for Western eyes and ears. We will rely especially on her presentation of the role of mediation in Confucianism, Taoism and Buddhism, because that aspect of mediation comes substantively closest to our theme – the non-Western Jesus.

Mediation in Confucianism

Confucianism was the official state religion for more than two thousand years. The transition from dynasty to republic in 1912 also indicated the considerable decrease of Confucianism's influence. It became the religion of the past, of old China. But from the 1880s on, there seems to have been a slow and careful change in the tide. Some even speak of revival. Obviously, it is not a revival of the old, hierarchal Confucian structure of society but a revival of the old Confucian values concerning social ties and solidarity with nature, which appears to lie more deeply anchored in the Chinese soul than many in China in the last century would have liked.[14]

Like so many other writers, Ching also begins her explanation of the meaning of religion in China with an explanation of the veneration of ancestors and the meaning of family relationships in connection with that. Without this, nothing of religion in Asia (and also Africa) can be comprehended. The veneration of ancestors and, we would almost say, the "honouring" of family relationships in the history of China, go back further than the history of the three religions mentioned. As a kind of *cantus firmus*, reference to these two phenomena – the meaning of ancestors and of family relationships – will continue to be made throughout this chapter.

The concern with ancestors and family relationships is also expressed in the word for religion, *zongjiao*, that the Chinese have adopted from a Japanese translation of the Western (Latin) word for religion, *religio*. Thus they do have – indirectly – a word for religion. *Zongjaio* means "lineage teaching" and refers especially to the receiving aspect. It refers to those who tell us where we come from. In addition, the word also refers to *zhuzong*, the ancestors: *zong* refers to lineage. Ancestors were honoured as protective, life-giving spirits in the sense of the Roman Catholic patron saints.[15]

With regard to the deceased, Confucianism assumes two souls: a higher one and a lower one. The one rises and is preserved, whereas the other descends into the grave and disappears. The grave does remain the place where the memory of a person is honoured, which is why graves play a major role in the lives of Confucians. At certain times food and drink are brought as a sacrifice to the grave, and people kneel before the gravestone.

The manner in which the dead continue to be remembered against this Confucian background in Asia has led up to this very day to a great deal of tension in Asian Christianity. The example given in the first chapter of the ecclesial incorporation of the veneration of ancestors in Korea already insinuated this and the above-mentioned "battle of rites" also has everything to do with this.

Ching typifies Confucianism as "humanism that is open to religious values," as "religious humanism"[16] that has coloured the Chinese culture for almost two and a half millennia (Confucius lived from about 552 to 479 BC). As a classification of the character of Confucian thinking, reference is often made to the "negative" formulation of the so-called "golden rule" of ethics in Confucius' Analectica (15, 24): "Do not do to others what you do not want them to do to you."

Confucius drew up this rule with a view to the five connections he used to characterize human existence, variations of which we also encounter in the Bible:[17] master–servant, father–son, husband–wife, older–younger brother and friend–friend. Although these relationships are all mutual, they are also hierarchal. Even in the case of friendship, the oldest has priority. Once a year, the entire Confucian hierarchal social system was dutifully confirmed in the sacrifices that only the emperor could bring directly to the highest god, Heaven.

The emperor thus also fulfils an important mediating role between Heaven and Earth.[18] He is the one with a personal mandate from Heaven; he is therefore also called the "son of Heaven" and is the only one who maintains a strong ritual prayer relationship with the "Lord in the highest" via his sacrifices. In that respect he occupies a solitary – in the sense of unique – place between Heaven and Earth. As a mediator, he literally stands alone.

A prayer by Emperor T'ang is even quoted in the Analectica (20, 1), in which, during a period of drought, he asks Heaven – "O, most great and sovereign God" – to see him as the one who has sinned, rather than his people. He clearly serves as a substitute for his people.[19]

This passage is remarkable because here sin is seen as sin against God, which is not usual in Confucianism. Sin is usually viewed in the sense of evil deeds linked to the unfavourable factors in the environment that can divert someone from their original goodness. Sin can also be viewed as the result of the choices that have been given to humankind.[20]

Western theology also contains these two approaches. Explaining evil with reference to the unfavourable factors in the environment assumes that humans are originally good. That goodness can be destroyed by the environment, and sin is then seen as *privatio boni*, robbery, the taking away of the good.

The second approach expresses the ambivalent character of human freedom, which is always a freedom to make good and bad choices. Thus, bad choices have nothing to do with the essence of human existence but rather with the factuality thereof: they are more a matter of the factual *existence* of humans than of the *essence* of humans, their being.

In Western theology these two approaches are always paralleled by a third approach that strongly emphasizes the inner impotence and the compelling power of the historical character of evil. Concepts such as guilt and original sin therefore also play a role. Here one needs to be liberated from one's own impotence or from an actual historical situation of evil. In Confucianism, that need arises less often because the internalizing and historicizing of guilt so typical of Western theology have not occurred here. Instead of guilt, they speak rather of ignorance, which leads to merely inadequate spiritual growth.[21] Thus, there is also no need for a substitutionary "taking over" of guilt. The above-mentioned quote from Emperor T'ang seems all the more remarkable against this background.[22]

As an escape from the sin that results from a bad environment or from poor choices, Confucianism points to the mysticism of the heart, for the heart is, as it were, the point of contact between heaven and earth. The heart comes to us from heaven and leads us back to heaven. It is the symbol of the centre of life in each individual and transcends individual existence. Here Ching acknowledges the *exitus-reditus* (exit and return) model, which we recognize from the Greek church fathers (Gregory of Nyssa) especially and which can also be found in Thomas Aquinas. It is thinking in terms of a *micro-* and *macrocosmos*, whereby the idea is central that those (spiritual) powers present in the individual as microcosmos parallel those that are present in the entire universe as macrocosmos. Our spiritual and physical *microcosmos* thus mirrors the *macrocosmos* of the universe, and vice versa. For Ching, this is one of the most central thoughts in the Asian religious world: understanding the individual as a reflexion of the entire cosmos or, to put it in other words, the whole cosmos is inextricably connected with the inner self of each individual.[23]

Ching is very much aware of the "secularizing" tendency that has defined Confucianism throughout the centuries, through which "the path of

Heaven" has increasingly become "a path of the people." Because of this, Confucianism has acquired the reputation of being primarily a moral and ritualistic religion. Yet throughout her life, Ching continued to defend the thesis that the anchoring of the Confucian rules and certainly the veneration of ancestors presupposes a religious framework, and that Confucianism itself actually presents that.[24] The many references in the Analectica to "Heaven" as the source of all good and as that which decides our destiny are also a clear indication of that (1, 4; 3, 13; 7, 23; 9, 5; 12, 5 and 14, 36).

If this thesis can indeed be maintained, then the question of mediation between heaven and earth can also be posed in Confucianism in a time when there is no emperor. One can then also ask who assumes the mediating role of the emperor *now*. The role that Jesus takes in Christianity is not entirely new to Confucianism, even though he is seen by Confucian philosophers more as a wise man (*guru*), scholar or moral example than as a mediator between the divine and human.[25]

Mediation in Taoism

Just like Confucianism, Ching sees Taoism primarily as a wisdom tradition, as a religious tradition that is intended to pass on practical wisdom, directed at the concrete structuring of everyday life. But this concrete structuring always requires – and this is her central thesis as mentioned above – a framework that not only transcends individual existence but, more generally, our present, tangible existence as well. After all, our tangible, collective existence offers a still insufficient basis for the final motivations of human existence.

In Taoism, the wisdom to be gained is directed towards restoring the unity between body and spirit and subsequently also to maintain it even beyond death. Also as in Confucianism, a distinction can be made in Taoism between a more philosophical and a more religious variant. Here it is Ching's thesis that both philosophical and practical Taoism is based on religious presuppositions.

The ideal that Lao Tse had as the founder of Taoism was a return to nature. Nature is understood here as a kind of *status integritatis*, an original state of nature, which is also the destiny, the final purpose of human beings. It refers to a state in which not only the unity of body and spirit are assumed but also that of individuality and involvement with the world around us. The distinction between the I and the world thus disappears. Such thinking, i.e. in terms of unity, is usually called mysticism in the West. After all, the experience of unity does come to expression in a certain way of life, of conduct. *Tao* can mean both "word" and "way" and thus unites in itself the two meanings that Greek indicates by the two words *logos* ("word") and *hodos* ("way") (Tao Te Ching, XXII and XXXIX).[26]

In Chinese translations of the gospel of John the word *tao* is used to translate *logos* – for example, in the sentence "In the beginning was the Word" (John 1:1) – as well as to translate *hodos* – as in the sentence "I am the way, the truth and the life" (John 14:1).[27] Moreover, the word *tao* has, in fact, taken over the place of the word "heaven" in Confucianism. *Tao* is actually also a principle that is indescribable, that eludes any closer description. Sometimes the concept *tao* is seen primarily as *wu*, as non-being, described in terminology that reminds one of classical "negative" Christian theology, which uses only negatives to speak of God. The use of the superlative case that reference to the divine, human mystery of life – greatest, highest, etc. – always entails is, indeed, that it must be stated continually that this mystery is not *this* and not *that*. Continual denials (negations) are thus necessary (Tao Te Ching, I and XXV).[28]

As a way of life, the concept *tao* also includes, as stated, death. The acquiring of immortality is included among the "natural" unity of body and spirit. That is an idea that may, perhaps, evoke surprise initially. One could, after all, include the acceptance of natural death as belonging to the return to nature. Here, however, we see the ambiguity of the concept of nature, an ambiguity that has also caused misunderstandings in the Christian tradition.

Briefly, the concept of nature can have three different meanings: (1) as actual, organic and anorganic living space, (2) as a normative initial situation and (3) as a normative end situation, as ultimate destiny. The expectation that the natural unity of body and spirit also includes immortality usually presupposes the last concept of nature.

This belief in immortality is directly related to the Taoist teaching of the three life principles: *breath*, a *vital life-force* (or *seed*) and *spirit*. All three principles have two dimensions: an immanent one and a transcendent one. As such, they are simultaneously present in the human being as *microcosmos* and in the universe as *macrocosmos*. In this context people speak of the Taoist trinity, for these internal and external principles (*breath*, *vital life-force* and *spirit*) are essentially divine principles. They cannot be reduced to human existence. Rather, they support that existence – they are thus its presupposition. Such a tripartite division is also articulated in the concepts (which presuppose one another) of *wu* (the invisible, disappearing), *yu* (the visible, manifesting itself) (Tao Te Ching, II) and *te* (the divine power at work in the creatures) (Tao Te Ching, LI).[29]

This two-dimensionality expressed in an earthly and heavenly principle is also reflected in the actual view of immortality. Immortality can be conceived as both earthly and heavenly and, as far as the earthly aspect is concerned, is accompanied by a concrete search for elixirs of life in all kinds of alchemic practices. Because of their experimental character, they played a major role in the development of pharmacy and of preserving techniques for the human body.[30]

Taoism includes the phenomenon of confessing sins in healing rites. The sins are explicitly written down by those concerned, and these documents can be offered to heaven on mountain tops or commended to the earth or to rivers at funerals or drownings, as the case may be.

The rites express a strong sense of being placed in the hands of superhuman powers, which can have both an earthly and a heavenly character. Taoism has a complete pantheon of gods, to which deified humans can also belong. There is a clear hierarchy among them with a supreme deity at the top, often conceived as a tri-unity – *the heavenly, the earthly* and *the great*, later identified with the three life principles mentioned earlier but also sometimes briefly called one "lord of heaven."[31]

Comparisons with the Christian doctrine of the Trinity have, of course, not been lacking here. The heavenly God who reigns over the past is associated with the Father, the earthly one who reigns over the present with Jesus, and the great one, who rules over the future, with the Holy Spirit. Such a Taoist view of the Trinity can be traced back to the second century before Christ. It is difficult to determine the extent to which this was influenced much later by the above-mentioned Christian Nestorians.

In a text that dates already from the seventh century before Christ, Taoism includes a form of what in the Judaic-Christian tradition would be called messianism. The text mentions a divine man who possesses a heavenly book that speaks of the return of the ideal form of government in the fullness of time, the Great Peace *(Taiping)*. This divine man has the authority to transmit the revealed words to the "true man," a prophetic figure whose job is to transmit the texts in his turn to a ruler of great virtue. The ruler (prince) will rule by the authority of *tao*: he will lead his people into the kingdom of peace without force or threat of punishment.[32]

This text has actually functioned in Taoism the same way as the Sermon on the Mount and the parables of the kingdom of God have functioned in Christianity. In the course of the centuries new generations have time and again referred to them for justifying sharp criticism of rulers who were interested in peace least of all.

Taoism sees the current human situation as sinful and attempts to bridge the gulf between the divine and the human through extensive prayers in which penitence is central. Over against Buddhism, however, Taoism pointedly does not teach that earthly, human existence is suffering. The longing for physical immortality and thus of a continuation of earthly existence is certainly not an expression of that. It is rather an expression of attachment to life in this world.[33]

Of the three great Chinese religions, Confucianism, Taoism and Buddhism, Taoism can be called the most (mono)theistic. However, this exists next to a polytheism that does not undermine its (mono)theism but presupposes it. There is – as stated – a clear hierarchy among the many gods, in which one God is supreme. More than Confucianism and Buddhism, Taoism also appears able to inspire an "alternative" way of life that can serve as a fertile source of social criticism. It should not be surprising that it is precisely in Taoism that Chinese Christians seek motifs that can illustrate the "alternative" nature of Jesus' way of life.

The theologian Chen Yongtao, from Nanjing, is a good example of this. His starting point is that a "Chinese Jesus," i.e., a Jesus who is truly meaningful for the Chinese in their lives, must be the embodiment of the integration of biblical original experiences and Chinese experiences of recognition (see the section "Must Jesus Always Remain Greek?" in Chapter 1). Yongtao develops a *tao* Christology in which the incarnation is understood as an embodiment of the *tao* of God. He elaborates on the *tao* concept subsequently via three metaphors: the bowl, the sun and the suffering mother.

The first metaphor points to a *kenotic* (self-emptying) Christology in which the Word (*tao*) can be compared with a round, open bowl, ready to receive food and then to distribute it again. This relation between *kenosis* (emptiness) and *plerosis* (fullness) returns frequently in various forms of mysticism. Emptiness is then the condition for fullness. In Tao Te Ching XI, reference is made not only to the cavity of the bowl but also to the hole in the axis of a wheel with thirty spokes and the door and window of a house. It is the emptiness, the space left open, that continually makes the bowl usable, makes it possible for the wheel to be attached to a cart and makes a house livable.[34]

The second metaphor refers to the *cosmic* (universal) Christology in which *tao* can be compared with the sun that rises on the just and the unjust. This metaphor is a model for the non-exclusive way in which the church should deal with the Gospel. Instead of the domineering image of the "good shepherd" with its "rod and staff," the metaphor of the sun emphasizes the image of the emerging seed and the plant that grows because of fresh air, rain and sun.

The third metaphor of the suffering mother is a model for the di-unity of love and pain with which the contemporary world is borne in the hope of rebirth (resurrection). The Chinese have the same word for love and pain, and the labour pains that accompany the pain of birth are especially seen as *the* example of the di-unity of love and pain.[35] Yongtao borrows the image of the suffering, loving mother primarily from the time of the Cultural Revolution (1966–1976), when thousands of men were imprisoned and died, and the mothers not only had to look after the households but also had to bring in income for the family.[36] He connects the motif of the suffering mother with the above-mentioned female *bodhisattva Kuan-Yin*. In the West we would probably refer to the *pieta* motif, the grieving mother (Mary) with her suffering son (Jesus) in her arms.

It is striking in Yongtao's elaboration of the three metaphors how he seeks a connection in his *tao* Christology not only with Taoism but also with Buddhism and Confucianism (e.g. referring to the ideal image of the *junzi*, the true "lord"). He sees his Christology as a non-exclusive, inclusive contribution to that which always resounds in every form of Chinese religiosity, namely the unity of Heaven and Earth, in this case the unity of Heaven and Humankind (*tian ren heyi*).

Yongtao seeks his (hermeneutical) keys to the "Chinese Jesus" via four ways: Bible, tradition, religious context and daily life. The aspect of tradition is (still) the least independently developed here. For that, he writes to his Chinese audience, the Chinese must search much more intensively for their own Chinese Paul, John, Augustine and Thomas Aquinas.[37] To do so, we could add, they should look more to Chinese church history, beginning with people like Adam and Alopen, mentioned in connection with the *Sian-Fu* tablet. We will come back to another example of an Asian Christotao in Part V.

Mediation in Chinese Buddhism

Buddhism should be mentioned as the third religion in China, in particular, *Mahayana* (the great vehicle) Buddhism, which should be distinguished from *Theravada* (*Hinayana* or little vehicle) Buddhism. *Theravada* Buddhism, which has taken root primarily in Sri Lanka, Burma, Laos and Cambodia, teaches that salvation (*nirvana*) can be reached only via a long path of concentrated practice. In fact, it means that salvation is then reserved only for life-long monks (*arhats*) who are able to follow that long road of practising meditation and recitation without being distracted by worries about their material existence. *Theravada* Buddhists are oriented exclusively to the historical Buddha.

Mahayana Buddhism, which is present primarily in China, Korea, Vietnam and Japan, assumes that *nirvana* can in principle be attained by anyone and orients itself to that end to several *buddhas* and *bodhisattvas*. The latter are already far advanced on the path to enlightenment and, although they are on the point, as it were, of attaining *nirvana*, they nevertheless return because they are moved by pity for those who are still far from *nirvana*. It is obvious that the figure of the *bodhisattva* exercises a great power of attraction and is often compared with Jesus because of his concern with the lot of his fellow human beings.[38]

That Buddhism has taken root in China may cause surprise. In contrast to Buddhism, both Confucianism and Taoism have gods and assume that a life can be continued in the heavenly spheres, in an embodied or disembodied state. This belief leads to a practical attitude directed at the here and now that is borne by a hierarchy imposed from above. Being connected with the ancestors plays a major role in this hierarchy of life. The idea of a rebirth in one of the heavenly spheres, as taught in Buddhism, gives a dynamic all of its own to the veneration of ancestors. After all, a person's stay in the heavenly spheres is only temporary. Heaven does not offer any lasting escape from suffering. Only *nirvana* does that, the place that people can reach from heaven if the chain of rebirth (*samsara*), which is kept in motion by the law of cause and effect (*karma*), is broken. By honouring one's ancestors one builds good *karma* – and that can also have a positive effect on the deceased ancestors. Thus, Buddhism can also allow veneration of ancestors. This veneration emphasizes how much a person owes those who have preceded him. It is typically an expression of a strong sense of community, even beyond death. Without the integration of such aspects of solidarity, Buddhism in China would never have had much chance. The idea that was developed in *Mahayana* Buddhism as being connected to everything links up with this better than the emphasis on a celibate monastic life in *Theravada* Buddhism. That monastic life is much less easily compatible with the Confucian and Taoist emphasis on family connections and procreation.

The Chinese form of Buddhism is so specific that it is a major point of discussion as to whether the Buddhists *conquered China* or the Chinese *conquered Buddhism*. In any case, it is clear that in China Buddhism showed a great capacity for adaptation. That also evokes the question what would have happened to Christianity in China if Christianity had shown a similar capacity for adaptation. In later centuries already, people could point to the capacity for integration that the Nestorians, mentioned at the beginning of this chapter, displayed.[39]

The unique Chinese form that Buddhism has taken is primarily that of *Ch'an* and *Pure Land* Buddhism. *Ch'an* Buddhism is known in the West primarily in its Japanese variant as *Zen* Buddhism. One could speak here of simplifying – Ching even uses the term "short cuts" – with respect to the more traditional Buddhism. The major difference between *Theravada* Buddhism and *Mahayana* Buddhism on the accessibility of salvation (*nirvana*) is resolved in the two above-mentioned variants in favour of an idea of accessibility that is, in principle, free for everyone, and the question of fundamental knowledge of the Buddhist writings is considered to be of secondary importance. Salvation is acquired in *Ch'an* Buddhism through "self-development" in the sense of a process of breaking free of one's own self (the ego) via meditation or through a sudden experience of enlightenment. In *Pure Land* Buddhism it is acquired by calling on the name of Amida, one of the four heavenly *buddhas*. If Amida grants grace to a dying person, then he is allowed to stay in one of the heavenly spheres (the *Pure Land*).

A parallel is drawn sometimes between the emphasis on "good works," including one's own enlightenment, in *Ch'an* Buddhism and the emphasis on "grace alone" (in Amida) in *Pure Land* Buddhism on the one hand and the classical dispute on good works between Protestants and Roman Catholics in the sixteenth century Reformation in Western Europe on the other. In this comparision *Ch'an* Buddhism's position approximates the Roman Catholic position (good works) and *Pure Land* Buddhism the Protestant position (grace alone) in that debate.[40] We will consider this point further on the latter parallel in Chapter 7 in the section on "The Attitude of the Japanese Christians towards the State." The former parallel – that between *Ch'an* (Zen) Buddhism and Roman Catholicism – provides less insight than the latter. The sober character of *Ch'an* Buddhism (no images, strongly oriented to one's own existential processing, etc.) could also be closely associated with sober Protestantism. *Ch'an* Buddhism teaches that salvation – *sunyata* (emptiness) – can be acquired by direct intuition to which meditation (concentration) can open the way. That gives this form an iconoclastic character (i.e. the rejection of images), because various other matters such as study and the recitation of sutras, veneration of Buddhist statues and performing all kinds of (sacrificial) rituals are then relegated to a secondary level.[41]

Here we see a radicalization of an idea that is characteristic of *Mahayana* Buddhism, namely that the absolute can be experienced in the relative. In Buddhist terminology, that means that *nirvana* (enlightenment) can already be experienced in *samsara*, in the chain of things that cohere with one another. *Anatman*, one's own emptiness, which is to be attained through detachment (the "Great Death"), thus does not lead to isolation with respect to the surrounding world but rather to a feeling of ultimate connnectedness with everything, to the sense of the interconnectedness of all that exists (*pratiya-samutpada*). *Nirvana* is therefore the di-unity of *anatman* and *pratiya-samutpada*.[42]

Concretely, this means great appreciation for life in the current world. It also leads to greater freedom in one's own articulation of the "breakthrough" experiences of the sense of *anatman* and *pratiya-samutpada*. It is more a matter of one's own, personal experience of openness than something towards which one develops slowly throughout a whole lifetime via discipline in prayer and careful study of the holy writings as in *Theravada* Buddhism.

One can, of course, pose the critical question if this form of Buddhism, in which no prominent place is ascribed to the Buddhist writings or even to Buddha himself, is an authentic form of Buddhism. The accent on one's own internal, spiritual development, without the help of an external teacher can itself take the form here of the cry repeated again and again: "Kill the Buddha; kill the Buddha" – a cry that must then be understood in the same way as the classic adage *etsi deus non daretur* (as if God did not exist). It was primarily the German theologian Dietrich Bonhoeffer (1906–1945) who gave renewed currency to this adage by connecting it as a motto to his argument for a "mature" faith. One should live before and with God as if one has to live without God. This understanding of life is the opposite of that of faith in a *deus ex machina*, an absolute dependence on a God who intervenes unexpectedly whenever he pleases. The parallel between Bonhoeffer's appeal to this classic adage and the Buddhist cry described above lies in the summons to view the divine not as an external factor in human life and thus as an excuse for not changing one's own life but as an internal power that changes human existence.[43]

Ch'an masters will answer the critical question of the authentic Buddhist character of this form of Buddhism by saying that the essence of a religion does not lie in the letter of its holy writings but in the *spirit* – in other words, in the religious experience that is seen in these holy writings themselves as the essence of (Buddhist) belief. One arrives at this experience best, they will say, not so much through study but through meditation in which the "art" of letting go is practised. For that matter, the question of what precisely the characteristics of authentic – in the sense of the oldest form of – Buddhism were is still open – just as the question is open in all the great religions.

By placing the emphasis on one's own meditative possibilities, the *Ch'an* masters could come paradoxically close to the *Theravada* monks who emphasized the individual's own achievements. A spiritual attitude could then be displayed that would be called pride (*hubris*) in the Christian tradition and is viewed as one of the greatest sins. Both the *Ch'an* masters and the *Theravada* monks presuppose a high level of consciousness. The broad accessibility of salvation that the *Mahayana* Buddhists teach is then in danger of being pushed aside.[44] That is a risk that each form of theology of experience always runs. One's own experience is then also an achievement, and an elite quickly comes into existence with regard to experience.

Pure Land Buddhism assumes a heavenly paradise that can be reached from *nirvana*. This form of Buddhism constitutes the clearest parallel with Western monotheism as we know it in Judaism, Christianity and Islam. *Amida Buddha* is the central figure in the expected paradise. He is assisted by the above-mentioned *bodhisattva Avalokitesvara*, in the female form *Kuan-Yin*. This Buddhism can be traced to the *Pure Land sutra*, the longer form of which emphasizes that good works are just as important as revering Buddha. The shorter form emphasizes only the revering of Buddhism, which comes to expression in explicitly calling on his name.

The latter variant has to do with an experience of faith in which three aspects are central: (1) a heavenly Buddha, *Amida*, (2) a mediator, *Kuan-Yin*, and (3) a doctrine of grace in which the "faith alone" comes to expression in calling Amida's name (in Japanese: *Nembutsu = Namu Amidabutsu*: Amen, Amida Buddha), the only one that counts. The female *bodhisattva Kuan-Yin* has become especially loved in China. She is called the "goddess of grace" and is also revered as the "giver" of children. In addition to the already mentioned parallel with Jesus, there is also an obvious parallel here with the role of the veneration of Mary in Roman Catholicism.[45]

All in all, one can say that Buddhism in China has taken on more "worldly," earthly forms than elsewhere. The process of becoming internally empty is closely connected with the (taken over from Taoism) idea of the connectedness of all things. From a "foreign" religion, it has become a Chinese religion. One can speak here correctly of *double transformation*: the Chinese have made their own choice from the Buddhist reservoir of transmitted meanings – and this form of Buddhism has also changed China.[46] In the original *Ch'an* Buddhism, the individual's own fundamental attitude is emphasized greatly, and in *Pure Land* Buddhism the letting go of one's own self is connected to the surrender to Amida and the expectation of the gift of grace. Such a surrender and expectation of grace was not part of Buddhism originally.[47]

While Confucianism primarily supports and ritualizes the social connections in society in its hierarchical rules, and Taoism allows all space to polytheism in relation to monotheism and supports its own, alternative lifestyle in solidarity with nature, Buddhism stimulates individual piety strongly. It can correctly be called the most devotional religion of the three Chinese religions.

The above discussion of a number of aspects of China's religious context compels some reservation with respect to general judgements on what the Chinese should or should not have in their religion. It is indisputable that they have a practical bent in their religion.[48] People are involved intensively in a large-scale way in many rituals for marking daily life. It is a religiosity that asks something of those involved in it. According to the Protestant Chinese theologian Pui-lan Kwok, the idea of "transmission of guilt" and especially of a unique transmission does not fit the Buddhist-Confucian Chinese context very well.[49] Nevertheless, the idea is not completely missing in Confucianism, as we just saw, even if the idea of forgiveness received "from elsewhere" is not dominant. People in the West should realize what it means to speak about guilt in a shame culture.[50]

To speak openly about guilt is already unusual, let alone about the assumption of guilt. We must be wary of absolutizations here as well, however. We also saw that the idea of guilt and confession of guilt is present in Taoism.

On the basis of the texts of anti-Christian polemic by a number of prominent Buddhists at the time of the first missionary attempts by Jesuits, we can now state that, historically, the idea of substitution was the primary stumbling block for Buddhists.[51] In early Buddhist reactions to Christianity, the forgiveness received "from elsewhere" was even called a dangerous idea that could undermine the moral order.[52] No one would then have to hold back in doing evil because the boomerang effect would no longer work. That is an argument that Christians have also heard with respect to the belief in heaven and hell. The argument is that belief in heaven and hell should be maintained in order to provide an incentive for enforcing morality.

According to the Polish Roman Catholic missionary Roman Malek, the publisher of the five-part work *The Chinese Face of Jesus Christ*, this has been the most controversial point in China from the beginning, thus also in the seventh century.[53] Already in the *Jesus Messiah Sutra* of 635 the Nestorian Christians did not allow any misunderstanding regarding the meaning of Jesus' death (especially at the end – nos. 198–206 – of this text).[54] For that matter, Eskildsen sees a not unimportant shift in the Nestorian texts. Whereas the *Jesus Messiah Sutra* from 635 speaks very explicitly of Jesus' death for sinners, the inscription on the *Sian-Fu* tablet from 781 makes no mention of it. There Jesus is primarily the one who precedes us in a virtuous life and restores true human nature. An important shift appears here that Eskildsen traces primarily to the increasing influence of Manichaeism.[55]

The phenomenon of spiritual leaders in the role of martyrs is not usually as present in Buddhism as it is in Christianity, even though the notion is not lacking entirely. The monks themselves illustrated that when they set themselves on fire during the Vietnam War in the 1970s. The current position of the Buddhist monks in Burma is another case in point. Nevertheless, it cannot be denied that the belief that one person can act as a substitute for the other and thus liberate him is not an idea that fits in well with the idea of *karma*. The latter teaches that a human being will have to bear the consequences of his own bad deeds, just as he will be rewarded in a future life for his good deeds. Suffering as a result of the evil that one has done thus remains connected to the one in question, and no one can remove it from him.

Nevertheless, there are, primarily in the stories about the *bodhisattvas*, examples of their intention to take the suffering of others upon themselves. That notion is also not completely alien to the Chinese religious culture in the broader context. Within Confucianism we encountered the idea of the substitutionary role with the Chinese emperor T'ang. All in all, there is enough reason to return in detail to the mediating work of the *bodhisattva* in Buddhism in relation to Jesus in the subsequent chapter.

The Current Theological State of Affairs in China

From the above summary of some central aspects of Chinese religiosity with a view to the concept of mediation, an approach to religion emerges that is different in a number of respects from the three Abrahamic religions. But it is not a matter of "ships passing in the night," even if many Western observers are surprised. For the time being it remains a riddle as to how a typically Western, atheistic ideology like Marxism could have been so successful in such a typically Asian, religious China.[56] Perhaps the same question can be posed here as we already posed in relation to Buddhism: Did communism *conquer China* or did the Chinese *conquer communism*? Given the high rate of current changes in China, the latter could very well be the case.[57]

How the Christian faith is given concrete form against the background of the above-mentioned religious context can be illustrated by the views of Bishop Ting, the most powerful man in the strongly (through Confucian influence) hierarchically organized, official Chinese (patriotic) Church for the last fifty years.

Especially since the 1980s, the church in China has been growing spectacularly. Christianity can even rejoice in such popularity among intellectuals that in 1987 the government spoke of a "Christian fever" sweeping the country.[58] Protestantism especially has a great power of attraction. Through more informal (and often part-time) leaders, it could usually be set up more flexibly than the Roman Catholic Church, which is still divided between a wing loyal to Rome and a "patriotic" wing.[59] It is difficult to check the reliability of estimations of the number of believers. In 2000 Edmond Tang spoke of 10, 12, 20 or more million Protestants and 10 or 12 million Catholics.[60]

Bishop Ting was the motor behind the so-called *Three-Self Patriotic Movement*: *Self-government, Self-finance, and Self-propagation*. In addition, Ting used the so-called "Nevius method" that the American missionary John Livingston Nevius (1829–1893) had advocated in vain at the end of the nineteenth century as a method for mission in China. Thus Ting attempted to refute the communist reproaches that Chinese Christianity was governed and financed from outside the country and was being used as an anti-communist propaganda instrument. He wanted to show that the church in China was truly a church of the Chinese. That is why the word "patriotic" is used in the name of this movement.[61]

Theologically, Ting has articulated his ideas primarily under the term "cosmic Christ" in various speeches and articles. In Jesus' self-effacing love for the suffering, Ting sees him as moving completely in harmony with the true nature of the universe (the creation) that emerged from the divine love. This approach to Jesus makes it possible for him to say to his comrades in the communist party that Jesus' love is not limited to believers but extends to the whole creation, thus also to them. In that context, Ting can sum up a row of "heathen saints" – from Nebuchadnezzar to Egypt and Assyria – similar to what we saw already in Song in the paragraph "From Israel to Asia: A Theological Leap" in Chapter 3 above as an illustration of the role of "foreign peoples" in God's plan of salvation.

Ting calls his fellow believers not to limit their concept of sin to their own sense of individual sin. He sees very socially active Christians burdened down with a strong sense of individual sin and hears them sigh à la Paul (Rom. 7:15) over their lack of power. There is forgiveness if they come up short individually, Ting argues, if we realize that Jesus applied the concept of sin primarily to make clear the question of who it is who is continually sinned *against* ("the sinned against").[62] Jesus had pity on them, and Ting sees many of his fellow believers and his party comrades taking pity on them. For him, sin has to do primarily with social injustice. The sense of sin is primarily a sense of knowing who the victims are, i.e. the people who have been sinned against the most. That should result in actual aid for victims. He considers the sense of also coming up short in that respect as a "minor problem" over against the necessity of lending aid. This sense of coming up short is not to get in the way of lending aid.

We see the concept of sin shift here from a moral concept to a social one. This shift occurs repeatedly in Asian theology,[63] and has everything to do with the fear of "punishing the victim doubly" by talking him into an individual guilt complex. They thus want to avoid the phenomenon of "blaming the victim." In Chapter 17, in the section "The Nature of the Mediation," we will discuss the question of whether this legitimate struggle does not throw out the baby with the bathwater.

Ting's choice for a concept of sin that reflects Jesus' pity has everything to do with the salvific meaning that he ascribes to Jesus. For him, that meaning lies in daring to say yes whole-heartedly to creation, just as God intended that in Jesus. Here Ting is concerned not so much with the question of whether Jesus is "God-like" enough – such a question often reflects criteria for divinity derived from Israel's religious environment that do not, in his view, bring us closer to Jesus. Rather, he is concerned with the question of whether we think of God sufficiently as "Christ-like."[64]

In his emphasis on the "cosmic Christ" Ting fully endorses the widespread notion in the Chinese religious context that the same divine principle that supports the whole creation also gives form to individual life. This was earlier referred to as the di-unity of the macro- and the microcosmos. But Ting does not propose many concrete suggestions. The church could play a role and to that end the Chinese view of the church is needed. But Ting never gives any impetus for it. Apparently, he did not grant himself the latitude or he was convinced that the Chinese church would not be given that latitude under the communists. That probably showed a sense of reality but not prophetic courage. Ting also kept quiet during the Cultural Revolution (1966–1976) that cost millions of lives and also during the violently suppressed student protest on Tiananmen Square in Peking in 1989.

Against this background one can ask if speaking of the "cosmic Christ" does not, after all, have something of an escape about it. In addition to Jesus' love that comes to expression in creation, one can also speak of Jesus' love as a bearer of the cross.[65]

In an overview article in the journal *Ching Feng*, "Theological Reorientation in Chinese Protestantism, 1949–1984, II," the Protestant American China expert Philip Wickeri states that the Cultural Revolution, however terrible it was, was never a subject of theological reflexion in China. At least not explicitly. No "theology of the wounded" was developed in the same way that the Chinese intellectuals developed a "literature of the wounded" after the fall of the so-called "Gang of Four" following Mao's death in 1976.[66]

The above-mentioned shame culture is perhaps present in this as well. Against the background of the inevitable psychological processing of the millions of victims of the Cultural Revolution, Chinese inculturation of aspects of the Western guilt culture could be beneficial. The phenomenon of the inculturation does presuppose that cultures are not closed blocks but are again and again capable of absorbing new elements in an independent way. If the concept of guilt is discussed in China in the way argued for in this study – namely the way of *double transformation* – that concept will undoubtedly be given a different (more Taoist) timbre, but the Chinese shame culture will also undergo a change.

The example of Ting's theology illustrates that there is no theology at this time in China with its own explicit Chinese face. Throughout the centuries, Christianity in China has come up against the powers that be in the form of Taoist, Confucian or communist emperors who have limited the latitude for the development of a Chinese theology. The situation is now changing quickly.[67] Yongtao's "Tao christology" is a first example of this.

Part IV: Jesus as *Bodhisattva*

Among the many meanings that can be attributed to Jesus in a Buddhist context – such as exemplary monk (arhat) or Amida Buddha – bodhisattva is the one that easily stands out the most. In all the different East Asian contexts, the figure of the bodhisattva more or less colours the nature of the mediation between finite and infinite existence. This simply begs the question of a comparison with the role of Jesus in Christianity. But this comparison raises several questions. First, given the method by which enlightenment is attained, can one speak of mediation in Buddhism? Does the notion of mediation not conflict with the essence of Buddhism? After all, Buddhism teaches one how to attain enlightenment on one's own. And, second, if there is room for mediation, what is the role of the bodhisattva in this? Third, how personal can the relationship with him be? After discussing these three issues we will close the discussion of Jesus as bodhisattva with a number of conclusions in which we will apply the principle of double transformation that was developed in Chapter 1.

6   Jesus in a Buddhist Context

A Historical Comparison

To get a somewhat clearer view of the figure of the *bodhisattva* central to *Mahayana* Buddhism, we will turn once again to the first traces of a theological discussion between Christianity and Buddhism in eighth-century China. Although the translation of a number of passages of the *Jesus Messiah Sutra* cited in Chapter 5 is disputed and scholars are anxiously awaiting better translations, a few striking observations can be made on the basis of the translations now available.

In one fragment, the *buddhas* are associated with angels and their work with the fruit of the Holy Spirit. In the other, Buddha even seems to be placed directly alongside God. But then the question arises immediately as to which dimension of existence (*kaya*) in the doctrine of the Buddha's three dimensions, the so-called *trikaya*, is associated with God here. Is it the *nirmanakaya*, the visible (historical) Buddha and those who became *buddhas* after him because of how they lived on earth? Or is it the *sambhogakaya*, the heavenly *buddhas*, who are present in a beneficial way for us? Or is it the *dharmakaya*, the non-physical essence of a *buddha*, the buddhahood that can in principle be attained by anyone?

This teaching of the *buddha's* three dimensions of existence – (1) as a historical *buddha*, (2) as an auspiciously present heavenly *buddha*, and (3) as an internal ideal that every believer can in principle attain – seems to play a key role in the way in which Christians attribute meaning to Jesus in a Buddhist context now as well. Does the meaning of Jesus lie primarily in the reference to the historical Jesus, the *nirmanakaya* dimension? Or does it lie in the notion of Jesus sitting at the right hand of the Father and thus auspiciously near to us, i.e. the *sambhogakaya* dimension? Or does it lie in the *dharmakaya* dimension, the Christ-in-us of which Paul speaks so emphatically in Galatians 2:20 and where a Buddhist would say: not I, but the *dharma*? Thus, all three dimensions of existence find an analogy in the Bible.

The fact that the one fragment in the *Jesus Messiah Sutra* appears to emphasize the relationship between the God of the Christians and Buddha more strongly than the other could be an indication of the fact that the differentiations that the *trikaya* doctrine allows were known – if not to Alopen himself then to the anonymous Buddhist writer of this sutra.[1] That this is not a simple comparison but a theologically well-thought-out analogy (= similarity in the midst of clear differences) is apparent from the fact that further on in the text he calls those who are thinking about returning to Buddhism to understand what distinguishes the two religions from each other. He himself is thus very aware of the differences.

The aspects that Alopen cites from Buddhism for comparison with certain aspects of the Christian faith come back often in the interreligious dialogue between Christians and Buddhists. Thus, Alopen already referred to the Buddhist idea of emptiness to indicate that God transcends our understanding. All the terms he uses for Jesus come close to concepts that are used for Buddha himself or for one of the *bodhisattvas*. The expression "Lord of the Universe," for example, which Alopen places above his exegesis of the part of the Sermon on the Mount from Matthew 6 and 7, can also be found in the *Lotus Sutra* and elsewhere as a designation for Buddha.[2]

On the famous *Sian-Fu* tablet we find qualifications of Jesus' compassion for those who mourn that evoke a number of associations with the *bodhisattva Avalokitesvara* and his later female form, *Kuan-Yin*. The same images that are used for her – for example in the story of the rescue from drowning – are also used for Jesus.

D. Scott sees these linguistic and functional overlappings as affecting the theological attitude of the monk Adam towards Buddhism as well. They – as Adam remarks, obviously referring to the Buddhists – who have grasped only partially the fullness of the Gospel or who do the works their faith prescribes with a sincere heart will inherit heaven.[3] That the Nestorian monk Adam also practised this solidarity in his life is apparent from the story that he helped a Buddhist monk translate the *Satparamita Sutra* and even translated at least seven parts himself. The conclusion can be none other than that he considered the content of those parts to be worthwhile.

In itself, the solidarity that Adam obviously felt is remarkable, because there were fierce Nestorian anti-Buddhist polemics from other parts of Asia in the same period (the seventh to tenth centuries). Frankly speaking, Buddha and the Buddhists were called embodiments of the Antichrist. But there is no record of this kind of polemic coming from China. Scott's explanation of this is that, in contrast to other parts of Asia, people encountered one another "in the flesh" as neighbours in faith.[4]

A Contemporary Comparison

The parallel that is most striking in Scott's report is that between the *bodhisattva Kuan-Yin* and Jesus. This brings us to a broader discussion on the parallel between the role of the *bodhisattvas* and that of Jesus. A good introduction to that discussion is the contribution by the Korean theologian Hee-Sung Keel to the journal *Buddhist-Christian Studies* called "Jesus the Bodhisattva: Christology from a Buddhist Perspective."[5] The subtitle of the article seems to suggest that this article was written by a Buddhist, but that is not the case. The author does not disguise his Christian background. "From a Buddhist Context" would probably have been a more appropriate subtitle than "From a Buddhist Perspective."

His starting point is: What power made Jesus who he is and what power makes a *bodhisattva* a *bodhisattva*? He presupposes that it is the same power, i.e. divine love, and the further elaboration of this analogy is seen by Keel as contributing to an indigenous Asian Christology.

Let us attempt first to sharpen our conception of the figure of the *bodhisattva*. A *bodhisattva* is not a Buddha but is on the way to Buddhahood. Originally, the term *bodhisattva* was used for the path of enlightenment (*bodhi*) that made Gautama a Buddha. Since the time that *Mahayana* Buddhism saw enlightenment as an ideal accessible in principle to everyone, the term *bodhisattva* is used mainly for those who are just about to enter *nirvana* but who, motivated primarily by compassion for others, choose not to do so.

Thus, *bodhisattvas* are not concerned in the first place with their own enlightenment but with that of others. Their care for the well-being of others extends so far that they simply postpone their own arrival at *nirvana*, towards which they have made great progress, even if that means that they are still bound to the suffering that belongs to earthly existence. A *bodhisattva* is thus rightly called a helper. He never refers to himself but always to something above himself, namely to the *dharmakaya* to be reached through *sunyata* (emptiness), the Buddhahood that is, in principle, accessible to everyone.

The parallel with Jesus here is obvious. For Keel, the heart of the comparison is the fact that both the *bodhisattva* and Jesus "point to something else." They reveal the meaning of the divine in an exemplary way, but the fullness (emptiness) of the divine is somewhere else, not in them. Keel illustrates this identification extensively while maintaining the non-identity of the divine with the figure of Jesus. As much as Jesus constantly showed his spiritual connection with the Father, he never takes the Father's place. Jesus reveals who the Father is but does not take the place of the Father.

To illustrate this, Keel refers to the first chapter of the gospel of John. There it is said that the divine Word became flesh. But it does not say that the divine Word was completely absorbed into human flesh through its associating with human physicality. Keel refers here to the well-known adage that Jesus is *totus Deus* (fully God) but not *totum Dei* (the whole of God). He reveals God like no other; he is as God is. But that identification does not imply that God has been completely absorbed in Jesus. Even if God cannot be known apart from Jesus, this does not entail that God and Jesus are completely identical. The Christian tradition has always spoken of the *identification* of the Son with the Father while at the same time maintaining a clear *distinction* between them.

Identification alongside *non-identification* is an intellectual construction often used in other contexts in the history of Christian theology. For example, Calvin employs it as support for his starting point that the finite human cannot grasp the infinite divine (*finitum non capax infiniti*).[6] The well-known Calvinist theologian Karl Barth applies the same construction to Jesus' relation to the Church. The Church is the embodiment of Jesus' message, but Jesus is not the same as the Church.[7]

Protestantism, in particular, also uses this type of reasoning with respect to the appeal to the Bible as well. The position is that the adage "Scripture alone" (*sola scriptura*) should obtain as the final norm: each position to be defended in theology is to be based on the Bible. But that does not entail that the "biblical theses" exhaust the meaning of the Bible completely. In other words, the demonstrable biblical character of a thesis does not mean that the complete Bible (*tota scriptura*) is present in this thesis. The *sola scriptura* is, therefore, not identical with the *tota scriptura*. One can speak of a strong *identification* in all these contexts (Word-Jesus, Jesus-Church, and theology-Bible) but not of a complete *identity*.

Keel elaborates on this line of thinking in different contexts in Christian theology when he wants to make clear that, whereas Jesus does reveal God's salvific nearness in a unique way, he does not exhaust the way of salvation. The purport of his argument is that other analogous ways of salvation can be revealed to us in his wake. To that end, he appeals to the idea, also widespread in Christian theology, of the limited knowability of God. This idea is intended to leave room, despite the revelation of God's true nature in Jesus, for a hopeful, expectant treatment of the always open mystery of the experience of God's presence.

There has been an extensive discussion in Western systematic theology on the question of whether God is exactly the same as how he revealed himself in history. To cut short all kinds of theological speculation, it is usually argued that, as believers, we know no other God than that revealed in the Bible. We cannot go back any further than that God. But that truth that we are to endorse does not at all mean that we therefore know God completely. God reveals his true nature in Jesus, but that does not imply – as was just shown – that God is revealed completely in Jesus.

Keel thus adds the obvious thesis that our knowledge of God is not completely exhausted in our knowledge of Jesus – God is too great for that and our ability to understand too small. That is why the New Testament also refers innumerable times to the immeasurability of God and the limits of our knowledge (e.g. Rom. 11:33–36 and 1 Cor. 13:9).

These two motifs – the non-identity between Jesus and God in the midst of a unique identification and the recognition of the limited nature of our knowledge of God – bring Keel to the following two conclusions. (1) The divine Word is more than its embodiment in Jesus. (2) Therefore, Christians cannot claim to have exhaustive (exclusivistic) complete knowledge of the divine Word. This does not deny that the Word is revealed decisively and finally in Jesus; it demonstrates only that the Word which the New Testament says is the Creator of all things (John 1:3 and Col. 1:15–17) simply cannot be present in one finite human being. That would, after all, be a denial of the fact that the Creator is present in all things.

If we take the all-encompassing power that the New Testament calls "Word" seriously, then all expressions of the Spirit in the world must also be related to this power. That is why Keel can also raise the questions of the terms with which Jesus' meaning for Asians would be associated if he had been born in East Asia. Then the title of *bodhisattva* would also have been applied to him – the term for this mediator of salvation who does not seek his own salvation exclusively but gives himself to the world of suffering through his unlimited mercy. For him, Jesus is *the* example of a *bodhisattva*, of the embodiment of compassion that transcends itself.

For the rest, Keel does not explore the differences between the Buddhist and Christian views of suffering. *Dukkha* (suffering in the sense of insufficiency) can refer to suffering associated with pain and sorrow but also to suffering that accompanies change and transience (*anitya*). In addition, suffering can also refer to ignorance (*avidya*), through which the human being places his own "I" constantly at the centre of his knowing and acting. People can be liberated from these forms of suffering through detachment. In the Christian tradition, suffering has a somewhat different meaning. Suffering from the transience of human existence does play a role – Romans 8:21 even speaks of the "bondage to decay" – but this colours the concept of suffering only in a limited way. Next to physical suffering, in Christianity the notion of suffering as a consequence of guilt is prominent, culminating in Jesus in the idea of substitutionary suffering as a consequence of *taking over* our guilt. We will return to this in our conclusions at the end of this chapter.

According to Keel, by ascribing the title *bodhisattva* to Jesus, Asian Christians do not differ in any respect from the first Christians who attributed the Judeao-Greek titles of Christ, Son of God and Lord to him. Many generations of Christians throughout the whole world have followed the first Christians in this. At issue here is the continuing process of understanding, in which new terms are continually applied to Jesus, in all historical variety and relativity, that articulate his meaning in a certain time and place. Until now, the Asian churches have scarcely been involved in this process. This is so partly because they are still so young (Korea) and partly because they have been dominated by the West for so long (China, India and Indonesia).

Keel writes as an Asian Christian who lives in a Buddhist context and can therefore express the meaning of Jesus in no other way than in the religious terminology supplied by his Buddhist culture. He does not consider it out of the question that that terminology will also add new elements to the conceptualization that has thus far primarily been Western. Of course, the concepts borrowed from Buddhism have their shortcomings, but – he argues – these shortcomings do not need *per se* to be greater than the Greco-Roman concepts that Western theology used exclusively for so long.

In essence, Keel constructs his argument along two lines. These lines are characteristic for most contemporary, contextual theology, especially those forms of contextual theology that are formulated in the situation of being a religious minority in the midst of a dominant majority religion. The one line is a matter of arguing that the knowledge of God is not exhausted in the knowledge of Jesus. Following this line of reasoning, it can be argued – as stated earlier – that God was in Africa and Asia already before the missionaries came. The other line argues that new meanings can be attributed to Jesus now as well. These concepts can also be borrowed from other religions, just like in Jesus' time.

In fact, for most non-Western theologians, the first line of argument functions to make the second possible. They want to retain Jesus' key role but can do so in their African or Asian context only by referring to concepts that actually play a role in their context. But these concepts are often – to use Pieris' terminology – already "occupied" by other religions. The only way to justify their use is the reference to the presence of God in other religions as well. Here we come across the idea of the "overlap" that can only be established by analogy, which we discussed in Chapter 2 in the section on "Double Transformation."

An External Mediator of Salvation?

Before looking further at Keel's Christian interpretation of the role of the *bodhisattva*, we should ask what precisely the role of the Buddha – and thus also the *bodhisattva* – can be as mediator. After all, one can always ask if Buddhism includes the idea of an *external* mediator of salvation.

Does it fit well with the Buddhist view of the way of salvation that each believer must travel *himself?*

Is the Buddha actually a bringer of salvation in the same sense that such a term is used in Christianity?[8] The historical Buddha, Siddharta Gautama, was called the teacher and pointer of the way. But he was also called the caravan leader. In the strict sense of the word, however, he is not a "saviour." The *dharmakaya* dimension, which embodies the road to enlightenment that is to be travelled by everyone, does not allow that. Instead of a bringer of salvation, a saviour, Gautama can be characterized more as one who is the first, who blazes a trail so that everyone in principle can follow it. Gautama's example does not, as such, make that path easier or shorter. He only shows the possibility of following the path.[9]

But the mediating role of the historical Buddha should not be minimized too much. He is more than merely an initiator. If that was all he was, then he would be comparable to the founder of a philosophical school, such as Plato or Socrates. But the legend that grew up and the iconography surrounding his person are clear indications of a role that goes beyond that of an initiator. In *Theravada Buddhism*, docetism (*lokottarvada*) is considered to be a misunderstanding – even a heresy – of the meaning of Buddha's concrete life. It is apparent then that a great deal of salvific meaning is attributed to his earthly life. A way became visible in his life as in no other life, and to that extent that life also includes an aspect of granting salvation. On that basis he is also revered personally.

Other aspects that have been worked out more in *Mahayana* Buddhism leave room for a mediator of salvation. The *sambhogakaya* aspect especially (the auspicious heavenly presence of Buddhas) offers that possibility. More so than with reference to the historical Buddha, one can speak, with reference to the heavenly Amida Buddha of Pure Land Buddhism, of the salvation he grants. The related concept of *adhisthana* (blessing understood as "empowerment" to break through attachment) also allows some talk of "saving," as indeed happens frequently in the case of the *bodhisattva* Avalokitesvara.

Surveying the role of the *buddhas* and the *bodhisattvas*, one could say with Pieris in terminology that reminds one of Christology that Buddhism has two possible routes for acquiring salvation: an ascending one and a descending one. The way of salvation for the historical Buddha and that of monks (*arhats*) within *Theravada* Buddhism is clearly one of ascent. They live a life that slowly but surely approaches a higher state of enlightenment. The attitude that this ascending line presupposes is one of great personal detachment. On the other hand, the way of salvation to which the Amida Buddha and *bodhisattvas* point is one of descent. In their *karuna* (compassion), they descend to the believers[10] and grant them the possibility of enlightenment. The attitude they presuppose is one of expectant receptivity.

To characterize both attitudes, the terms "activist" *Theravada* Buddhism and "passive" *Mahayana* Buddhism are used paradoxically.[11] The "activism" of *Theravada* Buddhism, the active way in which, for example, the monks memorize and recite and the strictness in which meditation techniques are taught, is directed towards the quieting and emptying that should lead to the final enlightenment. To express it in a paradoxical way: *Theravada* Buddhists work hard actively at living passively or at receptivity. In the same paradoxical way, the passive attitude of the *Mahayana* monks, which only comes to expression in their calling on Amida's name, is directed towards the active acquirement of the gift of enlightenment.

In short, the same di-unity of activity and passivity that is present in Christianity with respect to the question of how one can acquire salvation is also encountered in Buddhism. Further on in this study, in Part VI, we will see that Hinduism has the same di-unity. In the course of the history of these religions, Buddhism, Hinduism and Christianity, this di-unity has sometimes been neglected and has then sometimes deteriorated into sharp oppositions between separate groups.

The recognition of this di-unity can help us in answering the question of whether one can speak of salvation in Buddhism that is "bestowed" on someone. Does that not contradict the emphasis that one must oneself travel the road to the non-self? Here we are faced with a question that concerns not only Buddhism but all religions that talk about "salvation." No matter how the concept of salvation is defined, it always forms a di-unity of both an external and an internal aspect. Salvation must always come from without – otherwise the human "self" would suffice – but it must also have an internal component, for otherwise it could not be experienced as something that affects a person in her essence. It causes a person to transcend himself and drives him internally. These two aspects often come together in a unique way in the form of a (salvific) mediator. An image that expresses this well is that of "strength of mind." It involves both something on which one can call – which therefore comes "from outside" in a certain sense – and something that motivates him/her internally and thus also comes "from within."

In effect, salvific mediation is always a three-part event, consisting of a source of salvation, a mediation of salvation and a power of salvation by which a bridge is built to the source and the mediation. Classic (Western) dogmatics always distinguished three aspects of the *mysterium salutis* (mystery of salvation): an external *fons salutis* (source of salvation), a *medium salutis* (means of salvation) and a partially externally and partially internally operative *virtus salutis* (power of salvation). It is not difficult to recognize the Christian Trinity of the Father (*theos*), Son (*logos*) and Holy Spirit (*pneuma*) here. In Chapter 2 we pointed to Burrel's recognition of a similar three-part division in the three Abrahamic religions, and Pieris even saw it in all the great world religions.

The di-unity of the external and internal aspects of each concept of salvation concerns both the means and power of salvation and, ultimately, the source of it as well. The latter is usually viewed not only as external but also as a "fountain in us." The whole of the three-part mystery of salvation is recognized as having both an external and an internal power. The external and internal aspects of salvation in Christianity emerge most strongly – but not necessarily exclusively – when discussing the Holy Spirit. Paradoxically, one could speak of the *potentiality* here that is *granted*. This characterization also fits in with the image of strength of mind used earlier. The concept of "inspiration" comes close to what we mean here. This concept always assumes a di-unity of "without" and "within." Buddhism expresses this phenomenon in the concept *citta*, the driving power behind the path to *nirvana*.[12] In Buddhism as well, this potentiality is evoked by something that transcends the process of detachment: it is the knowledge revealed by the Buddha (*dharma*) that points the way to the absolute of *nirvana*.[13]

The individual path that one must take to enlightenment is thus always only in a certain sense an "individual" path. One of the most important characteristics of religion is that a person must not be seen as a being in isolation but as one who is influenced by forces. A person always lives within a field of forces to which he or she can react. If the definition of three-part religion as defined in the section "Must Jesus Always Remain Greek?" above, is adequate, the adjective "individual" could possibly point simply to personal experience, to authenticity, and never to being "enclosed within oneself." It was precisely that which was seen as characteristic of sin (Luther).

The di-unity emphasized above of the character of the concept of salvation as coming from without and from within makes it impossible to view the essence of the individual separately from the forces that influence his or her existence. Taking this into account excludes every oversimplified expression of a contrast between the internal (proceeding under one's own power) or external (granted) path to salvation. Therefore, the question if Buddhism allows external mediation on the path to enlightenment cannot be answered by a simple yes or no. Where religion is concerned, there are too many questions to pose as to what exactly is meant by "external" and "internal" to be able to answer that question in a simple way.

Certainly when it concerns – as in Buddhism, and most Asian religions – a religion that emphasizes the unity of the "within" and "without" (the micro- and macrocosmos), all terms that describe one of the two aspects without the other are, by definition, inadequate. The distinction between this approach and that of the three Abrahamic religions is expressed by the Protestant philosopher of religion, Hendrik Vroom, when he speaks of "cosmic" and "theistic" concepts of transcendence. In a "cosmic" approach, of which Buddhism is an outstanding example, the divine cannot be distinguished from the cosmos or universe. In a "theistic" approach, the world is seen as a creation of God and thus clearly distinguished from God (the divine).[14] Here, too, the exception proves the rule. Within Christianity, for example, Maximus the Confessor (580–662) is the model for a way of thinking begun by the fifth-century Pseudo-Dionysius the Areopagite in which the unity of the micro- and macrocosmos is central;[15] and within Buddhism, Pure Land Buddhism with its accent on a merciful, transcendent power (Amida) is an exception.[16]

And yet these exceptions leave the clear distinction between a cosmic approach and a theistic one intact. In a theistic approach, where the idea of God as creator is prominent, creation always has its own (relative) independence with regard to the creator, similar to the relative independence of a work of art from the artist who made it. In this connection, a medieval philosopher, Nicholas of Cusa (1401–1464), spoke of the creation as other and, at the same time, as not-other with regard to the creator. Despite the emphasis on the interwovenness of the creator with the creation as "the work of his hands" (Ps. 138:8), such an approach makes every conception of a "cosmic" merging impossible.[17]

The differences are so evident that the Japanese Buddhist scholar Shinryo Takada can speak of the *shock of revelation* that a Buddhist meets in Christianity and the *shock of non-being* that a Christian encounters in Buddhism. There are completely new ideas for both that speak, on the one hand, of a creator as "over against" and, on the other, of a process of setting free as a "not-being" of the "self."[18] The challenge that this distinction entails for the dialogue between Christianity and Buddhism is that speaking of a creator must never lead to an "externalization" of the faith that does not touch the essence of human existence, and that an inner releasing process must never lead to a neglect of the social and historical dimensions in which a human lives and, therefore, also of the forces that are exerted on him or her.

The Freedom of the *Bodhisattvas* and of Jesus

Keel outlines numerous parallels between Jesus and the *bodhisattvas*. He describes these parallels in terminology borrowed from Buddhism. How Jesus acted and how *bodhisattvas* act are both characterized by freedom and love. They are "in the world but not of the world." They are involved in the world of birth and death (*samsara*), but the world does not have them in its clutches. Free of greed, anger and ignorance, they see through to the true nature of human existence as selflessness (*anatman*), connectedness with everything (*pratiya-samutpada*) and suffering (*dukkha*). Although they appear in our world, they are of another. Just like Jesus, they see through the reality of everyday. As Jesus saw the things around him from the perspective of the "true" reality of the kingdom of God, so the *bodhisattvas* are capable of seeing the visible reality as a false reality, full of projections, that can be escaped only through the emptiness (*sunyata*) that becomes available through detachment.

Bodhisattvas are spiritually free not only from the world of birth and death but also from being concerned with reaching *nirvana*. Birth and death and *nirvana*, illusion and enlightenment, finite beings and *buddhas*, the false and the true, the secular and the religious, the impure and the pure are always linked together in the wisdom of the *bodhisattvas*. The one can never be viewed without the other, and the one always accompanies the other. In their wisdom, which is characterized by non-duality, they are free from all forms of contrasting discernment and attachment, including that of *nirvana* and of enlightenment from this world. They do not sacrifice the true and holy for the false and profane, but neither do they sacrifice the false and profane for the true and holy. They see *nirvana* in the midst of birth and death, and birth and death in the midst of *nirvana*. Not living in either of the two realms, the *bodhisattvas* move freely back and forth between the present reality and ultimate reality.

Just as the *bodhisattvas* rejected – as Keel contends – the *Theravada* wisdom in which a clear distinction was always made between true and untrue, so Jesus also rejected the legalism of his time that distinguished clearly between holy and profane, pious and non-pious, just and sinful, and clean and unclean. He knew the paradox of the just person who became a sinner, and the sinner who became just. Jesus taught freedom to the children of God. Whereas the *bodhisattvas* appeal to the wisdom of Emptiness in their call to detachment, Jesus appeals to the unconditional love of God (his mercy). Thus, emptiness and mercy constitute the basis of the unlimited freedom of both with respect to everything around them. In this way, both the *bodhisattvas* and Jesus personify the truth of the "non-self" (*anatman*).

For the *bodhisattvas*, the true self, which is the "non-self" (*anatman*), refers to underlying human solidarity. In this way, the individual can be freed from the false notion of a permanent, substantial self. In this way, he can live in openness towards others without being centred on himself. In Jesus' case, the true self, the self that has emptied itself (Phil. 2:6–8), refers to the solidarity with the Father and one's neighbour. In both cases, detachment appears to be an essential condition for surrender.

In its concentration on suffering, Buddhism has always focused on the vulnerability, changeability and thereby inadequacy of human existence. This is, as it were, the Buddhist *primal experience*. Along this line of thinking, birth is not the opposite of death but its beginning, namely, the beginning of our transient existence. The confrontation with human transience (first the encounter with an old man, then one with a sick man, followed by one with a dead man) was also all-determinative biographically for Gautama, the historical Buddha. After all, the denial of the transient aspect of life is impossible and only brings more suffering with it. That is why confrontation, followed by detachment, is the first essential condition for every form of attachment that will not bring suffering with it anew.

This does not mean that one must keep all things to which one can become attached at a distance. Rather, it means that one must view the relativity of all forms of attachment. Not doing so will lead inevitably to suffering. Viewing life as inadequate does not exclude joy and love, but it does call us not to view that form of attachment as a final, definitive attachment.[19]

Throughout the history of Christian theology, a distinction has often been made between *the last things and the things before the last things*.[20] If we do not make that distinction, then we become susceptible to illusion. That is also why Paul calls us to live in the midst of all the attachments belonging inevitably to daily life as though we are not bound by these attachments and thus preserve our inner freedom. He calls those who have wives to live as though they had none, those who mourn to live as though they did not mourn, those who are happy to live as though they were not happy, etc. (1 Cor. 7:29–31).

Detachment, however, has never become the dominant, religious experience. Christianity is typically – as in Judaism and Islam – a relational religion in which attachment (the covenant) is central. The relational covenant between God and humans and between humans and humans is primary. Relationality is the positive *primal experience* (the experience of salvation) and the breaking of that relationship is regarded as the *primal sin*, as the commencement of original sin. The essence of sin is also seen, in line with Augustine, as *amor sui*, the exclusive love for oneself. It is being "enclosed within oneself," "bent into oneself" (*incurvatus in se ipsum*), which Luther would say later along the same lines.[21] Christianity thus sees this extreme form of "detachment," i.e. breaking the bonds with God and fellow humans for the benefit of the self, as the ultimate sin. But we call this an improper form of detachment, because it arises from an extreme form of attachment to oneself.

Paul speaks of detachment in a more literal sense, in the example mentioned in 1 Corinthians 7 and the earlier citation from Galatians 2:20 and Philippians 2:6–8. He speaks of a form of detachment via loss of self by letting go every form of frenetic self-preservation. Here the Christian view of loss of self approaches that of Buddhism.[22] In both cases, it concerns a process of detachment or emptying and is the first step of a negative freedom, a "freedom from" as an experience of liberation. The freedom of the *bodhisattvas* and that of Jesus arises through their freedom from the world, from religious attachments, from moralistic distinctions and, finally, from the attachment to their own "self."

It is clear that this freedom is not simply a negative "freedom from" but is also a positive "freedom for." We are deliberately not employing here the more obvious preposition "to." "Freedom to" is usually seen as the counterpart of "freedom from," but this always entails the danger of going from the one galling attachment, from which one has just freed oneself, to another galling attachment, to which one now attaches oneself. One can speak of true freedom, however, only when there is a kind of intermezzo, a certain pause, between both concepts of freedom, a marking of time, during which one opens oneself to that which ultimately supports human life. Both "freedom from" and "freedom to" carry a fundamental activist concept of freedom in which a great deal is "obligatory." One remains attached, and only that to which one is attached, the object of attachment, has changed. Only the attachment has shifted. Old attachments are immediately replaced by new ones. Only the receptivity of a "freedom for" – the emptiness of a receptive concept of freedom – can protect us from this. That freedom alone is the true basis for selfless devotion.[23]

This "freedom for" is optimally expressed in the lives of both the *bodhisattvas* and Jesus. It is a "filled" freedom, a freedom filled with love (devotion). It is apparent from their lives that there is no love without freedom and no freedom without love. Forced love is not love and freedom without loving surrender is, in the end, the lonely freedom of the desert inhabitant or the ocean sailor. In contrast, true freedom arises from the awareness of being able to surrender oneself to the supporting ground of our existence, to life-giving love.

Just as it is for the Chinese theologians Ting and Yongtao, so too the all-encompassing divine love is central for the Korean theologian Keel – a love that allows the sun to rise on good and bad people, and the rain to fall on the just and the unjust (Matt. 5:45). In short, the divine love is seen as a principle of life that conquers earthly and interpersonal contrasts. The *bodhisattvas* and Jesus were able to demonstrate this insight because they drew from a transcendent well called Emptiness or Love. They do not elevate themselves above earthly concerns but see through everyday reality and yet see what is before their eyes. Part of the wisdom (*prajna*) of the *bodhisattvas'* emptiness and love was that they are related to each other in a fruitful way.

Here Keel introduces in his argument a discussion on the relationship between form and emptiness that is typical of the Buddhist way of thinking, elaborating on the adage phrased in the famous *Heart Sutra* that *form is emptiness and emptiness is form*. Free of every attachment to form, *bodhisattvas* are dependent on nothing. Viewed this way, form is emptiness. But, encompassing all forms, *bodhisattvas* are at the same time moved by the well-being of everyone. For emptiness is, after all, identical to non-selfish "attachment." Emptiness stripped of all forms makes true freedom possible and, subsequently, this same emptiness can assume all forms of involvement. Thus, emptiness is also form.

In Keel's view, the parallel between the *bodhisattvas* and Jesus has everything to do with the parallel between the concepts of emptiness and love. Keel thus arrives at his central thesis that that which makes a *bodhisattva* a *bodhisattva* is the same reality that makes Jesus an embodiment of God's love.[24] It is the all-encompassing love that finds itself only by losing itself. Sharing in this love implies, from a Christian point of view, dying and rising with Jesus. Only that love binds us together. It is the self-transcendence through loss of self that links us together as human beings in an unpretentious and, therefore, unconditional way.

Thus both Buddhism and Christianity are concerned with an emptiness (loss) that is the condition for true solidarity. This shift from loss to solidarity is called emptiness in Buddhism and love in Christianity. In both cases it concerns a reality, a force, that supports human existence. Following Keel's logic, when this force is called Logos in the New Testament, it could also be called Emptiness. It is, after all, a love that empties itself in order to be able to devote itself completely to another.

What Keel actually does here is link the tradition of wisdom that is Buddhism to the tradition of love that is Christianity. It is a linking that goes back a long way in both religions. Christianity contains the di-unity of love (*agape*) and knowledge (*gnosis*) in the Logos and Buddhism understands Buddhahood to be the fullness (*pleroma*) of wisdom (*prajna*) and loving care (*karuna*).[25] The parallels are evident here, providing that one remembers that the doctrine of the Logos in Christianity always presupposes the doctrine of creation and can only be understood from that perspective (see above).

How "Personal" is the Relationship?

A question that Keel does touch upon but ultimately leaves unanswered is the question if the source of the above-mentioned all-encompassing love, called Logos or Emptiness, can be seen as a personal force, as Christianity is wont to do in contrast to Buddhism. A brief reference to the history of (Western) theology will make clear that this question cannot easily be answered.

Anyone who is familiar to some degree with the doctrine of God in Western theology knows that speaking about God as a person was always done in a nuanced way. Speaking about God as a person is never the same as speaking about a human individual; it has always been viewed as an analogical way of speaking, i.e saying something about God based on a number of similarities with human persons amongst even greater differences. It is on the basis of this reluctance that the simple thesis that God is not human lies. Concepts applicable to humans cannot be transferred to God straightforwardly.

At times in the history of theology this has led to an argument for an *apophatic* theology: a theology that remains silent about God's attributes. This has led at times to an argument for a negative theology: a theology that only states what God in any case is not. Following from this line of thinking is the *theology of the comparative*, i.e. a theology that holds that, in comparison with us, God is always greater – for example, *more than* love, *more than* a person, etc.

With respect to content, the various forms of theology arise from the awareness that the concept of God confronts us with closeness and distance, with immanence and transcendence. If the first aspect dominates, the concepts deemed fitting are taken from the interpersonal context. If the second aspect dominates, and God is viewed especially as a *mysterium fascinans et tremendum* (a fascinating but terrifying mystery), one speaks rather of a power or force and the personal terms disappear into the background.

The di-unity of in themselves opposite – more distant and more intimate – aspects can be found not only in the relationship to God in the Abrahamic religions but also in the way in which Buddhism speaks about the relationship to the Buddha. The *trikaya* doctrine mentioned above on the three dimensions of existence of the Buddha (historical nature: *nirmanakaya*; heavenly: *sambhogakaya*; and internal: *dharmakaya*) creates the possibility of a more varied use of language. The concepts that presume more distance give the concepts that presume nearness more depth and prevent them from becoming trivial or too familiar, whereas the more personal concepts that presume nearness give warmth and emotion to the more distant concepts. Thus, they presuppose one another.[26] There is room for both the more personal and more impersonal concepts.

The considerations above also entail the answer to the third question we posed at the beginning of this chapter, i.e. the question of the personal nature of the relationship with the mediator. The answer to the second question – that of the nature of the mediator – will follow that. We determined that speaking of "personal" in the relationship to God can never be derived too immediately from the interpersonal realm, for God is not human. Moreover, we determined that in Buddhism as well the relationship to Buddha has many shades.

The Nature of the Mediation

In addition to the question regarding the nature of the personal relationship, the comparison with the *bodhisattvas* also raises the question of the nature of the mediation. As far as we are concerned, this is a question that has to do directly with the meaning of resurrection in Christianity and reincarnation in Buddhism. In the latter, reincarnation is not – in contrast to the concept of resurrection in Christianity – something positive. It entails the continuation of being bound to the finite life with all of its suffering, even though it is sometimes viewed positively in the sense of a process of maturation or purification. But in that case it is always a matter of ascent and not of descent. The choice between the two can only be attributed to or blamed on the person himself. In the case of an ascent – as a process of purification – parallels have been drawn with the Roman Catholic concept of purgatory. The resurrection is viewed as a passage to another existence that is seen as "heavenly" or "spiritual" and not as earthly.

The idea that at some point body and spirit can be reunited has ancient roots in Christianity. This is why the Apostolic Creed also speaks of the resurrection of *the body* – albeit in a later addition. No one knows what that would be like, but the intention is clear: resistance to a (docetic) undervaluation of the body. There was much at stake here in the discussion with the Gnostics. The argument of a church father such as Irenaeus, for example, was that if the *recreating* God of the belief in resurrection did not concern himself with the body, the created, then the *creating* God would not have been able to do even that, and the Gnostics, with their denial of the fact that the God of Jesus was also the creator, would then have been right.[27]

Christianity is convinced that Jesus' own death and resurrection pave the way for the death and resurrection of his followers. This death and resurrection is seen as both a psychological process that occurs during a human life as well as a physical process that occurs at the end of each human life. Buddhism sees this death and resurrection as an internal process, called the "Great Death," also in relation to the concept Emptiness. Neither religion truly succeeds in creating a clear idea of what the continuity between the "old" dead person and the "new" reborn one is. It is clear that the two most extreme possibilities – complete discontinuity and unaltered continuity – are rejected in both religions.[28]

It is difficult to express positively the identity between the old and new person in Christianity and between the various rebirths or between the last rebirth and Buddhahood in Buddhism. After all, every concept that could be used would suggest that something in a person could be removed from the process of dying, and that is difficult to maintain with respect to the radical nature of the idea of dying, of emptying, in both religions. And yet the person who is reborn, the one who has entered *nirvana* in Buddhism, and the one who is resurrected in Christianity has not lost every form of identity with their previous lives. If that were so, then a completely different person would be reborn, enter *nirvana*, or be resurrected.

The idea that believers can follow the path of Buddha and of the *buddhas* and *bodhisattvas* and thus attain *nirvana* fits in with the Christian views regarding the imitation of Jesus, but in Buddhism it is never linked with the idea of the incarnation of the divine. The transient human being can be called the personification (*huashen*) of the immortal eternal one, but there is no divine descent that serves as its basis. Rather, there is a human ascent. A person can achieve such a state of enlightenment that, as a finite being, he or she approaches the eternal divine. In Christianity, that way of thinking runs parallel to so-called *adoptionism* in which Jesus' devotion to the kingdom of God is seen as a reason for God to adopt him as a son. But that line of thought always has – so as not to be considered one-sided – the incarnation (descent) as a counterpart.

Buddhism, and especially *Mahayana* Buddhism, also contains a line of thinking in which the descent – in this case in the sense of granting salvation – is central. One of the aspects of the dialogue between Christians and Buddhists that offers the most perspective lies enclosed within the bearable tension between both lines.

The strongest parallel between Jesus and the *bodhisattvas* lies in their devotion that arises through loss of self. Both have a mediating role. They are both preparers of the path. In Jesus' case, however, it is not only a psychological process of death but also a concrete death on the cross that is linked to the forgiveness and the opening of life for many. Thus, the nature of the mediation is somewhat diverse. Jesus is not only a preparer of a path who can be followed but also someone who, in a very unique way, breaks open a dead end – namely, that of human guilt – with his own death and resurrection.

Double Transformation

Are the points of difference such that it would be better not to explain the meaning of Jesus by referring to the role of the *bodhisattva* in Buddhism? We stated in Chapter 2 that a syncretic event always involves *double transformation*. And that is what we see happening here. More emphatically than in many other well-known conceptions of Jesus in the history of Western theology, we see the image of Jesus moved by compassion (*karuna*) emerging from the comparison with a *bodhisattva*.

This is the *transformation* that appears on the Christian side. Jesus is seen primarily as one moved by compassion and who puts aside all aspirations to power. Viewed against the background of the reproach against Christianity for its lack of solidarity with the great poverty of the Asian population, this is by no means a slight transformation. As *bodhisattva*, Jesus is the one who is unequivocally concerned about the fate of the Asian poor.

The *transformation* on the Buddhist side is that Asian Christians will see the personification of their God in this *bodhisattva* – a God who "descends" in human form. Furthermore, there is the belief that the death of this *bodhisattva* opens a path to salvation for his followers. He does not simply show solidarity (concern) with the lot of his fellow human beings but enters the fray on their behalf as well. In this way he breaks through the snarled relationships between God and people and between people.

Here we touch on the issue of the *taking over* of human guilt. The *transferability* of guilt is not an issue for people, for they are accustomed to calling people to account for the guilt of others (ancestors or descendants, family members and kinsmen). We speak relatively easily of historical, collective guilt. In Asia, *self-sacrifice* is certainly not an unknown phenomenon: millions of Asian women have been forced into it. There are also more specific examples. Many still see clearly in their mind's eye monks immolating themselves during the Vietnam War in the 1970s. By sacrificing their lives, the monks wanted to shock world opinion and thus contribute to the end of the Vietnam War.

But the idea of *taking over* the guilt of others so that those who were truly guilty would not be punished has thus far been found only in the Analectica by Confucius (20,1) in a passage on Emperor T'ang. The notion of possibly *taking over* the guilt of another is not unchallenged either. Kant's and Sartre's comments on this are well-known. For the great

Enlightenment philosopher Immanuel Kant (1724–1804), the highly personal nature of the guilt of sin entailed that sin cannot be taken over – is not *transferable* – and can be borne only by the sinner and not by an innocent person. From the perspective of his existential philosophy, Jean Paul Sartre (1905–1980) went one step further and stated that a person has to bear responsibility for his own existence and need not justify it to anyone else; therefore he cannot be declared guilty.

The New Testament tells a different tale. It sketches human guilt as a power that can best be characterized as the lack of freedom – a lack of freedom with regard to the powers of evil that is expressed especially in its powerlessness to renounce itself. This lack of freedom (powerlessness) has become so overwhelming through its historical and collective character – often viewed as original sin – that one can be freed from it only by sharing in Jesus' death as a sinner. This participation takes place in Christian baptism: dying and rising with Jesus. One's guilty separation from God by being enclosed within oneself can be undone – so goes the argument – only by identifying with the one among us who is closest to God (Jesus) and who, by taking our place, has most deeply experienced the abandonment of God. One becomes free only by identifying with the one who grants him or her a new identity as one reborn. In this approach, guilt is the lack of freedom and participation in (the identification with) the events of dying and rising in baptism is the gift of freedom. Thus, a Christian receives his or her freedom (= his/her identity) through identification and in that identification there is a *taking over* of guilt.[29]

In conclusion we could say that the *Christian bodhisattva* is different from the Buddhist *bodhisattva*, just as the Christian Lord is different from the Greek-Roman *kyrios-dominus* and the Christian *Saviour* is different from the Germanic *heliand* (saviour). Regarding the comparison between Jesus and the *bodhisattvas*, one can then rightly say that this is an analogy: a similarity amidst even greater differences. In fact, this is – as we argued in Chapter 2 – the normal inculturation pattern.

Only within the framework of this dynamic process of attributing meaning can the designation of Jesus as *bodhisattva* be called an enrichment of the Asian Christian theology. Separated from this process of transformation, the differences are evident. Jesus is a historical and not a mythological figure like the *bodhisattva*. Moreover, he is not, as the *bodhisattva* is, on the path to enlightenment. Rather, he is the personification of divine enlightenment ("I am the light of the world" (John 8:12)). Jesus is not a Buddhist *bodhisattva* just as he is not a messiah in the Jewish sense, a son of God in the Jewish or Greek sense, a *kyrios* or *dominus* in the Greek or Roman senses, and a *heliand* in the German sense. In all of these cases, the moment that these concepts are applied to Jesus, their meanings change.

This is also the case with the concept *bodhisattva*. But this in no way means that Jesus cannot be described meaningfully by concepts that have been borrowed from the worship of the *bodhisattva*. Perhaps this is the only possibility in a Buddhist world for making clear how unconditional God's compassion is, especially for the Asian poor. After all, the *bodhisattva* is pre-eminently the one who displays *karuna* or, as Christians would say, God's compassion.

Part V: The Japanese and Korean Jesus

In Japan – more than in any other country – the self-emptying that the not-I requires is linked with suffering, i.e. with human pain and with the pain of God. This fascination with suffering is reflected not only in theology but also in Christian literature (Endo). In the Japanese not-I theology (Takizawa and Yagi), the human is, in effect, the place where the divine (the not-I) manifests itself, whereas in the Japanese theology of the cross (Kitamori and Koyama) the divine is the place where the human aspect (suffering) manifests itself. In both cases there is a strong link between the divine and the human. With respect to God, this link could be characterized as vulnerable immanence and with respect to humans as a vulnerable desire for transcendence. This link also means that divine and human suffering cannot be kept separate from each other. But that immediately evokes the question of who can relieve the suffering, assuming that mere sympathizing with those who suffer does not relieve it.

One's relationship with one's ancestors is all-determinative in Korea. At the same time, that relationship is the major point of dispute among Korean Christians. Does that relationship stand in the way of one's relationship with Jesus or does it clarify the latter?

In Korea as well, religion is very directly involved in the practical issues of sickness and death and material well-being. The cause of prosperity and adversity can always be found close by, rather than far away, in one's own way of life or in that of the ancestors, which is why ancestors are also involved in the question of salvation. In Minjung theology especially, salvation is viewed as having historical implications as well: there is a concrete expectation for the future. The non-Asian externalization of salvation that can accompany it is sometimes dealt with by linking the internal and external worlds inextricably together by means of the yin and yang principle. But this principle does not at all presuppose a harmonious society; rather, it presupposes one with sharp contrasts between good and bad and between good and evil spirits. Forces mediating the good can appear in the midst of these contrasts, whether in the shape of a mudang or instruction in the di-unity of word and path (tao). It is particularly with respect to this mediation that analogies with Jesus occur.

7   The Japanese Jesus

The Attitude of Japanese Christians towards the State

Although the palette of colours in the religious climate in Japan is the same as in China, Japan nonetheless has its own accent. We have already made references to *Zen* and *Pure Land* Buddhism, strongly influenced in Japan by early medieval thinkers such as Honen and Shinran. The *Jodo-Shin* (of the Sect of the Pure Land) school, established by Honen (1133–1212), teaches that good works and mercy (received by calling Amida's name) bring redemption. The *Jodo-Shin-Shu* (of the True Sect of the Pure Land) school of Shinran (1173–1262) maintains an almost Lutheran concept of sin. There is nothing in a human being that can bring him salvation – not even calling Amida's name. Salvation comes from the "beyond," from somewhere else. Having to rely on mercy "outside of ourselves" (Luther would say: *extra nos*) causes all believers to be essentially equal. That is why Shinran sharply criticized the inequality between monks and "normal" believers in the Buddhism he knew. The parallels with Luther here are rather obvious.[1] The Swiss theologian Karl Barth (1886–1968) even speaks of the most "comprehensive and illuminating heathen parallel to Christianity" and considers this form of "Japanese Protestantism" to be the *symptoms* of the mercy and truth appearing in Jesus Christ.[2]

Shinran's criticism of a religious hierarchy is exceptional in Japan. The Japanese respect for authority displays more of a Confucian philosophy of life, albeit in a secularized form today. Taoism has never been prominent in Japan but a link with nature that is also characteristic of Taoism is apparent in the refinement and almost divine cohesion that can be seen in their ornamental art.

A fourth and, after Buddhism, possibly most important colour that must be added to the Japanese religious palette is Shintoism (literally: path of the gods). This is a form of original Japanese religiosity that actually only consists of rituals and feasts around the Shinto altars. These rituals and feasts celebrate the unity with nature, the ancestors and the Japanese nation.[3]

Shintoism was the explicit state religion and the cult of the emperor from 1868 to 1945. The Confucian and Shinto worship of ancestors and rulers converge in this cult. The emperor becomes a divine ruler who is part of the unbroken line of canonized ancestors that ultimately goes back to the sun goddess, Amaterasu-o-mikami. One of her direct descendents, Jimmu-Tenno, became the first emperor of Japan around 660 BC.

We are dealing here with a state ideology based on rituals in which the emperor plays a crucial role. This structure was supported by a governmental regulatory framework that gradually became more detailed with regard to the participation in the rituals at the Shinto altars. Students of religious studies describe the altars as the "state in worship." In fact, the state more or less appropriated the old, Shinto rituals of the people.[4]

From the middle of the 1930s on, all churches were forced to participate in Shinto ceremonies: the argument was that these ceremonies were not religious but national. This argument could also be used in the West for keeping the church neutral; but, in a society in which the state ideology has not (yet) been exposed as a religion, the enforcement of a new religion is a nasty business, whereas subjugating the church in the interest of the state is not.

Apart from exceptions, most Protestant churches and the Roman Catholic Church have participated wholeheartedly in this state ideology and even sent "missionaries" to Korea and China, which had been colonized by Japan, to convince their fellow believers of the "innocent" (= non-religious) nature of the Shinto altars.[5] In Korea especially, as we will see later, this led to great tension among Christians. After the war, the Japanese churches explicitly confessed their guilt with regard to this position.

To this very day, the role of Shinto worship in Japan in relation to emperor worship and Japanese nationalism is a point of contention. Even though the above-mentioned state ideology was officially abolished in 1945, it has far from disappeared. The Yasukuni altar, erected in 1879 close to the emperor's palace in Tokyo in honour of Emperor Meiji, is still the place where the more than two and a half million Japanese (including a large number of notorious war criminals) who died for the honour of the emperor in the various wars Japan fought in the twentieth century are honoured. Official visits by Japanese rulers to such altars have led in recent years to massive and violent anti-Japan demonstrations in China and Korea.

Religion in Japan, including Christianity, is linked very emphatically with recent state history. This complicates the position of the churches, which is probably also one of the reasons for the fact that Christianity has spread widely in Korea but not in Japan. In Korea, Christianity was quickly viewed as an important ideological power factor over against Japanese colonization. For Koreans, identification with Christianity became a means for fighting for their national identity over against the Japanese occupation. The Christianity brought over by American missionaries was just what was needed in Korea in the beginning of the twentieth century. The missionaries had nothing to do with this aspect; it was the Koreans themselves who allotted Christianity this role.[6] The Koreans were able to do this because in 1890 the Korean Presbyterian Church, in contrast to the Chinese Presbyterian Church, adopted the so-called "Nevius method," which consisted of self-rule, self-support and self-propagation.[7]

Christianity has always found itself in an entirely different position in Japan. For two centuries it was a forbidden religion. It then allied itself, albeit under pressure but without massive protest, with the rising Japanese nationalism and, even after the shock of the atom bomb – in Japan ironically called the "baptism of the atom bomb"[8] – little changed in the attitude of the majority of the Christians towards the state. This is all the more remarkable if one considers that the history of Japanese Christianity – a history filled with cruel persecution! – gives the least cause for loyalty to the state.

The *Kakure* Christians

At the end of the sixteenth and the beginning of the seventeenth century, from 1549 to 1639, Christianity in Japan underwent strong growth due to the Jesuits. Around 1614 there were approximately 400,000 Christians. That is almost half of the current one million Christians in a population of about 120 million. In the middle of the seventeenth century, the Buddhists began an extraordinarily fierce persecution that lasted more than two hundred years and resulted in 10,000 victims. Only a small group of 35,000 believers were able to survive all those centuries as "hidden Christians" (*Kakure Kirishitan*) in southern Japan in Kyushu (near Nagasaki) and on a number of islands near the coast. It is due in particular to the Japanese writer Shusaku Endo that their situation has become known in broader circles in the West.

When Tokugawa Ieyasu came to power in 1603, the missionary work of Portuguese and Spanish missionaries in Japan became impossible due to cruel persecution and forced conversions to Buddhism. It was not until 1872 that the Tokugawa ban was lifted and the remaining Christians joined the Roman Catholic Church. One of the most famous examples of a forced conversion is the Portuguese Jesuit Christovao Ferreira who, after his "conversion" in 1633, assumed the name Sawano Chuan as a Buddhist and later made an important contribution to the development of science in Japan.[9]

Just like the first Christians in China, these Christians developed their own form of Japanese Christianity. This development was strengthened, to a limited degree, by the isolation into which they were forced for two centuries. For example, they had their own holy book entitled *The Beginning of Heaven and Earth* (in Japanese shortened to *Tenchi*), in which the first two chapters are devoted to the creation, the fall and the flood, and the next thirteen chapters to the lives of Mary and Jesus, arranged according to the rosary.

The book contains many traces of Buddhist and Shintoist, typically Japanese, influences. For instance, the flood is conceived of as a tsunami sent by God, from which Noah barely manages to escape in a canoe with his children. A great deal of attention is paid to baptism and to burial rites, including the care for one's ancestors. Mary appears to fill the mediating role of the Holy Spirit in the doctrine of the Trinity. Pentecost is not mentioned.[10] It was not until 1853, when, under Western pressure, Japan was once again opened to foreigners, that these *kakure* Christians were rediscovered. The ban on Christianity was lifted in 1873.

The image that arises from what has been discovered about their piety is not very different from how religion functioned elsewhere in Japan. (1) Harmony between the gods, people and nature is presupposed; (2) the maintenance of relationships with both living and dead family members is important; (3) cleansing rituals are an essential part of religious festivals; (4) the festivals occupy an important place in the religious self-awareness of the local population; and (5) all religious customs are part of the rhythm of daily life and are not experienced in a particular way on a particular day – in contrast to how Christians celebrate Sunday, for example.[11]

Christianity has never been an independent, ideological factor in Japanese society. We referred in the penultimate section in Chapter 2 to the di-unity of confirmation and denial (critique), of the incarnation and of the cross and resurrection as a condition for a successful inculturation of the Gospel. Japanese Christians voice this critique only sporadically. Apparently they are too content with their society. Nor is there any room for something new, such as a new religion. There must first be a certain discontent with the existing religion for that to happen.[12]

That is why the epilogue of the volume *A History of Japanese Theology* (1997) edited by Yasuo Furuya states that Japan itself constitutes the greatest obstacle to the development of it own Japanese theology. As long as Japanese theology is not capable of conquering the regular flaring up of Japanese ethnocentrism, it adds nothing to what is already very common in Japan. In that volume, theology in Japan is therefore called to view its task primarily as a relativizing one with respect to the Japanese nationalistic self-awareness and subsequently as a catalyst in a broader, global consciousness by, for example, appealing more strongly to the tradition of peace that also belongs to the history of the Japanese church.[13]

A Jesus for the Japanese?

A chief exponent of the peace tradition is the *Nonchurch movement* founded by Kanzo Uchimura (1861–1930). Uchimura championed a radical kind of Protestantism without spirituality, without sacraments and without church membership but with a strong concentration on Bible studies and a strong expectation of Jesus' return. He founded a lay movement within Japanese Christianity that saw itself as pacifist and wished to build on Japan's pre-Christian past. For example, he dedicated the following short text to the relationship between Buddha and Christ:

> Buddha is the Moon; Christ is the Sun.
> Buddha is the Mother; Christ is the Father.
> Buddha is Mercy; Christ is Righteousness.
> ... I love the Moon and I love the night; but as the night is far spent and the day is at hand, I now love the Sun more than I love the Moon; and I know that the love of the Moon is included in the love of the Sun, and that he who loves the Sun loves the Moon also.[14]

Referring to the Confucian background of his Chinese father, Uchimura wished to Christianize the *bushido* tradition of the samurai class to which he himself belonged. The samurai class was the warlord class, whose high ideals could be summarized in the concept *bushido*. For Uchimura, those ideals stood for independence (from the state and from money) and loyalty (to Christ). If we look for a Western analogy of the movement that he had in mind, then we would probably end up somewhere between the Quakers and the Mennonites. He saw the best of Confucianism and Buddhism (especially Amida Buddhism) united in the form of Christianity he championed.[15]

In addition to the *Nonchurch movement*, which is a subject of interest for many intellectuals, Japan also has numerous other typically Japanese Christian movements such as The Way, The Heart and The Spirit of Christ.[16] Outside of the "mainline" mission churches, an extensive process of the inculturation of the meaning of Jesus has taken place in the characteristically Japanese way of thinking and rituals. It is estimated that those typically Japanese Christian movements comprise ten per cent of Japanese Christianity. The theory that a lack of inculturation is one of the most important reasons for the restricted distribution of Christianity in Asia certainly does not hold for Japan.[17]

The Japanese have their own way of dealing with religion. A Japanese person can bring a newborn to a Shinto altar for a blessing, can go to a Christian chapel to get married, and can be buried with Buddhist rites.[18] And religion comprises only a small part of Japanese life. This holds for the so-called "new religions" in Japan as well. They generally have a vital impact and presuppose a primal cosmic force, often described in maternal terms, that permeates all of life and ensures that our efforts bear fruit. It is estimated that about twenty per cent of the population lean toward these new religions that have often taken shape around charismatic leaders. These new religions include various elements not only from Buddhism, Confucianism, Taoism and Shintoism but also from Christianity.[19] As such, Jesus does play a role in Japanese culture, something that is expressed in literature, the visual arts, etc. But one seldom encounters direct identification with Jesus, including becoming a follower of Jesus.[20]

In the midst of all these religious hybrids, post-Second World War Japanese theology did acquire its own identity. We will look especially at the work of individual theologians such as Kazoh Kitamori, Kosuke Koyama, Katsumi Takinawa and Seiichi Yagi. We will attempt to trace a number of common perspectives in their theology.

The Pain of God

Immediately after the Second World War, Kitamori (b. 1916) published his *Theology of the Pain of God* (1946). Finding his way between the Buddhist view of suffering and the Christian theology of the cross, Kitamori developed a theology of the *pain of God* as an expression of the conflict in God himself between his love and wrath. Aside from the fact that this book does not directly examine the suffering and pain of the Second World War that ended so disastrously for Japan, it still seems to have been the right book at the right time.

The word *tsurasa*, borrowed from classic Japanese stage drama, is central to Kitamori's theology. The word refers to the emotion evoked by the decision to commit suicide or to murder a loved one for the benefit of the salvation of another. It is a very complicated emotion that represents suffering, sorrow and bitterness all at the same time. This emotion manifests itself most violently when it is repressed. Then it becomes a *pain*. According to Kitamori, this is exactly the same kind of pain that God feels when he allows his son to be killed on the cross.[21]

The history of (Western) theology provided only two options in answer to the question of whether God could suffer pain. Generally speaking, that possibility was denied God, by reference to his *apatheia*, his inability to suffer. Sometimes, such a notion was an expression of an image of God in which there was indeed no place for (co-)suffering on the part of God. That reserve sometimes arose from the fear that God would be swallowed up in suffering – who else could then free us from that suffering?

Also always present in Christianity, however, was the undercurrent of so-called *patripassionism*, which assumed that the suffering of the Son also affected the Father. This undercurrent has always been regarded as heretical. If Jesus' death is supposed to still God's wrath, God himself cannot be a fellow victim. But if there is an indissoluble link between the heart of God and Jesus' heart, one need not deny that the suffering of the Son also affects the Father. That is why – we would argue – patripassionism continues to surface as a *legitimate* undercurrent.

Kitamori, however, chooses neither option.[22] He sees God suffering as Father in a way that is very distinct from his Son, namely because he, as it were, "swallows" his anger about human sinfulness. This pain is an expression of a conflict in God himself. It is a reluctant expression of his love. The concept of *tsurasa* is the only fitting analogy that Kitamori can conceive for this readiness to suffer pain on behalf of others, even if they do not really deserve it. This last aspect especially is an element that Kitamori, as a Christian, consciously adds to the customary Japanese interpretation of the concept of *tsurasa*. In Japanese tragedies, the person for whom one offers his own or a loved one's life is always someone who deserves respect. In the case of Jesus, this is clearly not the case. God's *tsurasa* extends, in the case of Jesus, precisely to those who are reviled and with whom Jesus identifies.[23]

If we link God's pain with the concept of *tsurasa*, the Father's suffering is clearly different from that of the Son. God's pain is the result of his pent-up anger over the sinful behaviour of people and his readiness to allow his son to suffer for that (his love). His pain concerns both believers and unbelievers. Unbelievers do not realize this pain, but believers all the more so: they feel this suffering of God as their own. Kitamori speaks here of the *analogia doloris*, the analogy of pain.[24] This pain is not that of one specific experience but of all human existence, just as the pain does not merely affect God indirectly but literally strikes him in his heart.

This interpretation of sharing in divine pain also has consequences for the way in which believers can be a church – not in the sense of a "happy community" but in the sense that those who are aware of the pain of God and themselves carry the pain of human existence. It is a community that brings the contradiction between love and anger, which personifies the pain, to expression in its social protest. Kitamori's emphasis on the fact that Jesus was crucified "outside the city gate" (Heb. 13:12) in particular made him popular with the *Nonchurch movement*. Kitamori concludes from the phrase "outside the city gates" that Jesus died for the "outsiders," to "embrace those who were not permitted to be embraced." This is also why he likes to speak of the "outsidedness" of his theology and is horrified by the thought that his theology might become the "dominant" theology in Japan.[25] And yet he does not neglect to point to the practical application of his theology. Thus he is very much concerned with the continued effect of his theology. His main concern is an *analogia doloris* among believers, a love that is analogous to the way in which God "loves in pain," taking on the destiny of others. It should be clear that Kitamori's social position cannot simply be fit into an existing scheme, which is why the classification of "social quietism" that Inagaki and Nelson Jennings have given him goes too far.[26]

It is Kitamori's intention to show where God's heart is, and Jer. 31:20 is a key text here: "'Is not Ephraim my dear son, the child in whom I delight? Though I often speak against him, I still remember him. Therefore my heart yearns for him; I have great compassion for him,' declares the LORD." "This is why my heart brings me, so that I must have mercy on him" which is how Luther, in Kitamori's eyes, translates the last part of the verse very strikingly. "Love rooted in pain" is how Kitamori sums the essence of this text and thereby his own entire theology.[27]

Just as Jer. 31:20 is a key text for Kitamori, so Hos. 11:8 became a key text for his student Kosuke Koyama (b. 1929): "My heart is changed within me; all my compassion is aroused." This text from Hosea follows God's complaint that Israel has left him and serves other gods, which breaks God's heart. This is why God is aroused. Koyama paints a picture of a passionate God,[28] some of whose passion Koyama himself exhibits. Much more explicitly and personally than is the case with Kitamori, we see much more of Koyama's own personal and theological processing of the Second World War in his theology.[29] Although Koyama has lived most of his life outside of Japan (Thailand and the United States) and is therefore no longer seen as representative of the theology being done in Japan, his theology nevertheless so unmistakably follows that of Kitamori that – if only for that reason – he deserves mention.[30]

Personal experiences form the basis for his "theology of the cross." For him, the cross is not a static event in the past. It symbolizes a passionate God intent on encompassing all of humanity in his love. The cross, in Koyama's eyes, is a call to remain aware of the contrast, i.e. the contrast of an "other" world in which it is revealed to us "To act justly and to love mercy and to walk humbly with your God" (Mic. 6:8). Second, the cross reveals that the last judgement is not ours. "Brokenness" in the sense of the collapse of our ideologies is a characteristic of every theology of the cross. Third, the cross makes clear that there are "gods" in whose name people are nailed to the cross. And, fourth, the cross makes clear the distinction between the true God and false gods. The God who saves others does not listen to the call of the spectators at the cross to save himself (Mk 15:31). The true God does not save himself, only others.[31]

The starting point for Koyama's theology is his war experiences. Those experiences were apparently recognizable in other contexts as well –

especially in those of Thailand where he worked for years. And yet, at the end of his argument, Koyama often returns to examples from Japan, which reveal how critical he is of the renewed Japanese nationalism. Against that background, it is relatively shocking to see that he is only casually mentioned in the epilogue of the above-mentioned *A History of Japanese Theology*, with the remark that his influence in Japan is almost nil.[32] It is clear that the way in which the church in Japan has supported the state religion has left Koyama with deep wounds. His sensitivity to this has not always made him much loved in Japanese Christianity.

For both Kitamori and Koyama, the love of God expressed through the suffering Jesus is central. Their concentration on this suffering has to do with the recent history of the Japanese people but is also a clear symptom of the Buddhist context in which they formulate their theology. Whereas in classic Buddhism the believing individual attempts to escape suffering (*dukkha*) by means of repentance, Japanese Buddhists have reflected much more collectively and thus also more militantly on suffering.[33] That approach seems to have left its traces on Kitamori and Koyama as well. But neither of them engages in a fundamental discussion with Buddhism.

Militancy can be observed particularly in the Christian *Baraku* (also called *Eta*). Their name refers to the place where they were forced to live – "outside the village" – and how they were forced to live – "as dirt." Their position could be compared to that of the *dalits* in India.[34] Teruo Kuribayashi made their suffering the theme of his theology of the cross – *A Theology of the Crown of Thorns* – and turned it into a theology of the resurrection in which their liberation is central.[35]

Endo's "Japanese Theology"

The existential shape of this theology of the suffering of God can be gauged in the work of the Japanese writer Shusako Endo. For his image of Christians, he orients himself strongly to the *kakure* Christians mentioned earlier. They had integrated their forced betrayal of Jesus by the Japanese government into their perception of faith. Endo repeatedly mentions that, from 1629 on, these Christians were forced to betray Jesus by publicly walking over a copper plank, the *fumie*, that had his image on it. When they got home, they prayed for forgiveness for what they had been forced to do and performed a number of cleansing rituals, such as drinking the water in which they had cleaned their soiled feet. It was not until 1857 that the *fumie* was abolished, chiefly at the urging of the Dutch.

In the novel *Silence* (1969), a key role is played by the historical figure Sebastian Rodrigo, a Portuguese Jesuit who looked upon Ferreira as his master. It is Ferreira who incites Rodrigo to betrayal and forces him to walk on the *fumie* so as to end the torture of his fellow Christians who had been taken prisoner. Endo describes the moment he lifts his foot to step on the image of Christ as follows:

> He will now trample on what he has considered the most beautiful thing in his life, on what he has believed most pure, on what is filled with the ideals and the dreams of man. How his foot aches! And then the Christi bronze speaks to the priest: "Trample! Trample! I more than anyone know of the pain in your foot. Trample! It was to be trampled on by men that I was born into this world. It was to share men's pain that I carried my cross".[36]

The cock crows at the precise moment that Rodrigo allows his foot to fall. Released from prison because he renounced his faith, Rodrigo secretly continues to administer the sacraments and grants the one who betrayed him absolution. Rodrigo denies his faith and loses the last of his possessions, but God did not keep silent. Rodrigo heard His voice when he stopped being a Christian, when he betrayed all that was dear to him. What Endo has his main character, the unsuccessful student priest Otsu, say in Endo's latest novel, *Deep River*, is true: "Even if I try to abandon God ... God won't abandon me."[37] Most characters in Endo's novels are allowed, in the depths of their misery, only a glimpse of God, of the love that they themselves can no longer realize. It is not the believers and the martyrs who learn the true nature of faith but those who deny and betray, whereby, certainly in the case of Rodrigo, the question arises as to whether they have actually renounced their faith. His renunciation could, after all, be his way of keeping the faith. It was through his act that his fellow Christians could be saved.

In the novel *Scandal*, the main character's visit to the *kakure* Christians is important. The main character, who has defiled his own life in many ways with activities that could be viewed as betraying his Christian authorship, finds rest for his harried soul in the words of Matt. 11:28, which is recited by all during a church service: "Come to me, all you who are weary and burdened, and I will give you rest."[38] In his own biography – his mother had him baptized in the Roman Catholic Church at the age of eleven – Endo feels a link with these Christians who bore, with a great deal of pain, the fact of their being Christian as their destiny.

Endo does not, as one might expect, refer to the valour of these Japanese martyrs for the faith but, on the contrary, to their cowardice. This confronts us with a great number of questions. Is the act of stepping on the *fumie* indeed a betrayal of Christ, or is it precisely "the" place where one meets Christ? Is this capitulation a necessary condition for being truly liberated from ourselves by Christ? What does this tell us in connection with how Jesus dealt with Judas and Peter?[39] Each of the disciples – Endo argues –

stayed alive by abandoning Jesus and running away. He continued to love them, even though they had betrayed him. The result was that he was engraved in their guilty hearts and that they could never forget him. They went to distant countries to pass the story of their lives on to others. And thus he continued to live in their hearts. He died but was raised to life again in their hearts, because it also was true for them that their abandonment of God did not mean that God had abandoned them.

The betrayal of martyrs for the faith is a theme that returns often in Endo's work. He links that betrayal not only with the dark external world of the times of persecution but also with the dark, sadistic internal world of one's soul, in which the violence that is experienced externally also becomes internal. The image of Christ that emerges from this is a Christ who is closer to our weakness than our strength, closer to our lies than to our truth. It is the image that Heb. 4:15 sketches in the words: "For we do not have a high priest who is unable to sympathize with our weaknesses, but we have one who has been tempted in every way, just as we are – yet was without sin."

Endo's latest book, *Deep River*, cites Isa. 53:2–4: "he hath no form nor comeliness; and when we shall see him, there is no beauty that we should desire him.... He is despised and rejected of men; a man of sorrows, and acquainted with grief: and we hid as it were our faces from him.... Surely he hath borne our griefs, and carried our sorrows."[40] One of the two main characters in the novel, the failed student priest Otsu, identifies with this person. Endo sees a reincarnation of Jesus in him.[41] Otsu, who spends the last years of his life by the Ganges, carrying people to the holy river, prays: "O Lord ... You carried the cross upon your back and climbed the hill to Golgotha. I now imitate that act.... You carried the sorrows of all men on your back and climbed the hill to Golgotha. I now imitate that act."[42] But, for Endo, this identification is not an exclusive identification with Jesus, for after he had been crucified in Jerusalem, Jesus began to travel through many countries. Even today he wanders through all kinds of countries: India, Vietnam, China, Korea and Taiwan.[43] People can identify with him in other religions as well and thus he can be reborn.

Endo's God is strongly modelled on the image of motherly warmth.[44] It is the womb from which we, in our first death, our (re)birth, are cruelly torn and to which we return at our physical death, our second death.[45] There is hardly any growth on the way from the first death to the second, but there is a strong desire – a desire for warmth, which Endo understands as an enormous life-force that pours out mercy. This becomes especially clear in the novel *Deep River*.[46] It is the merciful nearness that rises above that which we view as the distinction between good and evil. This is why Endo has Otsu say during his failed attempt to become a priest in a French seminary: "I can't make the clear distinction that these people make between good and evil. I think that evil lurks within good, and that good things can lie hidden within evil as well."[47] Otsu concludes from this that God can even use his sins to send him towards salvation.

It is also clear here why Endo can give a place to betrayal (sin) in the Christian way of life. It enables one to make the striking comparison between quinine and sin: "Quinine produces high fevers if you drink it when you are well, but it becomes an indispensable drug for a malaria sufferer. I think sin is very much like quinine."[48] It remains a poison, but it can smooth the way to healing, for God makes use of not only our good deeds to save us but our sins as well. In the novel *Scandal*, in particular, Endo has elaborated on his summary of the role of sin in a human life. It is there that the ambivalence of this concept becomes clear in his work.

Within sin, there is always, on the one hand, the desire for rebirth. Within each sin lurks the desire to find an escape from one's current, suffocating existence, or even from life itself.[49] Within each sin seethes secretly the energy for a rebirth.[50] Sin is ultimately an expression of the desire to find a new way of living.[51] That is why he can say: "Even sin carries certain virtues in its make-up. The human hunger for rebirth lies within each sin we commit."[52] Endo also consciously leaves open the possibility that there are obvious parallels with Buddhist thought in the notion that the possibility of salvation lies within sin.[53] Thus, referring to the *kakure* Christians, among others, the Japanese Buddhist philosopher Soho Machida argues that there are also darker sides to Jesus' humanity and that, theologically, more emphasis should therefore be given to his sinfulness. He posits, for example, that Judas should be seen as an aspect of Jesus. After all, recognition of the dark sides of human existence emphasizes the need for this existence to cease.[54]

On the other hand, Endo himself also nuances this – we would almost say – functionalistic or utilitarian approach to sin. Not every form of sin "serves" something. He himself realizes that he has indeed seen a sign of salvation in every form of human baseness in many of his novels. To that extent there were always limits to sins. But there are also impulses on which no boundaries have been placed. But in that case we are no longer talking about sin but about a horrifying monstrous evil.[55]

Does that mean that Endo's God is an amoral life-force? Not in the least. It does mean that this God knows our weaknesses. Especially after becoming acquainted with the work of de Sade, Endo elaborates on these weaknesses in the direction of a shocking exploration of the dark forces of our unconscious, erotic-sadistic self. Judas has now become not only an external but also an internal figure. Thus, there is a strong psychologizing of evil here. Endo's accent on the inextricability of good and evil in a human soul comes close to Paul's speaking of "slavery" to the human will in Romans 7. This human inability, often expressed in the choice for evil and betrayal, is brought close to the face of the Christ figure, for it is, after all, the face of Christ on which the unfaithful person steps when he walks on the *fumie*. The face of Jesus always shines in the dark dungeon of our imprisonment in powerlessness and obstinacy. The most intimate aspect of Christ is not far removed from what is often most close to us: evil. That is why Endo can see Judas coming so close to the heart of Jesus. There, next to Judas, is where Jesus' compassion appears. That is why Otsu, when he is rejected by the other main character, the fickle student Mitsuko, also hears a voice call: "Come to me. Come. I was rejected as you have been. So I will never abandon you."[56]

Most likely, Endo expresses his own attitude towards this image of Christ most clearly through the quite ambiguous sadistic-masochistic main character in the novel *Scandal*, Madame Naruse. He has her say:

> This Jesus you believe in ... I wonder if he was murdered because he was too innocent, too pure....
>
> As Jesus, bathed in blood, carried his cross to the execution ground, the crowds reviled him and threw stones at him. Don't you think they did that because of the pleasure I'm always trying to describe to you? A naïve, pure human being is suffering right before their eyes. Can't we assume that it was the pleasure that comes from heaping further indignities on such a person which consumed the mobs that day? Jesus was too blameless, too unblemished ... so much so that they wanted to destroy him.... That feeling is shared by all of us. It inhabits the depths of our hearts. But no one wants to stare it in the face. That's how you've felt for many years, Sensei. Even in your novels ... in reality all you've written about are men who have betrayed Jesus but then weep tears of regret after the cock crows three times. You've always avoided writing about the mob, intoxicated with pleasure as they hurled stones at him.[57]

At first the writer, Suguro, the second main character in this novel, answers rather guardedly, saying that there are things about which a writer does not wish to write, but at the end of the book it is apparent just how accurately Madame Naruse has interpreted his own feelings. Then he describes that which he, on the Sunday after Easter, saw behind the altar in the stations of the cross: "Beyond the altar the emaciated man spread his arms wide, and his head drooped. Powerless to resist and soaked in blood, he had dragged his weary legs towards the execution ground. Along the way the crowds had jeered at him, hurled stones at him, and revelled in his torments. Suguro had not given any thought to that mob before. But he could not be at all certain that, had he been present, he would not have stoned the man and taken delight in his agony."[58]

It is Endo's intention, as he states in *Deep River*, "to think about a form of Christianity that suits the Japanese mind"[59] – which naturally immediately raises the question as to whether that intention is also recognized in Japan. He was criticized by liberation theologians for not tapping the sources of resurrection enough with respect to conquering evil, which causes him to land, obviously, on the side of the establishment. He is too fixated on the darker side of his "own" self and is therefore no longer able to see the darker side of society as a whole. The feminists argued that, while his concept of God does have its strong feminine aspects, his depiction of the holy female divinity still pedantically needed its dirty, female whorish aspects. Because of this, a more true-to-life image of women "between saint and shrew" is not expressed as well as it could be.[60]

Neither the critique by liberation theology nor that by the feminists need remain unchallenged. The main character in *Deep River*, Otsu, does make his ethical choices. After much wandering about, he decides to devote his life to carrying the dying poor to the Ganges, which is ultimately the cause of his own death. It is clear that Endo, partly due to having studied in France, was influenced by, for example, Dostoyevsky, Kierkegaard and by Julien Greene and Graham Greene. They all have the sinful, shadowy side of human existence and the ambivalence of the human will as a theme. Do these writers do something unbiblical? If that were so, then Luther and Augustine and, finally, Paul would have to be disqualified with them. But Theo Sundermeier, a German scholar of Third World theology, remarked in response to a much earlier work by Endo, *A Life of Jesus*: "Here a theology of the cross is depicted in Japanese garb that breathes the spirit of the man from Wittenberg."[61]

With regard to the feminist critique, it can be stated that internal and external evil certainly does not skip the main female characters in Endo's novel, but it can also be seen that their, at times, "gruesomely inhuman" appearance does not contrast sharply with that of the male main character. One could almost say that, in Endo's works, both sexes compete in evil and that the contest is undecided in the end. Nor does the divine in Endo have only female characteristics. In the novel *Deep River*, the main character Otsu has unmistakable Messianic characteristics. If, with Sundermeier, we want to discuss a "radical kenotic theology of the cross" in Endo and the self-emptying (*kenosis*) would involve the female figures in particular, then we would indeed be able to speak, with the Roman Catholic theologian Annelies van Heijst, of a destructive form of self-loss.[62] After all, we are then not concerned with a role that a woman herself freely chooses but with a role that is imposed upon her by an established gender pattern. But, as a conscious choice, removed from every form of compulsion, the idea of self-loss plays an important constitutive role in many mystical traditions and is not restricted to mystical traditions. It forms the core of the Christian theology of baptism.

We have examined the works of Endo so thoroughly because, in Japan more than in any other Asian country, it is writers and artists in particular who are exploring Christian themes.[63] This most likely suggests existential gaps in Japanese spirituality – gaps that have to do especially with themes such as guilt, forgiveness and mercy. And yet these themes are linked not so much with Jesus himself but with Jesus' God. That is also why Sundermeier asks if the Japanese theology of the cross – the most well-known works in the West are those of Kazo Kitamori, Masao Takenaka, Kosuke Koyama and Teruo Kuribayashi – is not more concerned with God than with Jesus.

For these Japanese theologians, the cross reveals God's presence as a presence in hiddenness. The cross is not so much a symbol of the reconciliation between God and humans but rather the door through which we can catch a glimpse of God's face. It is the (narrow) path by which we can approach his heart. From Kitamori up to Endo, Old Testament texts in which God indicates just how deeply his soul is touched by the fate of humans play a major role. In addition to the text mentioned earlier in Isa. 53:2–4, there are repeated references to such penetrating texts as Jer. 31:20 ("'Though I often speak against him, I still remember him. Therefore my heart yearns for him; I have great compassion for him,' declares the LORD.") and Hos. 11:8 ("My heart is changed within me; all my compassion is aroused").

Such an observation confirms the impression that this form of theology of the cross is concerned primarily with the suffering of God the Father and that we can therefore speak of theopaschitism, i.e. of the suffering of God. Christ is not the one who, in his suffering, fulfils the role of mediator over against God but is the one who reveals God's true face to us. The "Ecce homo" ("Behold, the man") here becomes an "Ecce deus" ("Behold, God"). This has revealed a dimension of speaking about God that has never received much attention in the West: namely, the vulnerably immanent God. In actuality, Endo is concerned with the hidden immanence of God's transcendence, of God being other.

In Dialogue with Buddhism

In Japan, an explicit discussion with Buddhism occurs within the circle of more philosophically oriented theologians such as Katsumi Takizawa (1909–1984) and Seiichi Yagi (b. 1932). Their attempt to express the nature of the Christian faith experience can be indirectly seen as an answer to the question discussed earlier of self-relativization in Japanese theology. Referring to the insights of the Japanese philosopher Kitaro Nishida (1870–1945), the founder of the Kyoto school in Zen philosophy, they develop a theology in which the confirmation of the non-being of things is the condition for every form of connection. They regularly draw parallels between Nishida's philosophy and Karl Barth's famous commentary on Paul's letter to the Romans in 1919–1920.[64] In both cases, it is an approach to reality that attempts to trace the true being of things by stressing the non-(true) being of all things around us.

Takizawa assumes two kinds of contacts between God and human beings. It obtains for all that, simply by being human, they are connected to the divine, the absolute, the "eternal Christ." Takizawa called this connection a (first) Immanuel contact. This divine nearness concerns all people, whether they are aware of it or not.[65] He prefers to refer to the nature of this contact via a poem, which Nishida often cites, by the Japanese Zen master Daito Kokushi: "Forever apart, and yet not separated for one moment; together for the whole day, but not together for one instant."[66] Sundermeier, in his introduction to Takizawa's *Das Heil im Heute*, calls this citation the key to Takizawa's theology.[67]

What the Christian tradition specifically says about Jesus' relationship to God applies to every person. For Takizawa, it functions as the starting point for an anthropology in which he (also), following Nishida, speaks of the "absolute paradoxal self-identity" or "contradictory identity" of the human being who will always find his true identity only in his non-self: in that which supports his existence. He can be distinguished from it, but he is also linked with it on the deepest level.[68] This contradictory identity is not elevated to a higher unity. The contradictory element consists in that every person is an expression of the One that encompasses all, who experiences a person as authentic by realizing his own non-self, that is, his own emptiness and thereby his identity with the One, while the contradiction between the One and the many is not removed. Here it also obtains that form (authenticity) is emptiness (non-self) and emptiness (non-self) is form (authentic connectedness with the One that encompasses and supports all things).[69]

When someone becomes aware of this nearness, an intense experience of enlightenment occurs and there is a second Immanuel contact. Takizawa sees both Buddhism and Christianity as being this second contact, although they obviously use different words. In both religions Buddha and Jesus are models for this second contact in which one loses one's (old) self and merges into the true Self via the path of negation. It is from the perspective of this second experience that the first contact is truly illuminated. The second contact does not create the first one but does make it reality. It is thus impossible to separate Jesus from the first Immanuel contact ("inseparable"), but the first Immanuel contact does occur first ("irreversible"), even though it becomes reality only in Jesus.[70]

In *Mahayana* Buddhism and in Christianity, the second Immanuel contact that fell to Jesus and Buddha can, in principle, fall to anyone who opens himself to it. In Christianity Paul's recollection of this experience in Gal. 2:20 is illustrative of this experience: "I have been crucified with Christ and I no longer live, but Christ lives in me. The life I live in the body, I live by faith in the Son of God, who loved me and gave himself for me." Jesus' concrete life thus clears the way for Christians to experience the "Christ in us" experience, the second Immanuel contact. This is the experience of our true Self: Not-I, but Christ in me. Takizawa's approach emphasizes that, while everyone already exists in relation to the divine state, this can be called the first contact only from the perspective of the second contact, the experience of enlightenment.

Yagi follows Takizawa in speaking of two experiences and elaborates on both experiences from the perspectives of the New Testament and Buddhism. He too sees a distinct parallel in Zen Buddhism to the way in which one understands the "self" within Christianity. In the experience of enlightenment in the New Testament, in the encounter with Jesus, the absolutization of the ego is negated and, from the "Christ in me" experience, the true Self, a new I, the Not-I, arises.[71]

The true understanding of the New Testament should penetrate to this core in "pure intuition" or in a "direct, unmediated experience." On this last point Takizawa and Yagi have had some intense discussions.[72] Takizawa was concerned with the question of the extent to which the individual experience of enlightenment does not become the measure for all things for Yagi. Essentially, this question has everything to do with Takizawa's thesis of the incorruptibility of our relationship with the Immanuel contact.[73] That incorruptibility assumes that we already have – before we are even aware of it – a relationship with the supporting ground of our existence (the first Immanuel contact). Yagi sees Takizawa making a wrong step in the direction of the objectification of God and, in fact, also of an ontologization of Jesus,[74] whereas Takizawa's purpose was to honour Karl Barth's "discovery," namely that "man is [not] able to be ... although not absolutely and ontologically, godless.... His godlessness ... cannot make God a 'manless' God."[75] We also encounter this same thought in Barth in the circular reasoning he deliberately employs: "He would not be man if he were not the image of God. He is the image of God in the fact that he is man."[76]

Here we encounter one of the most central issues between Christians and Buddhists. A person becomes liberated from himself only if he can let go of himself; but he can experience that as a freedom only if he can understand that situation of non-self simultaneously as new and as his own. The "true self" can thus be paradoxically expressed as "the self that is becoming non-self."[77] Subject and object then interpenetrate each other. But the balance can easily fall to either side, resulting in the accusation of subjectivism (on the part of the Christians) or of objectivism (on the part of the Buddhists).

A good illustration of this tension can be found in an article by Yagi on the I in the words Jesus speaks.[78] What does it means when Jesus says "I"? On the one hand, we see a strong identification with the Father: "Anyone who has seen me has seen the Father. How can you say, 'Show us the Father'? Don't you believe that I am in the Father, and that the Father is in me? The words I say to you are not just my own. Rather, it is the Father, living in me, who is doing his work. Believe me when I say that I am in the Father and the Father is in me" (John 14:9–11 and also 17:21). On the other hand, somewhat earlier in this same Gospel, Jesus makes a clear distinction between his own words and those of the Father: "For I did not speak of my own accord, but the Father who sent me commanded me what to say and how to say it.... So whatever I say is just what the Father has told me to say" (John 12:49–50). Here it is clear that there is one, Jesus, who obeys another, the Father.

For Yagi, in the first case, the Son–Father relationship concerns two concentric circles of which the centres converge. The second case presents more of an ellipse. Christianity has struggled with this di-unity of a concentric and elliptic relationship since the first century. Yagi reads this in the differences of opinion at Chalcedon. The Alexandrians (the Monophysites with Eutyches as their spokesman) saw the two circles converging in Jesus, while the Antiochenes (the Dyophysites with Nestorius as their spokesman) saw two centres in Jesus, of which the one obeyed the other. In the well-known double formulation of the "inconfusedly, unchangably" (contra the Alexandrians) and the "indivisibly and inseparably" (contra the Antiochenes), the Council chose a position in which the divine and the human in Jesus remain clearly separate but also inseparably bound together.

Yagi recognizes this same di-unity in Paul when he, on the one hand, continually testifies that he, his own I, has died and now Christ lives in him (Gal. 2:19–20) and, on the other, also states that he is not the one who speaks but Christ or, the other way around, that he speaks and not Christ (1 Cor. 7:10–12). Thus there is a simultaneous continuity and discontinuity and the connecting link is, for both Jesus and Paul, the Holy Spirit (Rom. 8:4, 9-10 and 1 Cor. 12:3). In neither case is there self-deification – both remain fully human – but there is strong identification. There is – as Yagi argues following Nishida[79] – a paradoxal identity in which the Wholly Other becomes our own subject. If God were simply the Wholly Other, then he would remain far removed from us in absolute transcendence. If God were completely absorbed into our subjectivity, then it could correctly be called self-deification.[80]

It is fascinating how the Japanese Christian philosopher Hisakazu Inagaki and the American missiologist J. Nelson Jennings, in their joint study on Nishida's philosophy and current Japanese theology (*Philosophical Theology and East-West Dialogue*), link the role of the Wholly Other with the Japanese "shame culture." This shame culture is characterized by the continuous, threatening presence of the "eye of the other." In such a culture, everyone's psychological health benefits not when the "other" is eliminated and absorbed into the "self" (the non-self, the *anatman*) – in their opinion, that risk is always present in *Mahayana* Buddhism which has shaped the Japanese religious spirit – but when the identification with the continual presence of the Wholly Other makes a new self possible. In short, instead of a threatening other, the other becomes a beneficial other.

Conclusions

Whereas Kitamori and Koyama were mainly concerned with the "external" Jesus, we saw that Takizawa and Yagi were mostly concerned with the "internal" Jesus. But in both approaches self-effacement is central. That element, which plays such a major role in Buddhism, appears to determine their way of being Christian to a great extent. In the one case, there is a clear parallel with the Western *theology of the cross*. In the other case, there is a remarkable parallel with Western mysticism (Eckhart), a parallel that has been observed repeatedly by the West as well as the East during the last century.[81]

In both cases, the question of the relationship between the divine and the human can be posed. In the Japanese theology of the cross, the divine is in the human, and in the not-I theology the human seems to be absorbed into the divine, although we have just seen that Takizawa and Yagi reject that last step. They are completely aware that the historical Jesus continued to experience the closeness of the Father (also) as an "other."

The Christian doctrine of the sacraments can be seen as an attempt to involve the internal and external aspects of the faith with each other in a fruitful way. In the administration of the sacrament of baptism and of Communion, Christians who have gathered together are always called, like the one being baptized and those attending Communion for the first time, to "die with Christ and to rise with him." Thus, they are always called to an emptying experience, a not-I experience. But this emptying experience always has the life of the historical Jesus in the background. That background is the reason why dying and rising with Christ is never conceived without opening oneself up to a way of life in which the historical

Jesus is seen as a predecessor and substitutionary bearer of the cross.[82] As such, Buddhism also similarly connects the transhistorical, existential and historical in referring to Gautama's concrete way of life and that of the *bodhisattvas*, but there it is much less crucial.

In the Japanese not-I theology, the human is, as it were, the place where the divine (the not-I) manifests itself, whereas in the Japanese theology of the cross, the divine is the place where the human (the suffering) is made manifest. In both cases the divine and human are strongly interwoven[83] – an interwovenness that we found in Chapter 4 to be typical of Asian theology. But both give little space to the idea of liberating change, so emphatically inherent to the idea of a kingdom of God. And yet the weakness of both of these theological approaches is also their strength. Here God is so emphatically connected with humans that every idea of mutual alienation is completely excluded. Whether it is the divine that penetrates the human or the human that penetrates the divine, Japanese theology is always concerned with the connectedness that touches the hearts of those connected in life and in death.[84] For God, this connection could be typified as *vulnerable immanence* and, for humans, as a *vulnerable desire for transcendence*.

8 The Korean Jesus

The Confucian Veneration of Ancestors

However much the Japanese and Koreans wish to be distinguished from each other, they are very much alike in one area: their veneration of ancestors. The section on the role of Jesus in the veneration of ancestors in Japan and Korea that now follows forms the transition between the previous discussion on the role of Jesus in Japanese theology and the discussion on the "Korean Jesus."

In both countries, the veneration of ancestors confronts us with an anthropological given that we, as theologians, cannot go into in depth but is worth pointing out. In Chapter 3 we established via Pieris' observations that a new religion can catch on in an existing religious culture only if there is more or less room for it in the form of a lacuna or a credibility crisis in the existing religions. In Asia – and we will see in Part VIII that this also holds for Africa – new religions catch on only if they, in the eyes of the new believers, have something useful to say about the fate of those who die. Apparently, the fate of those who die is so strongly connected to the *basic insights* of religion mentioned in Chapter 1 that this theme cannot be ignored or declared taboo without penalty.

In a survey, almost 60 percent of the Japanese interviewed indicated that they felt spiritually connected with their ancestors and the same number also indicated that they had a family altar for them and, according to Buddhist custom, participated in one of the many rituals during *obon* (the special commemoration of ancestors in the middle of August).[1]

The Protestant missionaries in particular always took a completely dismissive position with regard to this phenomenon. In brief, their view was that death caused an immediate separation between heaven and hell and after death it was too late to pray for someone or honour them in some way. For the majority of the Japanese, this eternal separation from their ancestors was unacceptable, which is why the veneration of ancestors has long since returned in the independent Christian movements discussed earlier.

Appealing to the fifth commandment ("Honour your father and your mother") of the Ten Commandments, this new Christian movement cautiously seeks a means of veneration that does not conflict with the first commandment ("You shall have no other gods before me") and the second commandment ("You shall not make for yourself an idol") of those same Ten Commandments. The core words in such arguments for *rituals of remembrance* are "thankfulness" and "respect."

But this veneration often entails more, among Christians as well. Sometimes special "substitution" celebrations of Communion are held for the dead, in which the descendents receive the bread and wine on behalf of the deceased, believing that the deceased have received these gifts in heaven in a spiritual way. Those who have left their bodies have already taken their place with the Lord (2 Cor. 5:8) – after all, is Communion not a link with the Lord (1 Cor. 10:16–18 and 12:13)?

Most members of these new Christian movements also have a Buddhist altar at home to honour their ancestors, at times "Christianized" in such a way that there is only a cross with the names of the deceased hanging on the wall; sometimes a Buddhist mortuary tablet hangs next to the cross.

In the early church, the key texts that brought the deceased also within reach of the Gospel were 1 Peter 3:19–21a ("...he went and preached to the spirits in prison who disobeyed long ago when God waited patiently in the days of Noah while the ark was being built. In it only a few people, eight in all, were saved through water, and this water symbolizes baptism that now saves you also...") and 1 Peter 4:6 ("...the gospel was preached even to those who are now dead..."). These are key texts in Japan as well. For almost a millennium, Jesus' descent into hell was the most iconographic motif in the early church for depicting the resurrection. In the eyes of the early church, Jesus' resurrection included his descent into the realm of the dead in order to allow everyone – the righteous and the unrighteous – to share in his new life.

Western Europe is familiar with the eighth-century story of the Frisian king, Radboud, who, just before his baptism, asked the priest about the fate of his non-baptized ancestors. When he received the answer that they were in hell, he withdrew his foot from the baptismal font and chose solidarity with his ancestors. For many millions of Christian Asians and Africans, Radboud's question is theirs as well. Referring to 1 Peter 3:19–21a and 4:6, they would give a different answer from the one given by Radboud's priest.[2]

They would also refer to Acts 16:31, where Paul and Silas, in reply to their fellow prisoner's question of what he must do to be saved, answered: "Believe in the Lord Jesus and you will be saved, you and your household." To a good Japanese person, the "household" includes all deceased family members as well.

A third biblical passage would be 1 Cor. 15:29, where Paul asks: "Now if there is no resurrection, what will those do who are baptized for the dead? If the dead are not raised at all, why are people baptized for them?" But if the dead are indeed raised – and Paul is absolutely convinced of this – then it does make sense to allow oneself to be baptized for one's ancestors (the dead). On the basis of this text, a number of Japanese new churches make use of not only *substitutionary Communion* but also *substitutionary baptism*. In these churches a question such as Radboud's would be answered by the reply: "With your baptism, your ancestors are also baptized." In this way the ancestors are indeed brought within reach of the Gospel and the link with them is not broken.

The Protestant Taiwanese theologian Song, whom we discussed in the second section of Chapter 3, objects rather sharply in the third part of his trilogy *Cross in the Lotus World* to the tendency to explain the article "descended into hell" as the preaching of the Gospel to those who were either born before Jesus or to those who had already died before they could have heard him. He sees this as a "salvific altruism" or "salvific imperialism" by which adherents of other religions can yet become Christianized.

His second objection is that this entails that the horrors of hell, including the hell in our world, are lost to view. Does hell then not become little more than a neutral waiting room where the deceased wait for Christ's salvation? How can one still speak of Jesus' solidarity with those who are condemned to a god-forsaken hell?

As the former chairman of the World Alliance of Reformed Churches (WARC), Song is – consciously or not – following his Reformed (Presbyterian) tradition entirely. For Calvin, the article "descended into hell" had to do with the pastoral heart of his theology. He devotes an extensive and very emotional passage in his *Institutes*[3] to stressing the unconditionality of Jesus' solidarity with us in our godforsakenness. The Calvinist Heidelberg Catechism of 1563 follows the same line of thought in Answer 44 of Lord's Day 16 and speaks of the "unspeakable anguish, pain, terror of soul" that Jesus underwent to save us for that same "anguish and torment of hell."

Nonetheless, historically speaking, it cannot be denied that the Christianity of the East and the West viewed the descent into hell for a thousand years as an interpretation of the scope of the resurrection. In order to be able to honour this central motif, it is better to see Jesus' solidarity with those who suffer in terms of the cross than in terms of his descent into hell. In both the early church and contemporary churches in Asia and Africa, the descent is viewed as a *descent to the ancestors*. The word hell (*sheol* or *gehenna* in Hebrew and *hades* in Greek) does have two meanings, after all, and both meanings can be found in the Bible: *place of rejection* and *waiting room*.

Because of the significant role that one's connection with the ancestors plays in Asia and Africa, we, with Mullins, do not think it right to speak of "salvific imperialism."[4] Rather, it involves a pastoral concern that, viewed from an existentially experienced awareness of the "community of the saints," goes beyond the boundaries of death – a concern that we see expressed just as carefully in, for example, Africa and Indonesia.[5]

The above-mentioned biblical texts are only a part of the many biblical examples from which it is apparent that the New Testament, more so than the contemporary Western world, took a "world full of spirits" into account. For many Asians and Africans that "world" is the most real one and the communication between it and the world in which they live is one of the most intensive faith experiences they can have. Thus the veneration of ancestors assumes an understanding of reality (*cosmology*) that presupposes a lively *interaction between the world of the living and of the dead*. The living are always accompanied by the dead and the dead by the living. As long as Western theology does not develop any sensitivity for this interwovenness, it will never grasp the essence of the Asian and African understanding of reality and thus Asian and African theology as well. At least, that is our conclusion after more than ten years of studying these forms of theology, having had intense discussions on this with numerous Africans and Asians and having observed their perceptions of faith intimately in their churches and their homes. By the way, a Dutch missiologist, A. G. Honig, came to the same conclusion twenty years ago on the basis of his experiences in Indonesia.[6]

A number of Japanese churches are also familiar with the phenomenon of substitutionary baptism in connection with the so-called *mizuko*, children who are aborted or miscarry. Many women in Japan, where there is a high rate of abortion, feel guilty about their abortion or miscarriage and fear the curse that the wandering spirits of their children – filled with bitterness about their fate – could bring about. If someone else can be baptized for these undeveloped children and the forgiveness of sins is proclaimed in that baptism, as is customary in every baptism, then the reasoning is that these children too can be led, through Christ, from the kingdom of death to the kingdom of heaven.

Thus, the relationship with the deceased does not extend only to ancestors. It also includes those who have died an early death in a war, have died as a result of sickness or an accident, or have remained childless. In all these cases their spirits exude bitterness (*urami*), and sometimes malice as well. That is why the prayers and rituals have a dual purpose: they are meant to grant final rest to the wandering, bitter and sometimes malicious spirits of those who died too early. Here the focus is on those who died. But the prayers and rituals are also directed at protecting the surviving relatives. Those who died without bitterness are also sometimes expected to play an active protective role. They are asked to pray for the well-being of their relatives. They become, as it were, their "guardian angels."[7]

This last expression already indicates that the Japanese veneration of ancestors is considerably closer to Roman Catholicism than to Protestantism. In contrast to Protestantism, Roman Catholicism has numerous customs that are practised after someone has died – whether it be in grateful memory or out of concern for his or her fate. One can think here of calling on the saints to mediate; holding a mass for someone many years after his or her death, prayers for the dead and the belief that the lot of those who exist in purgatory can be improved, etc. All of these customs are taboo in Protestantism, even though many Protestant churches have recently introduced a prayer for the dead in the Communion liturgy. This could be an indication of a small change in the Protestant attitude.

Following Vatican policy in China, the Roman Catholic Church that was established in 1783 in Korea soon took a very critical attitude regarding the Confucian veneration of ancestors, leading to fierce persecution in Korea. By law (1800) the death penalty was even imposed in Korea on those who did not participate in the veneration of ancestors. But when the first Protestant missionaries arrived in Korea at the end of the nineteenth century, this law was merely a statute on the books. The suffering that the Protestants had to undergo because of their refusal to participate in the veneration of ancestors came not from the government but rather from their own family circles from which people were often cast out. A European can scarcely fathom the emotional pain that a Korean suffers through such a rejection. Koreans are raised from an early age to memorize and recite the names of their ancestors going back many centuries. That link is, to put it concisely, their *raison d'être*.[8]

The discussion on the veneration of ancestors in Korea grew rather heated when Korea became a Japanese colony, i.e. from 1910 to 1945. The obligation to worship the Shinto altars was introduced in Korea as well. That worship divided the Korean church deeply and led to the fanatic persecution of those who refused to do so by the Japanese. The antitheses arising out of this conflict can still be traced in the Korean church and play a role in the cautious attempts by the current Korean churches to give ritual and ceremonial shape to the thankful link with the ancestors in worship services.[9]

The same discussion regarding the veneration of ancestors took place in the previous century in Korea that had taken place in China three centuries earlier. Here too the distinction between a Confucian and a more popular – in Korea Shamanistic – veneration is not to be ignored. The Confucian veneration of ancestors is a man's job; it is patrilinear and the responsibility of the eldest son. Honouring the ancestors and thereby coming into spiritual contact with them (with their spirits) is, in Confucianism, so exclusively the responsibility of the eldest son that the Vietnamese theologian Peter Phan posited Jesus' relationship with his

Father in an analogy to this role of the eldest son.[10] If one considers how much weight is given to the "passing on" of the life of the father through the son in Confucianism, then one also realizes how shocking, if not unbearable, the crucifixion must be in Confucian eyes.[11] Only the resurrection that follows can make that idea bearable for them.

In essence, the entire Confucian image of society is reflected in the veneration of ancestors, from state policy up to and including family ties. This is also the reason for the fierce reaction to the Christian aloofness towards this phenomenon. In the strongly Confucian Vietnam, that aloofness led, in the period from 1825 to 1883, to more than one hundred thousand deaths among the Christians.[12] Thus, Phan is very much aware of what was at stake for the Christians. It is precisely for this reason that he is still trying to bridge the gap with the image of Jesus as the eldest son – because he is very much aware of the vital importance that is attached to the connection with one's ancestors in Asia.

The Shamanistic Veneration of Ancestors

For several millennia – it is thought since ca. 1000 BC – Koreans engaged in a more popular, Shamanistic veneration of ancestors, often led by a woman as the *shaman* (priest); it is therefore not patrilinear nor restricted to one's own parents. The spirits of the ancestors are not conceived of as exclusively passive, merely accepting the honours bestowed upon them, but also as active, achieving good and bad things and demanding offerings for themselves. Here, too, it is particularly the spirits of those who died young, with many unfulfilled desires, who can cause evil and must therefore be satisfied.

One could say that in Confucianism the ancestors are symbolic icons. They do not exercise any power themselves. It is those who venerate them who grant them their powers. But in Shamanism the spirits of the ancestors act much more independently and therefore cause more fear as well.[13]

With this background in mind, it should not be surprising that the first Christian missionaries in Korea were strongly opposed to Shamanism. Most of the Shamanistic gods are, after all, ancestral spirits that can do evil as well as good. Moreover, Shamanism has numerous spirits that inhabit stars, trees, stones, mountains and other natural objects and with whom the believer should have a good relationship. For many missionaries, it was a religion full of demons, an evil religion and, as a result, their publications contained an antagonistic image of the relationship between Shamanism and Christianity.[14] But the fact that Shamanism continues subtly to exert its influence, even among Christians, is becoming recognized more and more. Reference is made, for example, to the value that is attributed to material blessings, healings, spiritual exorcisms, charismatic leadership, fervent prayers and ecstatic experiences in Korean Christianity. Even the loud singing and the often cheerful services are linked to this.

Partly due to the Minjung theology that developed in South Korea in the 1970s, this antagonistic image now seems to be open to correction. Historically, it can also apparently now be shown that the first missionaries based their readiness to adopt the Korean Shamanistic name of *Hananim* as the term to be used for the God of Jesus on a thorough knowledge of the old Shamanistic *Tan'gun* myth in which they saw a prefiguration of Christian monotheism.[15] Instead of antagonism, there was a creative syncretism.[16]

This choice for the name *Hananim* is often seen as one of the most important factors for the rapid growth of Christianity in Korea. If it is true that Koreans have a Confucian head, a Buddhist heart and a Shamanistic belly,[17] then it is clear what is closest to the poor Korean masses. These were the masses who had seen their Shamanism maligned alternately by Confucianism and Buddhism and had even been persecuted. Now, in choosing this Christian name for God, they had recovered their God, enriched with numerous new associations. Thus, as we established earlier, Christianity not only gave the Koreans their own identity, as opposed to Japanese identity, but it also gave them back their own God.

In the meantime – as we already indicated in Chapter 2 – the role that the *Hananim* fulfilled in the lives of ordinary Koreans must not be overestimated. He is rightly called a distant God, and other gods are closer to them. As a description of the way in which the nearness of the gods in Shamanism is experienced, we will be guided by the penetrating outline by David Kwang-sun Suh in his partly autobiographical study *The Korean Minjung in Christ*.

The nearness of the gods is experienced especially during home ceremonies in which a female shaman, a *mudang*, leads a Shamanistic ceremony called *kut*. In actuality, these *kuts* constitute the only form of expression in Shamanism. All other religious forms of expression that we know of in all the world religions are lacking. There is no founder, no hierarchy among the spirits nor even among the many gods, no doctrine, no holy scripture and no temples.

In themselves, the Shamanistic gods are neither good nor bad. How they present themselves to people depends on the care that people take regarding their relationship with them. Thus, in times of crisis, extra attention must be paid to the gods in order to insure their aid. In a *kut*, the gods are first invited to "descend" by the *mudang* through songs and dancing and, subsequently, a dialogue with the gods is "acted out" through song and dance. The message of the gods is generally passed on by the spirits of the ancestors through the *mudang* and the spectators then respond to the message, at times by having the *mudang* ask the ancestors further questions. The sessions are closed with copious expressions of gratitude to the gods.

The *kut* for the dead is the one that is performed most often. The souls of those who died too early or tragically are especially suspected of wandering around full of bitterness ("*han*-ridden"). They are capable of all kinds of mischief. The *kut* is directed at taking away their bitterness (*han*) concerning their early or tragic death and finally giving them rest. We can best penetrate the theological implications of this ritual of the dead by taking a moment to reflect on the epic poem on *Parkongju*.

Pari is the mythical predecessor of all *mudangs*. She was the seventh and last daughter of a royal family that was desperately hoping for a male heir. Angry at the birth of yet another daughter, Pari's parents put her in a basket on the sea. But the sympathetic Buddha found her and entrusted her to the care of an old man. Pari grew up to be a beautiful and intelligent princess.

Her parents became sick – allegedly because of Pari who returned when she was summoned. But her parents did not get better. A heavenly messenger revealed that they needed a heavenly herb from another world. Only the sacrifice of a human life could bring the herb to this world. All of Pari's sisters refused to sacrifice themselves and so Pari decided to go. When Pari left for the other world, she met a mountain spirit (a Taoist divine figure) who asked her to marry him in exchange for the heavenly herb. Pari agreed and bore him seven sons.

Upon her return to the palace, she encountered her parents' funeral procession. Running up, she placed the heavenly herb on her parents' chests. Her parents came back to life and Pari was offered the highest place of honour in the royal court. She refused and asked instead to be allowed to become the predecessor of all *mudangs*. And that was how it came about. It became her task to lead the dead safely and peacefully to heaven.

Theological Implications

The epic poem above describes well the bitter position (*han*) and self-sacrifice of women in Korea. The poem is often still recited by *mudangs* in mourning rituals. In such a ceremony it is the task of the *mudang* to lead the soul of the deceased from hell to heaven. Explicit representations of hell and heaven do not exist in Shamanism, and images are often borrowed from Buddhism. Nor is there a doctrine of original sin or notions about punishment and reward. Even if the life of the deceased has been wretched, a good *kut* ritual can put that life to rest. That rest is necessary, for the spirits of all the dead stay close to the relatives. A person cannot allow vengeful elements to remain among the dead.

The entire *kut* event is a dramatic play between a person and the spirits that surround them. The spirits of the past continue to work in the present and one can only be certain of the nature of those works after a meticulous ritual. All human emotions are expressed in such a ritual: from loud wailing to loud laughter, from deadly silence to deafening shouting. Once such a ritual has been performed, one can openly ask the god for earthly blessings through the spirits of the ancestors. But a battle of life and death between the powers of good and evil must first be played out in the *kut* ritual.[18]

The *mudang* sometimes distinctly acquires the features of Jesus in this "game."[19] But stories of self-sacrifice, such as that of Pari, are not told about other *mudangs*, even though she is the model for all *mudangs*. Their vocational experience is often paired with deep spiritual and physical suffering, comparable to the suffering, dying and resurrection of Jesus. The "descent" to the souls of the dead in order to open the gate of the kingdom of heaven makes one think of Jesus' descent into hell. In any case, it is clear that the role of the *mudang* is a mediatory one. But who and what exactly in this mediation brings about a "breakthrough" remains unclear.

And yet all of this is relatively far from the way in which Christianity speaks of the meaning of Jesus as mediator. In essence, the entire *kut* event is closer to that which occurs in charismatic and Pentecostal circles than what is usually the case in so-called "mainline" churches. The leaders are the ones who drive out the evil spirits and thus bring about healing for the sick. In charismatic and Pentecostal circles the power or force that the leader has is always a derived power or force. It does not belong to the leader but to Jesus. The *mudang* first needs to have an ecstatic experience through which she can reach her power from elsewhere. Who exactly gives her this power remains unclear.

The most striking parallel with Jesus' work lies not so much in a comparison with his person as with his work. A *mudang* is the one who, *par excellence*, still gives hope in the most terrible situations. She knows the *han*, the terrible situations of Korea's very poorest, like no other and is very much aware of the position of women.[20] If we are to understand Jesus along these lines, then he must also be a "priest(ess) of *han*."[21] He must be involved in a *han-pu-ri*, in the liberation from hopeless ("*han*-ridden") situations.[22] *Han* is thus not only a reference to the terrible situation of the very poorest but at the same time a reference to the power on which they can call in their terrible situation.[23]

More direct parallels with the person of Jesus are also more likely to be attributed in Korea to the *bodhisattvas*. One can think of the fact that, despite the changing fate that Buddhism has suffered under various dynasties – from national religion under the Silla and Koryo dynasty (668–935 and 918–1392, respectively) to a forbidden religion under the Confucian Yi or Chosun dynasty (1392–1910) – Korea has always remained, most certainly culturally, a Buddhist country, even though the Buddhists are now a minority in comparison with Christians. The country continues to exude a Buddhist atmosphere.

In her speech at the seventh assembly of the World Council of Churches in Canberra in 1991, the Korean Presbyterian theologian Chung Hyun Kyung pointed to the parallel between the Holy Spirit and the *bodhisattva* *Kwan Yin* (= *Kuan-Yin*), popular among East Asian women and honoured as the embodiment of compassion and wisdom.[24]

In addition to the *bodhisattva* ideal, the expectation of the future Buddha, *Maitreya*, has left deep traces in Korean spirituality as well. This expectation is also an important part of Minjung theology and has many parallels with the Christian expectation of the return of the Son of Man.[25] While *Amida* Buddhism promises believers a heavenly paradise after death, *Maitreya* Buddhism promises them another existence on earth.[26]

Minjung Theology

We have already referred to Minjung theology a few times. Korean Minjung theology is part of the much broader, political Minjung reform movement, in which people arrived at a social-critical reinterpretation of Korean history. Minjung theology is but a small part of this movement. It is a theology that arose among intellectuals in the 1970s in South Korea during the student riots under the dictatorship of President Chung Hee Park and is derived from the Korean words *min* (people) and *jung* (masses). It identifies with the poor masses of the Korean people and seeks its identity partly in the biblical tradition and partly in the history of the resistance of the Korean people.[27]

The following aspects in particular from the biblical tradition are important: the Exodus, the role of the Greek word *ochlos* (people) in the gospel of Mark and the identification with the crucifixion and resurrection of Jesus.[28]

There are three events especially that are striking in the recent history of the Korean people: the Tonghak Revolution of 1894 (a social-religious resistance movement by farmers, once compared with the Farmers' War inspired by Thomas Münzer (1490–1525)),[29] the Independence Movement of 1 March 1919 and the Student Revolution of 19 April 1960 against President Syngman Rhee, later continued against the 18-year-old government of President Chung Hee Park.[30] Biographies and folk stories in Minjung theology play a large role even apart from these historical points of contact. Thus the gap between text and context is bridged in an entirely different way.[31]

Theologically, the concept *han* functions centrally as an indication of the wretched position of the very poorest among the Korean people and of their source of power.[32] After the death of President Park in 1979, a slow process of democratization began in South Korea, not least of all supported by the masses of the people (*minjung*) who, through the large demonstrations in the 1960s and 1970s, had become aware of the power of the alliance between students and labourers. But, due to this process of democratization – as we must matter-of-factly observe – Minjung theology lost its direct opponent (a dictatorial government). Of course, a change in government and the subsequent changes in the spiritual climate in South Korea did not mean an immediate change in the social circumstances of the very poorest. As a "messianic-political" movement of emancipation and inculturation, Minjung theology still embodies that which Song and Pieris encountered when they spoke of "Jesus as the Crucified People."[33]

Subsequently, in any case we can now say that Minjung theology stepped into a gap that until that time could not be filled by the intellectual and elite Confucianism, by the Shamanism so strongly directed at individual well-being or a good situation for the family, by devout Buddhism and the generally very Western-oriented churches. That gap still exists, having to do with the connection of religion and social ethics. Up until the present, this is one of the large areas not addressed in Korean religiosity.[34]

At this time, Minjung theology seems to have lost most of its appeal. It was probably too historically oriented, in line with Western thinking, to be able to develop a broad base in Korea. For example, in Minjung theology, the link that we said was characteristic of Asian theology, namely the link between the micro- and macrocosmos – between the (non)-self and the world around us – is merely a link between micro- and macro*history*.

This is the reason why some scholars, such as Heup Young Kim,[35] have at times sought a broader religious foundation, not to replace Minjung theology but to support it further via images borrowed from Confucianism and Taoism. Thus the Korean poet Kim Chi Ha, who felt a close affinity with Minjung theology, wrote a parable based on the unequal battle fought by hundreds of thousands of farmers during the 1897 *Tonghak* revolution on *Ugumch'i* hill against well-armed Japanese forces. Where did the farmers get their power and courage? His parable, which he calls "The Ugumch'i Phenomenon," attempts to answer this question.

The parable is about the familiar phenomenon of small fish swimming against the current. Their *sin-ki* (vital energy) apparently connects them with the water's *sin-ki* and, if their *sin-ki* is characterized by *yin* and *yang* and those streams of energy move in the same direction, then a powerful counter-movement arises in both the fish and the water (an undercurrent). Something similar must have occurred on *Ugumch'i* hill.

The word *ki* here stands for a power that comes close to the biblical concept of *pneuma* (*ruah*) and connects the commonplace, our breath of life, with a force of life that surpasses our life-force.[36] In Taoism, this force of life always swings back and forth from one extreme to the other, so that every movement forward always entails a backward movement as well. Thus, Jesus' descending movement in the gospel of John (as the Word that descends) is also the ascending movement of the other gospels (of the Son who follows the path to which the Father points him). And thus his self-effacement is also his preservation. In all essential matters in life, the truth lies not in the either-or but in the both-and. Sooner or later, extremes always turn to one's disadvantage. If *yin* and *yang* thus belong together, this also holds for the relationship of the divine and human, the horizontal and vertical, the male and female, the temporary and the eternal in Jesus.[37]

Yin and Yang

The American-Korean Protestant theologian Jung Young Lee in particular has made an original attempt to articulate the meaning of Jesus in Asian categories based on the *yin-yang* theory. For this purpose, he highlights the term liminality (*limen* = threshold), borrowed from the American anthropologist Victor Turner.[38] Turner, in turn, borrowed the term from Arnold van Gennep's triple classification of "rites of passages": separation, threshold and participation or reintegration. Turner uses the terms "preliminary, liminal and postliminary." Liminality describes what happens anthropologically when an individual or group is confronted with a radically new social situation. A person leaves behind what he must, stays in a transitional phase for a while and, with time, adjusts to the new situation. This three-phase stage can be recognized in almost every situation. Becoming an adult, coping with bereavement, moving (emigration), etc. – all are generally characterized by these three phases. Almost every culture has rituals, so-called *rites of passage*, for these transitional situations, whether they are officially formalized or simply informally arranged. Central to these rites is the threshold experience, which is the experience of living in a border for a time, living on the boundary of two worlds. Lee calls this liminality or marginality.

This term liminality is generally described from within the core group, and thus there are those who find themselves on the margins, always in a (more) disadvantageous position. They only count for half. And yet, from the perspective of those on the margins, their position can be described more positively. Their *in-between* situation can also mean being at home *in both* or – probably more realistically – being half at home in both cultures. The *in-between* that implies an *in-both* can also lead to an *in-beyond*: a rising beyond both cultures from within.[39] This could result in a source of creativity, as has been proven by writers, artists, scientists and journalists who often stay abroad.

Lee sees this "in-between" situation as very characteristic for Jesus, for both his interhuman relationships and his God–human relationship. Via his incarnation, he moved toward the margins of the divine and on the cross he moved to the margins of the human. According to Tao Te Ching (II, 40), re-entry is the essence of how the path (*tao*) goes. This means that Jesus' becoming human (incarnation) is not a threat to the divine and that the self-emptying (crucifixion) is not a threat to the human. Rather, becoming human is the way for the divine to re-enter itself (the human, "his own," John 1:11) and self-emptying is the way in which the Son of Man re-enters his own, the divine (Phil. 2:6–8). Lee compares the relationship between Jesus' divinity and humanity with that of *yin* and *yang*. Just as *yang* cannot exist without *yin*, so *yin* cannot exist without *yang*. In Jesus God is not separated from humans and humans are not separated from God.[40]

Karl Barth and Asian Theology

Lee's argument brings to mind Karl Barth's argument in his famous *Church Dogmatics*. There Barth argues that in Jesus the "Lord as Servant" is an indication of the way in which the divine wants to live among us and the "Servant as Lord" is an indication of how the human can be related to the divine.[41] In other words, the divine is expressed especially in the human and appears in what is truly human. Continuing along these lines, from the *yin-yang* principle, Lee could say that Jesus' divinity does not exclude his humanity and his humanity does not exclude his divinity.[42] In this way, from the perspective of the Taoist *yin-yang* principle with reference to the Korean term *ki* (power, energy), Lee connects the internal and external powers that Minjung theology could not. Heup Young Kim later elaborated on this reference to Karl Barth's "Lord as Servant" and "Servant as Lord" and Lee's reference to the *yin* and *yang* principle further in his monograph on *Christ and the Tao*.[43]

Again and again, Karl Barth's theology seems to exert a strong attraction on Japanese, Korean and even Chinese theologians. At first glance this is strange, because Barth so strongly thinks in terms "von Gott aus," i.e. from the point of view of God, whereas Asian theologians tend to draw the divine and human as closely together as possible. But they do see that Barth, thinking "von Gott aus," brings God and humans together in a way that Western theology has never conceived and that line of thought is what fascinates them. To be sure, Barth can think in this way only by placing himself in God's position, but that exchange of position is exactly what the Asian theologians are aiming at with terms such as self-emptying, emptiness, etc.[44]

For them and Karl Barth, this exchange of position has everything to do with *Hingabe*, with surrender, emptying – in short, with susceptibility. In this they do not escape the exclusivity of God – God's own decision – upon which Barth's inclusivity of God and humans is generally based.[45] Rather, it usually encourages them to look for an "open" subject, a broad concept of subjectivity within Buddhism, Taoism and Confucianism as well. Here, too, one can speak of "double transformation." Barth removes their prejudice against Western theology, which thinks purely transcendentally. In their eyes Barth can at least be transformed in the direction of Eastern thinking. At the same time, Barth confronts them with the question of how a "closed" concept of subjectivity can be avoided. In short, they "change" Barth, but Barth wants to "change" them as well.

Conclusions

In summarizing this section on the "Korean Jesus," there are a couple of aspects that stand out. Generally speaking, the religious contexts of Japan and Korea are the same as that of China. In all three Eastern Asian countries, the traditional religious context consists of old popular religions: Confucianism, Taoism and *Mahayana* Buddhism, supplemented in Japan by Shintoism and in Korea by Shamanism. Up until the present, Christianity has truly taken root only in South Korea. The successful association with Korea's own (Shamanistic) religious identity in a time of Japanese, Buddhist dominance can be given as one of the most important reasons for this.

One's relationship to the ancestors determines everything in Korea. At the same time, that relationship among Korean Christians is a true issue for dispute. In Korea as well, religion is very much applied to practical issues such as sickness and death and material well-being. The cause of prosperity and adversity is never to be sought far away but close by, in one's own way of life or in that of one's ancestors, which is why the ancestors are included in the search for salvation. In Minjung theology especially, that salvation also receives historical characteristics: there is a concrete expectation for the future. The non-Asian externalization of salvation that can accompany this is sometimes overcome by involving the internal and external world inextricably with each other by means of the *yin* and *yang* principle. But this principle does not at all presuppose a harmonious society but a society of sharp contrast between good and evil, between good and evil spirits. Forces can appear among these contrasts for the purpose of mediating for good, be it in the form of the *mudang*, or by instruction in the di-unity of word and path (*tao*). It is especially when that mediation is expressed that analogies with Jesus arise.

Part VI: The Indian Jesus

Within largely Hindu India is a form of Christianity that goes back to the end of the second century and claims apostolic origin (the so-called Thomas Christians). But a true dialogue, initiated primarily by Hindu thinkers, between Christianity and Hinduism did not start until the nineteenth and twentieth centuries. Just like Krishna and Buddha, Jesus was seen by Hindu thinkers mostly as one in whom the unity of atman *(the actual self) and* brahman *(the true self) was manifest in a way that was worth imitating. The words spoken by Jesus, "I and the Father are one" (John 10:30), became a key text in this interpretation.*

Within contemporary Indian theology, Jesus' role as mediator sometimes reflects very much the characteristics of the avatara "descending from" Vishnu, sometimes also those of the guru "ascending to" Shiva in the midst of his fellow human beings. Detachment is central in both types of mediators. Here the notion of guru seems to be more capable of integrating the often difficult path of Jesus' earthly suffering than the notion of the merely temporally "descending" avatara. Both approaches are far from a third, Christian, approach to Jesus, namely Jesus as dalit, *as an untouchable. In the Indian church, which is far from casteless, there is hardly any room for this casteless person, however much the majority of Indian Christians belong to this large group of "untouchables."*

9   Historical Encounters

The Thomas Christians in India

Christianity occupies a relatively modest place in India. In this densely populated country – which will shortly overtake China with regard to the number of inhabitants (more than a billion) – Christians account for more or less three per cent of the population. That means 25 million. Barret even estimates double that in his *World Christian Encyclopedia*, but his estimations are often generous.

Officially, according to the constitution of 1947, India is a secular state. Here "secular" does not refer to the (Western) separation of state and religion but to the fact that the state is neutral with respect to the religions. Gandhi and Nehru, the spiritual fathers of the constitution, sought very much to protect both the Muslim minority, fourteen per cent of the Indian population, and the Christian minority in the constitution. In fact, "secular" means primarily that India is not a Hindu state, according to the constitution. It does not mean that the state does not meddle in the different religions through its legislation.

Recent decades have witnessed a growing, nationalistic *Hindutva* movement that is striving for a Hindu state under the slogan "India for the Hindus." Through violent acts against Muslims and Christians and more subtle political pressure, this movement is explicitly making its presence felt in India today. That sometimes makes the position of highly placed Christians – of whom there are, proportionately, quite a few – somewhat ambivalent. When a Christian, a granddaughter-in-law of Nehru, was elected President of India, she was apparently subjected to so much pressure behind the scenes that, shortly after her election, she indicated that she would rather not accept the high office after all.

The constitution allows mission work, but many states have introduced so many limitations that "conversion" is actually possible only in the sense of a return (*shuddhi*) to Hinduism. Alleged missionary activities spark intense emotions among Hindus in some regions.

In recent decades, the Christian faith has become attractive especially to the *dalits*, the casteless people, who are also known as the "untouchables." They constitute fifteen per cent (150 million) of the Indian population and usually live a subsistence existence in rural areas. They have often converted as a group to the Christian faith. It is primarily their "mass conversions" that are criticized by the adherents of the *Hindutva* movement.[1] They now constitute the majority of Indian Christians. Therefore, the traditional image of Christianity in India as an elitist religion does not correspond (any longer) to the actual situation. Meanwhile, a highly educated elite in the Indian church still sets the tone, increasingly causing tensions, all the more so because the traditional Indian church is not at all a "casteless" church. At the present time, *dalit* theology, with its strong emphasis on Jesus as *dalit*, seems to be enjoying a better reception outside of India as a liberation theology than it does in India.[2] Only a stronger anchoring in caste-critical aspects of India's own religious context will be able to change this.[3]

Christianity's roots go deep in India's history. The so-called Thomas Christians in particular see their church as a direct continuation of the work of the apostle Thomas, tracing its origin to the end of the second century.[4] The seven million Thomas Christians live mainly in Malabar (Kerala) in southern India and are spread among different churches, of which the Syro-Malabar Church, which was united – though not without tension – with Rome, is the largest, with 3.5 million members. It is followed by the autocephalous (independent) Malankara Orthodox Syrian Church with about 1.5 million members. The considerably smaller Mar Thoma Church (about 700,000 members) has especially been busy on the ecumenical front because of its close contact with the Anglican Church.[5] The well-known Indian theologian M. M. Thomas (1916–1996) was a member of this circle. Christians account for twenty per cent of the population in Kerala.

A great deal of dissension among Indian Christians was sown when Portuguese missionaries forced the Latin liturgy on them, and a number of major schisms have occurred. Indian Christianity belonged originally to the Nestorian Persian (Seleucid) church and followed the East Syrian liturgy.[6] At the time of the conflict on the Latin liturgy, a large group moved more in the direction of Monophysitism, without much else in their church being affected by that. That seems to confirm the impression that the struggle between the Monophysites and the Dyophysites did not substantially affect the church in India.[7] At most, one could say that traces of the Dyophysitism (two natures) of the Nestorians protected the church of India from surrendering itself too eagerly to Monophysitism (one nature) to which it had, as it were, a natural inclination – as will be apparent later – because of its Hindu context. Because of that, the logos Christology that was so popular in its circles could always be given its own Indian content. This could also very easily become very abstract and, subsequently, nothing more than a vague reference to a wisdom principle.[8] In their logos Christology, the Indians have always stressed the ethical meaning of Jesus' concrete life.

Hindu Voices on Jesus

Hinduism has reacted much more strongly than Buddhism to Christianity. Because Hinduism contains gods and mediators, Christianity can be compared more easily with Hinduism than with Buddhism. In the nineteenth century especially there was a veritable wave of publications by Hindus on Christianity. The inculturation of the meaning of Jesus in Indian culture was brought about in the first place not by Christians primarily but by Hindus.[9]

Because we are focusing in this study primarily on the meaning that has been attributed to Jesus in the last forty years in the non-Western world, we will mention only a few well-known historical names here briefly. Since contemporary Indian theology continues to refer to them, we cannot skip them.

The first that must be mentioned is Ram Mohan Roy (1772–1833), the founder of the *Brahmo Samaj* movement (1828), a movement of Hindu intellectuals in Bengal whose goal was to arrive at a new understanding of Hinduism in relation to Christianity. In 1820 Roy published his *The Precepts of Jesus: The Guide to Peace and Happiness*. His Jesus is primarily an ethical Jesus. He does not concern himself with the historical Jesus or the Jesus of the church. Jesus' connection with God is what is expressed primarily in his teaching. For him, Jesus is, indeed, "the guide to peace and happiness."[10]

Keshub Chunder Sen (1838–1884) also became involved in the *Brahmo Samaj* from 1857 on. He was fascinated especially by the way in which Jesus brings the divine closer through self-emptying. Around 1882, he worked that out in his interpretation of the doctrine of the Trinity. Jehovah-Brahman descends in his Son, an emanation from his Self, encompasses and penetrates the whole universe and leads it through the power of his Spirit back to him. Sen sees direct parallels here with the Hindu view of *Saccidananda* (a drawing together of the three concepts of *sat*, *cit* and *ananda*. *Sat* means: being/truth; *cit* means consciousness/mind; *ananda* means happiness/blessing). Jesus is the embodiment of the consciousness (*cit*) of Brahman.[11]

Both Sen and his friend Pratap Chander Mazoomdar (1840–1905) emphasized very much the Asian character of Jesus' life. Mazoomdar thus published his thirteen meditations on the beauty, holiness and power of Jesus in a volume called *The Eastern Jesus*.[12] All three authors display great interest in Jesus without making the transition to the Christian religion.[13]

That was not the case with Brahmobandhav Upadhyaya (1861–1907). He was baptized and from then on expressed his Christian faith in the concepts that were available to him from his upbringing and context. He wrote a hymn on the *Saccidananda* that is still often sung in India. In that way he gave shape to the fact that he was "Hindu by birth" and "Christian by rebirth."[14]

Apart from the interest in Christianity associated with these well-known people, an increasing interest among the poor in India in Christian thinking on social justice could be observed at the end of the nineteenth century.[15] Whereas the intellectuals associated with the Brahmo Samaj movement emphasized Jesus' divinity, here it was the opposite. These two ways of thinking seem to be completely divergent but could also sometimes be connected with each other. Thus, for example, someone like Sathianathan Clarke, who wrote a study on *dalit* theology, sees the strength of Indian theology precisely in the connection between these two ways of thinking: they need each other. Otherwise, the divine "cosmic" Christ would lose contact with the earthly Jesus, and the latter would lose his divine cosmic power. Without power (*sakti*), the Jesus who suffers with us could not change the lot of the suffering in any way, and without Jesus' earthly existence, we would not know what powers the "cosmic Christ" could release.[16] This argument places Clarke in a tradition of reflection on Jesus that, as we already stated, was characteristic of the Thomas Christians.

In any case, we can distinguish four different approaches on the interaction between Christianity and Hinduism. (1) The inclusion of the Christian body of thought sometimes brought Indian Hindu thinkers (Ram Mahon Roy, Keshub Chander Sen and Pratap Chander Mazoomdar) to their "own" Jesus who was rather different from (and they were very much aware of this) the Jesus whom Christians talked about. (2) That sometimes led, as in the case of Brahmobandhav Upadhyaya, to conversion to the Christian faith while retaining Hindu intellectual frameworks. (3) Again, other Hindu thinkers, such as Mahatma Gandhi,[17] brought an aspect of the Christian faith (the ethics of Jesus' Sermon on the Mount in Matt. 5–7) to the fore that people missed both in the Christianity of the time and in Hinduism. (4) We can also point to the rather smooth inclusion of the Christian faith within Hinduism. Ramakrishna Paramahamsa (1836–1886) and his student Vivekananda (1863–1902) followed this route. For them, Jesus is an incarnation of God (Vishnu), just as Buddha, Rama and Krishna are.[18] But in that case Christianity is not, as it is for Roy, an extra dimension but a confirmation of what Hinduism had always taught. This form of integration can take on the characteristics of annexation and sometimes also be very critical of Christianity as a superfluous religion.[19]

Common to all these thinkers is that (1) they reject the notion of Jesus' uniqueness, (2) do not attribute any special meaning to Jesus' historical existence, (3) do not ascribe any importance to Jesus' death on the cross and his resurrection, (4) attribute great meaning to Jesus' self-denial and living as an example, (5) attach a great deal of importance to Jesus' message of love and non-violence, and (6) do not see any surplus value in Christianity as a religion and the church as institute. It is thus not necessary – for most of them, with the exception of Upadhayaya – to become a Christian and member of a church in order to worship Christ and to follow in his footsteps.[20]

The Di-Unity of Jesus and God

How Hindus respond to Christianity and how Christians look at Hinduism are very much determined by the form of Hinduism for which one feels the most affinity. Is it the oldest, Vedic tradition in which the cosmic and social harmony and worship play a major role? Or is it the later *advaita* teaching of the Vedanta school in which the personally experienced becoming one of the self (*atman*) with the divine (*brahman*) is central and the one who prepares the way is distinguished from other believers solely by his example? Or is it the *bhakti* tradition in which personal devotion to an exalted God is strongly emphasized and an *avatara* mediator (Krishna) plays an important role? For that matter, the latter two ways of thinking – *advaita* and *bhakti* – can sometimes go together. A good example of this is the Bhagavadgita.

All thinkers mentioned thus far stand in the *advaita* tradition, except for Sen who displays more of a *bhakti* type of devotion. *Advaita* thinking presupposes the non-duality of the individual soul (*atman*) and the world soul (*brahman*). There are usually two key texts from the Upanishads that stand at the heart of the *advaita* experience: one in the Brhadaranyaka Upanishad (1.4, 10) and the other in the Chandogya Upanishad (6.8, 7).

The first text fragment concerns the famous sentence: "In the beginning this world was only *brahman*, and he knew nothing other than himself (*atman*) (knowing): I am *brahman*." The closing sentence of the second fragment is: "The essence – that constitutes the self of this whole world – that is the truth, that is the self (*atman*). And you are that, Svetaketu!"

In both texts the subject–object split has disappeared. The human I has been absorbed into the divine I. That is the essence of the Hindu notion of salvation: the liberation (*moksha*) from the cycle of rebirth (*samsara*) through the merging of *atman* and *brahman*. Many Hindus see Jesus as reflecting this *advaita* thinking when he says "the Father and I are one" (John 10:30). Indeed, perhaps only someone who is familiar with this *advaita* thinking can truly understand this saying.

In modern variants of this thinking about Jesus from the *advaita* perspective, the individual self can also be understood more inclusively, so that the other (the neighbour) can also be understood as belonging to our *atman*. From the summons to love one's neighbour ("Love your neighbor as yourself" (Matt. 22:39)), and mindful of Jesus' words, "Whatever you did for one of the least of these brothers of mine, you did for me" (Matt. 25:40), the self and the other can indeed, including Jesus, be understood as a non-dualistic unity. Thus, *advaita* implies not only a vertical but also a horizontal unity. For that matter, one can add here by way of critique that the above-mentioned conceptual possibility leads only sporadically to a different attitude among (rich) Christians with respect to their fellow believers among the *dalit*. That is why the *dalits* still see brahmanistic *advaita* thinking as one of the greatest obstacles to the destruction of the caste system.[21] The focus on internal unification still seems to be at the expense of external unity.

The question of whether *advaita* thinking can indeed be seen as a key to understanding Jesus' relation with the Father depends to a great extent on the question of whether Jesus' connection with the Father is a goal in itself or must be seen primarily as a summary of his concrete life. That is a question that will constantly arise in this chapter. More than any other religion, Hinduism contains ways of thinking that can articulate the connection between the human and the divine. But less than the Abrahamic religions in any case, Hinduism does not contain ways of thinking that can articulate the importance of the historical – apart from the category of reward or punishment.[22]

We cannot discuss the question here of whether the human becomes divine or the divine human in the di-unity of *atman* and *brahman* that Jesus personifies *par excellence*, because it presupposes thinking in terms of two worlds. And that kind of thinking is precisely what Hinduism (just like Buddhism) wants to rise above. After all, the human state is never separate from the divine and the divine is never separate from the human. We encountered that as also a problem for Western thinking in the previous part.

In order to do justice to both God and human beings, the main tradition of Western thought has always clearly distinguished between God and human beings. In contrast, in the main tradition of Eastern thought, God and human beings, the finite and the infinite, are not distinguished. The intention there as well is to do justice to God and human beings.

The fascinating aspect of the Christological doctrine that the Council of Chalcedon so nicely formulated in the "inconfusedly, unchangeably, indivisibly, inseparably" phrasing is precisely the fact that this di-unity was articulated literally and figuratively on the interface between East and West. In this study as well – as the reader will in the meantime have observed – we are constantly entering this interface.

Just as the East cannot avoid the issue of this distinction, so the West cannot avoid the question of the connection. We therefore also repeatedly come across formulations in Western dogmatics that stress that God cannot be conceived without people and the human being cannot be conceived without God (Barth) or even go a step further and speak of the relatedness of each human being to God and the relatedness of God to human beings (Rahner, Pannenberg). Nevertheless, such an understanding – which is also present among the Western Church Fathers – of an internal connection between God and human beings could not prevent thinking in terms of distinction from gaining the upper hand. That thinking always arose out of the need to stress the freedom of both God and human beings. But that is, again, an aspect that is seldom heard in Asia, except in connection with the *bhakti* devotion in southern India.

The theology of a famous *bhakti* thinker such as Ramanuja (ca. 1050–1137), for example, is often called "qualified monism" in this context. He presupposes a fundamental unity of God, humans and the world but also asserts the distinction. Instead of the impersonal, all-comprehensive *brahman* or *advaita* thinking, he speaks of a divine form, Vishnu, with its own characteristics to whom human beings can surrender themselves in pious devotion.

In the thirteenth century, a difference of opinion arose in the school of Ramanuja on the way in which a person is thought to surrender himself to the divinity. That difference of opinion reminds one in many respects of the dispute at the time of the Reformation between Roman Catholics and Protestants on the question of how a person should see himself with respect to divine grace: as purely receptive (passively) or actively cooperative? In southern India this is called the "school dispute" between the northern school and the southern school. Both schools agreed that a human being depends on divine grace. The difference of opinion focused, however, on the question of whether the human can cooperate in the reception of grace. According to the northern school, the human being has to seize grace himself, like a young monkey who clings actively to its mother's back or belly while she is walking. The southern school disputes this. They argued that the human being cannot cooperate in his own salvation in any respect. Here the human being seems to be more like a kitten that is passive while its mother picks it up by the scruff of its neck and carries it. It is for that reason that the two schools are called, respectively, the "monkey school" and the "cat school."

The core concept of the "cat school" is "self-surrender." In the thirteenth century it was primarily Nimbarka who developed this thinking as a form of Krishna devotion in which *bhakti* stood for loving surrender to the gracious God. The surrender (to an Other) is expressed so strongly here that there is no longer talk of a "qualified monism," as in Ramanuja but of a "dualistic monism." His attempts to articulate the connection and distinction sometimes seem to approximate the wording that the Council of Chalcedon needed to express the di-unity of Jesus' divine and human nature ("inconfusedly, unchangeably, indivisibly, inseparably").

For Indian theologians, the gospel of John plays a strikingly major role. An exegetical basis for that attention to this gospel was provided primarily through the work of A. J. Appasamy at the end of the 1920s and the beginning of the 1930s.[23] In the history of Christianity, Indian theologians are perhaps those who have an outstanding conceptual apparatus for understanding this gospel. In the way in which the divine logos comes to "his own" (John 1:11) in this gospel and in which Jesus can say that he is in the Father and we in him and he in us (John 14:20), they saw the intended di-unity of *atman-brahman*, which concerns the divine that is present in each person but which must be brought to a higher level through union with the divine *brahman*. Jesus is then primarily the "cosmic Christ," the mediator of creation (Col. 1:15–17) or the Word (Logos) through whom everything has come into being (John 1:3).[24]

The Indian theologians are, of course, aware of the claims of uniqueness ("no one comes to the Father except through me" (John 14:6)) in the gospel of John in reference to the concrete person of Jesus of Nazareth. They interpret the I about which Jesus is speaking here as the I of enlightened individuals who thus indicate their unity with the divine. Therefore, it is not the I of the ordinary person who thus distinguishes herself from her fellow human beings but the I of an *avatara* or a *guru* who knows that his I, his connectedness to God, is the only way that leads to the divine. This does not say anything more or less than that only an enlightened one, an *avatara* or a *guru*, can lead a human being to the divine.[25]

10 Examples of Reflection on Jesus

Raimundo Panikkar's Cosmotheandrism

It is not our intention in this study to describe the thinking and development of individual theologians. Nevertheless, we cannot avoid discussing Asian (and African in Part VIII) theology without constant reference to individual thinkers. However much we want to trace its main lines and tendencies, rather than individual variations on these, theology – happily enough – remains something done by people of flesh and blood who arrive at their theological views through their entirely unique development. Acquaintance with this development often provides the best access to understanding the existential import of their ideas. This approach runs parallel to the starting point articulated in Part I, i.e. that worldwide recognition does not arise through abstraction from concrete situations but, rather, through the recognition of the authenticity of these situations.

In this section we will look at the development of two of the most influential Indian theologians. We will begin with the both respected and maligned Raimundo Panikkar. We could call the Roman Catholic Indian theologian Panikkar an embodiment of the "inreligionization" for which Pieris argues.[1] His father was an Indian Hindu and his mother a Spanish Roman Catholic. He himself could speak of a "double belonging," or even of "multiple belonging" because, as an Asian Christian, he saw himself not only as a Hindu but also as a Buddhist. "I left as a Christian, I found myself a Hindu, and I 'returned' as a Buddhist, without ever having ceased to be a Christian."[2]

We will indicate first, briefly and necessarily concisely, the essence of his theology so that we can then turn to the question of the meaning that he ascribes to Jesus. For him, just as for Pieris, it is the Christian doctrine of the Trinity that was the doctrine in which the most essential aspects of the God–human being–world relation can be understood. In essence, the doctrine of the Trinity is the "junction" where the authentic spiritual dimensions of all religions come together.[3] He views the first person of the Trinity, God the Father, from the perspective of the Hindu teaching of the *advaita* and the Buddhist teaching of *nirvana*. Both *brahman* and *nirvana* are beyond human ability to comprehend. The Father is thus also absolute and transcendent; he generates the Son. The Father can be known completely only in the Son; the Father himself is unknowable. He personifies only eternal silence. Panikkar speaks of "ontological apophatism" with respect to God, thereby intending to indicate that one cannot speak of the being of God.[4] In the course of his development, Panikkar elaborated more extensively on this way of speaking about the Father through images borrowed from Buddhism.[5] The *non-being* of the absolute (the Father) does not mean that the absolute does not exist but that the absolute exists in such a way that it cannot be included in the category of *that which is*. Otherwise, it would mean that we could then include the absolute among *that which is* and the absolute would consequently no longer be the absolute.

The Son is the one who forms the bridge between the finite and the infinite, the created and the uncreated. He is the *summus pontifex*, the ultimate, definitive bridge builder. One can enter into a relationship with him and not into one with the Father. Panikkar sees the personal relationship with God that the Son makes possible flanked, as it were, by the spirituality (which transcends our understanding) that we affirm with respect to the Father and the immanent power of the Spirit that works in us. The Father thus represents that which is not, the aspect of God that transcends being, and the Spirit represents the non-dualistic, immanent aspect.[6]

Panikkar applies this scheme to the central ideas in Hinduism as well. In the Upanishads, as *Nirguna Brahman*, *Brahman* can be conceived as self-sufficient, transcending all our terms and intellectual conceptions. The parallel with the Father is obvious. But *Brahman* can also be conceived as *Saguna Brahman*, i.e. the aspect of *Brahman* that is turned towards the world. *Saguna Brahman* is also called *Ishvara*, the dimension of *Brahman* in which the whole world exists and to whom all people are related.

Ishvara has an important place in *bhakti* devotion with its accent on a personal God. The use of the term in the Upanishads seems to have evolved from a name for God into a term for power and subsequently, into one for the person of God. Panikkar summarizes the function of *ishvara* as follows:

1. *Ishvara* can be considered to be *the revelation of brahman*.
2. He is *the personal aspect of brahman*, for *brahman* itself cannot enter into any relationships. That would endanger *brahman's* absoluteness.
3. *Ishvara* is *the creator*, for the absolute transcendence of *brahman* would be threatened if *brahman* were also the creator.
4. *Ishvara* is the one who *leads us back to brahman* again.
5. He is the *consciously acting brahman*.
6. As incarnations of the divine, *avataras* can be called *manifestations of ishvara*.

7. Because *ishvara* does everything for *brahman* and as *brahman* but is nevertheless distinguished from *brahman*, he is the one who, *par excellence*, can guarantee the immanence of *brahman*.[7]

It is clear from the last characterization especially how close the function of *ishvara* approaches that of Jesus as the "cosmic Christ."[8] Just like the Logos, *ishvara* is equal to God but also to be distinguished from God as the source.

Panikkar views speaking about the "cosmic Christ" as an expression of *theandrism*, a conception in which the cosmos, God (*theos*) and the human being (*anèr*) are woven together without lapsing into pantheism.[9] Panikkar defines *theandrism* as the classical and traditional term for the intimate and complete unity between the divine and the human that is realized paradigmatically in Christ and constitutes the goal towards which everything here below is directed in Christ and the Spirit.[10] Pannikar would later explicitly include the whole creation (cosmos) in this unity and preferred to speak of *cosmotheandrism* or the *cosmotheandric principle*.

Without denying that they are distinct from one another, God, human beings and creation are interwoven with one another in such a way that Panikkar can refer, by way of characterizing this interwovenness, to the same expression the Christian tradition used to express the relationship between Father, Son and Holy Spirit. But the Eastern church fathers especially also used this expression to indicate the relationship between the two natures of Christ. They did so by means of the concept of *perichoresis*, i.e. mutual interpenetration.[11]

We can become aware of this form of *cosmotheandrism* personified by Jesus if we understand the reality in which we live as ruled by the law of *ontonomy*. This neologism is Panikkar's attempt to get beyond the opposition between autonomy and heteronomy. The notions autonomy and heteronomy or theonomy deny the relational connectedness in which human existence alone can be given shape.[12] It is the Spirit that makes us aware of this connectedness with both the Father and the Son and which thus makes *advaita* possible: the connectedness of our deepest self with both the transcendent aspect of God (the Father) and that aspect that is turned toward us (the Son).

Since the first printing of his *The Unknown Christ of Hinduism* in 1964, in which he actually states that Hinduism is potential Christianity, Panikkar shifted in his radical revision of this book, now with the suggestive subtitle *Towards an Ecumenical Christophany* (1981), to the position that Christ is not so much the Jesus of Christianity but rather the symbol of *theandric* human existence. As such, this Christ transcends Christianity and the adherents of other religions do not need to refer to him necessarily by a name derived from Christianity. Then, not only can it be said that *brahman* is the "unknown Christ" of Hinduism, but it can also be said that Christ is the "unknown *brahman*" of Christianity. In both cases, at issue here is a reality whose full weight the individual religions can only gropingly articulate.

But Pannikar deliberately does not speak of the "hidden Christ" because he is concerned with the *presence of this one mystery* that can be experienced in both Christianity and Hinduism.[13] Essentially, Panikkar says here that "Christ" refers to an ontological (= something that is not conceivable apart from human existence) mediator who is a model for the connectedness of the relative and absolute in all religions.[14] In this way Panikkar can thus speak, indeed, of the "universal Christ" and of the "christic principle" that lies at the foundation of the whole of reality. That position belongs to him as the one who connects the eternal and the temporal, God and human beings. Each living creature is called in him and by him into existence and exists in and participates in the Son; each living creature is thus essentially a *Christophany*.[15]

Panikkar can state that Jesus is an epiphany (appearance) of Christ but considers that to be only partially true. This Christ of the Christophany is not exhausted in Jesus. For Panikkar, this does not deny the historicity of Jesus' life and the reality of the divine incarnation in him but only puts it in a larger context. The historicity of Jesus' life and belief in God's incarnation in him is necessary to come to faith in Christ. But the appearance (epiphany) of the Christ is not limited to Jesus. For him, Jesus' uniqueness is not at issue here because he characterizes the concept of uniqueness as a qualitative concept. Thus, there can be other epiphanies of the Christ – such as, for example, in Hindu *avataras* or Buddhist *bodhisattvas* – but no single one surpasses the ephiphany that Jesus embodies. In this context, Panikkar also makes use of the distinction between identification and identity.

A person can be identified via all kinds of details (historical, genetic, etc.). But these details do not yet establish someone's identity, i.e. that which is most characteristic of someone. For example, during an arrest the police can perhaps quite simply identify someone on the basis of available personal details, but that does not yet establish that person's (true) identity. To do that, an insight (epiphany) is needed that transcends the purely personal details. This means that the meaning of the historical Jesus does not exhaust the meaning of the transhistorical Christ.[16] We saw earlier that this is an insight that is constantly emphasized by Asian theologians and artists – not only in a Hindu context but also in a Buddhist one.[17] As such, one can agree with this insight, but if it is placed too emphatically in the foreground, it will inevitably lead to the trivialization of the importance of Jesus' own choices in life.

For Panikkar, historical mediators are more or less fortuitous manifestations of the second person of the Trinity who represents the (ontic) relation between the human and the divine. They are important as appearances but not essential for the relation in question. But one could ask if the identification of the divine (the Father) with the concrete life of Jesus of Nazareth is not so strong that the medium (his life, humanity) is in fact the most authentic expression of the message (divine nearness). And one could ask if it is not precisely that identification that also challenges us to become aware of the divine presence within the limits of the conditions for our historical existence. In other words, is human confidence in that which is historically concrete not precisely *the* characteristic of the human answer to God's desire to make his "dwelling among us" (John 1:14)?[18]

In fact, for Panikkar, Jesus is the *avatara* of *Ishavara* and *Ishavara* is the heavenly (and not the incarnate, the made flesh) divine Logos, the second person of the Trinity. Here we encounter aspects of Jesus' existence – his earthly and heavenly existence – that the Christian tradition always managed to connect with each other only with the greatest possible difficulty. It was always the intention of the Christian tradition to show that Jesus' earthly existence was essential for the way in which he was connected with the divine. To cite a few extreme comparisons: if his earthly life had been more like that of Stalin, Hitler, Hirohito or Pol Pot, then the way in which he could have been brought into connection with the divine would also have been different.[19]

The Spirit represents the divine power that inspired Jesus to his concrete life choices and the Word represents everything that he heard from the Law (Torah) and Prophets as coming from God. Without Jesus' concrete life, that Word would be a dead letter and without that Word, Jesus' concrete life could be applied to anything and could be subject to the wildest interpretations.

One could point to the patristic term *perichoresis* of which Panikkar also speaks. The term is derived from the Greek verb *chorein* and means "to stride" or "to dance." Both aspects of Jesus "dance through" each other. They penetrate each other without damage or loss and enrich each other in what is unique to both. Jesus' earthly life belongs inseparably to the way in which we know God. And the converse applies as well: God reveals himself only in Jesus.

It is striking that it is precisely in the *dalits'* view of Jesus that the importance of the historical concreteness of God's presence among us receives major attention. There it is even the pivot on which the central thesis of Jesus as *dalit* turns. After all, if God wants to be present in Jesus' earthly life, with the "impure" family tree containing two prostitutes (Rahab and Tamar), four "foreign" women (Rebecca, Rachel, Rahab and Ruth), someone who committed adultery (Bathsheba), a mother who had a child out of wedlock, a father belonging to the working classs, whereas Jesus himself led a life full of "impure" contacts with Samaritans, adulterous women and tax collectors, he would all the more want to be present among the *dalits*. The *dalits* are thus a *right place to find God*.[20] It is also not surprising that precisely the cross and resurrection occupy an important place in *dalit* theology, just as they do, by the way, in other forms of socially engaged Indian theology.[21]

Stanley Samartha's "Unbound Christ"

In contrast to Panikkar, Samartha does not want to speak of the "unknown Christ in Hinduism." He feels that that does not do justice to the historical Jesus. Moreover, he considers it insulting for Hindus to think of their religion as a kind of disguised Christianity.[22] He speaks rather of the "unbound Christ" who transcends the boundaries of Christianity. Just as Christianity is connected with and bound to Christ, so Christ is indeed connected with but not bound to Christianity.[23] This accent on the unbounded character and therefore universality of Jesus is a refrain that we have heard many times in Asian theology.

Samartha sees the fascination that Hindu India appears to have with Jesus as an indication of an "unbaptized koinonia" existing outside the doors of the church but connected with Jesus.[24] The prominent way – immediately obvious to any tourist – in which Jesus is present in Indian Hindu art is simply an indication of this fact for Samartha. Samartha finds this "unbaptized koinonia" with Jesus primarily in *advaita* thinkers, more so than in *bhakti* thinkers. He considers the comparison that emerges primarily in *bhakti* thinkers between the role of Jesus and that of the *avatara* dangerous because, within *bhakti* theism, the *avatara*, an incarnation of the divinity, is always considered to be lower than the divinity itself, always considered to be a limitation, in fact, in conflict with the being of the divine.[25] That is why for Samartha *advaita* thinking, in which a "non-duality" of *atman* and *brahman*, the human and the divine, is striven for, is more valuable than the concept *avatara*.[26]

Later in 1991, in his study *One Christ, Many Religions*, we see Samartha sketching a much more positive image. When *bhakti* theologians like Appasamy and Chakkarai speak about Jesus as the one and unique *avatara*, it is precisely the recognition of multiple *avataras* that seems to offer Samartha the opening for ascribing more value to this form of mediator. He calls the idea of multiple *avataras* "theologically the most accommodating attitude in a pluralistic setting." It is an attitude that "permits recognizing both the Mystery of God and the freedom of people to respond to divine initiatives in different ways at different times."[27]

But he still continues to emphasize that he cannot imagine any teaching about Jesus in India that would not make use of the terminology and ideas of *advaita* thinking, all the more so because this thinking shows itself to be open to reinterpretation when confronted with new ideas.[28] These reinterpretations should, as far as Samartha is concerned, be concerned with the meaning that can be attributed to history, social reality and individual responsibility. For Samartha, one can speak here truly of a lively interaction between Christians and Hindus ("Hindu Christian mutuality") because *advaita* thinking can, in turn, "lock" Jesus up in his own history and thus ignore his universal, cosmic significance. It can happen that the human ego becomes an independent entity between God and the human being. *Advaita* thinking can help us understand in an exemplary way the implications of the growth to a "not-two-ness."[29]

Samartha is well aware that Christianity and Hinduism each have their entirely unique histories in entirely unique contexts. That is why he also insists on taking differences into account in interreligious dialogue. Instead of asking from the Christian perspective, "Is there salvation in Hinduism?" as Christians, we should ask more subtly "Does Hinduism contain the form of liberation from sin, guilt and curse that Christians believe was achieved for them by Jesus on the cross?" The answer must be no: Hinduism does not think in those terms.

Conversely, the Hindu could ask: "Is there *moksha* in Christianity? Does the Christian faith offer liberation from being bound to *karma-samsara* (destiny and rebirth) in the situation of unity between *atman* and *brahman*? Here as well the answer must be no: Christianity does not think in those terms. Such a dialogue would never be fruitful. It would be more fruitful to look at our current societies, assess their needs and then search for words and concepts that can articulate in a specific context most adequately that from which and that to which Christianity and Hinduism wish to liberate human beings. That implies a reformulation of the event of the cross and resurrection as well as a reformulation of the *advaita* unity.[30]

Sometimes, where a sharp contrast is accepted, there can nevertheless also be recognition. Thus the Hindu accent on the sinful involvement with oneself – as articulated, for instance, in Bhagavadgita 16:7–20 – sometimes strongly resembles the way in which sin is described in the history of Western theology, for example, in Augustine's famous description of sin as *amor sui* (self-love). Even in a Christian theologian such as Aleaz, who makes a creative synthesis of the Christian faith and classical *advaita* thought his explicit goal and thus moves sharply away from the Western Christian doctrines of reconcilation and sin, we encounter formulations for characterizing sin – such as self-confirmation through one's own efforts apart from *brahman* – that approximate Augustine's description.

But that affinity is not that strange. *Advaita* thinking, based on the unity of the *atman* and *brahman*, presupposes that a human being must be brought back to his true self. That is why Aleaz does not want to speak about the sinful self, for that self is not sinful but divine! But he does speak of the sinful ego of the human individual. In fact, he is not that far from the doctrine that he rejects. The Christian tradition has always distinguished between two "selves": the inauthentic, sinful self (the ego) that isolates itself and concentrates exclusively on itself, *and* the true relational self of the human being as the image of God. Jesus brings the human person back to the latter "self." He restores the image of God in humankind again – Aleaz would say that he brings the *atman* and *brahman* back together.[31]

The constant attempt by Indian theology to bring the human and divine together in a specific way is crucial. Samartha is also a clear exponent of this. We see him searching for a Christology that approaches Jesus' divinity through, as it were, his humanity: "the way to the confession of his divinity is through his humanity." That does not mean that he wants to end up with an "impoverished 'Jesusology'" – which is how he refers to the often inadequate reconstructions of Jesus' earthly life – since he wants to begin with the historical Jesus. With his approach "from below," with the historical Jesus, he wants to show how a human being can approach the divine in self-denial and be accepted by God at his resurrection as a "son of God."[32]

It is in this context that Samartha's distinction between a "helicopter Christology" and a "bullock-cart Christology" has become famous. In its attempts to land on the religiously pluralistic terrain of Asia, helicopter Christology makes such a missiological noise and kicks up so much theological dust that those around cannot hear the voice nor see the face of the descending divinity. In contrast, a bullock-cart Christology always has its wheels on the unpaved roads of Asia, for without continuous contact with the ground the cart cannot advance. Moreover, this Christology has the advantage that the bullocks pull at a constant speed, even if the driver falls asleep. In other words, Jesus' earthly life had its own dynamic that was not dependent on historical circumstances.[33]

For Samartha, Jesus' theocentrism is central. It concerns God; it concerns his Kingdom.[34] For that reason Samartha also resists any simple identification of Jesus with God. To claim that Jesus is equal to God is the same as making God a tribal god over against the gods of other religions.[35] For him, the meaning of Jesus lies within the framework of the universal relationship between God and human beings.

We touch here on a crucial point for Samartha that has caused repeated emotional flare-ups in the history of the church. In the New Testament Jesus shows such a strong sense of connectedness to God that he could be called "son of God" and could say: "I and the Father are one" (John 10:30). Does that mean that it concerns two completely identical "persons"? No, for the Christian tradition has always said that Jesus is completely God but never that God is completely Jesus. It has never theologically come to the point of complete identification of the Father and the Son, to the *Christomonism* that Samartha rejects. But in fact – Samartha argues – Christianity has often shown itself to be very Christomonist and has ignored Jesus' own references to the Father.[36]

The purpose of Samartha's argument for a *theocentric Christology* in which the meaning of Jesus is seen in how he reveals God's love is to show the "distinctiveness" of Jesus' way without the possibility of other ways to show that "distinctiveness" has to be reduced.[37] The belief that God can best be defined by Jesus does not, after all, have to mean that (our knowledge of) God is limited to Jesus. Samartha sees Buddha, Rama and Krishna especially as pointing in the same direction. For him, therefore, it is not necessary to speak about Jesus as the *one avatara*. Precisely the existence of several *avataras* and thus of different ways to God makes us sense how great the divine mystery is – a mystery that is not exhausted by the truth of one religion.[38]

More than Panikkar, Samartha emphasizes the meaning of Jesus' concrete life. But he emphasizes the key role of the figure of the mediator less than Panikkar does. By giving the kingdom of God a central place in Jesus' proclamation, Samartha can preserve the social import of that proclamation. But, by giving that message several interpreters, he relativizes the role of Jesus in that proclamation.

11 Jesus as *Avatara* and *Guru*

Jesus as Avatara

Of the many meanings attributed to Jesus in India in Hinduism – *sannyasin* (monk), *yogi* (yoga practitioner), *guru*, *avatara*, etc. – the latter two stand out with respect to this study, because they are the two that are situated most explicitly on the interface between the divine and the human.

Avatara means, literally, "descent" but is often used in a broader sense as a term for the divine manifestation in human form and in that sense can also refer to an "ascending" movement. Strictly speaking, the concept *avatara* is not the same as incarnation, for the latter, from a Christian point of view, refers to the radical becoming human of the divine and not simply to taking on human form. One would do better to employ the distinction here between a *theophany*, a divine appearance among people, and an *incarnation*, in which the divine becomes completely human. An *avatara* is actually "merely" a *theophany*.[1]

The classsic place in the Bhagavadgita where the role of the *avatara* in the person of Krishna appears is chapter 4:5–9. There Krishna says:

"I have been born many times, Arjuna, and many times hast thou been born. But I remember my past lives, and thou hast forgotten thine.
   Although I am unborn, everlasting, and I am the Lord of all, I come to my realm of nature and through my wondrous power I am born.
   When righteousness is weak and faints and unrighteousness exults in pride, then my Spirit arises on earth.
   For the salvation of those who are good, for the destruction of evil in men, for the fulfillment of the kingdom of righteousness, I come to this world in the ages that pass.
   He who knows my birth as God and who knows my sacrifice, when he leaves his mortal body, goes no more from death to death, for he in truth comes to me."[2]

There are a number of elements in this passage that are striking. (1) The passage begins with a clear reference to immortality ("unborn") and thus the immutable nature of the divine, whereas, as God, he has entered human existence several times ("have been born many times"). (2) The divine supremacy over and independence from the infinite is stated unambiguously. (3) The immutable and independent divine enters the realm of the mortal and dependent. (4) It does this of its own accord. (5) The reason is explicitly stated: the decline of righteousness (*dharma*) and the rise of unrighteousness (*adharma*). (6) The purpose of the divine manifestation that occurs in every age ("ages that pass") is to protect the righteous, to destroy the wicked and establish *dharma* once again, and (7) thus to protect believers from rebirth.[3]

The belief in *avataras* is intended to give courage and inspiration in times of hopelessness. If evil supplants good, it is intended to remind the believers that the divine mystery always guides the world. Clearly, here the divine is the active principle. It is the divine in the form of a human but not in a human being who is subject to the cycle of rebirth. For that reason we could say, rather, that the divine is in the form of the truly human. So the belief in *avataras* is an indication of divine faithfulness to the human being, precisely as the human situation displays unfaithfulness. As unrighteousness (*adharma*) is a sign of the absence of the divine, righteousness (*dharma*) is a sign of its presence.

Thus, there is no notion of "flight from the world" here. Krishna's involvement in the human lot is a direct incentive to share his concern. People like Gandhi have thus also derived inspiration for their political views directly from the above-mentioned passage in the Bhagavadgita (4:5–9). In particular, in Bhagavadgita 3:19–25 Krishna shows how detachment does not lead to ignoring the lot of the poor but is precisely the indispensable condition for actual involvement – without any ulterior motive – in their lot.[4] But Hinduism does not indicate explicitly where this involvement will lead for the world as a whole. The conception of a kingdom of God as a future for the whole creation and the associated idea of the transformation of present reality are missing.[5]

It is striking that Hinduism is not at all interested in the historicity – in the sense of the historical traceability – of the appearance of *avataras*. Nor does that fit into the cyclical, non-linear experience of time.[6] After all, his "actual coming" means that he is always present; it penetrates the awareness of the believers. It means that people become aware of his presence and liberating power. This "knowing" is purely a psychological process of becoming aware. Here "knowing" is *becoming what we already are* – connected with *brahman*. Krishna is *in* the world but not *of* the world. We could say that he *is* among us, but we cannot say *where* he is, because his presence coincides with everything that is.[7]

In the passage in question from the Bhagavadgita, Krishna himself decides to descend. By way of a history of religion intermezzo, we can assert that, in the developments in Hinduism concerning Krishna, this constitutes a final step in his journey from human being, to demigod, to complete God, to descended God.[8] Viewed across several centuries, Krishna is thus first a divinized human being who at a later stage returns as God. The same discussion occurs in Hinduism with respect to Krishna as in Christianity with respect to the mediator: is it ultimately a matter of the descending God or one of an ascending, exalted – critics would say "extolled" – human being? In Christian theology this is called the difference between a descent model and an ascent model.[9] But such a history of religions approach always entails something unreal for both Hindus and Christians. First of all, the question arises immediately, of course, as to the correctness of such a tracing of a historical development and, subsequently, believers experience a great deal of alienation when confronted with such reductions. For them, in their experience as believers, neither Krishna nor Jesus *became* divine over the course of time; rather they were always divine.[10]

Also playing a role here is the question if one is thinking more from an *advaita* or a *bhakti* approach. In the first case, an "ascending" line of thought is somewhat more obvious. In the second case, a "descending" line of thought is to be expected. For the rest, moreover, one should recall that – as remarked earlier – *advaita* thinking does not actually need any *avataras*. The unity between *atman* and *brahman* is attainable for everyone individually.

As is also the case with the incarnation in Christianity, there is a search in Hinduism for a conceptual model with respect to the *avatara* that in any case transcends thinking that places the divine and human in competition with each other. Such a conceptual model is usually found where the divine can be seen as the truly human and the human as something that is revealed in all its dimensions only in the divine. Here God is always a God of human beings and human beings are always the "image of God." Then divine "descent" always means the "ascent" of people and vice versa.[11]

A crucial question remains as to where the divine primarily reveals the truly human and the truly human primarily the divine. The motif for the coming of the *avatara* is the expulsion of unrighteousness, as we read above. But the Bhagavadgita does not elaborate any further on that motif when it has Krishna describe thoroughly and even profusely his presence among human beings (7:8–11 and 10:20–39). Little of his specific motive for coming can be found in this description – in any case not as specific as we find in Jesus' beatitudes (Matt. 5:3–11) or in the "judgement by the Son of Man" (Matt. 25:31–46). We do not find anything of social import in the Bhagavadgita in the same sense as found in Matt. 25:40, i.e. "whatever you did for one of the least of these brothers of mine." But we do find social import in the Bhagavadgita in the sense that everything is connected to Krishna (15:12–15).

Here it is not about a mediator who also shares in the lot of humanity. The Belgian Jesuit and expert on India, Jacques Dupuis, sees here – even though he calls the Hindu idea of *avatara* one of the steps towards the Christian mystery that offers the most perspective – the core of the distinction between Christianity and Hinduism. It thus concerns a difference between a divine manifestation in human form (*avatara*) and God's personal involvement in the history of humanity (Jesus).[12]

This thesis seems generally justifiable if it is not made into an absolute opposition. It also appears to concern mutual love between Krishna and human beings. "In whatever way men approach Me and surrender to Me," Krishna says, "I reward them accordingly" (4:11) and he is prepared to forgive the greatest sinner if he shows a sincere intention in coming to Krishna (9:30; 7:28 and 18:64–66). That is why Samartha, for example, wants to speak about the "unknown Krishna of Christianity" as well as about the "unknown Christ of Hinduism." He says in so many words that Jesus can be discovered in Krishna as well.[13]

Krishna is the one who, as *avatara*, comes to restores the right order (righteousness) if needed. He is not a redeemer in the sense that he takes responsibility on himself for the unrighteousness and in that way "bears the sins of the world."[14] Here also we could say that this thesis is true – again if it is not made absolute. After all, we hear Krishna saying in the Bhagavadgita: "For I am the sacrifice and the offering, the sacred gift and the sacred plant. I am the holy words, the holy food, the holy fire, and the offering that is made in the fire" (9:16). He has mercy for the great sinner, without any respect for persons, who comes to him with a sincere heart (9:30–34; 7:28 and 18:66). Here one does find something of "self-sacrifice on behalf of others" and of forgiveness of sins, even if the concept of sin is not associated here in the first place with guilt but with ignorance. One could speak here of a guilty ignorance (9:11); Krishna comes to break through that ignorance (*avidya*).

In Hinduism, it is not so much sin or guilt from which one needs to be liberated as it is from ignorance concerning one's true nature. Ignorance comes to expression in the identification with finite things: a person remains closed up within himself and an unbreakable connection – so characteristic of karma – exists between his actions and the result of his actions. Over against this hopeless situation, the Bhagavadgita places detached, devoted, selfless acts (*karma yoga*) (3:7–9 and 25) that are performed for the well-being of the whole world (3:25). One knows *brahman* only through acting in that way, and knowing *brahman* means entering into *brahman* (8:24 and 18:55).

The ethics of the Bhagavadgita presupposes a conception of humanity with a high degree of awareness and does not seem to take account of the "unfinished" character of the lives of those who have died early – all those millions of Indian poor with their shockingly short life expectations. The comparison with the Roman Catholic idea of purgatory is unsatisfactory. The idea they have in common is that a human life is often too short to produce true godliness.[15] But is that what one would want to say to the hundreds of millions of poor in India? One cannot, after all, say that they are "still falling short"? The lot of the reborn is a hard one. Certainly for the poor Asian masses, the idea of a rebirth causes great fear that the current life of poverty, disease and decline will be repeated. In India alone, according to the standards of the World Health Organization, 300 million people live below the poverty line. In that situation, rebirth is then not much more than "a repeat of death" or, as it is also called a "redeath," a return of constant worry about one's existence.[16]

The law of the *karma-samsara* has difficulty accounting for the historical and social interwovenness of human existence and the effect of that on the room for human decisions. Should the notion of settlements for one's own deeds not be flanked at least by other ideas? It is in this context that Samartha explicitly discusses the Christian idea of cross and resurrection and all concepts connected with that – substitution, forgiveness, dying and rising with Christ[17] – ideas that, as we saw, are not completely lacking in the Bhagavadgita but certainly do not predominate.

The "harsh" aspect of settling accounts in the notion of reincarnation is often underestimated in the West. The notion of rebirth may enjoy a certain popularity in the rich West: it invokes feelings of a second, better chance or of a repeat of a current good life. Over against the Christian idea of a final judgement resulting in heaven or hell, the idea of rebirth seems to be a mild "compromise."

Appearances are deceiving, however. At first glance, it seems that there is no place for heaven or hell in the cyclical view of reincarnation. But, actually, the Upanishads appear to have incorporated the old Vedic notions of heaven and hell, and the deceased are said to stay, according to their deeds, some time in hell or heaven before they are handed over to the wheel of rebirth or ultimately enter the freedom of a final reality (*brahman*) after many reincarnations. In short, our deeds do follow us, but there can be a certain catharsis in the intermediate phase of a heaven and hell and, when the deceased arrive at the moon as their first accommodation on the journey after death, there also seems to be a certain moment of choice (Chandogya Upanishad 5:3, 1–10 and Kausitaki Upanishad 1:1–7).[18]

Just as Buddhism includes the notion of a future ("Messianic") *buddha*, the *maitreya buddha*, Hinduism also has a future *avatara*, Kalki(n), who has often been depicted with Buddha since 400–500 before Christ. Both are thus seen as the final *avataras* (in a sequence of ten) of Vishnu. Buddha is the one who prepares the way for Kalki(n), the restorer, completer of the whole universe. Depictions of him (preferably brandishing his sword, riding on a stallion) sometimes evoke the image of the apocalyptic rider from the Book of Revelation in the Bible.

The role that is attributed to those *avataras* makes clear that the idea that the good will not automatically be victorious over evil was widespread.

Free, independent divine intervention is needed. Krishna observes in the Bhagavadgita: "If ever my work had an end, these worlds would end in destruction, confusion would reign within all and this would be the death of all being" (3:24 and 9:19).

The question with respect to the *avatara* in the above discussion that arises as most central is that of the importance of the mediator's being completely human. There are a number of parallels between the roles of Jesus and Krishna that can be drawn. The most prominent is the *motivation* for both their ways of acting: *compassion*, *mercy*. But there are also important differences and these are concentrated on the question of *the irrevocability of the divine surrender* to the situation in which a human being lives.[19] Christianity is unique in holding that God is known pre-eminently on the interface of the divine and the human and that interface has everything to do with the most radical human situation, namely that of suffering and death and all the issues of collective and personal guilt that are part of that. That situation is the most penetrating eye-opener to God. The Christian symbol of the cross is also intended to indicate that interface (intersection). Both God who approaches the human and the human who approaches God cannot avoid that situation. The existential reflection on this aspect of the encounter between God and human beings seems to be one of the exciting challenges for Christian-Hindu dialogue.

Jesus as *Guru*

The term *guru* has become so popular that it has also found acceptance outside of Hinduism (in particular in Buddhism) and even outside any religious context. Thus, for example, people call Johan Cruijff, a former famous Dutch football player and now a football analyst, a "football guru," which means that he not only has an extensive knowledge of the game of football but that he also has such great authority that he is listened to and, as an authority, has gathered a following.

This meaning of radiating knowledge and authority and gathering a following lies very close to the original use of the term in Hinduism. The *guru* (mostly male but also female sometimes) is a venerable teacher who embodies divine wisdom that is hidden from those who have not been initiated into this wisdom. He is the one who undoes the darkness of human ignorance and allows his students to share in the light of the knowledge that is necessary to escape rebirth. He himself has crossed the ocean of *samsara* (the wheel of rebirth) and now helps others reach the other side.[20] Without his instruction, this knowledge cannot be attained (Katha Upanishad 2:8–9). In the Taittiriya Upanishad (1:11.2) people are even instructed "to treat your teacher like a god," but that is not meant exclusively for *gurus*. Parents and guests are also to be treated as such to a certain extent.[21]

In the course of the history of Hinduism, the position of the *guru* seems to have evolved slowly from the teacher treated with respect and deference to the revered and even divinized teacher.[22] Especially in Shaiva Hinduism, the *guru* is truly the mediator of the divine, in this case of Shiva. The identification of the *guru* with Shiva can be so strong that the *guru* in fact becomes Shiva, who confers his wisdom (*jnana*) on (specific) people as grace. The power of the *guru*, which comes to expression in the conferring of the grace of divine wisdom, is thus entirely Shiva's power. As a human being, the *guru* withdraws and becomes merely the messenger (the spokesman) of Shiva's grace.[23] That is why Thomas Thangaraj also points out that the *guru* can act on different levels: on the interhuman level, as the intermediary of the divine and as a spiritual power that leads to mystical union.[24]

In this respect, the *gurus* of Shiva can be clearly distinguished from the *avataras* of Vishnu, even though there are also several *gurus* in Vaishnavism, which is strongly oriented to Vishnu. The *gurus* are a pan-Indian and, thus, also a Buddhist phenomenon,[25] but they occupy a specific place in Shaivism, which worships Shiva. Shiva manifests himself only in the form of *gurus* in temporary visits to people and does not assume any physical forms, as is the case with the *avataras* of Vishnu in the stories of their births and youths (for example, of Krishna). The *guru* passes on the divine power (*sakti*) as purely as fire without smoke provides warmth (Katha Upanishad 4:13).

The *guru* is the one who can speak about God because he himself has experienced him. He himself has travelled the road to the divine and can now show others the way. It is the way to liberation from the wheel of rebirth. The *guru* does not teach so much by words as by example. He does not provide knowledge so much as an experience. That is why the relationship with him is always personal. Because of the divine nearness that he radiates as a person he can also be revered.

In this context, Jesus can also be revered as *guru* and he can be called the true *guru*, the *sadguru*, because he embodies all qualities of a *guru*. After all, he is the way to the Father (John 14:6). He has revealed God, whom no one has ever seen, because he is alongside the Father. He can say, "I and the Father are one" (John 10:30). He can also speak from the experience of unity (John 3:31–32) and he can invite the disciples to share the same experience with him (John 6:57 and 17:21). Just as it is said of the *guru* that he is "the dike to the immortal" (Mundak Upanishad 2:2–5 and Svetasvatara Upanishad 6:19), so it is said of Jesus that he is the mediator between God and humanity (1 Tim. 2:5 and Heb. 9:15).

And just as it is said of Jesus that we have not chosen him but he us (John 15:16), so it can be said of the *guru* that his wisdom is not attained through instruction and study but that only he choses the *atman* that can attain this wisdom: only he "whose body chooses this self (*atman*) as his own" (Katha Upanishad 2:23).

Roberto de Nobili (1577–1659), one of the first Christian missionaries in southern India, in the country of the Tamils, already spoke of Jesus as the *guru* (and also, besides, as *avatara*). He called him the *sadguru*, the divine *guru*, a term that Hinduism already used for *gurus*. Especially in the way in which the risen Christ can be manifested in our midst through the work of the Holy Spirit, his life-giving Spirit (1 Cor. 15:45), the Indian Jesuit Xavier Irudayaraj sees a parallel with the manifestations of Shiva as *guru*. Jesus is the "inner Guru" who works in us (John 5:15). After his resurrection, it is the Spirit who enables us to preserve the internal connection with him.

But there is still a striking difference from the Hindu *guru*. The risen Jesus can never be seen apart from his earthly life and cross and resurrection. The risen Christ also refers immediately to that in his first appearances (John 20:25–28 and Luke 24:37–47). But a *guru* never calls others, as Jesus did, to follow his path of the cross and suffering (Mark 8:34–35 and Rom. 8:17) and to die and rise with him (Rom. 6:4). The *guru* can call others to deny themselves and to die to the old man consumed by his own desires, but this call does not involve a reference to the liberating "substitution for" another who only then frees the way for the surrender of the self.

Conclusions

Whereas in the question of Jesus as *avatara* the discussion focused mostly on the question of the extent to which an *avatara* can truly be seen as a human being, the question with respect to Jesus as *guru* focuses on the question of whether a guru can truly be seen as divine. In the one case, the suspicion of *docetism* (apparent humanity) lurks in the wings and, in the other, that of *adoptionism* (the exaltation of a human being to God).

The *avatara* idea has been developed primarily as a "descent" by Vishnu. The *guru* idea has been developed primarily, although certainly not exclusively, as an "ascent" to Shiva. The relationship to Shiva can take three forms: that of a mystical relation, a theophany, and an interhuman relation. In the first case, Shiva himself is essentially the *guru* and a human being experiences his power. It then concerns the inner *guru*. In the second case, it concerns an external, incidental encounter with Shiva.

And in the third case, the issue concerns a true teacher–student relationship with a human *guru* merely as a travel guide. The human being must make the journey himself. In the last case there is no (ontological) relationship between Shiva and the *guru*. The role of the human *guru* here is purely functional. He does not point to himself but refers beyond himself. The *guru* can rise to a great height in this process.

Instead of focusing on the observation that the *guru* himself does not act as a subsitute for those who follow him and is fundamentally different from Jesus in this regard, we can, following Thomas Thangaraj, take up another line of thought and conceive of Jesus as a "crucified" *guru*. We thus consciously transcend the Hindu concept of the *guru*. Such a transformation of the familiar image of the *guru* can be very meaningful with a view to discussing the meaning of Jesus' cross in a Hindu context.[26]

In the call to self-emptying of this *guru*, his own self-emptying on the cross is included as a crucial element. Because of that, a considerable change occurs in the original notion of *guru*. Here a *double transformation* takes place. For Indians, Jesus' relation as a *guru* to his followers is more intense than can be expressed by any other image (rabbi, lord, etc.). Thus, for them, the *guru* Jesus changes from a distant "Lord" into an intimate teacher. That is the change that occurs on the Christian side. At the same time, for them the intimate teacher changes into a teacher who not only "loses himself" in his own devotion to the divine but who also – and even primarily – "loses himself" in devotion to his followers. His self-emptying is thus an *inclusive self-emptying* that also involves his students in his resurrection. That is also a change in the Hindu concept of the *guru*.

In the case of Jesus, the initiation rites between *guru* and student become the initiation rites of the church, i.e. the sacraments of baptism and communion. In those rites dying and rising with Christ are central, regardless of status or caste. Our old Adam must die in order for us to rise with the new Adam, Jesus. In these initiation rites, all initiation classifications that are associated with the *guru*–student relationship are questioned. Because of their own theological content, baptism and communion simply exclude the caste system.

By speaking of the "crucified *guru*" and connecting his message directly to the content of the central sacraments of baptism and communion, the concept of *guru* can then be given a socio-ethical dimension.[27] With this intention, Thangaraj joins a tendency seen in several Indian theologians. They are searching for images native to India for integrating the liberating aspect of Jesus into the Hindu notions of *avatara* and *guru*. Sometimes, as with the social-critical Jesuit, Sebastian Kappen, that intention is articulated in a critical attitude towards cyclical thinking, which is inherent to the Hindu way of thought.[28] For that matter, a form of "prophetic criticism" is also possible within that cyclical thinking of Hinduism, as is apparent from the critique of social abuses in the *bhakti* tradition.[29]

As soon as the comparison of Jesus with the figure of the *avatara* or *guru* is made, the question arises sooner or later whether such a comparison is compatible with Jesus' uniqueness. After all, there are many *avataras* and many *gurus*, but only one Jesus. This question arises also whenever Jesus is compared with a *bodhisattva*, ancestor or healer.

Sometimes an answer to the question is sought by calling Jesus the *sadguru*, the true *guru*. In Part VIII we will see that the same approach is sometimes chosen in Africa for speaking about Jesus as ancestor: Jesus is the "ancestor *par excellence*" or the "proto-ancestor." Jesus becomes a very special guru, ancestor, etc. If the approach lies within the framework of what we called a *double transformation* in Chapter 2, it can be a fruitful approach. It would then illustrate how concepts change when applied to Jesus and how Jesus also changes through them. But if all emphasis comes to lie on the indeed very particular character of Jesus' being a *guru*, ancestor, etc., then there is nothing more to compare and Jesus is essentially compared with Jesus.

But the purpose of a comparison is always to acquire a new point of view. By calling Jesus *guru*, a new aspect of the relationship to Jesus is revealed in the midst of other differences, i.e. an extremely intense teacher–student relationship that transcends the biblical images for the teacher–student relationships known thus far. Thus, a new dimension of Jesus is revealed that was not very well known to us up to that point, whereas that dimension is entirely in line with the way in which the New Testament speaks of Jesus as teacher (rabbi).

The fact that there are always several *avataras* and *gurus* in Hinduism, just as there are several *bodhisattvas* in Buddhism and several ancestors in the African religions, etc. does not affect the issue of the uniqueness of Jesus. Is the uniqueness of Jesus threatened by calling him *kyrios* or *soter* (saviour)? In the Greco-Roman culture there were, after all, thousands of the former and dozens of the latter.

The question of uniqueness is, of course, a legitimate question. But it must be posed with respect to the substantial point of comparison. It must refer to the *new insight* that this kind of comparison yields. It is a *qualitative* question and not a quantitative. It inquires about the way in which new comparisons contribute to the revelation of the unique position of Jesus as mediator between God and human beings.

Part VII: The Indonesian Jesus

After a short sketch of the political-cultural context of Indonesian Christianity, we will look at a number of examples from the Moluccas so that we can map the specifics of the inculturation of the gospel in largely Muslim Indonesia. To that end, we will also offer a brief overview of the way in which the Qur'an talks about Jesus. Two divergent approaches will serve to illustrate how, in their interpretation of the meaning of Jesus, Indonesian theologians draw from both their common pre-Islamic and pre-Christian past and make their own contribution to the Christian–Muslim dialogue. Each overview of the "Indonesian Jesus' thus always leads us not only to the treasures of Indonesian culture but also to those in international Christian–Muslim dialogue.

The old Indonesian, religious stories lead us to the guru who paves the way to the water of life with his own life. The question of how such a life can be a "sign" of God's presence among us brings us immediately to the unique Indonesian contribution to the international Christian–Muslim dialogue.

12 The Indonesian Religious Context

The Political-Cultural Context

Indonesia has the largest Muslim population of any country in the world. More than eighty per cent of the approximately 215 million inhabitants are Muslim. About ten per cent, more than 20 million, are Christian. Since the arrival of Christianity in Indonesia in the sixteenth century, Muslims and Christians have lived more or less together in peace. The Christians are most strongly represented in the outlying areas on the edges of the Indonesian archipelago, in the east in New Guinea, the Moluccans, Timor and North and Central Sulawesi, and in the West in North Kalimantan and North Sumatra.

After the independence of Indonesia, many were surprised that Christianity's significance increased rather than decreased. It should have been obvious that, as a "foreign" religion of the colonial powers, Christianity would have difficulty surviving and perhaps also decrease with respect to numbers. But the opposite happened. After the departure of the Dutch, Christianity increased faster in size than it had during the centuries that the Dutch had been present.[1] That means that the churches in Indonesia have become real Indonesian churches and that they also share in all the tensions and conflicts that accompany religion in Indonesia.

Since the proclamation of the Republic of Indonesia on 17 August 1945, maintaining the unity of the republic has been a constant source of concern for the Indonesian government. The five principles of the state ideology, *pancasila* (one God, humanity, national unity, democracy and social justice), must be the basis for that unity under the slogan "Many but One" (*Bhineka Tunggal Ika*). The question here is not so much how much difference this unity can tolerate but rather how much difference is necessary to guarantee the unity. After all, since the beginning it has been clear in the new republic that the state of unity would survive not only religiously but primarily ethnically only if a large degree of plurality was guaranteed. The Republic of Indonesia covers such a large area with so many different cultures that it is impossible to group them under one denominator.[2]

The official state ideology is accepted particularly by the Christians, because it does not express any preference for a certain religion and therefore does not support the introduction of *sharia* (Muslim law) as the constitutional law. But after more than fifty years, this ideology is under immense pressure. In fact, the majority religion is very much favoured by the Indonesian government. Tensions between Muslims and Christians flare up regularly in Indonesia, primarily in Central and South Sulawesi and on Ambon, and there have been hundreds – and on Ambon even thousands – of victims.[3] Attempts are sometimes made, such as during Suharto's New Order, to give *pancasila* an exclusive Islamic character by arguing that the first principle ("Belief in the one and only God") can refer only to (the Islamic) Allah because he alone is one.[4]

Both the threatened minority situation and the actual, often violent conflicts have not passed Indonesian Christian theology by – and this also applies to content. Although direct connections cannot be indicated straightforwardly and all kinds of other factors often play a role, it nevertheless seems undeniable that it is very much in the interest of Christian theology to remain "on speaking terms" with the theologians of the majority religion. Because of the power factor – the Muslims have almost always been in the majority – this can be a confusing factor in the theological dialogue. But it would not be fair to disqualify the Indonesian dialogue between Christians and Muslims from the start by referring to unequal power relationships.

That dialogue can also be a unique opportunity, if there are minimum guarantees for the limitation of external political influence. As long as there is a reasonably functioning democracy in Indonesia, the guarantees are more or less present and there is no reason to doubt the sincere character of the dialogue between Muslims and Christians. Just as was the case in the preceding chapters on Asia, here also we can show only a few examples from the broad spectrum of Indonesian theology of new meanings that are attributed to Jesus in the Indonesian context. It is not an accident that the examples come primarily from Java and the Moluccas because theology there has been done mostly in interaction with international developments. That gave people the candor to take even more radical steps in the direction of an Indonesian theology of its own than has happened elsewhere in Indonesia. Java and the Moluccas are thus certainly not representative but perhaps indicative of certain developments that can be expected in Indonesia as a whole.

Muslims and Christians in Indonesia also have much in common among all their differences. They share the same pre-Islamic and pre-Christian Indonesian, religious and cultural history and see themselves as confronted with the same problems of poverty, corruption, overpopulation (especially on Java) and dictatorship.[5] They sometimes simply adopt things from each other without further ado. A case in point is the choice of the name of God as Allah. Just as in Africa and Korea, in Indonesia as well Christians use the name of the supreme divinity in the area for the Christian God. For Christians, that means that God was addressed by the usual Muslim name of *Allah* since the sixteenth century; this can also be observed among Arab Christians as well. Conversely, many Muslims saw no harm in celebrating the Christian Christmas, which also occurs in Lebanon.

In 1981 a special *fatwa* (condemnation) by the National Indonesian Muslim Scholars' Council was needed to forbid Muslims to continue this practice. The reason for this was the suggestion of the implicit recognition of Jesus' divine sonship that could result from such participation.[6] Christmas is a very sensitive issue precisely because the "Christmas story" in the Qur'an, the nativity story of Isa in *Sura* 19:16–36, does report the special character of Jesus' birth but explicitly avoids calling him the son of Allah (v. 35).

After the minister for religious affairs had forbidden the dissemination of this *fatwa*, in the same year another measure was enacted in the form of a ministerial letter in which a distinction was made between "closed," strictly liturgical religious gatherings of the five officially recognized religions (Islam, Roman Catholicism, Protestantism, Hinduism and Buddhism; note: Roman Catholicism and Protestantism are seen as two different religions in Indonesia!), and more incidental gatherings that are open to everyone. The religious gatherings in question were mentioned explicitly in the letter.[7]

For that matter, at the present time there are various combined gatherings of Christians and Muslims in many places around Christmas. Moreover, the tradition still exists that the (Islamic) president of Indonesia is the first to light a candle on the Christmas tree in the stadium of Jakarta.

Christians and Muslims were confronted with the same questions with respect to the *adat* as well, i.e. the old, pre-Islamic and pre-Christian rituals and practices. Crucial to the success of the Christian mission was the attitude of the missionaries to these *adat*. The Moluccan anthropologist Simon Ririhena speaks in this context of the "adatization" of Islam and Christianity and means thereby the process of the integration of the *adat* into these two religions. Only if there was a fusion between *adat* and Islam or between *adat* and Christianity could these religions be considered "native."[8]

In fact, the relationship to the *adat* is still decisive for the way in which these two religions can be experienced as authentically Indonesian. The issue with respect to the *adat* is not exclusively a matter of a historical phenomenon – the relation with the old Indonesian religions that sometimes include a number of Buddhist and Hindu elements as well – but also that of the unwritten rules that are protected by the ancestors and order present life.[9] In recent decades, it is primarily the theologians from the Moluccan Theological Council (*Moluks Theologisch Beraad*) in the Netherlands who hammered away at establishing even more emphatically this connection between *adat* and Christianity. After all, the necessity of this connection is often denied by Christian missionaries in Indonesia and counteracted – when it does arise – "from below."

It is precisely this great importance of integrating old Moluccan and Christian practices and rituals to which the theologians of the Moluccan Theological Council are pointing. For them, this turn to their own culture marks a new phase in their theological existence in the Netherlands. Instead of the sense – fostered for decades – of living in exile in the Netherlands, waiting for a return (exodus) to the promised land, the Moluccans are now entering a situation of a new balance in which they are adjusting, on the one hand, to remaining permanently in the Netherlands but are identifying, on the other, more strongly than ever with their own Moluccan culture. The "in-between" situation of the Moluccans in the Netherlands is thus a source of creativity in which they are conscious primarily of the ancestor dimension of their exodus theology.[10] Biblically speaking, the God of the exodus is, after all, the God of Abraham, Isaac and Jacob. It is the God who fulfils his covenant with Abraham. In line with this covenantal approach, the theologians of the Moluccan Theological Council point to the role of their own ancestors.[11] At the same time, they are "rediscovering" their own old Moluccan religious culture and are relating that to reflection on their own faith. Thus, for example, they point to the custom of cleaning the whole village once a year – often during Advent – (*tjutji negeri*) according to the wishes of the ancestors, to the offertory plate (*piring natzar*) found in each house on which coins wrapped in paper are placed for all family members, and to the centuries-old connection between villages (*pela*).[12]

The same discussion is now going on between the theologians of the Moluccan Theological Council and a number of ministers within the Moluccan community in the Netherlands as that between the churches in the Moluccas and the theological faculty of the Christian university (UKIM: Universitas Kristen Indonesia Maluku) on Ambon. The Moluccan Museum on Ambon and the Moluccan Museum in Utrecht in the Netherlands play an indirect role in that discussion. The issue in this discussion is whether the pre-Islamic or pre-Christian history of the Moluccas belongs to the "heathen" past or contains a great treasure of religious wisdom that is vital for the contemporary proclamation of the gospel on the Moluccans. The discussion by the Moluccan Theological Council on the offertory plate in the home, the *piring natzar*, can be seen as a first cautious attempt to make a bridge between that "heathen" past and the Christian present. We will look at this example in more detail, because it is an example of the inculturation debate that is now taking place within Indonesian Christianity. Examples of the same debate can be cited from other areas in Indonesia. One could think here of, among other things, the discussions concerning the funeral rites of the Torajas on Sulawesi.

The example of the *piring natzar* is thus only one among many. The *piring natzar* is usually located in the parents' (bed)room. It is an offertory plate containing coins wrapped in paper on which the names of the family members are written. On the evening before important family events, all family members pray at the *piring natzar*, which has been usually moved to the living room for that purpose. This also happens on New Year's Day, birthdays, weddings, before and after church services and at a number of other important events. On these occasions extra coins, with or without a text or any other special statement, are added. On Sundays, preferably when communion is celebrated, the coins wrapped in paper are deposited in the collection box and replaced by new ones at home. Young couples will be given their own *piring natzar*, consecrated by the minister, at their weddings. It often already contains three wrapped coins – for the Father, the Son and the Holy Spirit – and two are added for the young couple. Although each family has its own *piring natzar*, the one in the parents' or ancestral home, the *rumah tua*, is given a special place. After all, all the high and low points of the family's life have occurred around the *piring natzar*. For the *piring natzar* is the place *par excellence* to thank God in times of prosperity and to ask him for help in times of adversity, whether or not accompanied by a vow. In addition, it is also a place where people can retreat for personal meditation at the beginning or end of the day. It is a place where both the connection to God and the ancestors is most intensely experienced.

The *piring natzar* is also called the Moluccan family altar. The money that is deposited on Sundays in the collection box (*peti derma*) in the church is not simply removed from one's wallet but has a prior history as a coin on the family altar. It has already been dedicated to something, sacrificed for something. The Moluccan religious culture is not conceivable without this dedication or sacrifice ritual. The connection with God is nowhere experienced so intensely as it is around this sacrifice ritual. In fact, the connection with the broadly defined family also arises around this offertory plate: both the living and the dead. Thus, the *piring natzur* is also a place where the *adat* constitutes the channel through which the Christian faith flows. For the Moluccans, it is a gracious sign through which God wishes to dwell among people. Human gifts are offered on this offertory plate in the light of the sacrificial lamb that Christ embodies for Christians. It is an offertory plate from the past that is experienced as a gift in the present. As such, it refers to the *tete manis* (dear ancestor) Jesus who assists the whole world with his cross, his sacrificial pole, as the centre pole (*tiang laki-laki*) in the traditional Moluccan home supports the whole roof.

The example of the *piring natzar* shows how Christians take up old Moluccan practices into their faith. The discussion among the Moluccans on these practices occurs primarily on the question of the extent to which the *piring natzar* is accorded an independent, magical effect and if the *tete manis* is simply the "dear ancestor" or the "dear God," Jesus Christ. In fact, the two forms merge together, which is why Ririhena can also speak of Jesus as the ancestor *par excellence*.[13]

The appeal to old Moluccan religious practices does not occur only within the framework of the Christian proclamation of faith but also within the framework of the dialogue with Islam. That dialogue is very much needed on the Moluccas. In recent years, thousands have been killed as a result of the troubles between Christians and Muslims, and hundreds of thousands have been driven from their villages. It is against this background that reference is made to the value of the centuries-old *pela* covenant between Moluccan villages.[14] This covenant transcends the oppositions between Muslims and Christians and can be concluded between a Christian village and an Islamic village without any problem.

A *pela* between two villages arises when the village chiefs meet to conclude an official peace. They drink together from a half-coconut of rice wine and sprinkle a few drops of their blood into the wine. During such a ceremony, the ancestors are invoked to act as witnesses and are asked to watch over the *pela* rules. A village can make a *pela* with several villages whereby each *pela* has its own, unique character. Mutual help in times of need, assistance in large projects such as building houses, a mosque or a church, providing food to a visitor or a traveller from a neighbouring *pela* village, and the mutual prohibition against marriage between members of two *pela* villages are all usually part of a *pela*. If these rules are transgressed, it is expected that the ancestors will intervene.

Just as the blood of Jesus is a sign for Christians of their connectedness with his death and resurrection, so the official conclusion of a covenant with rice wine containing a few drops of blood from their village chiefs is the ultimate sign of peaceful unity for Moluccans. And just as the bread and wine at communion symbolize Jesus' presence, so the blood of the village chiefs symbolize the beneficial presence of the ancestors. In this case as well Jesus can take on the characteristics of the ancestor. He is the ancestor *par excellence* who watches over the *pela*. Jesus is then their peace, their *pela*.[15] Jesus is the *tete manis*, the dear God, not only for Christians but also for Muslims. Within this framework, the Moluccan theologian Elshel Maspaitella proposes that both Muslims and Christians use the old Moluccan name for God, *tete manis* (literally: dear grandfather).[16]

This striving for a joint basis for faith is not limited to the Moluccans. It also fits in with the way in which religion in Indonesia, and primarily on

Java, is experienced. The ability of the Javanese religious culture to absorb other elements is often pointed out here. It is a culture that is, as it were, already syncretistic in nature and can also deal with the differences and similarities between Islam and Christianity in an entirely unique way.[17] To understand that properly, especially with respect to the meanings that are attributed to Jesus, we should first look at the contemporary Islamic context.

Tawhid and Jesus' Divine Sonship

For Indonesian Christianity, as a minority in a Muslim country in which the confession of Allah's *tawhid* (being one) is the most important expression of faith, reflection on the relationship of Jesus to God is one of the most urgent issues. Without determining Jesus' position with respect to the famous *Sura* 112:1–4, no serious form of dialogue is possible. That verse states: "In the name of Allah, most benevolent, ever-merciful. Say: He is God the one the most unique, God the immanently indispensable. He has begotten no one, and is begotten of none. There is no one comparable to Him." Because of this *sura*, Muslims will always be inclined to accuse Christians of *shirk*, i.e. of associating Allah with something non-divine, because of the position Jesus occupies with respect to God in Christianity. For Islam, that is the greatest sin conceivable, the only sin that, according to *Sura* 4:116, is unforgivable.

In line with the confession of the *tawhid* of Allah, the Qur'an also explicitly denies that Jesus was the son of God and calls such an idea blasphemy. For Allah has no son. If Allah did have sons, then he would have had to have them via a woman and Allah must not be conceived in such human terms (*Sura* 4:171; 5:72–73; 6:100–101; 9:30–31; 18:4–5; 19:35 and 92; 23:91). But this explicit denial – also quoted from Jesus' own mouth (*Sura* 5:116) – does not mean that the Qur'an does not attribute a special place to Jesus' proximity to God. *Sura* 3:45 includes him among those who are "placed next" to God, and *Sura* 5:19 warns believers that they are wrong in often thinking that no messenger of good news and warnings has come to them. Jesus, the son of Marjam (Mary), who is often called *Isa* or *Masih* (messiah) in the Qur'an, is here called "a bearer of good tidings."

But he is a messenger, a prophet, in a long line of prophets from whom he is not distinguished in any essential way. He is included in the line of Abraham, Ishmael, Isaac, Jacob and the patriarchs, Moses and the prophets (*Sura* 2:136 and 285; 3:84; 4:163; 5:75; 19:30). Jesus was nothing more than a servant, an example for the sons of Israel (*Sura* 43:59 and 4:172). He was "only an apostle of Allah" but, nonetheless, also "his command" and "spirit from him" (*Sura* 4:171). Jesus is seen as the one who confirmed in his teaching (*indjil*) what was told about him in the Torah (*Sura* 3:50; 5:46). His virgin birth (*Sura* 3:47 and 59; 19:20–21) and his ascent into heaven (*Sura* 4:158) do place him in a unique position, but that does not detract at all from his "normal" humanity. Just like his mother, he had to eat to stay alive (*Sura* 5:75). Jesus' crucifixion is explicitly denied in the Qur'an: Jesus was not crucified and killed by the Jews but was raised by Allah into his glory (*Sura* 4:157–58). Allah protected him against the Jews by taking him up into heaven (*Sura* 3:54–55).

It is self-evident that in this interpretation every foundation of the Christian doctrine of the Trinity disappears. *Sura* 4:171 and 5:73 state emphatically that in reference to Allah one is to think not of three gods but of one God, whereas *Sura* 5:116 gives the impression that the Christian doctrine of the Trinity consists of the tri-unity of Father, Son and Mary. From the fact that the Qur'an understands the doctrine of the Trinity as tritheism (three gods), one can see how difficult it was for Christianity in the seventh century to avoid the impression that it had in mind three gods when speaking of God the Father, God the Son and God the Holy Spirit.

Even though the monotheistic framework has never actually been questioned in a fundamental way, an adequate formulation of the doctrine of the Trinity has always had a difficult history. People read in the Bible that God's revelation occurred in a threefold way, but how were these three ways to be distinguished from and connected with one another? Are we talking about "persons" in relation to one another, "forms," "modes of existence," or "energies" of the one God? All of the above were considered in the history of doctrine – sometimes they were eagerly embraced and sometimes shoved aside as heresy.

In any case, it is clear that in the history of doctrine, people sought diligently for alternatives for speaking about "persons." The original meaning of the Latin concept of *persona*, "mask," moved quite quickly into the background. Since the Middle Ages, the concepts "person" and "individual" have become more closely interwoven. This development rendered the concept of person less well-suited to clarify the distinction that the Christian tradition wanted to apply to God in the Christian tradition. If "person" can only mean "individual," the doctrine of the Trinity will always be subject to the charge of tritheism.

But the need to talk about differentiations within the one concept of God is, biblically speaking, completely legitimate. One could even say that abandoning such distinctions would give rise to great problems with respect to understanding the Bible. That can be easily illustrated via the role of Jesus as the Son in respect to God the Father. Especially in the gospel of John, Jesus is called the Son of God several times, but Jesus himself rejects a complete identification of Jesus with God. Like no other, he reveals the true face of his Father, but that does not mean that he is identical with his Father.

We will repeat here once again the key texts that we quoted when discussing the views of Japanese theologian S. Yagi in Chapter 7. On the one hand, as Son, Jesus clearly identifies himself with the Father:

> Anyone who has seen me has seen the Father. How can you say, 'Show us the Father'? Don't you believe that I am in the Father, and that the Father is in me? The words I say to you are not just my own. Rather, it is the Father, living in me, who is doing his work. Believe me when I say that I am in the Father and the Father is in me; or at least believe on the evidence of the miracles themselves. (John 14:9–11; also 17:21)

On the other hand, Jesus can also indicate an explicit distinction: "For I did not speak of my own accord, but the Father who sent me commanded me what to say and how to say it.... So whatever I say is just what the Father has told me to say" (John 12:49–50). Here the issue is clearly that of the one, Jesus, who obeys another, the Father.[18]

With respect to the Holy Spirit, a similar distinction is necessary. "God is Spirit," we read in John 4:24, but in that same gospel we read that the Spirit will be sent by Jesus (John 16:7, 13), and in the story of Pentecost in Acts 2 it is stated in accordance with the Old Testament prophecy that God himself will pour out his Spirit. Here too a clear distinction can be indicated in the midst of a strong identification.

The distinction between Allah and the prophets in the Qur'an is undeniably clearer than the Bible's distinction between God and Jesus. But the Qur'an does contain some striking gradations, for example when Jesus' position is at issue. The Qur'an seems to display a certain ambiguity sometimes. With respect to Jesus, passages that put him on the same level as other prophets – "nothing other than" – are continually supplemented by passages that underscore his special character, which comes to expression in, among other things, his virgin birth and ascension into heaven. Along with Abraham, Noah, Moses, David, Mohammed and many other "prophets," Jesus is included among those who have been sent (*rasul*). In *Sura* 19:31 Jesus states frankly about himself: "And blessed me wherever I may be." That is why the way in which the Qur'an understands Jesus is sometimes paradoxically characterized as denying both Jesus' divinity and his "ordinary" humanity.[19]

The same ambiguous attitude also extends to Christians. Often characterized in both a positive and negative sense as "people of the Book," Christians are called "the closest in love" to Islam (*Sura* 5:82), but at the same time they are those who are guilty of the worst sin, namely undermining belief in the one God. But dialogue with them is not shunned

– both Jews and Christians are summoned: "O people of the Book, let us come to an agreement on that which is common between us, that we worship no one but God, and make none his compeer, and that none of us take any others for lord apart from God" (Sura 3:64).

Here as well we should pause a moment in connection with the Christian reference to Jesus as "Son of God." This expression is a well-known Old Testament expression that is used for kings (2 Sam. 7:14; 1 Chron. 17:13; Pss. 2:7 and 89:27–28) and the people of Israel as a whole (Exod. 4:22; Jer. 31:9, 20 and Hosea 11:1). The expression can have eschatological, Messianic characteristics and refer to a "royal Messiah" who is to be expected and can be called the "Son of God."

In Hellenistic culture the term has the same broad use for heroes like Dionysius and Heracles and philosophers like Pythagoras and Plato.[20] In the Old Testament, the expression refers to a special relationship with God and, in the case of the king, to the extent that the latter represents God to the people.

Within this widespread use of the term "Son of God," the term was given a unique connotation when applied to Jesus. His calling God father (abba) and the way in which he stimulated his disciples to follow him in his "experience of the father" contributed to this in an important way. In addition to all the passages cited earlier in the gospel of John on the Father–Son relationship, the other gospels also show that they attribute a special position to Jesus with respect to God by their use of the term "Son." Like no other, the Son knows the Father (Matt. 11:27; Luke 10:22); in the parable of the tenants, the assault on the Son ("the heir") is clearly the worst act (Matt. 21:33–41; Mark 12:1–9; Luke 20:9–16) and with respect to the knowledge of the last day, Jesus says that not even the Son is privy to that knowledge (Matt. 24:36; Mark 13:32). All these facts lead to no other conclusion than that a strong sense of "sonship" had a strong influence on Jesus' view of himself and that that is the basis for the authority with which he announces the coming of the kingdom of God. His birth does not play a strikingly major role in the question of the special aspect of his experience of sonship. His sonship is not connected specifically with one event but with four aspects of his existence: his pre-existence (his existence before his coming to earth) (John 1:14 and 18); his birth (Matt. 1:20; Luke 1:35); his baptism in the Jordan (Mark 1:11); and his resurrection (Acts 13:13; Heb. 5:5).[21]

The image that the Qur'an sketches of Jesus in no less than 99 verses confronts Christians with the question of how to articulate the divine nearness in Jesus without undermining the monotheism that it shares with Muslims and how to articulate Jesus' sacrifice on the cross so that it does not give rise to the image of a prophet forsaken by God.

13 Indonesian Images of Jesus

Two Approaches

Among the images of Jesus now articulated in Indonesia, a number of the same approaches surface time and again. Generally speaking, we see two divergent perspectives in the several variations: an approach that attempts to bridge the gulf between Christianity and Islam as much as possible by taking its starting point in concepts that it shares with the Muslims, and an approach that uses images from the religious tradition of Indonesia more or less as a bridge between Islam and Christianity. The first approach is called the dialogue approach and the second the contextual, even though we are of course aware that in Indonesia dialogue also has a strongly contextual character, and that the contextual approach on Java has certainly not lost sight of the aspect of dialogue. We have just stated that that approach even constitutes indirectly the bridge to dialogue. In the case of the contextual approach, we must point out that, sometimes, the "traditional Indonesian" can no longer be precisely distinguished from the Islamic. Indonesian Islam has sometimes (not always) simply become too Indonesian for that and the traditional Indonesian too Islamic. It is nevertheless meaningful to introduce this distinction for the sake of the bridge function.

It is clear that the two approaches can also give rise to the necessary questions. It should be asked critically if the Islamic interpretations of Jesus and the old Indonesian religions do not in fact determine the space for the "Indonesian Jesus." In a certain sense, that is in fact the case, as that was also the case with the New Testament Jesus and the early Christian Jesus. To put it in even stronger terms, the means for religious expression that were available at that time provided the contours for the image of Jesus.

But it was not for nothing that in Chapter 1 under the heading "Who Decides?" we also listed three criteria by which the Christian tradition could be judged. We called these criteria for the *catholicity of the church* and understood by that the interwovenness of Bible, church history and liturgy. Those three criteria – characteristic in fact of each religious community of transmission – must always be connected with one another and, for us, entail that each new meaning attributed to Jesus must be related to the way in which the church has read the Bible down through the ages, summarized the core of its own transmission, and celebrated the sacraments and the Christian feasts. These are not criteria that give a quick and ready answer, but they do yield – viewed over a not too brief period of time – a certain image (of Jesus). With respect to new Indonesian images of Jesus that arise in an Islamic context, it thus means that their "tenability" must be proven over time in the Indonesian churches and in global Christianity.

However different they may be, the two approaches cited above mark a new phase in Indonesian theology. They indicate the understanding that Christian theology in Indonesia can no longer be formulated without entering explicitly and constructively into dialogue with the Islamic context. It is this that distinguishes this form of theology from earlier forms of Indonesian theology that usually do take the traditional Javanese context into account but seldom discuss the Islamic context. And if they do discuss it, then it is usually as merely the opposite of Christianity.[1]

The Dialogue Approach

A good example of the first approach is found in an article that Stanley Rambitan, a Protestant theologian from Sulawesi, published in 2003 in the journal of the Reformed Ecumenical Council called "Jesus in Islamic Context of Indonesia." Here Rambitan concurs with recent, Indonesian Islamic interpretations of Jesus on the presupposition that new, Islamic interpretations of Jesus should also find a basis in the Christian tradition.[2]

Sometimes the appeal can be heard to come to a common interpretation of the nativity story about Jesus. Such a proposal has great topicality against the background of the *fatwa* we cited earlier. *Sura* 19:21 especially, where it is stated that Mary's child will be a sign (*aya*) by Allah for people as the personification of divine mercy, is a key text here.

Rambitan presents in detail the multifaceted image that the Qur'an sketches of Jesus.[3] The Qur'an uses many names to refer to Jesus. He is called *Isa* twenty-five times, often followed by the term *ibn Marjam*, son of Mary. Jesus can also be called *Masih*, the messiah. In addition, the Qur'an uses a large number of titles for the roles that Jesus fulfils: *nabi* (prophet), *rasul* (apostle), *abdi* (servant of God), *kalimah* (word of God), *ruh* (spirit of God), *aya* (sign) and *rahma* (blessing). The question is then of course: To what term or function does the Qur'an attach the greatest importance? Just as there is no simple answer to such a question posed to the New Testament, this is also the case with respect to the Qur'an.

Rambitan chose Quraish Shibab, a well-known scholar with a reputation for moderation in the contemporary Indonesian Muslim community, as a guide. Using Shibab's interpretations, he investigates a number of key texts in the Qur'an and, with him, comes to the conclusion that Jesus cannot be identified with the Word of God in the Qur'an (*Sura* 3, 45), that he was graced more than other prophets with the Spirit of God but was not himself the Spirit of God (*Sura* 2:87), that he was raised by Allah from the death that his persecutors had plotted (*Sura* 3:55) and that the identification of Jesus with the son of Mary shows that the Qur'an did not view him as divine (*Sura* 5:17, 72). On the basis of this interpretation of the Qur'an, Rambitan establishes that Quraish Shibab considers Jesus to be a person with a special position, special gifts and an exceptional role but not divine. For that matter, one can ask if it is so clear that Jesus cannot also be referred to as Word of God and Spirit of God in the Qur'an (*Sura* 3:39, 45; 4:71).

The approach of the Protestant theologians Rambitan and Rakhmat is not a confessional position. We find the same approach in Roman Catholic Indonesian theology. A good example is the Javanese Roman Catholic theologian Johannes Banawiratma. His approach is the same, but his conclusion is different. Indeed, if the Islamic reference framework is taken as the starting point, the interpretation of the meaning of Jesus will always go in one of two directions: either to the extreme of emphasizing his humanity at the expense of his divinity or to that of emphasizing his role as interpreter of the divine at the expense of his humanity. Rambitan and Rakhmat are inclined to go in the first direction and Banawiratma in the second.

The latter begins an article on the question of an "Indonesian" Jesus with a reference to the reactions of parishioners to the sketch of a fresco in the church of Saint Anthony in Yogyakarta. Two reactions struck him. The first indicated that, in the judgement of the parishioners, Jesus and Mary could not be depicted as Indonesians. They had to be represented as "foreigners," as Jews of their time. All other figures in the fresco, i.e. Nicodemus, the guests at the wedding in Cana and many others could be depicted as Indonesians. Further, it was indicated that it was the divinized Jesus "exalted" by God who was their inspiration and not so much the earthly life of Jesus of Nazareth. That earthly life was seen as a transitional situation.[4]

Banawiratma concludes from these two reactions that God's becoming human in Jesus is interpreted primarily as the incarnation of the Father and not so much as that of the Son. Jesus is God the Father in human form. This view is close to what the early church rejected as the heresy of docetism (the denial of Jesus' true humanity) or of Monophysitism (emphasis on only one nature, i.e. the divine). This emphasis has everything to do, he argues in a matter-of-fact way, with what people have heard in the church for years.[5] Has that preaching then been "heretical"?

Without Banawiratma himself probably being aware of this, in presenting these reactions he broaches an important point that merits further research. It concerns the question whether the "classical" preaching in the Indonesian church displayed more traces of the strict monotheism of Islam than people wanted to admit. After all, the strong "divinization" of Jesus seems, at first glance, to be directly in conflict with the Islamic denial of his divinity, but if the "divinization" in fact comes down to Jesus and God merging into one another, then one has arrived at the Islamic position that God is one. The Christian reservation at seeing Jesus as a human being could reflect the Islamic fear of connecting the human and the divine too closely to each other.

That Mary should not be depicted as Indonesian has nothing to do with her divinity, as is the case of Jesus, but precisely with her special humanity. In Indonesian Roman Catholicism Mary has a major role as a human being who brings believers close to God.[6] In relation to Jesus and Mary, the question is thus of direct contact with God or direct contact with a special, gifted person. That brings Banawiratma to the question of how we should understand the mediation, the encounter, between God and human beings.

Banawiratma argues that Islam itself has a way of bridging the gulf between God and human beings that is comparable with the role of Jesus in Christianity. In the Qur'an, according to him, Jesus is also not identical with the Word of God (*kalimat Allah*). The absolute Word of God is exclusively the Qur'an itself. That divine word can be heard and recited by people. When believers pray using the divine verses, their prayer is a human prayer. Their words are then human words. In that way the Qur'an mediates between the divine and the human without allowing them to merge. Jesus fulfils this role in Christianity. Banawiratma thus draws a parallel between Jesus and the Qur'an. But it is no more than a parallel. In any case, it is not a similarity of which Muslims would approve, for it should be clear that the Muslims would never put Jesus on the same level as the divine Word, as they do with the Qur'an.

For them, that could be done only if Jesus would, in fact, be considered to be completely divine. In fact, we see Banawiratma going in that direction indeed when he searches for an answer to the question of how the divine Word can become a word in human mouths. According to the Bible, that can happen only through the Holy Spirit: "No one can say, 'Jesus is Lord,' except by the Holy Spirit" (1 Cor. 12:3). Banawiratma thus arrives at a view of the Trinity as one God who speaks in his Word (Jesus) that we understand through the Holy Spirit. He sees Islam articulating the same thing in speaking of Allah, the Qur'an and God's power (spirit). In his view, if Christians understand the Trinity in this way, they would show that they took the Islamic critique to heart and all misunderstanding with respect to worshipping three gods would have been removed.[7] But it should be clear that the price for this accommodation is high: Jesus' humanity is seen exclusively in his influence on people through the agency of the Holy Spirit. There is nothing human about him any more.

Banawiratma's interpretation is one of the many examples of the difficulty Indonesian theologians have with the doctrine of the Trinity. For Banawiratma, the way out is the parallel between the Qur'an and Jesus.

The Contextual Approach

The Protestant theologian Andreas Yewangoe, from Sumba and now professor of dogmatics at Jakarta Theological Seminary, finds a way out through regauging Indonesian theology by means of images from the old Indonesian religions. Yewangoe is thus a representative of the second approach. He introduces the traditional Indonesian religions more or less as a third party in the hope of being able to build a bridge between Muslims and Christians. It is the same approach that we encountered in the members of the Moluccan Theological Council. He thus argues in two directions. He is searching for new images that are closer to the experiential world of Indonesian believers and at the same time can help Muslims better understand why Christians speak of God in a threefold way.

As an example, he cites a study by P. O. Tobing on the belief in one God among the Bataks on Sumatra.[8] Their chief God, *Ompu Tuan Mula Jadi na Bolon*, is called the lord of the upper world, *Tuan Bubi na Bolon*, lord of the middle world, *Ompu Silaon na Bolon* and lord of the underworld, *Tuan Bibi na Bolon*. He is *Debata na Tolu*, the divinity who is three and yet one. The one God can be differentiated in accordance with his functions. Yewangoe poses the question whether one can speak of the Christian Trinity in this way as well.[9]

Yewangoe follows the same type of reasoning with respect to the sonship of God. In the Timorese translation of the Bible, the term *Neno Anan* is used for Jesus Christ, Son of God. This term means Son of Heaven and is used on Timor as a greeting for kings. It is then given the meaning "prince of heaven" because it is believed that the prince receives power from above. That makes the term extremely suitable for Jesus because he, after all, also received the power of the Holy Spirit from above.[10] It concerns a human being here who is, as it were, "extolled." In his earthly existence, he also received power from above and in that way was increasingly distinguished from his fellow human beings. Such an approach is today called a "low" Christology, because it begins from "below." In contrast, Banawiratma's approach is an expression of "high" Christology: a "high" Christology portrays a Jesus who descends from divine heights and a "low" Christology describes a Jesus who rises from the depths of human existence. The former emphasizes *descent*, expressed in the *incarnation*, and the other emphasizes *ascent*, *rising up*, expressed in *adoption* as a son of God.

Another example of such a "low" Christology is found among the Mee Christians in West Papua. These Papuas, which became Christian at the end of the 1930s, have used an entirely unique terminology since the 1970s to express the meaning of Jesus. Their concept of salvation, *mobu*, is connected with all life situations in which satisfaction and satiation are experienced. That concerns, in the first place, not only food but also a good harvest, recovery from illness, health, peace and harmony. *Mobu* is received when the leading of *dimi* (the wise understanding) that God (*Gaiye*) gives is followed. This wisdom (*dimi*) can also be called *wauwa* (the eldest brother) and subsequently also become personalized in a concrete wise man, who can be called *iniuwai*, our wise brother. In principle, everyone who has this *dimi* wisdom can spread *mobu* and thus become a *wauwa* and become recognized as an *iniuwa*. He then serves as a moral example. In this way of thinking, Jesus can very easily become the *iniuwa par excellence*, the source of *mobu*.

The Roman Catholic theologian Neles Tebay, who belongs to the Mee tribe, points out that the Mee Christians are very well aware of the differences and overlappings between their traditional *wauwas* and Jesus. Here as well the process of *double transformation* can be observed. From the start their Jesus has something of the "holistic" aspect of a true *wauwa* and includes both the earthly material and the spiritual world within himself. But, in addition, he breaks through the image of the traditional *wauwa* because his influence extends beyond the limits of the tribe and the boundary of death. Each element of *quid pro quo* and force that surrounds the image of the traditional *wauwa* is lacking in their image of Jesus as *wauwa*. For that reason, the Mee Christians never call Jesus simply *wauwa* and not even *iniuwai* but only *iniuwai ibo*, the great eldest brother. They thus make the step that goes beyond the tradition.

They see Jesus' death in self-sacrifice as a confirmation of his self-sacrificial life. Only the greatest of all eldest brothers share that destiny. They see such a death as being of a piece with the message of love that they personified in their lives. Jesus can be full of love because he knows the *dimi* of his Father. For the Mee Christians, everyone is a child of God. For them, the term "Son of God" is not a special term. Someone is exceptional only if he can be called "the son of his father's *dimi*." It is then that there is true like-*mind*edness: then the son follows the will of the father and he can be seen as the one who reveals the will of the father.[11] We will see in the next chapter that this image of Jesus is close to the African image of Jesus as the one who bestows life. It is also striking that, in contrast to what Yewangoe stated about the Bataks on Sumatra and about the Timorese, here the meaning of Jesus from the perspective of a dialogue with Muslims is lacking completely. This must be put down to the dominant Christian character of West Papua. Muslims do not, literally, come into view in West Papua.

Thus, it is not always so that the traditional religious images are used for the purpose of constructing a bridge for dialogue with Muslims. The use of the traditional images has its own dynamic as well, apart from the dialogue between Muslims and Christians. More examples of this can be found primarily in West Papua. Thus the Protestant theologian Marthinus Mawene, who comes from there, points to the inclination of the Koreri people around Biak to see Jesus as the *Manseren Koreri*, the Master of the Koreri, and even as the *Manseren Manggundi*, the Master himself, i.e. the creator (*Manggundi*), God himself. In their *Koreri* myth – a myth with clear Messianic overtones – they expect the return of the *Manseren Koreri* and, as a sign of this return, the dead will arise. The identification with Jesus, including his divine origin, is obvious.

Mawene also sees such an identification occurring in the Sawi tribe in South Papua. He sees a parallel with Jesus' sacrifice primarily in the custom of handing over a peace child, a *Tarop Tim*, to a hostile tribe as a guarantee of peace. Only when Jesus could be viewed as a *Tarop Tim* did the Sawi tribe turn to the Christian faith in complete conviction – expressed in, among other things, their own hymns.

The inclination to see Jesus as *Manseren Koreri* and as *Tarop Tim* has led to a great deal of discussion in the church in West Papua. A breakthrough in this kind of discussion was reached only when it was recognized that these were not cases of seamless identification but of creative synthesis, in which, in addition to the recognition of overlappings, there is also room for the recognition of differences.[12]

Contextual Theology as Interreligious Dialogue

It is clear that these theologians from West Papua follow a much different path in the area of the contextualization of their faith than the theologians who have to articulate their faith in the midst of a large and sometimes threatening Muslim majority. Rambitan is a clear-cut example of the latter category of theologians. His approach places us, in fact, in the midst of Christian–Muslim dialogue. That fact makes us aware that *the internal Christian dialogue to which this study is intended primarily to contribute has also, to a great extent, become from within – namely from the local situation – an interreligious dialogue.* If Christians want, from their minority position, to become comprehensible in a religious way to a Buddhist, Hindu or Islamic majority, they cannot escape searching for a common conceptual frame of reference.

In Rambitan's situation, this means that the dialogue with the Muslims must begin with concepts such as "prophet of God" and "servant of God," the two concepts of Jesus that Jesus uses as an infant in the Qur'an (*Sura* 19:30) to describe himself: "I am a servant of God.... He has...made me a prophet." In such a dialogue Rambitan wants to do full justice to Jesus' nearness to God as well as to his humanity (47–48). But the question then is what the expressions "prophet of God" and "servant of God" mean. In any case, it is clear that the contexts in which the New Testament uses these terms is different from those in the Qur'an, without intending to deny that the meanings of these concepts can fluctuate in both holy scriptures.

The following image of Jesus as prophet emerges in the New Testament:

1. Jesus appeared against the background of a certain Jewish pattern of expectation with respect to the advent (or return) of a prophet, following the example of Elijah (Mal. 4:5–6; Mark 6:15; 8:28), Moses (Deut. 18:15, 18; Acts 3:22–23 and 7:37) or an anonymous prophet who brings peace in the end times (Isa. 61:1–3 and 52:7; Mark 6:15 and 8:28; Luke 9:8, 19; John 6:14 and 7:40, 52).

2. As with so many prophets, Jesus was expected to provide a sign, but he refused to give any other sign than the reference to Jonah who spent three days and nights in the belly of a whale. Jesus would also spend three days and three nights in the heart of the earth. Jesus found this implicit reference to his death and resurrection to be sufficient (Matt. 12:38–42). But the expectation of a sign constantly arose around him (John 30; Mark 11:27–33).

    Neither aspect – the Jewish expectation and the question of a sign – leads to a clear image. The Jewish expectation is not clearly defined and the question of a sign is rejected, whereas it was clear meanwhile that he performed impressive signs – such as that of feeding the multitudes with a few loaves of bread and some fish (Mark 6:30–44 and 8:1–10).

3. Jesus himself uses a number of sayings about prophets, such as "Only in his hometown, among his relatives and in his own house is a prophet without honor" (Mark 6, 4), and in the Beatitudes (Matt. 5:3–12) he seems to refer consciously to the words of the prophet of the end time (Isa. 61:1–3). Furthermore, many of Jesus' acts, such his exorcisms and healings, can be associated with the appearance of the Old Testament prophets.

4. Can what Jesus says about John the Baptist – i.e. that it concerned "more than a prophet" (Luke 7:26) – be applied to Jesus himself? The story of the transfiguration on the mountain (Mark 9:2–10), especially where Jesus literally leaves Moses and Elijah behind, points in that direction.

The above points bring us to the conclusion that Jesus was considered by many in his immediate surroundings to be a prophet, that he saw himself standing in the tradition of the prophets, but also that he saw himself rising above the traditional prophet as the prophet of the end times who did indeed proclaim new things. In particular, the parable of the tenants (Mark 12:1–9), with a clear climax that focuses on what is done to the son of the owner of the vineyard, can be seen as an indication of his status as "more than a prophet."[13]

With respect to the proposal to speak about Jesus preferably as "servant of the Lord" we are confronted with precisely the same questions. In the book of Acts (4:23–31) the expression "servant of the Lord" can be used for both Jesus and David. As a Messiah, who stands in the line of the Messianic king David, Jesus is called "your holy servant whom you anointed" (4:27). There this expression comes very close to the term "Son of God," for that is the term for the Messianic king of Israel: "You are my Son; today I have become your Father" (Ps. 2:7). This verse is quoted literally in Acts 13:33 and applied to Jesus. Thus, instead of the expression "servant of the Lord" leading us away from the discussion on the sonship of God, it leads us precisely to the heart of the discussion.

This is also apparent from the second New Testament association that is connected with the concept "servant of the Lord." In addition to the association with the Davidic king who is called the "son of God," there is also reference to the suffering servant of the Lord in Isaiah (52:13–53:12). At the last supper, Jesus cites Isa. 53:12 and applies it to himself: "It is written: 'And he was numbered with the transgressors'; and I tell you that this must be fulfilled in me. Yes, what is written about me is reaching its fulfillment" (Luke 22:37). And when Philip hears the Ethiopian official in his chariot reading the passage from Isaiah 53 about the sheep that is led to the slaughter, he asks him: "Do you understand what you are reading?" and then explains to him how this passage refers to Jesus (Acts 8:26–35).[14]

In short, neither the expression prophet nor that of servant of the Lord brings us immediately closer, biblically speaking, to Islam. Jesus appears to have seen himself as a very specific prophet of the end times who was clearly to be distinguished from the Jewish prophets before him. And the expression "servant of the Lord" in the New Testament appears to come very close to the meaning of the expression "Son of God." Both expressions emphasize Jesus' unique nearness to God. The meanings still differ from those in the Qur'an.

The *nabi* (the prophet) is a key figure in the Qur'an, and can be identified, it seems, with one who is sent (*rasul*). Prophets are usually part of a long line. There is a succession of prophets in which a new prophet is considered to confirm the message of his predecessors – an idea that is also not foreign to the Old Testament. In contrast, Islam has not developed any further the Old Testament idea of a prophet to be expected in the end time. The idea of Mohammed as "the last prophet" or "seal of the prophets" (*Sura* 33:40) seems to stand in the way of that.

In addition to the term "prophet," "servant" (*abd*) is a second key concept. This word is also used repeatedly in the Qur'an for Jesus, without being given any specific meaning. It refers to the relationship between God and human beings in general. In the Christian–Muslim dialogue the term "servant" is used quite often to indicate that Jesus was "only" a servant of God and nothing more (*Sura* 43:59).

Thus the concepts "prophet" and "servant of the Lord" cannot be used to construct a bridge between Christians and Muslims in Indonesia. The possibility for that can perhaps be created if Indonesian theologians succeed in adding aspects from their own culture to these concepts that Muslims also share. That would then constitute a common Indonesian basis. To that end, we will cite a few initiatives in the following chapter.

14 Other Indonesian Interpretations of Jesus

The *Agama Jawa*

It is not always possible to trace as clearly as in the two approaches discussed in the previous chapter a certain method in the reflection on Indonesian images of Jesus. It is sometimes more a matter of tracing a certain attitude that can be brought into association with the context. Here a traditional view of life and, in connection with that, the traditional religions often play an indirect role. Especially on Java, where such an attitude is determined by – what Western observers call – the *agama Jawa* (the religion of Java) in which elements of Islam and the old Javanese Hinduism and Buddhism are included, it is difficult to make sharp distinctions.

Because of this typical Javanese syncretism, people speak of the *santri* wing, which strictly follows the rules of official Islam, and the *abangan* wing, which also includes elements of Hinduism, Buddhism and the traditional religions. It is usually assumed that Hinduism and Buddhism especially have contributed to the mystical character of Javanese Islam, even though that mystical character is strongly rooted in the nature of the Javanese people and Islam itself also has highly developed mystical schools.

The important role of the *kurban*, the sacrifice for warding off danger and receiving blessing, the *slametan*, the peace meal, and the role of the ancestors can be explained as deriving from the traditional religions.[1] Religion on Java cannot be understood if the role of sacrifices, meals and ancestors are not taken into account. In the same way – and that is a new development in Indonesian theology – the Javanese attitude to life, including that of Christians, cannot be understood without taking the meaning of central concepts in Islam into account. It would, of course, be easy to make caricatures here. Thus Yewangoe points out that the alleged Javanese fatalism is brought into association with the Islamic concepts of surrender (*nrimo* or *narima*), patience (*sabar*) and purity of intention (*ikhlas* or *rila*), but he also states that these concepts are certainly not interpreted within Islam as purely fatalistic.

As a form of *tawakkul* (trust), *narimo* (*nrimo*) represents the laying of a human life in God's hands. That does not exclude human activity but does imply the conviction that divine acting transcends the human.

In addition to patience, *sabar* can also mean perseverance in matters of faith and in the fulfilment of religious duties and acceptance in the face of disasters and other catastrophes. It also expresses the acceptance of current suffering in expectation of a reward in another world (Paradise).

Ikhlas is primarily an inner virtue that stands over against external legalism and has everything to do with the liberation of the selfish I. The term refers to detachment from everything that binds a human being. The influence of Hinduism especially can be seen in that concept.[2]

All three concepts are the expression of a form of maturity of faith that allows the believer to persevere in the midst of overwhelming suffering. They do not at all imply that believers on Java are inclined to accept everything around them in resignation, fatalistically. In this connection, Yewangoe shows that the Javanese experience of faith is characterized not only by a mystical bent but also by a messianism that is disposed to change, which often includes very old myths.[3]

By way of illustrating the effect of traditional Javanese aspects – thus including the Islamic – on the image of Jesus, we will look again at three examples. First we will explore a study that was done by the Dutch New Testament scholar Barend Drewes under the guidance of Hans-Ruedi Weber of the World Council of Churches between 1972 and 1974 among Protestants on Central Java into the meaning of the cross for Javanese Christians. Second, we will look at an extensive article by the Roman Catholic practical theologian P. G. van Hooijdonk, who goes into the results of Baniwiratma's master's thesis published in Indonesian (Bahasa) on Jesus as a Javanese *guru* (*Yesus Sang Guru*). In the third place, we will study the sketch that the Dutch Roman Catholic theologian and Islamologist Karel Steenbrink gives of Jesus as a Javanese prophet.

A Javanese Crucifix

Barend Drewes, a Dutch New Testament scholar who taught in Indonesia for years, points out that Javanese attitude, directed at internal and external harmony, is reflected in the preaching of the cross and how that preaching is processed in the Javanese churches. Through the reconciliation brought about on the cross, the way to heaven, to eternal life, is again open. That appears to be the tenor of many sermons and that is how the believers understand that preaching as well. That gives them rest and peace and gives them the patience to endure their own situation. Their position as Christians in the midst of an Islamic majority and the "break" that that entails in many respects – for example in family contexts – is related to the suffering of Jesus. The identification with Jesus' cross bestows balance, wholeness. The symbol of the cross is also used to ward off illness or evil spirits. Thus, many Indonesian Protestants wear a cross as well, a custom that Dutch Protestants, for example, rarely do. Energy for living is ascribed directly to the symbol of the cross.

It is fascinating what Drewes observes in connection with a life-sized depiction of Jesus in the house of a Christian *guru*, the leader of a Christian mystical group. It is a relief in plaster (of Paris) and was then painted, according to the artist, in a half hour of holy ecstasy. A figure from the *wayang* puppet play has been hung above the cross. It is *Kolo bendona*, a figure who dies because of his honesty and faithfulness to his dying friend. Above the cross on the right a star has been depicted, the symbol of the first pillar of Indonesian state ideology, *pancasila*, and refers to the acceptance of the one God (*ketuhanan*). The inscription on the cross is not the traditional INRI (*Iesus Nazarenus Rex Iudaeorum*: Jesus of Nazareth – King of the Jews). Written in Arabic-Indonesian is: "I myself." The left side of the cross beam is shorter than the right; this reflects Javanese symbolism where right stands for truth and goodness and left for lies and falsehood.

The face is not visible. It is black, the colour of rest and wisdom. The bowed head looks at a chest that has been forced open; the chest symbolizes repentance. Jesus looks into his soul, his innermost being, which lies open. The meaning is clear: just as Christ is open to God on the cross, so believers are open to God. On the outside wall of this *guru*'s house is a depiction of the head of Jesus crowned with thorns. Above it are the words: "I did this for you. What are you doing for me?" The internal and external worlds, micro- and macrocosmos, are thus brought into relation with each other. Underneath the cross is a yellow snake with a red crest that is biting Jesus in the heel. The yellow symbolizes the pride, the search for oneself and the red colour points to rage. In an allusion to Gen. 3:15, this says that Jesus' heel has not yet been crushed and neither has the head of the serpent. The struggle against evil has thus not yet ended. But next to the cross is a glass of water as a sign of eternal life (John 4:14).[4]

Yesus Sang Guru

The second example of the effect of Javanese spirituality on the image of Jesus concerns speaking about Jesus as a *guru* (*sang guru*). Next to the child-rearing tasks of parents and grandparents and, in essence, all adults, traditional Javanese society also has tasks that belong more or less to the monopoly of certain families. Here one can think, for example, of the task of the smith and the medicine man. A separate task (*empu*) is also exercised by people who could be called priests.

When the Hindus came to Java, those who were leaders in religious matters were called *Berahmana*. Their training included a type of education that the students of their teachers received in the form of joint private education, called *guru-kula*. In that way one could become a *Berahmana guru*. In addition to being a guide in all kinds of practical matters, the *guru* was also considered to be a guide to heaven and, in line with that, could also be identified with the divine (Vishnu, Shiva or Brahma). He personified, as it were, the visible divine. In Buddhism he can be seen as a *buddha*. The royal families gave the *gurus* special tasks in a wide area that included politics and education in addition to religion. Outside the court, their way of life was sometimes characterized by asceticism (abstinence). As hermit *gurus*, they could sometimes exercise great moral authority and they were often present at the cradle of many social reform movements.

With the coming of Islam, many *gurus* also became Muslims and the whole population usually converted with them. Within Islam, they primarily represented mysticism, a movement strongly oriented to interiorization. They were often, now in an Islamic context, closely associated with the royal families.

The relationship of the charismatic *guru* to his student(s) is always an unequal relationship and can be characterized using word pairs like above–below, full–empty, perfect–imperfect. This unequal relationship changes only when the *guru* dies. He is succeeded by his best student.

In fact, the *gurus* are the source of the knowledge of good and evil. Those who desire their teaching, desire – at bottom – God, the ultimate source of the knowledge of good and evil. A person can approach that source. The image that is often used for the unity (*soca-ludira*) to be attained is that of the smelting of copper and gold into a new alloy.

It is not surprising that the gospel of John especially, in which there is such a strong teacher–student relationship, offers a number of parallels for the *guru*–student relationship. Here also, the *guru* (Jesus) embodies the way to God and the student can never take the place of the teacher. For Banawiratma, this also entails a direct line from the Javanese *guru* to the New Testament "guru" Jesus, whom he sees as a unique *guru* because of his exceptional nearness to God.[5]

Banawiratma uses two works as sources for his description of the role of the *guru* in Javanese society. The first is a didactic poem, *Serat Wulangreh*, written in the nineteenth century by the prince of Surakarta, Pak Buwana IV, who reigned from 1799 to 1820 and advocated an open Islam that was expressed in, among other things, the fact that he had his court writers edit older Hindu writings. Included among these writings was the *lakon Dewa Ruci*, a description of the *wayang* play that Banwiratma uses as his second source, probably dating from the fifteenth century.

This play shows the same motifs that are present in the very popular *Serat Dewarutji*, an addition to the major collection of stories in the Hindu epic that is difficult to date, the *Mahabharata*.

In both the *Serat Dewarutji* and in the *lakon Dewa Ruci* the issue is the *guru*–student relationship in which *Wrekodara* is the student and Dewa Ruci the true *guru* who bears, as it were, the visible *guru Durna*. Durna gives Wrekodara the task of seeking the water of life. Wrekodara finally finds it with the god Dewa Ruci. He stays for some time in Dewa Ruci's belly where he is given all kinds of lessons and instructions. In Dewa Ruci, Wrekodara finds the true knowledge of God and thus also the true knowledge of himself, but he cannot stay in Dewa Ruci's belly. He needs to practise what he has learned in the hard reality of everyday.[6] The story is one of the many versions of the motif popular on Java of the search of the student for the water of life to which the *guru* points the way.

In his master's thesis, Banawiratma focuses primarily on the experience of mystical unity to which the *guru* is a guide. This experience of mystical unity is not intended to be a flight from harsh, everyday life but to enable one to face it. But he does not give the experience of unity any content based on the life of Christ and does not make any connection with the death and resurrection of Jesus, even though the material in question – the rebirth of Wrekodara in Dewa Ruci's belly – could have given cause for that.

Jesus as the Javanese Prophet

Steenbrink bases his portrayal of Jesus as a Javanese prophet on the *Serat Anbiya*, the Indonesian version of the well-known Islamic phenomenon of the prophetic narratives. He takes a nineteenth-century version as his starting point, but the thought in that version is much older. The Indonesian narratives are distinguished from the prophetic narratives of the Middle East in a number of respects. The main gist in both versions is constituted by what the Qur'an relates about Jesus. But not inconsiderable differences regarding shifts in accent in that line do appear. The general view in the prophetic narratives, the so-called *Qisas Anbiya*, from the Middle East is (1) that Jesus is one of the important prophets in a line that can vary in its extent. (2) Next, most of the narratives follow the Qur'an with regards to the statement that Jesus absolved his mother of all unchastity when he was still in the cradle. (3) His miracles are usually considerably more extensively talked about than is the content of his preaching. (4) And, finally, it is usually reported that Jesus was rejected by the Jews as a prophet and that they attempted to kill him. But God saved Jesus by taking him up into heaven.

The Indonesian prophetic narratives have a number of other emphases. (1) Jesus is compared with Seth, the third son of Adam, born without a mother, whereas the Qur'an draws the Jesus–Adam parallel, both of whom are born through God's powerful word: "'Be' and he was" (*Sura* 3:59); (2) instead of comforting Mary while in the cradle, as the Qur'an reports, Jesus comforts her while still in her womb; (3) in contrast to the Qur'an, the angel Gabriel comes to Mary a second time, the first time to announce the birth, the second time to comfort her in connection with the accusations that were to be expected from the Jews; (4) and, again in contrast to the Qur'an (*Sura* 4:157) which mentions the crucifixion explicitly, these narratives do not mention the crucifixion.[7]

In themselves, the differences are not exceptionally spectacular, but a few conclusions can nevertheless be drawn. Steenbrink sees the differences in emphasis as an indication of the fact that the literary sources of Islam, just like those of Christianity, were subject to cultural influences. Just as ethical (Jewish), philosophical (Greek) and juridical (Roman) influences can be seen in the literary sources of Christianity, so also ethical (Arabic), philosophical (Persian) and juridical (Turkish) influences can be seen in the Islamic sources. These influences coexisted for centuries and are an indication of a "culture of tolerated differences." The prophetic narratives that reflect these differences place Jesus in a long line of important prophets, from twelve up to as many as twenty-five. And although it is constantly stated that all the prophets are equal in standing, nevertheless some do appear to receive considerably more attention than others. Thus, there seems to be some room for a certain differentiation within the term "prophet" with respect to Jesus as well.

Indonesian Islam fits within this range. Javanese Islam especially is – as remarked earlier – a synthesis of Islamic, Hindu and traditional Indonesian religious ideas. This sometimes seems to disqualify Indonesian Islam in the Islamic world from the very start. In essence, the same discussion that we raised in Chapter 1 with respect to Christianity occurs in Islam. Just as there is no *Reinkultur* in Christianity, so there is none in Islam. And just as there is the inclination in Christianity to declare the culture in which Christianity arose the normative culture, so the same phenomenon appears in Islam. The role that is attributed to Arabic is the strongest example of this. Given the argument in Chapter 1, it should be clear that we definitely do not consider the cultural attire of Indonesian Islam to be an obstacle to understanding Islam.

The *Serat Anbiya* includes not only Seth in Jesus' genealogy but also Hindu gods like Vishnu, Rama and Krishna. In addition, the Javanese narratives pay explicit attention to Mary's (beautiful) physical appearance, in accordance with the Javanese literary tradition, in which someone is always introduced with an extensive description of his or her physical appearance. If Jesus' speaking from the cradle, as reported in the Qur'an, was miraculous, his speaking from within the womb is even more so, in accordance with the Javanese narrative tradition in which a story's imaginative power is determined by its miraculous character. And, finally – to give only a selection of the characteristics listed by Steenbrink – it is striking that Mary does not flee to the desert to escape the Jewish gossip but goes into the forest and ends up at the foot of the mountains under a tree by water (of life).[8]

Any kind of anti-Christian polemic is strange to these old Javanese narratives. The rediscovery of this peaceful tone in Javanese Islam would make Indonesia in principle – if it were not that the current political reality is often different – into one of most suitable places for a fruitful Christian–Muslim dialogue.

Conclusions

On the basis of the above, we can conclude that not only is there an entirely unique Indonesian Christianity but also an entirely unique Indonesian Islam. From of old there appears to be room in that Indonesian culture for a *guru* who clears the road to the water of life through his own commitment. Thus, we could state somewhat generally that "mediation of salvation" is not foreign to Indonesian culture. This culture also allows the personal appropriation of another's sacrifice of his life as the sacrifice of "my own I," as the Javanese crucifix makes clear. In Indonesia, more than appears to be the case in the rest of Asia, there seems to be the right soil for a *guru* who substitutes himself for others.

Yewangoe connects this notion to the concept *kurban* in the traditional Indonesian religions. It can mean both victim and the one who sacrifices. There is a close connection between both meanings. People who have become the victim of something often seek their salvation from the gods by means of sacrifices in the hope that the alleged disturbed relationship with them can be restored. Usually an animal is sacrificed for that purpose. The blood of the sacrificed animal is then sprinkled on the (human) victim – the one who is ill or who has transgressed a law. The sacrifice of the animal is a substitutionary sacrifice. That sacrifice results in both satisfaction as well as a new relationship. In this context Yewangoe also speaks about Jesus as *kurban*. He shows solidarity with the victims but also brings about a new relationship by sacrificing his life for others.[9]

But this fertile soil for a unique Indonesian image of Jesus is reflected only rarely in Indonesian theology and not at all in the Indonesian Christian–Muslim dialogue. This could be explained by the fact that up until now both Christianity and Islam have dared to go their own way in Indonesia only hesitantly. But it is undeniable that there have been a number of inspiring initiatives, and we hope that we have given a first impression of these in the foregoing.

If, by way of evaluation, we concur with the two approaches to Jesus that we have discussed thus far in this chapter, then a quite different picture emerges. This picture is so differentiated because the image of Jesus that the Qur'an holds before us appears to lend itself to both a minimalist and a maximalist interpretation. It is thus clear, for example, that the application of the terms "prophet" and "servant of God" to Jesus in the Qur'an fulfil an entirely different role than in the Bible, but that does not at all mean that the Qur'an does not attribute a special place to Jesus. But it seems that the question is whether this special position – expressed in, among other things, his virgin birth or ascension into heaven – can be expressed best via the concepts of "prophet" and "servant of God" that are interpreted so differently in these two religions.

We would rather refer to the concept of sign (*aya*), as Rakhmat did and as the Norwegian Islamic expert Oddbjørn Leirvik proposes in his 1999 study on *Images of Jesus Christ in Islam*.[10] If we do that, then Jesus is pre-eminently the sign of divine nearness. In the Indonesian culture, so rich in images, the choice is more or less obvious. In the Qur'an Jesus is called innumerable times – whether or not together with Mary – a "sign" for humanity. *Sura* 19:21 speaks of a "sign for men" and "a blessing from Us." In *Sura* 21:19 it is said of Mary and her son that they have been made a "token for mankind" and *Sura* 23:50 adds that the son and the mother have been given "shelter on an elevated ground, sequestered, watered by a spring."

In both the Qur'an and the New Testament, the value of signs (*semeia*) is not obvious and their meaning is not simply there for the asking. The unbelievers will not understand them (*Sura* 6:109–11; Mark 8:12). Only the believers will understand them (*Sura* 25:73; John 6:26). It appears that signs reveal and conceal: without text and context they cannot be understood. Without speaking in both traditions about Jesus' concrete work and identifying ourselves with that, we will never be able to discover their meaning. This cannot be done solely from behind a desk or in a nice study centre.

In connection with Jesus as a sign, on the Moluccas we should think primarily of the *pela* concept. Not only could that concept play a fruitful role in the tense relations between Christians and Muslims, it could also open up new perspectives in relation to the question of who Jesus is in the Indonesian context. In the case of the *pela* concept that is primarily the integration of the personal commitment of one's life (symbolized by drops of blood from the village chiefs), the connection with the ancestors and the practical, ethical working out of this in peaceful relations between the villages.

In a wider context one could also think of the cross as a sign. In that case, it would concern the cross in the first place as a sign of substitutionary suffering. We already pointed to the many possibilities of identification that the cross and the suffering associated with that offer Indonesian Christians. At first glance, perhaps, it seems that making this image central is still confrontational with respect to Islam, but that does not necessarily have to follow. The Qur'an denies Jesus' death on the cross (*Sura* 4:157) but does attribute great significance to substitutionary suffering elsewhere. The suffering of prophets to which the Qur'an repeatedly attests speaks volumes in this context (*Sura* 3:146–47). Especially in the Shi'ite tradition, it is not strange to attribute a positive significance to the suffering of the prophets for others. The television images of their processions in which the participants strike themselves until they bleed are well-known.[11] The most well-known example in the Qur'an of "substituting for another," of "redeeming," is the story of the testing of Abraham in the demand that he sacrifice his son Isaac. Concerning this sacrifice Allah says: "We ransomed him for a great sacrifice" (*Sura* 37:107). Muslims continue to celebrate this "substitution" right up until the present on the yearly Sacrifice Day. It is clear in this story that God himself is the one who ultimately saves.[12]

Therefore, the theme of substitutionary character of suffering at God's initiative through the commitment of his own life is not foreign to Islam. But the Qur'an does not connect this idea with the crucifixion. That it does not make this connection could have to do with the way in which the Qur'an and the prophetic narratives speak of the fate of the truly great prophets. These stories all follow the same line. A prophet proclaims a message from God, is persecuted, threatened with death, but God shows himself to be trustworthy in the end and saves his prophet from the threat of death. The Qur'an's presentation of Jesus' death is in line with these stories. At the moment that his life was in danger, God intervened and saved him from the hands of his enemies, for God does not abandon the prophets that trust him.[13]

It is striking that the Qur'an does not speak about Jesus' resurrection. It speaks only of a resurrection at the end of time, on the day of Judgement. That makes it possible for the Qur'an to classify the crucifixion as a case of "being abandoned," whereas for Christians the resurrection is precisely the sign that God did not abandon his prophet. Thus, with respect to the cross, both religions say that whoever trusts in God will not be put to shame. But, in Christianity, Jesus is not rescued from the cross but from death.[14] That is the death of our "old Adam": he is crucified. In the dialogue with Islam the discussion on the meaning of the sacrifice of life before God (Allah) would be of great topical interest.

Indonesians would certainly be sensitive to such a discussion on Jesus' sacrifice of his life. If it is true that poets are usually the most sensitive to what lives in a culture, then they could be our witnesses *par excellence*. Of course, it is not a complete, finished image that emerges, but some shading occurs that will perhaps give more relief to the images sketched thus far. We think then, for example, of the poems of Willibrodus Surendra Rendra called "Ballad of the Crucifixion," "After Confession" and "Litany for the Holy Lamb."[15] As an illustration of the way in which the sacrifice can be integrated into a "theology of the light" we will cite a fragment from the poem "Litany of the Holy Lamb" from 1955 as the closing for this chapter:

Litany for the Holy Lamb (fragment)

Tiny Jesus, holy lamb.
Open your heart, O holy lamb!
You, slaughtered in the afternoon.
Let your blessing flow like water!
You, flowing with blood like wine.
Let forgiveness surge from the flood of your love!
You, blazing with light like a torch.
We all belong to you!

Part VIII: The African Jesus

Since the 1990s, there has been a great deal of discussion on the "new African theology." This refers to a theology that tried to bridge the gap often indicated in the 1970s and 1980s between African inculturation theology and African liberation theology. To do so, an image of Jesus is being used in which social concern and prophetic social critique is founded not only on the New Testament but also on the millennia-old religious culture of Africa itself. While certainly aware of the great cultural and religious differences on this continent, theologians are also daring to speak – after this had been declared taboo for decades – of what is common to all of Africa.

As far as content is concerned, this has to do with the belief in a supreme God with whom people come into contact, preferably through mediators. In the search for appropriate African images for Jesus, comparison with the mediating role of ancestors and healers is obvious. In this chapter we will also discuss the effect of this kind of comparison from the perspective of double transformation. Concretely, this means that, when applied to Jesus, the traditional African images of ancestors and healers change; but so does the image of Jesus. The key question in this process of change is what role is attributed to the cross of Jesus and to his ethics – which transcends family and tribal relationships – against the background of the "cross" of the African people.

15 The African Religious Context

Missions in Africa

Before we turn our attention to current African images of Jesus, we will first sketch briefly an outline of the position of Christianity in Africa, after which we will look briefly at the discussion on the characteristics of African theology and then give a short outline of how the supreme God is worshipped in Africa. We will conclude the first part of this section with a description of what is now called the "new African theology." In this theology reflection on the cross and the suffering of Jesus in relation to the cross and the suffering of the African people forms, as it were, a bridge across the gap – previously thought to be unbridgeable – between African inculturation theology and liberation theology.

We will examine the content of the African tribal religions more closely than we examined the tribal religions of Asia. This is because in Africa the old tribal religions have been pushed to the background by less regionally bound religions to a much lesser degree than in Asia. Because of the emphasis on the variety of African religiosity, it was also difficult to describe its content up until now. This seems to be changing within the so-called "new African theology." Even without a broad consensus, certain trends are becoming clearer than they previously were, and this is why we will attempt an outline.

A drawback (or advantage?) of such an outline is that we will not – as much as possible – look at any specific content that each region or tribe gives to the images of Jesus. Thus, in speaking of the "African Jesus," we consciously choose an approach that is distinguished from the approach we used for the "Indonesian Jesus." There we consciously chose a number of illustrations from Java and the Moluccas, assuming that the theological developments there are indicative of what will occur in Indonesia as a whole in the coming decades. We see no convincing arguments for such an approach to Africa. Here again, as in the previous chapters, we choose a thematic approach that can be given more specificity by looking at the work of various leading theologians.

At first glance, it seems impossible to write a coherent chapter on the "African Jesus." After all, theologically speaking, Africa is a very complicated continent. Up until the arrival of Islam, there was in North Africa, in what is now Libya, Algeria, Tunisia and Morocco, an influential Christian church with a Greek-speaking section in the East and a Latin-speaking section in the West. The "Greek" Christians in the East of North Africa were called Alexandrians after the city of Alexandria and the church fathers Origen (185–254) and Athanasius (296–373) were their most important leaders. The "Latin" church in the West of North African had its centre in Carthage and its most important leaders were Augustine (354–430), Tertullian (160–220) and Cyprian (200–258). Both parts of the North African church have left a distinct impression on Christianity in the northern hemisphere – the "Greek" mainly on the Greek and Russian Orthodox Churches in eastern Europe and the "Latin" mainly on the Roman Catholic Church and later on the Reformation churches in western Europe.

Ironically enough, we must immediately add that this type of Christianity, which was so influential outside of Africa, was the classic example of failed inculturation *within* Africa. Due to the collapse of the Roman Empire because of the attacks by the Vandals who expanded into North Africa and the later conquest of this area by the Arabs between 670 and 705, North African Christianity became isolated and began a slow process of starvation. The cause for this failed inculturation is often said to be internal division, too strong a fixation on the cloister at the expense of building up the community and the lack of interest in the native language of the area.[1] Nevertheless, most monasteries were situated in Egypt and Ethiopia rather than North Africa, and played an important role in the continuation of Christianity there, while the *lingua punica* (the language of the Carthagians), in addition to Latin, also played an important role. The mutual division that was focused primarily on the strict Donatist concept of the church – a church of the elect where the wheat was sifted from the chaff – undoubtedly played a role in this but cannot serve as the only explanation. In other areas this division among Christians had less disastrous consequences, which is why we tend, together with the New Zealand African specialist Elizabeth Isichei, to view the centuries-long process of the dying of this church as one of the great mysteries of African history.[2]

It was not until many centuries later that a second attempt was made to Christianize Africa. First, Portuguese missionaries came in the fifteenth century (mainly) to southern East Africa, and in the nineteenth century, when Western European countries had acquired their colonies in Africa, the English, French, Belgian and German missionaries came. Moreover, from the seventeenth century on, large groups of Dutch Christians, including many Huguenots who had been driven from France, settled in South Africa without, incidentally, doing much mission work at first.

Christianity therefore reached Africa in three waves. The first wave of missions to North Africa and the Nile basin in Egypt, Ethiopia, southern Sudan, Eritrea and Somalia has, up until today, held its own rather strongly. The above-mentioned obstacles to a good inculturation in North Africa –

internal division, lack of attention to building up the church and a lack of interest in the native language – did not appear here. In these areas there was a relatively early development of a characteristic African type of church, with its own liturgy and its own way of giving leadership.

The traces of the second, relatively small Portuguese missions invasion had all but disappeared after two centuries, whereas the third, massive missions wave led to Africa being divided confessionally in accordance with the borders between the colonies.

From the second half of the twentieth century on, in the wake of decolonization, there was increasing attention to Africa's own ancient religions. At the end of the 1950s and the beginning of the 1960s, in the French-speaking part of Africa, this tendency followed in the footsteps of a partly theological and partly literary movement that was called *négritude*. In the English-speaking part of Africa, this concept acquired an equivalent term in the concept *African personality*.[3] (We should add, as an aside, that we are aware that it is neo-colonial and thus strange to speak of French-speaking or English-speaking Africa. At most, in both cases French and English are second languages.)

Among anthropologists especially, there is much discussion on the implications of the concepts *négritude* and *African personality*. We will not take up this discussion but will assert that reflection in the 1990s on what is or is not typically African was more or less the prelude for a new and less biased reflection on the characteristics of African theology. A growing African cultural self-awareness is being expressed. Some people even speak of an African Renaissance.[4]

Indirectly and unintentionally, the native, independent African churches – usually called African Instituted Churches (AICs) today – have contributed much to this search for what is typically African. They are called "independent" because they were not established by European missions and therefore have no link via personnel or finances with the traditional European churches. They can often be traced partly to missions activity from outside – usually American revivalist movements – but then they proceeded to develop as true African churches. They are characterized by (a) leadership from within, (b) an orientation towards oral tradition, (c) little attention for the written word, given the illiteracy of most of the members, (d) integration of African dance and song, and (e) the assimilation of numerous aspects of the role of the African priest, healer and prophet in an extensive culture of prayer, healing and exorcism.[5]

The existence of these churches as well as their spectacular growth in the twentieth century has led observers to many remarkable conclusions regarding the characteristic nature of the development of Christian theology in Africa. For example, the Scottish theologian Allan Anderson points to the striking synthesis of aspects of the African traditional religions and

African Pentecostalism,[6] and the Kenyan theologian Philomena Mwaura demands that attention be paid to the central role that women play in these churches as founders, prophetesses or healers.[7] In addition to the renewed African self-awareness that arose from decolonization, these independent churches' power of attraction can also be seen as one of the main reasons for renewed reflection on the characteristics of African theology.[8]

In this part we will look specifically at the question of the African face Jesus has received in recent decades. We will skip over the development of the image of Jesus in the Egyptian and Ethiopian Coptic Church, even though there are interesting developments with regard to the interpretation of Jesus. But these developments are related primarily to the discussion that has been going on for 1,500 years concerning the Council of Chalcedon in 451. A small minority in the midst of an overwhelming Islamic majority, Christianity in the Middle East is preoccupied with overcoming its own historical division relating to the interpretation of Chalcedon. Undoubtedly, the current tense political context indirectly plays a role in this. Now, because of renewed research into the source material, the mutual condemnations are being retracted. But however fascinating this development is ecumenically, it is not directly concerned with the current inculturation of the image of Jesus. Rather, it is a processing of "old sores" from the distant past. That is why we will exclude it from our present discussion.[9]

We will also exclude the remarkable attraction that the Ethiopian or Abyssinian Church has in contemporary Africa and in the Caribbean, especially in reggae for example.[10] An extensive mythologizing of the African inculturation that took place in the Ethiopian Church has occurred in the *Kebra Nagast*. This mythologizing turns it into a model for many African independent churches. "Ethiopian" then represents a typically African way of being Christian and church that stems from biblical, Old Testament times (the queen of Sheba!).[11] The fact that that power of attraction extends far beyond the original boundaries is unique in the world of the Orthodox churches. Being nationally – if not nationalistically – oriented, these churches do not engage in missions. The Ethiopian Church is an exception and Ethiopian Orthodox churches can be found in the furthest reaches of southern Africa. From time immemorial their churches have reserved a major role for priests and prophets (including women) and for African music and dance. Because of this, they appear to have hit a nerve in Africa.[12] The old African Orthodox Churches – often included within the so-called eastern churches – are certainly, with their specific inculturations in mind, worth further examination on their own. But they do not present new inculturations and that is why we will not discuss them here.

Characteristics of African Theology

In many respects Africa is a very complicated continent – and this applies to religious Africa as well. Eastern, western, northern, central and southern Africa have very different histories, languages and religious customs; it is not possible to lump them together into one. The quest for what is typically African appears to be an impossible search right from the beginning, just like the quest for what is typically Asian. We saw this in Chapter 4 as well: the theologians who argue for the "critical Asian principle" searched for what was common to all of Asia more on a political and social level than they did on a cultural and religious one. Given the diversity of the Buddhist, Hindu and Islamic contexts, that would be an impossible task.

And yet we see that many theologians in Africa continue to search for what is theologically common. They do not want to be deprived – we could perhaps summarize their intention thus – of a common African theological identity in the midst of all the African diversity.

This tension between the accent on the variety of African religiosity on the one hand and the accent on what is common to Africa on the other will be heard throughout this section – it is a tension that is expressed primarily by African theologians themselves. It should be obvious that it is non-African foreign observers especially who speak about what is "typically African" and that the Africans themselves defend their common variety. In contemporary African theology, however, the opposite is true.

African theologians such as the Roman Catholic theologian Efoé Julien Pénoukou from Benin[13] and philosophers such as the Ghanaian Kwasi Wiredu[14] themselves show less hesitation in speaking of what is "typically African." They candidly write their articles and books on topics such as "African theology," "African philosophy," "the African Jesus," etc. They are aware, of course, of the great differences between the various African cultures, which are often discussed in detail as well. But that variety does not impede the search for what is common.

At times something of an internally African imperialism is expressed. "The African Jesus" sometimes appears to be remarkably similar to the religious concepts of the people or tribe to which the theologian belongs. Thus the "African Jesus" sometimes acquires very Ghanaian Akan or Nigerian Igbo features.

But a new African self-consciousness is unmistakably being expressed in the candid talk of the "African Jesus." This talk is the result of an honest search for the sources of the life-force of the peoples on this continent which is ravaged internally by outbursts of violence, dictatorial governments, corruption, mismanagement and AIDS. Thus, the accent on the "African Jesus" is a powerful protest against the Western tendency to write this continent off as a "lost continent" that, despite its enormous wealth in minerals, has emerged from the period of decolonization noticeably worse than many Asian countries without minerals. In this situation of continuous exploitation, poverty and violence after decolonization, the "African Jesus" appears to be the unique "ancestor" and "healer" that links the accent of the traditional African religions on the life-force, community and harmony with all that lives with the history of Jesus' crucifixion and resurrection in a liberating manner.

Therefore, the increasing openness in speaking of an "African Jesus" is, in the eyes of many African theologians, not a superficial generalization but the expression of a deeply experienced awareness that there is also another Jesus, in contrast to the "Lord" or "Messiah" of the Western missionaries, a Lord who always seemed to be distant. Certainly in theological literature the "African Jesus" is a latecomer to Africa. It took a comparatively long time before anyone dared to take up this theme. To do so, theologians first had to give their own interpretation of what Bediako, following Kenneth Cragg, calls *integrity in conversion*. Such integrity assumes that someone in a process of conversion does not have to give up his African identity but can deepen it instead. This is possible only if the break that conversion always entails is not experienced in such a way that what one was can no longer be a part of what one has become.[15]

Before going into any more depth as to what this means for the African image of Jesus, let us first examine a number of methodological questions. The first question is that of the most appropriate language. Because of the large diversity of languages, African theologians need to communicate with one another and the non-African world in a "second" language – a language that is not their own and one in which it is difficult to translate many African religious concepts. In Asia, the same problem exists. There necessity dictated that the common second language be English; English is dominant in Africa as well, but French is also a good second "second" language. The language chosen is almost by definition the language of that area's previous colonizers because people also know that language beyond the country's borders. In order to be able to experience the emotional value of these African concepts, those concepts in English and French studies are also stated in the African language in question. That language, in turn, is by definition always the language of a specific tribe. For many African theologians, an English or French book on African theology will therefore often evoke a double alienation: first, the confrontation with a language that one does not know or does not know as well as one would like and, second, the confrontation with concepts of a foreign tribe or foreign people.[16]

A second methodological question concerns an issue that is closely connected with the previous one: not only the great diversity of African languages, but also that of African religions. Should we not always speak of African religions in the plural? Because of the ethnic nature of Africa's religious concepts, the Kenyan Anglican John Mbiti does indeed argue in his *African Religions and Philosophy* (1969) for the plural form. It is simply true that religion in Africa is tribal bound. That is why there was never any missionary zeal among the various tribes.

Apart from the ethnic aspect, there are many other aspects to religion in Africa that make transmission to outsiders difficult. For example, religion in Africa is not a "religion of the book"; this makes religious communication very much dependent on one's readiness and ability to engage in interhuman contact. Moreover, African religions are linked to festivals and rituals more than they are to founders or reformers. Their concrete manifestation, however old that form may be in principle, actually strongly depends on leaders that arise by chance. As a third aspect, Mbiti points to the often quite varying historical and geographical background of the various African religions. Agricultural tribes have always had more rituals that were bound to certain places than nomadic tribes had, and they conceive of the functioning of their gods as more earthly and local than the nomads, who are more directed towards the heaven(ly bodies).

But twenty years later, in the foreword of the second printing of his *African Religions and Philosophy* (1990), Mbiti indicated that he was also open to the arguments by those who nevertheless prefer to speak of Africa's traditional religion in the singular.[17] The Nigerian Methodist Bolaji Idowu is one of the spokespersons for this group. He especially sees belief in an almighty creator God as an important argument for not losing sight of commonality in African religiosity.[18]

Leaving the language problem for what it is, with respect to the second methodological question we will follow those African theologians who assume a certain dominance of the belief in an almighty creator God. For them, African religion is ultimately monotheistic, even though that approach does not exclude the acknowledgement that a large number of lower gods are also worshipped. Before going any further into Idowu's rendering of the most important characteristics of African belief in God, it would be good to take a moment to look at the "battle of schools of thought" among anthropologists on the question of whether such characteristics are authentic.[19]

As a rule, in this debate a distinction is made between the "devout scholars" and the "de-Hellenists." Most of the theologians discussed in this chapter can be included among the "devout scholars." The Ugandan poet/writer/social anthropologist Okot p'Bitek and the English anthropologist Robin Horton can be included among the "de-Hellenists," but so can the Ghanaian philosophers Kwasi Wiredu[20] and Kwame Appiah.[21] The designation "de-Hellenists" comes from their argument for stripping African religion of the Hellenistic "garb" (transcendence, omnipotence, immutability, providence, etc.) that the "devout scholars" have draped around the African gods.[22] Thus, the discussion concerns the exact status that is to be given to the supreme God in African religions and the relation of this supreme being to the ancestors, the spirits and the believers.

The "devout scholars" in particular emphasize the authenticity and originality of African ideas concerning a supreme God, whereas the "de-Hellenists" see these ideas exclusively as a pious (devout) construction by the "devout scholars" that no African reality can live up to. They see such constructions as an overreaction to the Western tendency to undervalue what is typically African both culturally and religiously. According to the "de-Hellenists," Africans did not concern themselves with metaphysical (Hellenistic) issues such as the omnipotence, omnipresence, transcendence, eternity and providence of their gods before the arrival of Christianity and Islam. For Africans, religion had a pragmatic slant, directed at the here and now, health and welfare, personal success and a happy and fruitful marriage.[23]

In this functionalistic approach, religion is restricted to searching for a number of constant factors in the continually changing circumstances of everyday life. This approach does not deny that Africans worship a supreme God, but there is a difference of opinion as to the significance that should be attributed to this supreme being. In their view, this is more a matter of explanation or prediction and thus has to do more with everyday life rather than "communion" with the holy as a goal in itself. In this approach the tendency to see God as a transcendent force is an African (over)reaction to the modern worldview of the Enlightenment introduced by the Europeans. If many things in everyday life are simply the product of coincidental historical developments of social conventions, then belief in God can no longer function as an explanation of the everyday. It then disappears or "repositions itself" by distancing itself from everyday life. According to them, that process was completed in Africa in the second half of the last century.

But belief in a supreme God simply as a product of relatively recent historical changes and socio-political factors is not confirmed by the meanings that the names of God have had since time immemorial in many African languages. Analysis of those names shows that the African names of God often express the dimension of nearness as well as that of distance. On the one hand, God is a distant God, exalted high above all that is earthly and human. On the other hand, through the mediating role of the ancestors, spirits and lower gods, God is also near. These two aspects are not in competition with but rather presuppose each other. If there is no distance, mediation is unnecessary; if there is no mediation, distance would merely imply estrangement. But in many respects it can be said that the supreme God is characterized by "immanent transcendence" – a transcendence that can be seen in the everyday.[24]

This di-unity (dialectic) of distance and nearness, which the "de-Hellenists" misunderstand, can be seen as the key to understanding African traditional religion.[25] This does not at all deny the pragmatic or functional role of religion in Africa. Nor does it deny the often inadequate application of Western theological concepts to African religious concepts. It denies only that Africa's religions play only a functional role and that each more transcendent interpretation would be, by definition, "Western." Such generalizing "doctrines" seem, as they often do, to be inadequate. In Africa, the idea of a supreme God often refers precisely to the intangible, to the simultaneously immanent and transcendent.[26] Thus, the relationship to the supreme God cannot, generally speaking, be described otherwise than as a relationship with the *irreducible exterior*, with a power that can be reduced to nothing else, that transcends our existence. It is a relationship "l'au-delà de la relation normale," a relationship that is different from a normal interhuman relationship.[27]

Concepts such as transcendence, omnipotence and providence, occasionally used for lack of better terms to indicate what is meant in Africa by a supreme God, are, strictly speaking, unknown concepts in African languages. The words used in those languages for the supreme godhead can actually be explained only in their theocentric impact with reference to their own context. Only then will it also become clear that the words that describe the special position of the supreme God are distinguished from the words that are used for the mediating function of the ancestors, spirits and lower gods.[28]

The Relationship with the Supreme God

The special position of the supreme God can be clarified by how the supreme God is worshipped as creator in most African traditional religions. That worship is closely linked with his absoluteness and uniqueness. His exaltation usually makes direct contact impossible. Ancestors, spirits and lower gods are the objects of ritual worship, but the supreme God seldom is. It is sometimes incorrectly concluded that there is no place for a supreme God in traditional African religions. We encounter the same phenomenon here that we observed in the first section of Chapter 2 and the second section of Chapter 8 concerning the Korean God *Hananim*, and in the second section of Chapter 5 concerning the way in which the supreme being Heaven could be the only direct object of worship in the sacrificial service of the king. In all of these cases the highest God cannot be approached by an ordinary believer. For that matter, every schematization that is too rigid collapses when confronted with the colourfulness of Africa's spirituality in which the distant God – at times even without mediation – can be close to and approachable by everyone.

The fact that the supreme God is usually not an object of regular worship does not say anything about the importance that must be attributed to the supreme divinity. After all, it could be that the supreme divinity is considered to be so exalted that every form of direct worship does not do enough justice to his exalted status. At first, this attitude towards the divine seems somewhat similar to the "negative theology" that we mentioned in the fifth section of Chapter 6 in connection with the role of negations ("is not" statements) in Buddhism. But, upon closer inspection, this is actually a different attitude.

The attitude towards the supreme God in Africa is determined primarily by the nature of the *mediation*.[29] In contrast to so-called negative theology, it is possible to approach God but only via specific persons. Many African religions also assume a certain hierarchy with regard to the supreme God. This hierarchy consists of the (lower) gods, spirits and ancestors who mediate between the supreme divinity and the members of the tribe. They are the direct objects of worship and sacrifices can be made to them. This is why there are sacrificial places and altars for these "mediators" but not for the supreme God himself. There are also usually no set rituals or festivals for the supreme God.

These mediators – lower gods, spirits, ancestors – are not rivals or competitors of the supreme God. Rather, they serve the supreme God and worshipping them also implies worshipping him. It is not possible to characterize this relationship simply as monotheistic or polytheistic. In addition to the supreme God, there are indisputably other gods as well, but at the same time it is also absolutely clear who the highest God is.[30] In conjunction with this, Idowu also speaks of "diffused monotheism," a monotheism dispersed behind the presence of many other (lower) gods.[31]

One of the main reasons for this hierarchy is the conviction that the supreme God, the creator, is not seen as the cause of adversity or suffering. Suffering and adversity are associated more with the lower gods, evil spirits, insulted or disowned ancestors and one's own wrongdoing.[32] In the case of adversity and suffering, the gods, spirits and ancestors must be placated and sacrifices must be made to them. Only in the latter instance, when all other attempts at reconciliation have failed, will the help of the supreme God be called upon.[33] Thus, the idea of creator is not immediately connected with the idea of a direct divine involvement in all human actions.

The great distance between the supreme God and the members of the tribe is not usually seen as something that always was but rather as the result of the alienation that has arisen between the supreme God and the tribe. The supreme God has, as it were, retreated from everyday human life for which humans themselves, whether or not under the influence of good or evil spirits, are now responsible. This alienation is not considered irreversible: many religious efforts are directed at restoring contact with the supreme God.[34] Thus, the supreme God here is not one who has definitively retreated to the background.[35] Both physical and moral evil are seen as an indication of the disrupted relationship with the supreme God; the emphasis usually falls on physical evil here.

A great deal of attention is paid to tracing the cause of that evil. A whole range of causes can be produced, varying from evil spirits, witchcraft, magic, broken taboos, broken promises or the corrective or educative punishment by the gods or ancestors.[36] There can be several causes for all kinds of evil, but there is little speculation as to the origin or source of evil in itself. Many of these texts undeniably have something of the air of "paradise lost" about them, but there is no explicit reference to something like the "Fall of Man."[37] Because of this, there is also no notion of a sinfulness passed down from generation to generation, i.e. "original sin."

That there are many causes of evil means that not only tracing the causes of evil but also negating them or reconciling the forces that lead to those causes take a great deal of energy. That is the purpose of the many sacrifices. When (animal) blood is shed, it indicates the fact that serious matters are at stake that will affect the life of an individual or a group. Blood and life are, after all, intrinsically connected with each other. The shed blood of the animals is said to have a reconciling force for the lives of people.[38]

This concern for life extends beyond death. It is hoped that after death one will be accepted among the ancestors and be able to use their powers for the well-being of the family and tribal members. The contrast of this hope is the fear of being condemned after death to be a wandering spirit, cut off from one's own family and tribal community. We came across the notion of such a spectre in the second part of Chapter 8 when we discussed the role of the (spirit-exorcising) *mudang* in shamanistic rituals in Korea. In his study of the parallels between the African (Ghanaian) worship of ancestors and the Japanese, the Ghanaian theologian Elom Dovlo compares the dwelling of these wandering spirits with a dwelling in hell.[39]

The ancestors do not necessarily inspire fear. They do not represent hostile powers that must be sorted out by means of various rituals. They are too trusted, too much a part of the family for that. They are there to serve the living, who can call upon them for help by means of sacrifices and prayers. And yet, there is a certain ambivalence regarding the attitude towards them because the ancestors can become angry if they are neglected or if someone violates the rules of the community for which they are responsible. Then the borderline between angry ancestors and evil spirits tends to blur at times – all the more so since there is a question as to whether one should speak of ancestors or of ancestral spirits.

In this study we prefer to speak of ancestors because of the concrete and earthly nature of communion with them. Otherwise, their presence might be spiritualized. It is clear that when the mediating role of Jesus is compared with that of the ancestor, the latter is always a caring ancestor and not a wrathful or avenging one.[40] It is the type of ancestor (1) to whom one can turn as an intermediary if one is seeking contact with the supreme God, (2) through whom the Supreme God can also seek contact with them, and (3) who functions as the "guard" of the community rule within the family and the tribe.[41]

In emphasizing the function of the ancestors in actual everyday life, the Cameroon Roman Catholic theologian Jean-Marc Ela goes one step further. It is very important for him to view the veneration of ancestors as "worldly" and to keep them outside the sphere of a religious force. He sees the relationship with the ancestors "simply" as the continuation of family relationships beyond the boundary of death. This is also why the ancestors are to be distinguished from the spirits.[42] He quotes with approval John Mbiti, who is famous for his reference to the ancestors as the "living-dead" members of the family.[43]

In his denial of the religious nature of the veneration of ancestors, Ela endorses the distinction often made between *ancestor worship* and *ancestor veneration* or honouring the ancestors. Generally, because of the first of the Ten Commandments ("You shall have no other gods before me," Deut. 5:7), Christians see worship as crossing a boundary but do leave some room for veneration. Theologians such as Ela stress the point that in Africa people venerate the ancestors but do not worship them.

But the distinction between venerating them, calling on them for help, invoking, praying to and worshipping them is very small.[44] Ela also discusses at some length the sacrifices to the ancestors and attributes a mediating role to them in reconciliatory rituals to the spirits and the supreme God. Thus, such a sharp distinction seems forced. Such a distinction, especially in Roman Catholic theologians, seems at times to be determined more by church politics than anything else. Thus, the veneration of ancestors, as presented to the Vatican, which has a critical view of African inculturation theology, seems to be "more innocent" than it actually is. It will become apparent in the next chapter, however, that it is the thankful recognition of the religious, mediating function of the ancestors that can offer fruitful perspectives for creative reflection on Jesus' role as "eldest brother-ancestor,"[45] as "proto-ancestor," as "unique ancestor" or as "greatest ancestor."[46]

Here we should also remember that the idea of a religious mediator – someone who assumes the fate of another with the intention of restoring that person's good relationship with the supreme divinity – is in itself unknown in Africa, even though the Zimbabwean Methodist Zvomunondita Kurewa refers to the fact that the idea of a scapegoat in the form of a rooster, chicken or goat is not strange to most African people. Often, it is the traditional healer who evokes the idea that an evil spirit that makes people ill can be transferred to sacrificial animals. The animal is subsequently cursed and chased away.[47] The notion of a human being who sacrifices his life in a substitutionary way for the well-being of the community is not completely unfamiliar in Africa. Sometimes this human scapegoat was a slave who was forced into this role, but sometimes – like the priest Eleguru of the Ijebu Ode people of Nigeria – also an individual who once acted voluntarily for his people.[48]

It is, after all, possible that – outside of Europe – such a strong internalization of guilt cannot be found virtually anywhere as in Western theology and philosophy, and yet not a single culture nor a single individual would call himself "guiltless." Even where a shame culture rather than a guilt culture could be said to exist, people still dirty their hands and carry a guilty past around with them in many respects. In Asia and Africa as well, there is a great deal of guilt in the mutual relationships between countries and tribes and between individuals. Any religion that wishes to cover all aspects of life will therefore also always have to answer the question of guilt. Given this background, it is still advisable to search in Africa and Asia for typically African and Asian forms for dealing with the question of guilt and the possibility of forgiveness.

Later on in the next chapter, when we pose the question as to what Jesus *acquires* in the role of the ancestor in comparison with the Western tradition, it will be only fair to indicate at the same time what he *loses* in this comparison. That is, of course, the emphasis on his substitutionary death on the cross. That idea is never associated with that of the ancestor. But the fact that the comparison fails here does not mean to say that *that is the reason* why the mediating role of Jesus cannot be compared with that of the ancestor. One must rather conclude that the image of the ancestor can never be the sole image for Jesus' role in Africa: just as, for example, the Greek image of *kyrios* (Lord) can never be the sole image, for that image does not carry the notion of substitution either. But that was not sufficient reason not to apply this image to Jesus. It could have shed light on another aspect, namely, that of his authority. The same holds for the image of the ancestor: it can, as no other image can, express Jesus' concern, beyond his own death, for us in life and death.

The previous sentence refers to dying, to death. Physical death at an advanced age is seen in Africa as natural – it can even be called "God's death."[49] But that death need not be regarded as the end of someone's role in the community of life. What is crucial for the place that people assume in the community after death is the relationship they had with the ancestors during life and the help that people can expect from them because of that. Given this, one need not be surprised that many theologians in Africa see a starting point especially in the role of ancestors for the explanation of the role that Jesus can play for Africans.[50]

The New African Theology

The room for such a creative link between the role of Jesus and that of the ancestor seems to have arisen in African theology only since the end of the 1980s. The Ghanaian Presbyterian theologian Kwame Bediako speaks of the rise of a "new" African theology.[51] At that time most of the wars for liberation had ended. A sharp distinction between African liberation theology and inculturation theology can no longer be made.[52] Rather, as social-critical theologians such as Ela[53] and the Congolese Roman Catholic Bénézet Bujo[54] argue, now is the time to discover liberating aspects in what is typically African.

Attention to one's own creative contribution in Christian theology then fits in with an African "theology of reconstruction" that is distinguished not only creatively and critically from non-African theology but also offers a constructive social perspective within one's own African community in the midst of the many disillusions regarding decolonization.[55]

In the period since about 1950, the "discovery" of Africa's characteristic religion was central to African theology. That religion is directed primarily towards the continuation of life contexts. For an African to live without the community of living and dead family members and tribal members is unthinkable, which is why Mbiti, in characterizing the African way of life, could also paraphrase Descartes' famous *Cogito, ergo sum* (I think, therefore I am) as "I am, because we are; and since we are, therefore I am."[56] We find an almost identical paraphrase in the Ghanaian Anglican theologian John Pobee, in his *Cognatus ergo sum* – "*I am related by blood, therefore I exist*," or "*I exist because I belong to a family*."[57]

The African theology of that time (1950–1985) is clearly theocentric and appears to have more affinity with the Old Testament than with the New. After all, African religions usually do not have founders or reformers. In 1972 Mbiti could thus comment that African Christologies did not exist.[58] Reflection on an "African Jesus" can thus rightly be called a latecomer in African theology.[59] Given these facts, it is understandable that the Nigerian Baptist theologian Yusuf Amah Obaje argues for a "theocentric Christology" because he does not wish to be seen as a complete "stranger" with respect to African culture.[60] In this regard, the Nigerian Presbyterian theologian Enyi Udoh speaks of Christ as the "alien" image in Africa.[61]

And yet that image of Jesus – of actually being a stranger in Africa – has been rapidly changing during the last decade. The typically African reflection on the meaning of Jesus now seems to form, as it were, the theological counterpart of the "theology of reconstruction" generally strongly directed toward social issues.[62] Moreover, an African "theology of the cross" functions more or less as a bridge between more explicit theological reflection on "the African Jesus" and the social background of that reflection.

In our search for what is common in contemporary African theology we will not introduce African concepts by their African names. In a continent with such a diversity of languages and cultures, that would constantly require describing the specific social and religious context of that concept. Within a short time we would not be able to see the forest for the trees. But that does not mean that in this study we will simply abstract from the concrete African context. Rather, the opposite is true: both the following section on the cross and the subsequent chapter on Jesus as ancestor and healer will demonstrate how much theology in Africa is interwoven with everyday life.

The Cross and Suffering in Africa

Just because traditional African religions lack a crossbearer comparable to Jesus, we cannot therefore conclude that "bearing the cross" is alien to the people of Africa. Just as we saw in Chapter 3 with the Taiwanese theologian C. S. Song, so also in numerous African theologians we see an identification of the cross of Jesus with the cross that an entire people bear or that the poorest of that people have to bear. In 1983, during the last intense convulsions of the apartheid government, the South African Protestant black theologian Takatso Mofokeng wrote his doctoral dissertation on *The Crucified among the Crossbearers: Towards a Black Christology*,[63] and in 1994 the Eritrean Lutheran theologian Yacob Tesfai published the volume *The Scandal of a Crucified World: Perspectives on the Cross and Suffering*.[64]

In this volume, Ela comments in one of the two chapters on Africa that for five hundred years the West has chosen the Christ without the cross (i.e. the actual crossbearers), whereas the people of Africa have borne the cross without the Christ. He characterizes the situation of many in Africa as "passion without redemption," suffering without redemption, whereas he reproaches the West for preaching redemption but not seeing who actually bore the cross.[65]

The identification of Jesus' cross with the cross that millions of people still carry can be regarded as an intensification of the analogy between Jesus' suffering and the suffering of the early Christian martyrs. Parallels were drawn even then. To that extent, Jesus' cross was never a lonely one. In the New Testament (Phil. 1:29 and 3:10–11) and in early Christian literature and art, the cross that people have always had to carry refers to the cross of Jesus. And yet references to the cross are found, in the course of Christian history up until today, in so many varying situations that certain distinctions are in order. There are at least four very different interpretations:

1. The cross as symbol of indescribable human suffering: this is a cross without the resurrection, without prospects.
2. The cross as symbol of conquest, as symbol of "Christ the victor," as the banner of Christ as conqueror: here it refers more to the triumphant resurrection than to terrible suffering.
3. The cross as internal experience of analysis, as symbol of the "dying with Christ," the dying of one's own ego.
4. The cross as reference to Jesus' substitutionary sacrifice made for us, human beings, and creating new life (resurrection).

In Tesfai's volume mentioned above, we encounter three of the four interpretations mentioned here. Only the third is missing. We discussed that third interpretation, dying *with* Christ, the death of the "old person," thoroughly in chapters 6–11. This concerns a key Christian experience to which the gospels and Paul's letters witness and which form the basis of the experience of Christian baptism.

In baptism a person discards his old life, dies with Christ and subsequently rises with Christ to a new life (Col. 2:12–13). This is not a one-time – and, in infant baptism, even unconscious – experience but an experience that believers re-live time and again throughout their whole lives. Western theology has always spoken of this experience as a key Christian experience throughout the ages, and yet this interpretation of the cross of Jesus has not set the tone for Western spirituality, which is certainly not the spirituality of self-analysis, of self-effacement. We could probably say: only in a Hindu and Buddhist context does there appear to be extensive and fertile soil for this way of thought.

The second interpretation is often linked with the way in which the Spanish and Portuguese conquered Latin America, but can also be more widely associated with the way in which the church has proclaimed the cross of Jesus as a symbol.[66] Thus the Indonesian theologian Andreas Yewangoe begins his explanation of the relationship of the cross of Jesus with concrete suffering in Asia with the remark that in most Asian countries the cross is not seen as the symbol of suffering but rather as the symbol of the pride and arrogance of the church.[67] And in the same volume, the Brazilian Protestant theologian Walter Altmann concludes in his contribution on "A Latin American Perspective on the Cross and Suffering" that for the majority of the Portuguese and Spanish there was no contradiction between the sword and the cross – both worked together to spread Christianity.[68] It is a cross of which every righteous Christian should be ashamed. It is a theology of the cross (*theologia crucis*) that is in fact a theology of victory over the powerful of the world (*theologia gloriae*).

In the first interpretation the cross is that cross that Song spoke of as the "crucified people," hopeless in a situation of "overwhelming poverty" (Pieris). It is also the cross of those marginalized during the apartheid government, which Mofokeng distinguishes from the "crossbearers." For him, crossbearers are those who consciously and freely take up their cross in order to change the situation of injustice in which they exist, along with so many others. But is that also the case, Mofokeng asks, for all those millions of people who have not chosen their cross and in whose situation no change can be found? Is God's power of resurrection also expressed in them? Is their existence not one long Good Friday that just does not end? That is indeed so, he concludes, but just as God stayed close to Jesus in the garden of Gethsemane on the eve of his crucifixion and afterwards, on the cross, with his painful praying and calling in his godforsakenness, so he also stays near to this "crucified people" in their godforsakenness. Every godforsakenness in these circumstances is also always a sign of divine nearness, because this godforsakenness shows who it is for whom God is concerned.[69]

Mandela's twenty-seven years of captivity, of which eighteen were spent on the desolate Robben Island, can serve as one of the best examples of the hidden powers that can hide in hopelessness. His speeches, published under the title *In His Own Words: From Freedom to the Future*, witness to that with their numerous references to that troubled period of imprisonment. In that period he seems to have tapped into something unheard of, something that was the exact opposite of what happened to him. Afterwards, Mandela himself probably realized that, because in one of his speeches he commented: "In this sense, the worst in human beings as represented by the ideology and practice of apartheid helped bring out the best in its opponents."[70]

Despite itself and unconsciously and unintentionally, in this way the hopeless cross of the first interpretation still acquires a meaning that comes close to the fourth interpretation, the substitutionary suffering that offers new life (the resurrection). But we do not encounter an explicit theology of substitution in African theology. We know the "suffering of the just" and we are also aware of the power that can arise from such suffering.

But that suffering is not generally linked to the substitutionary assumption of the guilt of others. Rather, it is an identification that derives hope from a "passage" similar to that of Jesus' passage through his suffering to his resurrection. Jesus is thus the representative of millions of sufferers who, full of hope, can identify with him.

And thus the Roman Catholic Ugandan theologian John Waliggo shows by the key word "rejection" how Africa, rejected by external and internal violence, can reflect the way in which Jesus, who was rejected by the builders, became the cornerstone for the hope of millions (Acts 4:11: "He is the stone you builders rejected, which has become the cornerstone."). Waliggo deliberately makes use of the biblical image of the "touchstone." In the position regarding this stone it becomes clear how God acts and how people act (1 Cor. 3:10–15). That stone can therefore also become a stumbling-block (Isa. 8:14–15). Thus, Africa also demands judgement against those who cause Africa evil from without as well as its leaders who erode peace and justice from within.[71]

The identification of God's suffering with human suffering or, vice versa, the identification of human suffering with God's suffering is usually intended to emphasize three aspects. (1) We are asked to pay attention to the concreteness of suffering. (2) The decisive nature of the way in which one works out spiritual suffering is pointed out. (3) And reference is made to a power of God that can, it seems, be revealed precisely in suffering and the emptiness experienced because of it.

The cross of the innocent whose suffering seems to be a power to change is the cross as it appears in the contribution to Tesfai's volume by the South African Lutheran black theologian Simon Maimela. In his contribution on the South African anti-apartheid struggle, he gives a short survey of Luther's theology of the cross.[72] To that end, he cites the famous theses from Luther's *Heidelberg Disputation* of 1518 in which Luther distinguishes between a *theologia gloriae* (theology of glory) and a *theologia crucis* (theology of cross). There Luther posits that only someone who desires to see what can be seen of God in suffering and the cross can be called a theologian (thesis 20). Luther's theology of the cross reflects a God who himself suffers in the human suffering on the cross. This God "hidden" in suffering is the real God, the God that Jesus wants to reveal to us.[73]

In essence, in Luther's theology of the cross we see the first, third and fourth interpretations of the cross converge. Luther elaborates on the third interpretation in his doctrine of sin in particular, in which he characterizes human beings as those who ultimately stand empty-handed before God. Sooner or later the individual will have to let go of all of his claims and references to his own accomplishments. Luther's last words, written in 1546 just before he died, were that we are all, in the end, beggars in the presence of God ("Wir sind Bettler, das is wahr!"). This accent in Lutheran theology on the poverty (emptiness) to which Jesus calls us – "He must become greater; I must become less" – found an echo in Japan in particular, as we saw in the fourth and fifth sections of Chapter 7.

The above makes clear that the thesis that African theology does not know what to do with the cross and the suffering of Jesus needs to be qualified. A more powerful identification of the suffering of the people of Africa with the suffering of Jesus than the one Ela expressed in his *African Cry*[74] is hardly imaginable. In countries like Rwanda, where the genocide that occurred will leave traces for generations to come, we see something like a revival of a theology of the cross formulated "from below," expressed primarily in the songs that are sung during Christian gatherings. It is a theology of the cross soaked with pain but also, just as much, with the hope of resurrection.[75]

We encounter an entirely new, typically African point of view in the Ghanaian Methodist Kwesi Dickson who has described the role of death in the African community in more detail in connection with the interpretation of the cross in African theology. He demonstrates how a number of aspects of the African experience of death also have direct consequences for the experience of Jesus' death.

1. Even if there is a clear physical reason for death – a snakebite, for example – an African will continue to look for a cause of death. He continues to look for the *real* cause, and searches in the domain of the ancestors, of the spirits or, finally, of the supreme God.

2. Death is not the end of life but rather a passage to another. The deceased makes a journey to another world. Sometimes he or she is given food for along the way. After he has arrived at the kingdom of the dead, his physical existence is continued, modelled on the example of the life he lived on earth. This rightly concerns the *living dead.*

3. There is a personal link with the dead. Funeral rites should contain all the ingredients that are necessary for this relationship. Such a personal link is crucial because the dead remain an important reference point for the living.

4. The dead are seen as an opportunity to improve living conditions of others or for oneself (through reincarnation). To this end, the dead are given messages and requests for the ancestors. In the event of belief in reincarnation, the dead are often asked to request the ancestors for a good reincarnation, so that the next life will be better than the current one.

5. Participation in a funeral rite does not at all stand in the way of spontaneous and sometimes even cheerful expressions of life.

People often dance at funerals. Dancing in Africa is one of the most powerful confirmations of life. The communal eating and drinking will give a Westerner the impression of a party rather than a funeral.

6. Funerals are not only an activity for the family alone but for the whole community. The number of those present during the funeral therefore says nothing – even though it will of course often be the case – about the social position of the deceased as such.[76]

Given the background of all of these facets of the African experience of death, it should not be surprising that the celebration of the Lord's Supper is experienced very intensely as a meal on the occasion of a deceased person who nonetheless lives (the "living dead"). Thus Dickson also sees, with little difficulty, the African experience of death in a phrase such as: "Is not the cup of thanksgiving for which we give thanks a participation in the blood of Christ? And is not the bread that we break a participation in the body of Christ? Because there is one loaf, we, who are many, are one body, for we all partake of the one loaf" (1 Cor. 10:16–18). It does not take very much to imagine an African funeral meal in these sentences.

Paul says here that to eat and drink at the table of the Lord is to share in his death and also to share in the life of the community. Thus the meal of the Lord has a twofold purpose: to strengthen the community with the Lord who is no longer among us and to strengthen the community of believers. The African funeral meal has the same purpose.

Since Jesus was not guilty of anything, in Africa this means that after his death he would certainly be counted among the ancestors, since only those who have lived an exemplary life can rise to the position of an ancestor. He will never stop being one of the "living dead" because there will always be people who *know* him, whose lives have been irrevocably influenced by his life and work. He is the one whom people can call on for help and to whom people pray. Just as seats and staffs, among other things, are the symbols of the presence of the ancestors, so the wooden cross is the symbol of Jesus, the "ever-living."

Thus three important elements of the African religious background influence the experience of Jesus' cross: (1) only the ritual meal allows one to participate truly in his life, (2) he fulfils the mediating role of the ancestors in an exemplary way, and (3) his death is viewed as a passage to another, happier existence. Dickson sees these three biblical elements (participation in his life, mediation for the living, and expression of the expectation of life after death) experienced intensely in the African culture of death. He does not see those elements experienced as deeply in the West, which is why he wonders if the West has not lagged behind Africa when it comes to the existential integration of the richness of the rituals and ideas that the Bible presents regarding Jesus' death.[77] And therefore, following Dickson, Bujo can ask: "Could not the recognition of the place which the ancestors and elders occupy in the life of the Africans stimulate theologians to construct something new?"[78]

We commented in the third section of this chapter that it would be difficult to reconcile the image of Jesus as ancestor with his substitutionary death. Indeed, the step to the notion of substitution is not taken. Rather, the image has to do with Jesus as a representative of God to the people and of the people to God. The intensity with which participation in his life is experienced in the Lord's Supper, the high expectations that are nourished because of his intervention, and the character of reality that is attributed to a life after death are strong witnesses to a powerful belief in the *effect* of this representation. But that does not at all affect the fact that the notion of sacrificing one's own life for the sins of others so that they can be forgiven is lacking.

16 African Images of Jesus

Jesus as Ancestor

Much has been published in the last decade on the different images of Jesus in African theology. Two of these images that stand out the most are that of Jesus as ancestor and that of Jesus as healer. They are the most widespread of a broad range of images: Jesus as chief, king, master of initiation, eldest brother, etc.[1] In all these images Jesus' role as the bestower and protector of life is the central concept on which everything turns.

African theology can thus be correctly characterized as a "theology of life."[2] It is also from this that it derives its "earthly" character. The earthly aspect is so important that it can even be called "holy": "Life is so central that it must be characterized as sacred."[3] Human beings cannot ascribe value to their own lives and that of others solely by themselves, for their own lives are also involved here. The questions that life evokes take precedence over those of the individual human being, which explains the step towards a power who bestows life. In African religiosity, God is primarily the giver, the protector of life. Life thus means participating in the source of all life, participating in God. This participation concerns all facets of the created world, for God's presence is not limited to human lives: God can also manifest himelf in the material world and in the animal world.

But that manifestation – as is argued in all the passages on the supreme divinity – always occurs through mediation and has gradations, for all of life is ordered according to higher and lower sections. That hierarchy extends to both the material world and the spiritual world, to visible and invisible things, the living and the dead. There are constant forms of exchange between the different sections, and the ancestors and healers play a key role in these exchanges. God is the one who grants life but people are the ones who should preserve the unity of life, the connection of the biological with the spiritual.

Africa's religiosity can be seen as both monotheistic and anthropocentric. Without the mediation of human beings, the power of the most high God cannot be experienced. With reference to John 10:10 ("I have come that they may have life, and have it to the full"), Jesus is seen pre-eminently as the one who distributes the gift of life. As Gal. 2:20 ("I have been crucified with Christ and I no longer live, but Christ lives in me") proved to be a key text for Asian theologians, so John 10:10 has become that for African theologians.[4]

In this study we will limit ourselves to mediation by ancestors and healers. Their role is central to the whole world of African religions; they are a model for the way in which contemporary African theology deals with Africa's religious heritage. In the image of Jesus as ancestor, the continuity of life beyond death is central. The image of Jesus as healer is concerned primarily with the restoration of life on this side of death.

In our concentration on the role of ancestor and healer, we thus choose a "functional" approach to the meaning of Jesus. The *functions* that Jesus fulfils in the faith community are central for us. This does not entail an argument for a purely "functionalistic" approach that deliberately avoids the question of who Jesus is. Function and being (nature) are not separate here either. It will appear time and again that the function that *Jesus* can fulfil in a faith community has everything to do with the question of who he is according to that faith community. This latter question always has to do, in Jesus' case, with the question of how divine nearness comes to expression in him.[5]

The primary reason for choosing a functional approach is found very simply in the fact that this approach fits the "African Jesus" best. Who Jesus is is deduced here primarily from the way in which one experiences his life-force. Each experience does presuppose, of course, some conceptualization – otherwise, the experience cannot be "placed," cannot be named – but certainly in a culture that is so focused on experience as African culture, such experiences continually renew the available frameworks.

Without ascribing a prominent place to the role of Jesus as ancestor, each study on the meaning of Jesus in Africa (and essentially in Asia) would fall short of its goal, as several African theologians have claimed.[6] Up until now in this study we were faced with the role of the veneration of the ancestors most prominently in the chapter on Korea, but the veneration of ancestors plays a conspicuous role in all of Asia and Africa. The veneration of ancestors is closely connected with the role that family relationships play in the non-Western world. These relationships extend beyond death: death does not break one's relationship with the (deceased) family members. Family relationships are, in fact, unbreakable.

There is almost no people in Africa whose ancestors do not play a prominent role, even though they are venerated differently by each people. The presence of the ancestors can be sensed at the graves especially, for a deceased person is never completely in his or her grave. In Africa, a grave is the primary place where the invisible (the invisible ones) is concentrated, for the dead are not dead. An African will not say too quickly that someone to whom he stands in a living relationship is dead.

He would sooner say that he has left, has abandoned us, is no longer there, and has gone on, etc.[7]

Concretely, this means that the relationship of an African Christian to Jesus always presupposes the relationship of his ancestors to Jesus or – conversely – Jesus' relationship to those ancestors. That sense of an inextricable connection with the ancestors has largely been lost in the West, but the idea was not strange to the European peoples right up until the early Middle Ages, as the story of the unsuccessful baptism of King Radboud – to which we referred in Chapter 8 – testifies.

In his 1984 study *Christ our Ancestor*, the Tanzanian Roman Catholic theologian Charles Nyamiti lists five characteristics of ancestors. Ancestors are always characterized by:

1. A natural relationship with the earthly family or tribal members;
2. A supernatural status received at death;
3. Mediation between the divine and the human;
4. A morally exemplary life;
5. Regular contact with the earthly family members.[8]

In particular, Nyamiti looks at the brother–ancestor as an object of comparison, because Jesus' divine sonship can be compared with our "sonship," in which case, then, there is a parent we have in common.[9] Just as we saw in Chapter 5 in Asia, so also in Africa, at issue here is the special role that is ascribed to the *eldest brother* in the comparison between Jesus and a brother.[10]

But here as well Nyamiti is aware of the clear differences between the role of Jesus and that of the eldest brother–ancestor. He summarizes the differences as follows:

a. With Jesus, as human beings we are connected as *children of Adam* and not as *members of a certain family, tribe, or nation*. Moreover, his divine nearness gives his humanity a special character. It is a humanity that is connected with the divine that we can approximate through adoption, but because of his special position, we can never match it.

b. Jesus is not *only an example* for people, but, through his Spirit, he is also the supporting principle of our knowing and acting. He is thus both object and subject of our actions. He acts in us and we act in him.

c. The way in which Jesus comes into contact with us in the sacraments of baptism and communion is intended to *change* our lives. The contact with him thus not only confirms or restores a relationship but also changes it in that we become participants in a process of continual change (conversion), which is expressed in the continual dying and rising with Christ.

d. Brotherhood or sisterhood is, in Christ, a matter of *free choice* in comparison to the connectedness with family or the tribe, which is more of a given in which people participate.

e. Moreover, Jesus' presence is not experienced in animals or trees or cemeteries, as is most often the case with the ancestors, but in *people* and in the *sacraments*.

Because of these differences, the *analogous* character of the comparison should not be forgotten. Here, as has been remarked several times, "analogous" refers to the indication of similarities in the midst of (larger) differences.[11] But despite these differences, an analogy can – Nyamiti argues – reveal striking parallels.[12] In the midst of all these differences, the similarities will be so striking for many Africans that the image of the brother–ancestor will reveal more of the significance of Jesus to them than all the traditional images in the history of doctrine in the early church. But in the midst of all the associations that the image of ancestor evokes, it is necessary to focus the comparison somewhat. As far as Nyamiti is concerned, that focus should be directed towards the characteristics we mentioned earlier: *(1) having a parent in common, (2) being removed from death, (3) being able to mediate with respect to God, (4) constituting a behavioural example, and (5) being the object of regular ritual contact.*[13]

If, indeed, it can be made clear that the African belief in ancestors can be taken up in a transforming way in the role of Jesus as ancestor, then that will prove to many African theologians that it is very possible to be both authentically African and authentically Christian.[14] Jesus is then the "new" ancestor who breaks through the ethnic boundaries that are observed so strictly in the traditional belief in ancestors. He is "the ancestor of all mankind."[15]

In the Jesus–ancestor comparison, much depends on the place the ancestor is accorded in his mediating role with respect to the supreme God. Can their mediating role clarify that of Jesus or does it obstruct one's view of Jesus' unique role? The same discussion more or less took place in the Western history of theology between Protestants and Roman Catholics concerning Mary and the saints. There too the question was if there could be any other mediating figures alongside Jesus as the unique mediator. The churches of the Reformation rejected this. They did acknowledge a kind of "place of honour" of great names from church history to show respect – such as those of Augustine, Luther, and Calvin – but there was no veneration of them, let alone any mediation of salvation by them.

But unfortunately, in this kind of discussion, people often thought in terms of competition. The mediating role of saints or, in this case, ancestors is then seen as being in competition with Jesus' unique, mediating role. Nyamiti wants to break through this competition model. It can also be said of the ancestors that they exercise their authority "in Christ" like those who represent Christ in ecclesiastical office. The role of the ancestors is then held up, as it were, against the light of Jesus' words and deeds. Stated in a Christian way, they can only fulfil their role properly "in him."

It is for that reason that the Ghanaian Presbyterian theologian Abrahm Akrong then also remarks: "The ancestorhood of Jesus Christ has transformed our conception of the ancestors."[16] The ancestor thus resembles Jesus and Jesus resembles the ancestor.[17] Here, then, we find the phenomenon of *double transformation*. When the term is applied to Jesus, the ancestor can be nothing other than a bringer of salvation – that is how Jesus changes the concept of ancestor. Subsequently, Jesus appears to be able to fulfil a greater role amidst the connectedness of the generations beyond death that we have cited so often than many in the West have conceived. That is how the concept of ancestor changes Jesus' role as well.

This "transformation" of the meaning of the ancestors will require a not negligible conversion for many Africans. It is not for nothing that Nyamiti also speaks of a "profound Christianization" of the concept of ancestor.[18] Because the role of the ancestors overlaps that of Jesus in a number of respects, allowing two different circuits for Christians in Africa is not an option. Therefore, in a creative and critical synthesis, Nyamiti wants Jesus to be called the ancestor *par excellence*. The term could place a number of the biblical aspects of the celebration of the Lord's Supper in a clearer light. Nyamiti is thinking primarily of the following aspects:

1. People will be able to experience the Lord's Supper more intensely as a *community meal* that connects the participants with Jesus, the ancestors and one another.

2. People will be able to experience the spirit that makes Jesus present during this meal exclusively as a powerful and good spirit, a Holy Spirit, that connects the believers not only with the members of one's tribe but also with all of humanity.

3. The salvation that is experienced during the meal will not be experienced exclusively as spiritual but also be involved in the more physical or material facets of life.

4. An internal growth process will be started that allows us to share in Jesus' status as a child of God, just as the ancestors also allow us to share in the communal child.

5. Just as the ancestors are involved in the whole community, so participation in Jesus' death and resurrection in the Lord's Supper will be related to the transformation of the whole community.

6. The nearness of the dead in their "Being with God" will be experienced more intensely.[19]

This summary does assume that changes can occur on both sides. The Lord's Supper adds new dimensions to the traditional meal honouring the ancestors. And the comparison with the traditional meal in honour of the ancestors adds, in turn, new – or better – forgotten dimensions to the Lord's Supper. Thus the Lord's Supper teaches us that Jesus' spirit is always a Holy, good Spirit who connects us not only with members of our tribe but with all of humanity. And thus the meal in honour of the ancestors teaches us that salvation in Jesus is not exclusively spiritual. At the same time it shows us how concretely the nearness of those who have died can be experienced.

To this summary Akrong adds the point that speaking about Jesus as ancestor also makes it possible to integrate both masculine and feminine properties into this image[20] because the masculine and feminine can be transcended in him. But we should not overestimate how far we can take this. Because ancestors are usually considered to be male, the number of female images is quite small.[21] We do see, for example, how someone like the Cameroon Roman Catholic theologian Fabien Eboussi-Boulaga explicitly relates the African mythical representations concerning motherhood – i.e. the cosmic mother, the agricultural mother and the mother of the hero – to his outline of the "Christic model."[22]

The presupposition of this creative and critical synthesis of faith in Jesus and the veneration of ancestors is that the supreme God in respect to whom the ancestors occupy a mediating position is the same as the one who is called the father of Jesus in Christianity.[23] This presupposition has been and is, of course, the subject of much discussion. The idea behind it is that God was already in Africa before the missionaries came.[24] In fact, this idea was also already implicit and sometimes also unconsciously and unintentionally given form for decades in a number of African translations in which the name of the supreme God was chosen as the name for God.[25] The Kenyan Presbyterian theologian James Kombo could also add in an appendix to his 2000 dissertation on *The Doctrine of God in African Christian Thought*[26] a list of least eight closely printed pages with the traditional divine names that Africa's peoples and tribes connected with Israel's God.

For that matter, Kombo himself takes an intermediate position, in which he, on the one hand, rejects the customary identification of the African gods with the idols, the Baals, of the Old Testament. On the other hand, he does not simply identify the African gods with the Father of Jesus Christ. In order to build a bridge, he argues both for a "Christianization" of the African gods[27] as well as for an African inculturation of a number of classical concepts such as substance, person, and the father–son relationship from the classical Western doctrine of God.[28] He thus also arrives, in fact, at the notion of a *double transformation*.

The identification of Africa's God with the God of the Bible is, in fact, now the *communis opinio* in African theology. That is a remarkable fact, certainly against the background of other inculturations in the history of Christianity. It has been already discussed in Chapter 1 that it can be assumed that the Greco-Roman and West European cultures also left their traces on the Christian concept of God. But it was never a matter of an explicitly confessed identity between the Greco-Roman or Celtic, Frankish and Germanic gods and the God of the Bible. In these areas Christianization was a matter of "God against the gods."[29]

Probably – Walls suspects – Greco-Roman and West European polytheism stood in the way of such an identification. Africa's monotheism stands out sharply against that polytheism. Despite the recognition of the existence of lower gods, the acknowledgement of that monotheism in any case belongs to one of the hardly disputed any more and highly nuanced presuppositions of contemporary African theology. That makes the comparison and even the identification with Israel's God somewhat simpler.

A milestone in this process of acknowledgement was the conference of the All African Conference of Churches in Ibadan, Nigeria, in 1966. At this conference, where most of the participants were West African Protestant theologians and the above-mentioned Nigerian professor Idowu played an important role as president and speaker, the following statement was formulated in the final declaration: "We believe that the God and Father of our Lord Jesus Christ, Creator of heaven and earth, Lord of history, has been dealing with mankind at all times and in all parts of the world. It is with this conviction that we study the rich heritage of our African peoples, and we have evidence that they know of Him and worship Him."[30] This statement expressed well not only the opinion of contemporary Protestant theology but also that of many Western missionaries who worked in Africa for a long time.[31]

Roman Catholic theology was certainly more reserved in the 1960s, one of the reasons for which was the resistance of the Belgian lecturer (in the Congo) Alfred Vanneste to an "Africanization" of theology.[32] Now, however, Roman Catholic theology is undergoing a similar development.[33] Vanneste, then dean of the theological faculty at Kinshasa, first wanted to do "real theology" ("d'abord une *vraie* théologie") before creating room for African experiments.[34] By "real theology" he meant a theology for which account could be given universally and then later be adapted to the local situation. He came out, in fact, at the existing Western theology. His student, the future bishop Tharcisse Tshibangu, argued precisely that "couleur locale" be given a greater accent in every form of authentic theology.[35]

"Local," contextual theology will always develop in dialogue with theology done elsewhere and in dialogue with the Christian tradition. The history of dogma contains more or less all the moves that are made on the chessboard of attributing meaning to Jesus. Knowledge of these moves keeps us from being naïve, from the inclination to want to reinvent the wheel and from becoming derailed. But knowledge of the history of doctrine can also deteriorate into a fixation on history at the expense of everything else, in which more value is always ascribed to the past than to the present. Then the indispensable, historical orientation can also turn into a straitjacket; it becomes a kind of mould into which everything that can be said about Jesus has to fit.

The latter seems to be the case when both Bujo and Nyamiti justify their interpretation of Jesus as ancestor by referring to a Christology "from below" or "from above."[36] With that distinction they intend to answer the question of whether Jesus derives his meaning from his earthly existence ("from below") or from his being sent by God from on high and from afar ("from above"). In the former approach, Jesus is raised by God after his crucifixion to a higher glory, as it were, and in the latter, he descends from on high to us. Bujo chooses the first and Nyamiti the second.[37] In both cases it is a matter of further specifying the relationship of the divine and human in the person of Jesus. Each doctrine about Jesus will always be concerned about this relationship. If one of these poles disappears, then it will no longer be about Jesus. The Ghanaian Anglican theologian John Pobee calls the holding together of the two aspects "non-negotiable points" in each image of Jesus.[38] But one does not need to appeal as such to older ways of thinking in order to do so.

The risk is then too great that what is new in the African contribution to the ascription of meaning to Jesus will be counteracted too quickly. But Nyamiti himself gives an impetus to another approach by calling Jesus' death the centre of his approach to Jesus.[39] Indeed, if the death of family or tribe members is, as it were, the starting point for the veneration of ancestors, then Jesus' death must be the starting point for the meaning that can be ascribed to him as ancestor. Of course, that meaning is connected intrinsically with his previous life, but his death also reveals to us how he remains connected with the Father in life and death and how we subsequently also remain connected with him as "(eldest) brother" and as children of one Father.

But the Christian tradition adds an essential aspect to the veneration of ancestors that is not found in the tradition of the ancestors. That is the aspect of the forgiveness of sins. Our being connected in our death with Jesus' death is, after all, not only a question of a continuing connectedness with a now definitely finished life but is also a question of a new beginning in which our old life can be literally "put aside." It is not for nothing that

Jesus' descent to the realm of the dead was the most important depiction in Christian art for almost a millennium. Not only in a country like Korea, as we saw earlier, but also in Africa, Jesus' "descent into hell" is one of the most liberating passages in the Christian confession of faith.[40]

Thus, death is not a definite judgement about someone's life – that would, in any case, be too harsh a judgement. After all, not everyone is in a position to get her life and relationships straightened out before she dies. Moreover, on a continent like Africa there are certainly hundreds of thousands who have, partly through their own doing and partly due to circumstances outside their control, become victims of serious disease or violence. To call them to account for what their lives have in fact become would be extremely unmerciful.

The Christian faith does not speak to them about being pinned down in the life they are now living; it is considerably more merciful. It speaks about the possibility of "laying aside" one's old life in connection with Jesus' death. The new aspect that Jesus' death adds to these "unfinished" lives is his substitutionary act for their guilt, for their lot in life. This removes every aspect of merit from their life after death and places it within the framework of divine mercy.

Conclusions

Jesus can truly be called the ancestor *par excellence* only if the most important aspects of being an ancestor are connected with the most important aspects of the African reflection on the meaning of the cross of Jesus discussed in the previous chapter. It is only in that way that he is not only the ancestor but also the liberator and displays the nearness of the supreme God, who can be honoured *par excellence* in an African theology that recognizes both God's nearness and distance (his otherness).[41]

Contemporary African theology appears able to give its own entirely unique accents in ascribing meaning to Jesus even more than it does in its views concerning the supreme God.[42] Very concretely, it means that the concept of ancestor is stripped of every aspect of merit and seamless continuation with one's earthly life. That is the transformation on the African side. At the same time, Jesus is seen, more explicitly than has been the case in the last millennium in the West, as the one who connects the living and the dead with each other. That is the transformation on the Christian side.

Is this *double transformation* sufficient to ascribe a central role to Jesus as ancestor? From field research in Kenya, Uganda and Ghana by Diane Stinton, a Canadian Protestant theologian at Daystar University in Nairobi in Kenya, it appears that believers in Africa as a whole are not yet convinced of that.[43]

She ascribes this partly to missions, which for more than a century saw the belief in ancestors as competition for belief in Jesus and through its fierce resistance left deep traces of reservation behind in African Christianity. With a nice understatement, Stinton remarks that in any case the Africans were not prepared for this from the West.[44] A source of much misunderstanding is, of course, the language problem. Actually, not a single West European language is a good equivalent for the emotional value of the many words that the African languages have for the concept of ancestor. That is the reason for the argument often heard that one should write an African theology primarily in one of the African languages and only later – if desired – translate it.[45]

The belief in ancestors has a number of elements that can lead to some reservation. After all, how can someone like Jesus, who never married and had no children, be an ancestor?[46] And how can someone with whom we have no blood relationship be called ancestor? Moreover, an ancestor is considered to have died a "good death." Physically speaking, that was not at all the case with Jesus. In the midst of a number of fruitful analogies, there are thus some very obvious questions – questions that, according to Stinton, are posed less by Roman Catholics than by Protestants.[47] This probably has to do with the Roman Catholic veneration of the saints.

For that matter, the relationship between the classical veneration of the saints in the Roman Catholic Church and the veneration of ancestors is also disputed among Roman Catholic theologians. Thus Ela makes a sharp distinction between the veneration of saints and the veneration of ancestors. He considers the classical veneration of saints in the Roman Catholic Church to be, historically and contextually, primarily a European phenomenon with which Africans have little affinity.[48] He differs in this from Nyamiti, who in fact considers the classical Roman Catholic saints to be better examples of his Christian interpretation of ancestors than the African ancestors themselves.[49]

Thus, despite some unmistakable reservations, the reference to Jesus as ancestor contains, in the view of many African theologians, so many elements that make him more understandable to Africans than do terms such as *kurios, Messiah, Christ, Son of David, Son of Man* and *Logos*, that this analogy deserves to be worked out (more) carefully rather than abandoned.[50] Crucial here is the extent to which African believers have succeeded in effectuating the *double transformation* described above.

Jesus as Healer

The second image of Jesus that surfaces quite powerfully in the African "theology of life" is that of Jesus as healer. It is a challenging image, for it immediately invokes the question of the effectiveness of the healer in an Africa that is crying out for effective healers. Can Jesus protect a child from disease? A woman from infertility? From evil spirits who cause disease?[51] Whoever calls Jesus the great healer has a great deal to explain to the millions who are dying in the Sahel, the millions of victims of corruption and exploitation and apparently uncontrollable viral diseases like malaria and AIDS.[52] The image comes back like a boomerang, as it were, on the head of the user in the question: Where can the life that Jesus bestows be found in Africa? Is the "face" of Jesus in Africa not more likely that of the disease than that of the healer?[53]

We already remarked earlier that the physical cause of disease in Africa is only one side of the coin. The actual cause of disease is found elsewhere and has everything to do with the world of the spirits and the ancestors. Disease is an indication of disturbed relationships between human beings and between the human being and the spiritual powers surrounding him or her.[54] An African would never consider the preaching of exclusively spiritual salvation to be true salvation, and he would find a purely medical approach to disease superficial. On the one hand, the physical effect of spiritual evil would, in his view, be underestimated. On the other, the spiritual background of many diseases would be denied. Both too spiritual an approach and a medical approach ignore the many questions that physical suffering invokes. True salvation in Africa will always be viewed holistically, relating to both spirit and body.[55]

The preaching of Jesus as healer is suggestive against this background. It is expected that his spiritual power will also have a physically cleansing effect. Is that expectation realistic? The Guinean Roman Catholic theologian Cécé Kolié points out that many Christians in Africa live more or less in two worlds: the world of the church and the world of traditional healers, miracle workers, etc.[56] It is not easy, apparently, to build a bridge between those two worlds. Brave attempts to do so are not always appreciated either, as the Zambian Roman Catholic bishop Emmanuel Milingo, the archbishop of Lusaka from 1969 to 1983, experienced. His exorcism and healing practices were not appreciated by Rome, and he was suspended in 1983 and offered a "harmless" function in Rome.[57]

But Stinton shows, in her above-mentioned field research, that the image of Jesus as healer is close to the heart of many Africans and is seen as the most powerful, convincing image of Jesus.[58] This image is undoubtedly necessarily connected to the many stories about Jesus' healings in the New Testament. Furthermore, the image of Jesus as healer is strengthened by the earlier cited identification of the God of Jesus and the God of African monotheism. Healers, miracle workers and soothsayers are always seen as instruments of God. If Jesus can be called the Son of God in the New Testament, it is clear to all Africans that the therapeutic gifts that the other healers already possess on behalf on the Most High will be expressed most powerfully in Jesus. In addition to the New Testament, the traditional relation of the healer to the supreme God forms a rich soil for the image of Jesus as healer.

And, as a third argument, the appeal to one's own experience plays a major role here. Many Africans have had personal experience with religiously charged healing practices. They are familiar with the relationship between prayer and healing. It can perhaps even be said that nowhere else has that relationship been developed as strongly as in Africa.

In the image of Jesus as healer, therefore, a large number of aspects converge that are closely connected to the African experience. As the giver of life, Jesus is an "all-round healer" who also heals "wounds" in the spiritual and social realms. In addition, he himself makes frequent use of symbolic acts well known in Africa, such as the laying on of hands, exorcising evil spirits, etc. Therefore, his healings can be easily placed in the same perspective as those of many traditional healers. It is not a healing power that goes out from him with respect to individual, physical problems, but the forcefield around this healer extends to the whole weal and woe of the community. Moreover, he is also often prophet, soothsayer and counsellor, and he is considered to personify exceptional wisdom.

Despite the broad perspective in which both Jesus' work of healing in the New Testament and that of the traditional healer stands, the image that is evoked with the accent on Jesus as healer is not without risk. When Jesus, as a "newcomer," is presented primarily as a healer, he almost always comes in second place after the known, familiar healer. The same question of the "newcomer" or the "latecomer" who needs to go to the end of the queue also arises with the image of Jesus as ancestor.[59] In both cases, only by emphasizing the "transforming" character of the designation of Jesus as healer or ancestor can one break through the traditional ranking and orders.

Furthermore, the image of Jesus as healer can be narrowed into that of Jesus as First Aid, a glorified first-aider. He then soon becomes either a competitor of or an extra aid in reserve next to the "regular" medical care. He can then even function as an *excuse* for the lack of medical care. It is then all too easily forgotten that Jesus' healings are never isolated healings but *signs* of the coming kingdom of God. The expectation of that kingdom stands in sharp contrast to the current situation of health care in Africa. In Africa, that care is "class health care," where the rich receive an entirely different care than the poor. The effect of Jesus as healer could be much greater if this kingdom perspective was more often present in the preaching about his miracles, and that proclamation would contribute to a more social structure of the health care system.[60]

It was remarked in conjunction with the image of Jesus as ancestor that a distinction should be made between good and bad ancestors. "Bad" ancestors are those ancestors who act badly and are disowned, who can have an evil effect. The analogy with Jesus does not extend to them. A similar distinction should also be employed with respect to the image of the healer. Africa is, after all, full of fraudulent healers who fall into the same category as dangerous manipulators and evil sorcerers. This is also a complicating factor for the independent African churches as well.[61]

Stinton's research into the extent to which Christians are inclined to compare Jesus with their traditional healers thus yields an ambivalent picture. The identification appears – as indicated above – to have a strong basis, but a considerable group also has second thoughts, if not objections to it. Clear majority and minority views cannot be indicated. The hesitations centre primarily around two issues:[62] Should a normative image of a healer not be developed first, before that image can be applied to Jesus? And does the image of Jesus as healer not raise the problem of the recognition of Jesus' divinity?

With the first question, we find ourselves in the midst of the question of the dynamic of the process of *double transformation*. In fact, here what is requested is that the image of the healer be purified against the background of the image of Jesus as healer. But then Jesus is compared with Jesus and the comparison cannot yield anything new. That inclination does sometimes also exist in the case of comparing Jesus with the ancestor. The ancestor is modelled on Jesus and Jesus is called the ancestor *par excellence*. Here as well Jesus is compared with Jesus and the comparison does not yield anything new.[63]

It is much more interesting if the *transformation* is introduced only as the result of the tensive sifting process that occurs in the comparison rather than at the beginning. For only then can changes occur on both sides and new perspectives that have been hidden until now can be revealed. Then, as a result of the comparison, one can very well speak about Jesus as the ancestor or healer *par excellence*. After all, it will then be apparent that he can be an ancestor or healer only in a very specific sense. How specific is apparent, for example, from the fact that the Ghanaian Methodist theologian Mercy Amba Oduyoye can speak in this context of Jesus as "the wounded healer," the healer who knows what it is to be wounded, even to suffer.[64]

Whatever is specific about Jesus' healing will also have to be apparent from his role as healer against the background of the society in which he is active. His healing activity does not leave that society undisturbed. In contrast to the role of the traditional healer, Jesus' role does not have to be a confirming role as such, certainly not a confirmation of the current, often unjust African system of health care. He can also fill a critical role here, just as Jesus' healings filled a critical role with respect to a number of prejudices about people. His role as healer cannot be isolated from the context in which he works. Because of that, the forces that are released in the prayer for healing should not be viewed in too limited a way. They are not only related to the sick person in question but to the whole community.[65]

The second critical question concerned that of Jesus' divinity. Is that not denied by comparing Jesus with a human healer? This question appears to rest on a misunderstanding. The identification of the meaning of Jesus with that of human roles such as that of the priest, prophet, king and healer does not detract from Jesus' divinity at all. After all, an analogy always concerns a similarity in the midst of greater differences – differences that the history of doctrine has often expressed by speaking of Jesus as a divine or heavenly (high) priest, prophet, king or healer. But that is not at all intended to deify the priest, prophet, king or healer.

The same argument also obtains for the designation of Jesus as ancestor. The ancestor does not first have to be divine, and thus the divinity of Jesus is not thereby denied either. The divine nearness that Jesus personifies is always manifested, after all, precisely through his humanness, his all too humanness, and does not leave an exalted divine trail in our human trail that can be clearly distinguished from the human. After all, revelation is always a concealing as well, and is visible only to those who have eyes to see (Matt. 13:13–14).

Conclusions

The image of healer appears to evoke as many ambivalent feelings as does the image of ancestor. We thus see many theologians hesitating or adding a great many "ifs and buts" to the use of this image.[66] There could be two reasons for this reservation. In the first place, there is the reason of excuse, which we already indicated above. In an Africa that has been engaged in internal slaughter for the last four decades, Jesus can be spoken of credibly as healer only if the Christian churches themselves in Africa also display their manifold "gifts of healing" and thus show in deeds that they are inspired by a healer of old and new diseases.[67] If they do not do so, then speaking about Jesus as a healer soon becomes an excuse for their own negligence and then the image is rightly to be criticized.

In the second place, the hesitation of theologians with respect to the image of the healer can also indicate a gulf between the theology of the seminaries and the theological faculties and the "popular theology" in the villages. The Dutch anthropologist Matthew Schoffeleers has advanced the thesis of that gulf and associated the central position of the healer primarily with "popular theology."[68] But the reserve with respect to the use of the image of the healer that Stinton encounters in her field work precisely at the grassroots seems to counter his thesis. This does not deny the gulf between academic theology and "popular" theology; but it is only the focus on that gulf on this point – the central role of the healer – that is nuanced. For that matter, it is difficult for both Schoffeleers and Stinton to get a proper handle on "popular theology."

Much more than is the case with the Asian images of Jesus as *bodhisattva*, *avatara* and *guru*, with the African images of ancestor and healer, we are now in a world full of ambivalences. In Asia, *double transformation* has to do primarily with the question of how Jesus is God and how he is human. In essence, it concerns the question of the extent to which the concrete, harsh, earthly life can be connected with the divine.

In Africa, it is precisely God's relation to the concrete, earthly reality that is not in question. To the contrary, it is the focal point of everything. That also explains the preference for the Old Testament. In Africa, the central question is how Jesus can be spoken of in the midst of the ambivalences to which all forces, powers and spirits under the supreme God are subject. It is deliberate on our part that we are not speaking here of "transcending the ambivalences," as if Jesus should be exalted above them. Then it is precisely concepts like ancestor and healer from which we would have to keep our distance.

Rather, in the African setting, the question is if an earthly Jesus can also be a bringer of salvation in his earthliness.[69] Pénoukou characterizes this "earthliness" as a "being-there-with." He sees the nearness of the most high presented so unconditionally in Jesus that all ambivalence concerning the nature of his mediation is removed. He speaks of an "ontological solidarity." It is clear in Jesus not only that our humanity is always a "being there with" God, but it is also a "being-there-with" nature and fellow human beings around us. He thus personifies a threefold "being there with" and is the culmination of a "cosmotheandric" relation in which a human being lives in connection with the cosmos, with God (*theos*) and (fellow) human beings (*anèr*). We encountered this same term in Chapter 10. It is a term that Pénoukou sees as a description of that to which Paul refers in 1 Cor. 15:28 when he expresses his desire "that God may be all in all."[70]

Essentially, Jesus is then the person who – both as ancestor and as healer – maintains life's connections. The image that transcends both ancestor and healer is that of the giver and thus the saver of life. This is also the central motif that can be heard in the images that African women associate with Jesus. The New Testament stories of Jesus' approach to women are an occasion for them to see him as the one who shares in their primary concerns and is solidary with them, in contrast to many of their husbands, in their struggle for themselves and for their children to survive.[71] Thus, for them he is a life-force, as they testify repeatedly when asked in interviews about their personal image of Jesus.[72] It is striking in their answers, for that matter, that the image of the healer in relation to Jesus remains so male, whereas the traditional healers in Africa very often are women.[73]

Amongst all the *functions* Jesus could apparently fulfil in Africa to connect with the existing African religiosity, it is primarily the testimonies of African women that are decisive for us with respect to the concrete biblical stories about Jesus' earthly activity.[74] Eboussi-Boulaga, especially, in his call to imitate the concrete "Christic model," wants to direct attention to Jesus' own concrete life decisions, which also often go "unheard" in Africa and are of a "different" order than that which people are used to. That is why he also argues for an "ethical conversion," i.e. a conversion that also comes to expression in a different ethical behaviour.[75]

It is characteristic in this context that in those African countries where the majority of the population is Christian, there is no "different" sexual lifestyle with a view to the danger of contracting AIDS, little is done structurally with respect to discrimination against women, corruption is not forcefully combatted, and there has been no breaking through tribal thinking. Actually, only in South Africa, in the resistance to apartheid and later in the institution of a Truth and Reconciliation Committee, did the (black) church in Africa have an active, political role. That is remarkable against the background of the strong accent on Jesus as giver of life in all conceivable contexts. Also, if we take seriously the argument formulated at the end of Chapter 2 for modesty with respect to the social role a religion can play, that does not at all mean that we should not expect anything of a social nature from a religion like Christianity. Rather, we agree wholeheartedly with Bediako that the proclamation of the "public" meaning of Jesus' message in Africa should not be neglected.[76] Could that proclamation lead, with respect to the violence in many African countries where the majority of the population is Christian, to a mitigating and yet condemning role (regarding the distressing social contradictions)?

Such voices are rare at this time. That makes one think and brings to the fore that which should always be borne in mind as the flipside for every argument for contextuality in theology. Contextuality can, namely, also mean that the Gospel comes to nothing in that context: Jesus can also be *too much* "at home." The answer to the question of an African Jesus – just as, by the way, that of an Asian Jesus – will therefore always have to navigate in affirmation and negation between the Scylla of what is native and the Charybdis of what is foreign.[77]

Speaking of Jesus as both ancestor and healer brings us to a final aspect that up until now has only been touched upon indirectly. We already discussed earlier the point that Jesus is more or less a "latecomer" in African theological reflection. Reflection on God the creator has priority. Perhaps we should go a step further and say that reflection on the meaning of Jesus in Africa is, in fact, reflection on the work of the Holy Spirit. Africa is, after all, pre-eminently the continent of spirits, which play a major role with respect to both the ancestors and the healers. For that reason perhaps, the thesis can also be defended that only a more expanded, African reflection on the relation between God's Holy Spirit and the many good and evil spirits that populate the African universe can place Jesus' work in a perspective that is beneficial for Africans. Perhaps Jesus, even though he is called a latecomer, has yet come too early, and the entirely unique form that Pentecostalism has taken in Africa as a synthesis of Christian and traditional belief must first be judged more closely on its merits.[78]

Part IX: Conclusions

This study has been written from the perspective of the principle of double transformation *that usually accompanies a process of inculturation: a concept applied in another context changes the context but is also changed in turn. This creative process belongs to the "in-between" situation of each transfer event. This liminality also characterizes the transmission of the Gospel in non-Western cultures. Theologically, that event can be interpreted as both the confirmation (incarnation) and negation (dying and rising) of an existing culture.*

The meaning that is ascribed to Jesus depends very much on how people think about the nature of his mediation between God and human beings. That mediation can be directed towards having the human share in the divine but also towards the descent of the divine into the human. Both lines of thought have points of contact in the Bible and the history of the church and must be assessed in terms of the degree to which they leave room for Jesus' actual life, including the cross and resurrection.

In this presentation of non-Western images of Jesus – Jesus as bodhisattva, avatara, guru, prophet, ancestor and healer – two questions continually arose: (a) How is Jesus' divinity related to his humanity? (b) How can his "substitution" be understood as liberating, as bringing salvation?

Ultimately, the question of the non-Western Jesus is focused on the question of whether Jesus was already in Asia and Africa before the Western missionaries arrived. Affirmative theological, historical and anthropological answers can be given to that question. The latter has to do primarily with not allowing Jesus' presence to be absorbed into an anthropoligical possibility but also giving it shape on the basis of his actual life.

17 Methodical Conclusions

Too Western?

It is a rather risky matter to assess the "non-Western Jesus" from a Western perspective. After all, what is to be the basis for such an assessment – the author's Western framework? In connection with this question, Philip Jenkins makes use of the following illustration.[1] Suppose that in the seventh or eighth century – the time of Willibrord's mission to Western Europe – a traveller from distant Western Europe gave a report on the rise of a new Christianity there to the theologians living in the centre of Christianity at the time (Syria and Mesopotamia). They would probably have been very enthusiastic about the growth of faith in these areas that were considered to be stubbornly barbarian (= unbelieving). Undoubtedly, they would also have been very curious about the nature of the new Christianity: Were they Antiochenes or Alexandrians, Dyophysites or Monophysites, Nestorians or Eutychians? How would they have looked upon the iconoclasm that had broken out in the East in the meantime? They would probably have been disappointed to hear that not all their central questions were central for those new Christians in distant Western Europe. Consequently, they would have wondered if it was truly a matter of a new form of *Christianity* or a remarkable synthesis of Christian and Celtic, German and Saxon ideas. Undoubtedly, many would have used the word syncretism immediately in a negative sense.

A Western theologian could react in a similar way now to the many forms of non-Western theology. Western theology continues to be stamped by the concepts that became current during the sixteenth-century controversy between Rome and the Reformation. It is to these concepts (guilt, penitence/remorse, cross, justification, reconciliation, resurrection, being born again and renewed, hell and heaven) that every Western Christian attaches the central terms of his faith. He or she always wants to see those concepts in his fellow believers elsewhere as well. After all, it is difficult to believe that concepts that are crucial for the articulation of one's own faith would be declared to be of no value elsewhere. But that brings us to an impasse: Western concepts can no longer, as was customary worldwide since the missions of the nineteenth century, be imposed as normative. But Western concepts cannot, as a rule, be declared by the West to be non-applicable to a non-Western context. The non-Western theologians themselves need to decide what they do or do not take over.

One risks being accused of arrogance both in accepting the concepts without question and in declaring the concepts in advance to be inapplicable. The example of the worldwide use of medicine can clarify that well.

The usual Western pharmaceutical industry cannot declare the Western instructions to be binding as such in the non-Western world. Other circumstances (eating and living habits, climatological circumstances, family relationships, etc.) can make different instructions necessary. But, in general, the Western instructions cannot be declared inapplicable to the non-Western world either. The pharmaceutical industry could then undoubtedly be accused of employing double standards and using other – less broad – rules for the non-Western world. Only a well-motivated explanation of the differences in the rules will be able to offer a way out here.

We decided to choose such a differentiated approach in this study. In the "Preface" we characterized this study as a "Western study" on non-Western theology allegedly written mainly for a Western public. We thus indicated that we cannot and do not wish to jump over our own Western shadow. However much this book is written from an attitude of listening, the Western training of the author has played a role in the conclusions at the end of every chapter and will also do so in these final chapters. Openness about the cultural limitations to which this listening is always subject will always be one of the first conditions for a worldwide dialogue on the meanings ascribed to Jesus. But at the same time – as the example of the instructions for medicine makes clear – being connected to a culture is not only a disadvantage when approaching other cultures. As the Western instructions for medicines can also be of use to the non-Western world with regard to their strictness – and Eastern healing practices in the West – so a Western presentation of non-Western images of Jesus can fulfil a beneficial mirror function. Here it should be recognized that each mirror always distorts the object to some extent but nevertheless also presents the truth.

We also need to account for the use of the Bible in this study. In the second section of Chapter 2 we announced that we would do this in the final part. It was in Part VII on the "The Indonesian Jesus" that we made some biblical-theological digressions on biblical concepts such as "prophet," "son of God" and "servant of the Lord." This was not intended to introduce an external power factor but to bring to light in a reasonably objective way the broader, biblical range of meanings. Every reader will have to make choices from among those meanings. By exposing the breadth of the choice of possibilities, we intended to make the choices that had been made more explicit.

Less direct, but more decisive with respect to content, is the role played by the reference to Jesus' actual life and his cross and resurrection in this book. That will also be apparent in the rest of this section. That reference presupposes that these aspects of the "remembered Jesus" must also have a place in an African and Asian context. That can happen in a great variety of ways, as the history of the church clearly testifies. There was always a wide range within which the meaning of the cross and the resurrection was discussed, and that also applies now. We sometimes see meanings return in non-Western theology that were rejected long ago by the West, such as understanding the resurrection, viewed as a "descent" into hell, as solidarity with the deceased, often non-Christian ancestors.[2] Also, the way in which the crucified Jesus is often seen in "crucified" fellow human beings testifies to an intensity of the experience of phrases from Jesus' Sermon on the Mount (Matt. 5:1–48) and judgement by the Son of Man (Matt. 25:31–46), which do not have any equal in contemporary Western theology. In short, the reference in Asian and African theology to the historical Jesus is certainly not always a reference to an external factor.

In addition to the direct and indirect appeal to the Bible, the appeal to the Bible as such requires closer justification. We discussed the role of the holy scriptures of other religions primarily in Chapter 3 on the "Sources of Asian Theology." During this study, it has become clear that Asian Christianity cannot be understood without knowledge of the content of the holy scriptures of Buddhism, Hinduism, Islam, Confucianism and Taoism. This is less true for African Christianity because African religions do not have scriptures. In Asia, the holy scriptures of their neighbours and often of their ancestors, parents and family members form a natural reference framework for Christians. Without that framework, their articulation of their own faith is not conceivable and not comprehensible. The other holy scriptures do not take the place of the Bible for them, but they do form the surroundings of the place where the Bible lands. Pieris even spoke in this connection of other religions that already "occupied" the landing area.[3] A comparison with the way in which Greek and Roman and later Celtic and Saxon myths and sagas occupied life in Western Europe and "occupied" the landing place of the Gospel there as well is probably too weak, but that conclusion could also be Western naiveté.

Many Christians in Asia are well aware of the influence of their religious context and they also realize that they cannot simply shake off that context. Nor, because of the communication with their direct living environment, do they wish to do so. Inevitably, they will continually have to connect the content of the Bible with the content of the other holy scriptures. This will sometimes happen in an antithetical kind of way but often also in a creatively synthetic way, in a search for common points of faith for equipping and encouraging individual believers, for fighting social injustice and avoiding violence. Within their own faith community, it will be clear for Christians that the Bible possesses great authority,[4] but outside that community the Bible will again and again have to acquire authority (= accepted power) in intense dialogue with the representatives of other religions. That intense dialogue – comparable to the dialogue in the Middle Ages between Muslims, Christians and Jews in cities like Baghdad and Cordoba – was conducted in the seventh, eighth and eighteenth centuries in China and in the nineteenth and twentieth centuries in India and Indonesia. Now, it seems that that dialogue in both India and Indonesia has been brought to a halt through the activity of, respectively, Hindu and Muslim fundamentalists. Perhaps at this time China is still the most fruitful soil for such dialogue because there, after more than fifty years of Communism, religion has been rediscovered as an inspiring phenomenon.

Double Transformation as Liminality

With regard to method, we have tried to avoid partiality, primarily by applying the principle of double transformation consistently. That principle was explicitly distinguished from two other principles that are often used, namely that of the sharp contrast and that of striking similarity. The former assumes that there are unbridgeable oppositions; the second presupposes that two religions are a perfect match. Both principles ignore the dynamic that is a part of each encounter and the mutual osmosis (penetration) that often accompanies this.

At the beginning of the institutional ecumenical movement, at the third world conference of the Commission on Faith and Order of the World Council of Churches in Lund (Sweden) in 1952, the method of the principle of contrast and similarity that usually lay at the foundation of the comparative ecclesiology was rejected. The former led to entrenching oneself in one's own position, as it were, so as to be able to make the observation that unbridgeable oppositions exist. The other is lost to view because of the ramparts one throws up around oneself. In the latter method, that of similarity, one always runs the risk of more or less annexing the other and ignoring the ways in which it is different. That concepts are context-relative suddenly seems to no longer play a role.[5]

A separate, isolated description of the different traditions and schools in Christianity and other religions is a questionable undertaking not only from an ecumenical but also from a religious point of view. Not enough account will be taken of the historical dynamics, regional differences and mutual interaction. The phenomenon of double transformation described by us does not exclude sharp contrasts and striking similarities but does alert one to the fact that there is often a third factor – a *tertium datur* – namely, that of mutual interaction. That is a creative process that occurs precisely in new situations of transmission – in "limit situations" as it were.

At the end of the section on the Korean Minjung theology in Chapter 8 we discussed the concept *liminality*. The concept refers to a border or threshold (= *limen*) experience and allows one to describe anthropologically what happens when an individual or group is faced with a radically new situation. Then one leaves behind what is known (1); stays for a while in a transitional phase (2) and in the course of time adapts to the new situation (3). These three aspects can be observed in almost every transitional situation. Whether it is a matter of becoming an adult, coping with grief, moving (emigration), etc., in every case the same three aspects occur. Officially formalized or arranged informally, almost every culture has developed rituals for these so-called rites of passage. Central to these rites is the threshold experience: the experience of living on the border between two worlds for a time.

The concept of one who lives on the border can be interpreted negatively in the sense that that person does not belong anywhere, that he or she is literally and figuratively marginalized. But it can also be interpreted positively: in that "in-between" situation one can make a virtue of necessity. It means being at home in two cultures. This "in-between," which can imply an "in-both," can also lead to a creative "in-beyond": a transcending of both cultures from the inside out. That can be a source of creativity as writers, artists, scientists and journalists who do not stay in their home country prove.

The concept of *liminality* described in this way then comes close to the concept of *double transformation* that is the foundational principle of this book. The transmission event that is inherent to every inculturation process necessarily entails alienation. Old concepts no longer suffice and new ones have not yet been adopted. Many contemporary Christians in Asia and Africa thus find themselves in an "in-between" situation. They have been raised with a Western Christianity based on nineteenth- and twentieth-century missions. For many, therefore, that form of Christianity is thus actually "true" Christianity. In the meantime, they also (still) carry with them all the religious concepts from their non-Christian parents and grandparents. Sometimes, this leads to a very double attitude or to a feeling of belonging to different groups. Thus, many African Christians pray in the church for healing and then also visit traditional healers. But sometimes that leads to the emergence of creative theology in which both the "in-between" and the "in-both" are transcended in an "in-beyond" situation that does not alienate them from their own cultural context but does add new aspects to it. Thus, in a South African township at Easter we saw an extremely charismatic preacher wearing the emblem of the traditional healer and heard him preach on resurrection as "empowerment." Such an adaptation is a good example of how the phenomenon of *double transformation* works. Without alienation and annexation, a process of radical change does occur – a process of change that, because of the creativity that accompanies it, can be seen not as an impoverishment but as an enrichment.

In the second section of Chapter 2, under "Accounting for Methodology," we quoted the famous sentence from the letter by Diognetus on Christians feeling at home and not feeling at home: "For them, any foreign country is a motherland, and any motherland is a foreign country." We also referred to the debate between Heidegger and Levinas at the beginning of the 1960s. Gagarin's space flight made it clear to Levinas that, in a time of space travel, no one can or wants to be bound to a permanent place on earth. In contrast, Heidegger emphasized precisely the indispensable anthropological meaning of being "at home" somewhere. Heidegger's sense of "needing a base" can lead to a dangerous nationalism – as we argued – and Levinas' "wanderlust" is all too often the lot appointed to the poorest of all, against their will. Those are thus the two extremes that are to be avoided.

Later on, in the fourth section of Chapter 2 we discussed the ambivalence between being "at home" and not being "at home" through the image of the incarnation on the one hand and the cross and resurrection on the other. Incarnation can never be described without describing the experience of the cross and the resurrection – an experience of dying and rising. This experience is symbolized in the Christian sacrament of baptism, which teaches that a believer must first die (with Jesus) before he can rise (with Jesus). It teaches us that *indwelling* can never occur without change and that *change* can never occur without solidarity (identification). However much the distinction between the *old man* and the *new man* is emphasized, it is the same person. That person does assume a new identity but does not lose his integrity. That is why the African theologian Bediako prefers to use the expression "integrity in conversion" for this event.[6]

The Nature of the Mediation

In the section "Accounting for Methodology" in Chapter 2 we remarked that the figure of Jesus is inseparably connected with the notion of *mediation*. All the terms used to refer to Jesus in this study – *bodhisattva*, *avatara*, *guru*, prophet, ancestor and healer – refer to the mediation between God and human beings. This mediation can take many forms and serve many purposes. We distinguished three directions in Chapter 2. Jesus can be conceived of as the one who:

(a) restores the *right relationship* between God and human beings;
(b) opens the way for the *deification* of the human being;
(c) opens the way for the *humanization* of God.

We saw especially in an Islamic and African context that the mediation of the *guru*, the ancestor and the healer move in the direction of the right relationship between God and human beings. The mediator does have exceptional knowledge and gifts but is not himself viewed as divine, even if he is clearly venerated. Thus, he can be given Jesus-like characteristics in various respects, but this does not help us a great deal in the discussion of the God–human relationship. For the rest, it does not yet say anything – as we will later explore more closely – about whether or not these are adequate terms for Jesus. Although the *guru*, the ancestor and the healer are not divine, they are considered to have exceptional insight into what the divine requires of human beings. We will return to that in the next chapter.

The mediation can also be intended, as it were, *to be taken up into the divine existence* as the end of the transformation process. The discussion here thus focuses on the question of how close a human being can get to God and the extent to which he can leave his humanness behind him. According to Paul, from a Christian point of view what human beings leave behind is always connected with dying with Jesus. That is precisely the clause that precedes the so-often cited passage in Gal. 2:20. Immediately prior to "I no longer live, but Christ lives in me" is the sentence "I have been crucified with Christ." The New Testament scholar James Dunn sees the heart of Paul's theology articulated here. Paul can formulate that centre both in the "Christ in us" passages and in the "we in Christ" passages. These passages can refer to the present state of believers but also to their future. They refer, thus, to a process of growth and the issue is that of the impact of the dying and rising with Jesus in the life of the believers, with their spiritual growth and the ethical consequences of their choice.

Thus, for Paul, "sharing in" always has to do with something outside of ourselves – Jesus' cross and resurrection – in which we can participate through loss of self and being born again, symbolized by baptism. But Paul's own experience of faith reaches further than merely a reference to baptism. Romans 6:4–8 is one of the key texts here:

> We were therefore buried with him through baptism into death in order that, just as Christ was raised from the dead through the glory of the Father, we too may live a new life. If we have been united with him like this in his death, we will certainly also be united with him in his resurrection. For we know that our old self was crucified

with him so that the body of sin might be done away with, that we should no longer be slaves to sin.... Now if we died with Christ, we believe that we will also live with him.

On the basis of this identification, believers can be called "children of God" and even "heirs of God," and Paul can say: "We are heirs – heirs of God and co-heirs with Christ, if indeed we share in his sufferings in order that we may also share in his glory" (Rom. 8:17).

This "sharing in" thus receives mystical characteristics in Paul indeed. But it is a mysticism that refers to something that could only occur internally in someone because something had happened "outside" him, i.e. Jesus' cross and resurrection. That weaving together of external and internal aspects demands that the recognition of a mysticism of identification in Paul must always honour the reference to the salvific meaning of the cross and resurrection.[7] The specific character of this form of "identification" also characterizes the later Christian references to "sharing" in the divine. Two examples can illustrate that.

In the history of the church, the debate on "becoming one with Christ" occurred mainly around the Greek church fathers. An echo of that debate can still be heard in ecumenical dialogues concerning the Eastern Orthodox concept of *theosis* (deification).[8] A key text here is always the statement – first used by Iraneaus (*Adversus Haereses* V) – by Athanasius in *De Incarnatione* 54: "He, indeed, assumed humanity that we might become God."[9] In the biblical support for this statement, reference is usually made to 2 Peter 1:4, which states "so that through them you may participate in the divine nature." Other Bible texts that play a more indirect role in the discussion are those that refer to human beings as the image of God (Gen. 1:26–27), to the implications of being children of God (Gal. 3:26; Rom. 8:15) and to perfection (Matt. 5:48; 2 Cor. 3:18).

For Athanasius himself, this adage stands within the framework of undoing the consequences of the Fall. The human being has been driven far from God through sin and is now brought close to God in the incarnation. Here it concerns a nearness that is comparable to how the Son (the Logos) is near to the Father in the sense of Jesus' words: "that they may be one as we are one" (John 17:22). The "deification" is thus placed within the framework of the *imitatio Christi*, discipleship, and has the character of a process of sanctification that is *communal* and *directed at daily life*.[10] It concerns a *change* in the human being that is produced by following Jesus. This change occurs on earth and thus does not mean that the "deified" human being should stop being human. That is not even the case when the human being is taken up into God's glory. In the above we have given the so-called "broad" interpretation of Athanasius' adage. Because of the changing contexts in which he speaks of deification (*theosis*), a narrower interpretation is possible that is limited to the restoration of the original immortality through the incarnation.[11]

As a contemporary example of the "unity" with God, we refer to the interpretation by Jung Yong Lee we discussed in Chapter 8. We referred earlier to him in connection with the concept of liminality as a characterization of an "in-between" situation. Lee considers this "in-between" situation to be pre-eminently characteristic for Jesus, both for his interhuman relationships and for his relationship with God. In the incarnation Jesus moves to the margins of the divine and on the cross he moves to the margins of the human. According to Tao Te Ching (II, 40), return is the essence of the way (*tao*). That means that becoming human (incarnation) is not a threat for the divine and the self-emptying (crucifixion) is not a threat for the human. Rather, the incarnation is how the divine returns to itself (the human, "his own" (John 1:10)) and the self-emptying is how the Son of Man returns to his own, the divine (Phil. 2:6–8).[12] Lee compares the relationship between Jesus' divinity and humanity with that between *yin* and *yang*: just as *yang* cannot exist without *yin*, so *yin* cannot exist without *yang*. In Jesus, God is not separate from the human being and the human being is not separate from God.[13] In short, he employs here, via the concepts *yin* and *yang*, a concept of unity that does not threaten the differentiation between God and human beings but presupposes it. Instead of Lee, we could also have referred to the Japanese theologian also cited in Chapter 7, K. Takizawa. Following Nishida, he frequently quotes the poetic lines: "Forever apart, and yet not separated for one moment; together for the whole day, but not together for one instant." Both examples are an indication of the fact that in Christianity, including that in the Asia of today, the sense has survived that the distinction between God and human can be neglected in the idea of "becoming one" with the divine.

In Chapter 2 we also pointed to the intended *humanization* of God as a third purpose of Jesus' mediation between God and human beings. Here the question is if the true humanity that Jesus reveals can also be seen as the true destiny of God. And the next question is what this humanization exactly means. This question is central for the Taiwanese theologian Choan Seng Song and the Sri Lankan theologian Alois Pieris when they relate the suffering of the poor in Asia directly to the suffering of Jesus and speak of him as *crucified people* (Chapter 3). In Western theology it is primarily Bonhoeffer who made this question his own and responded to it in pithy sentences such as "The cradle shows the man who is God"[14] and "Man becomes man because God became man."[15] Theologically, we are then speaking of God's self-emptying, his *kenosis*, for which Phil. 2:6–7 is the star witness: "Who, being in very nature God, did not consider equality with God something to be grasped, but made himself nothing, taking the very nature of a servant, being made in human likeness." The idea of God's "suffering with" becomes central: Jesus' cross is placed, à la Marc Chagall, amidst many other crosses.

The critical question that always comes up is that of the liberating character of "suffering with." Does that relieve the suffering of those who suffer? Song and Pieris both show that solidary suffering always occurs from a certain perspective. In this context Song points to the fact that the Chinese language has the same word for love and pain and sees the two concepts coming together in the labour pains of a woman. That is "the pain of love" that can be endured from the perspective of the imminent birth that will mean liberation from pain.[16] We saw the same notion in the Chinese theologian Yongtao in the third section of Chapter 5. In Pieris as well, poverty and, with it, suffering are not discussed without perspective: he emphasizes that religion cannot do without poverty and poverty cannot do without religion. He thus says, in so many words, that religion cannot do without concern and poverty without perspective (Chapter 3). We translated this di-unity in the first section of Chapter 4 by the clause "poverty without religion is hopeless and religion without attention for poverty is merciless." We saw that same perspective in the Japanese theologian Kuribayashi as resurrection faith (Chapter 7) and in Minjung theology as Messianic expectation (Chapter 8) and it was also strongly emphasized by the Filipino Roman Catholic theologian Virginia Fabella in her publications on Asian female images of Jesus.[17]

But that does not yet say everything about the identification of the cross of Jesus and the cross of millions of others. After all, the cross is intrinsically connected to human sin and not exclusively to human solidarity. Especially in Asian theology we often come across the expression "the sinned against." We referred in the last section of Chapter 5 to the concept of sin held by the Chinese bishop Ting. This reasoning can be found in the Japanese theologian Kuribayashi[18] and in Korean Minjung theology as well.[19] It thus concerns those who have especially been sinned *against*, i.e. the victims. This change in the use of the concept of sin can be understood – as already remarked above – primarily against the background of resistance to the phenomenon of "blaming the victim." Saying to the victims of poignant injustice that they are in principle no better than those who commit the injustices may be a truism, but it glosses over the question of who is guilty and who is innocent and makes the victim guilty as well.

In his dissertation on *theologia crucis* in Asia,[20] the Indonesian theologian Yewangoe A.A. Yewangoe keeps posing the question of individual responsibility and thus also of individual guilt. We find this same question in the Korean theologian Hong Eyoul Hwang.[21] Indeed, hopefully victims do not remain nothing more than victims, and sooner or later one should be able to call them to account with respect to their own individual conduct. After all, no one can escape the corrupting influence of sin as selfish *amor sui*, self-love.[22] That is why Christianity has never seen the incarnation of God solely as solidarity but also as a liberating "substitutionary activity for" our weakness. It is understood as a substitutionary act for our lack of detachment, for our failure to deny ourselves. We are thus liberated *from* the prison that we have made of our "self" (Rom. 7:23) and liberated *to* the freedom of the children of God (Rom. 8:1–30).

Thus, where both *deification* and *humanization* are central, the reference to the cross and resurrection remains crucial. Both deification and humanization bring an important aspect of the event of the resurrection to the fore. The former has to do – to use Barth's expression – with "the servant as Lord" and the latter with "the Lord as servant." These two aspects cannot be separated from each other. If they are, either the solidarity, the "suffering with" (the Lord as servant), disappears, or the goal at which the solidarity is directed, namely redemption from suffering, does (the servant as Lord).[23]

18 Substantial Conclusions

Jesus as *Bodhisattva*

The strongest parallel between Jesus and the *bodhisattvas* lies in their commitment that is expressed in loss of self. In both cases there is a mediating role – they are both preparers of the way. But in Jesus' case, at issue is not only a psychological process of dying but a real death on the cross that, for many, is connected with forgiveness and the opening up of life. The nature of the mediation is thus quite different. Jesus is not only a preparer of the way who can be imitated but also someone who breaks through an impasse – namely that of human guilt – in a unique way with his own life.

Are the differences such that it would be better not to compare Jesus with a *bodhisattva*? We said in Chapter 1 that a syncretic event always concerns a *double transformation*. We see that happening here as well. More explicitly than in many other well-known images of Jesus from the Western history of doctrine, in the comparison with a *bodhisattva* we see the image of Jesus moved with compassion (*karuna*) emerge. That is the *transformation* that occurs on the Christian side. Jesus is seen primarily as the one who is moved by compassion and discards all aspirations of power. Against the background of the reproach to Christianity of lack of solidarity with the enormous poverty of the Asian population, that is no minor transformation. Jesus as *bodhisattva* is the one who unambiguously takes pity on the lot of the Asian poor.

The *transformation* that occurs on the side of the Buddhist context of this concept is that Christians will see the embodiment of their God in this *bodhisattva*: a God who "descends" in human form. Further, the belief arises that the death of this *bodhisattva* opens up salvation for his followers. He is not only solidary with (anxious about) the lot of his fellow human beings but also sacrifices his life for them. He thus breaks through the relationships between God and human beings and between human beings that have run aground.

We touch here on the question of the *assumption* of human guilt. The *transferability* of guilt is not usually a point of discussion among people. People are in the habit of holding one another to account for the guilt of others (ancestors or children, family members, members of one's own tribe or people). *Self-sacrifice* is certainly not an unknown phenomenon in Asia. But the idea behind the assumption of guilt, i.e. that those are truly guilty will not be punished, has been been found in the Asian world thus far only in the Analectica (20,1) in a passage on King T'ang (Chapter 5) and in the *kurban* sacrifice in Indonesia (Chapter 15).

In summary, we can say that the Christian *bodhisattva* is something other than the Buddhist *bodhisattva*, just as the Christian Lord is different from the Greco-Roman *kyrios-dominus* and the Christian *Heiland* is different from the Germanic *heliand*. One can thus also rightly say with respect to the comparison between Jesus and the *bodhisattvas* that this is an analogy, a similarity in the midst of still greater differences. But this is, in fact – as we argued in Chapter 2 – the normal pattern of inculturation.

Only within the framework of this dynamic process of ascribing meaning can the designation of Jesus as *bodhisattva* be called an enrichment of Asian theology. The differences are evident apart from this process of transformation. Jesus is a historical and not a mythological figure like the *bodhisattva*. Moreover, he is not like a *bodhisattva* on the way to enlightenment; rather, he is the personification of divine enlightenment ("I am the light of the world," John 8:12). Therefore, Jesus is not a Buddhist *bodhisattva* in the same way that he is not a Messiah in the Jewish sense of the word, not a Son of God in the Jewish or Greek sense of the word, not a *kyrios* or *dominus* in the Greek or Roman sense of the word and not a *heliand* (*heiland*) in the Germanic sense of the word. In all these cases a change in meaning occurs when these concepts are applied to Jesus.

That is also the case with the concept *bodhisattva*. This does not at all mean that Jesus cannot be described via concepts derived from the veneration of the *bodhisattva*. It is perhaps the only possibility in the Buddhist world to make clear how unconditionally God has mercy for the Asian poor. The *bodhisattva* is, after all, the one who pre-eminently displays *karuna* or, as Christians would say, God's compassion.

Jesus as *Avatara*

Just as Christianity does with respect to the incarnation, so Hinduism also searches for a conceptual model for the *avatara* that transcends the competition between the divine and the human. Such a conceptual model is usually found where the divine can be seen as the truly human and the human as something that is revealed in all its dimensions only by the divine. God is thus always a God of people and people are always the "image of God." Divine "descent" therefore always means "ascent" of people and vice versa.

A crucial question remains as to where primarily the divine reveals the human and where primarily true humanity reveals the divine. The *avatara* comes to drive out injustice, but the Bhagavadgita does not elaborate on that reason when it has Krishna describe extensively and even profusely his presence among people. Little of the specific reason for his coming can be seen in that description. An expression such as "whatever you did for one of the least of these brothers of mine, you did for me" (Matt. 25:40) is thus not found in this social meaning in the Bhagavadgita, although it is present in the sense that everything is connected with Krishna.

The *avatara* is not a mediator who shares in the vicissitudes of humanity. Krishna is the *avatara* who comes to restore the right order (justice) if the earth requires it. He is not a redeemer in the sense that he takes upon himself the responsibility for that injustice and thus "takes away the sins of the world," even though – as we saw in the first section of Chapter 11 – the contrasts should not be absolutized too much. In the case of Krishna, one can speak of a "self-sacrifice for" and of forgiveness of sins, even though the concept of sin here is not primarily connected with guilt but with ignorance. One could speak here of a guilty ignorance.

The question that emerged most centrally with respect to the *avatara* is that of the importance of the mediator's being completely human. There are a number of parallels to be drawn between the roles of Jesus and Krishna. The first is *why* they both act – out of *compassion, mercy*. But there are also important differences and those are focused on the question of *the irrevocability of the divine surrender* to the situation in which human beings live. In Christianity God is known pre-eminently *on the interface of the divine and human* and it is stated that that interface has everything to do with the most radical human situation, namely that of *suffering and death*, and with all the questions of collective and personal guilt that accompany that. The Christian symbol of the cross is also intended to indicate that interface (intersection). Neither God who approaches human beings nor the human being who approaches God can get around this situation. Reflecting existentially on this aspect of the encounter between God and human beings seems to be one of the most exciting challenges for Christian–Hindu dialogue.

Jesus as *Guru*

Whereas the issue of Jesus as *avatara* is focused mainly on the question of the extent to which an *avatara* can also be seen as truly human, the question regarding Jesus as *guru* is focused mainly on the question of whether a *guru* can be seen as truly divine. On the one hand, the suspicion of *docetism* (apparent humanity) lurks in the background and, on the other, that of *adoptionism* (raising a human being to divine status).

The *avatara* idea developed primarily as a "descent" of Vishnu. The *guru* idea developed primarily, although not exclusively, as an "ascent" to Shiva. The relation to Shiva can assume three forms: that of a mystical relationship, a theophany or an interhuman relationship. In the first case, Shiva is essentially the *guru* himself and a human being experiences his power; it thus concerns the internal *guru*. In the second case, it is an external, incidental encounter with Shiva. The third case reflects a true teacher–student relationship with a human *guru* who is merely a travel guide. It is up to the individual himself to make the trip. In the last case there is no (ontological) relationship between Shiva and the *guru*: the human *guru*'s role is a purely functional one. He refers not to himself but beyond himself, and in this referring process the *guru* can attain great heights.

Nor does the *guru* act as a substitute for his own. The image employed by Thomas Thangaraj of the "crucified" *guru* transcends the traditional Hindu image of the *guru*. Such a transformation of the familiar *guru* image can be meaningful with respect to making the meaning of Jesus' cross discussible in a Hindu context.

In that event, Jesus' own self-emptying on the cross is taken up as a crucial element in the summons for the *guru* to empty himself. Now one can rightly speak of a *double transformation*. For Indians, Jesus as *guru* is connected more intensely with his followers than he would be if any other image (rabbi, lord, etc.) would be used. Thus, for them the *guru* image changes Jesus from a distant "Lord" into an insightful teacher. That is the change that occurs on the Christian side. At the same time, for them, the intimate teacher also becomes a teacher who not only "loses himself" in his own devotion to the divine but who also – and even primarily – "loses himself" in his devotion to them. His self-emptying is thus an *inclusive self-emptying* that involves his students in his resurrection. That is the change that occurs on the Hindu side.

The initiation rites between *guru* and teacher are, in Jesus' case, the initiation rites of the church, i.e. the sacraments of baptism and communion. In those sacraments dying and rising with Jesus are central, regardless of rank or status (caste). All initiation classifications stemming from the caste system associated with the *guru*–student relations are criticized in these initiation rites. Simply on the basis of their own theological content, baptism and communion exclude the caste system. Speaking of "the crucified" *guru* and relating his message directly to the content of the central sacraments of baptism and communion can give the *guru* idea a socio-ethical dimension.

More than in Hindu India, Islamic Indonesia appears to have room for the *guru* who sacrifices himself. In Indonesian culture from of old there was always room for a *guru* who cleared the path to the water of life with his own life. We could thus conclude that "mediation of salvation" is not strange as such to the Indonesian culture. The personal appropriation of the sacrifice of one's life for another as the sacrifice of "my own I" is also part of this culture, as the reference to the Javanese crucifix made clear.

As soon as Jesus is compared with the figure of the *avatara* or *guru*, the question always arises sooner or later if such a comparison is compatible with Jesus' uniqueness. But the fact that there are several *avataras* and *gurus* in Hinduism, just as there are several *bodhisattvas* in Buddhism and several ancestors in African religion, does not at all affect the question of Jesus' uniqueness. This is not threatened by calling him *kyrios* (lord) or *sotèr* (saviour) either. In the Greco-Roman culture there were also thousands of the former and dozens of the latter.

The question of uniqueness is, of course, a legitimate question. But it must be posed with respect to the substance of the comparison. It must be related to the new insight that such comparisons yield. It is a qualitative question and not a quantitative one, one that inquires into the way in which new comparisons contribute to the revelation of the unique position of Jesus as mediator between God and human beings.

Jesus as Prophet

The image of Jesus as prophet is closer to the language of the Bible than are images of him as *bodhisattva*, *avatara*, *guru* and ancestor. That obtains as well for the image of Jesus as healer. Jesus as prophet is a central motif primarily in Christian–Muslim dialogue. The image is subject to fluctuations, however, on both the Christian and the Muslim sides. The Qur'an testifies on the one hand to the equality of all prophets but, on the other, also introduces important distinctions. We saw that in the Indonesian prophetic narratives the Islamic image of Jesus as prophet can still be given a number of its own accents. Theologically, they are not of exceptional importance but they are indicative of a certain interpretative space that is appropriated in the Islamic exegetical tradition as well. This was, of course, known for a long time from the medieval Islamic exegetical tradition, but in the current polarized relationships it is threatening to become lost to view again. It is apparent from the New Testament that, while Jesus saw himself as standing in a prophetic tradition, he also saw himself as occupying a unique position in that tradition: the prophet of the end times primarily. This specific position has everything to do with his relationship to the Father.

Thus, despite the fact that the acknowledgement of Jesus' status as prophet constitutes some common ground between Christianity and Islam, the understanding of the nature of his status as a prophet is quite different in each religion. Given that that understanding is also subject to several nuances in both religions, one wonders if the term "prophet" will yield all that much mutual understanding. For that reason, we ourselves were inclined in our conclusions to Chapter 14 to take the concept of "sign" as a starting point for reflection on the meaning of Jesus. That concept plays an important role in both the Qur'an (aya) and the Bible (semeion) in the designation of the meaning of the work of Jesus and prevents us from getting into an endless discussion on the degree to which a human being can personify the divine.

Jesus as Ancestor

Jesus can be called the ancestor *par excellence* only if most of the aspects of being an ancestor are connected with the most important aspects of African reflection on the cross of Jesus. In addition to solidarity via identification, the cross radiates the power of life mediated primarily by the Spirit (of Jesus). Three important elements from the African religious background influence the experience of Jesus' cross: (a) only the ritual meal provides a real share in his life, (b) in an outstanding way he fulfils the mediating role of the ancestor, and (c) his death is viewed as a passage to another, happier existence.

Contemporary African theology appears to be able to provide its own accents in giving meaning to Jesus more so than in its views concerning a supreme God. Very concretely, this means that every aspect of one's own merit and a seamless continuation of earthly existence is removed from the concept of ancestor. That is the transformation on the African side. At the same time, Jesus is seen, more explicitly than has been the case in the West for the last thousand years, as the one who connects the living and the dead with each other. That is the transformation on the Christian side.

Is that *double transformation* sufficient to attribute a central role to Jesus as ancestor? Indeed, how can someone like Jesus, who was unmarried and had no children, be an ancestor? Despite the many questions that can be asked here, the reference to Jesus as ancestor has so many elements, in the view of many African theologians, that make Jesus more comprehensible for Africans than terms such as *kyrios, Messiah, Christ, Son of David, Son of Man* and *Logos*, that this analogy deserves more to be worked out carefully than to be abandoned. Crucial here is the extent to which African believers also succeed in making the *double transformation* described above effective.

Jesus as Healer

Much more than is the case with the Asian images of Jesus as *bodhisattva*, *avatara* and *guru*, with the African images of ancestor and healer we find ourselves in a world full of ambivalences. In Asia, the *double transformation* primarily concerns how Jesus is divine and how he is human. Essentially, it concerns the extent to which the concrete, harsh, earthly life can be brought into connection with the divine.

But in Africa, God's relation to actual, earthly reality is not a point of discussion; rather, that relation is the foundation and centre of everything. There the issue concerns an earthly Jesus who can be a bringer of salvation in his earthiness. In essence, Jesus is the person who – both as ancestor and as healer – maintains the contexts of life. The image that transcends both that of the ancestor and that of the healer is that of the giver and thus of the saver of life. Against the background of the strong emphasis on Jesus as the giver of life in all conceivable contexts, it is remarkable that Christianity in Africa does not present itself more explicitly as an influential factor for the protection of human life over against all kinds of violence (ethnic, sexual, political). If we take seriously the argument formulated at the end of Chapter 2 for modesty with respect to the social role religion can play, that does not at all mean that we should not expect any social involvement from a religion like Christianity. Rather, we endorse the appeal of an increasing number of African theologians not to neglect the "public" meaning of the proclamation of Jesus' message in Africa.

19 Was Jesus Already in Asia and Africa before the Missionaries Came?

At various points in this study we cited the claim that God was in Asia and Africa before the missionaries came. Our own experience is that Asians and Africans usually agree with this remark wholeheartedly. They can indeed make the claim in a theological sense. The confession of God as creator of heaven and earth also implies, after all, the creation of Asia and Africa and, as he is praised in Israel in the psalms as the creator through references to nature, that should also be possible in Asia and Africa. The choice of an existing divine name as the name for Israel's God in Asian and African translations of the Bible[1] confirms this understanding: Israel's God is not a strange God for Asians and Africans.

Can the same remark be broadened to include Jesus? There are three, rather divergent affirmative answers to this question: a theological, a historical and an anthropological answer.

1. Christ as Logos, as eternal Word, is also called the creator in the New Testament (John 1:1–4; Eph. 1:20–23; Col. 1:15–20). The same reasoning that was just used in reference to the Father applies to him. Especially in Asia, where the image of Jesus as Logos, as creative power, has found wide acceptance, we see this argument used often.

2. The historical answer refers to the early proclamation of the Gospel in Africa (North Africa and Ethiopia) and in India and China.[2] It is actually stated that when the missionaries came proclaiming Jesus in the fifteenth and sixteenth centuries, and later in the nineteenth century, they had already heard about him a thousand years earlier. Both the theological answer and the historical answer can count on wide support.

3. That is undoubtedly different with respect to the anthropological answer. We encountered this difference most explicitly from the Indian theologian Panikkar, but we also saw it in the Japanese theologians Takizawa and Yagi. For Panikkar, each living creature is a manifestation of the "Christic principle" and embodies a "Christophany." For him, Christ is the symbol of the mediation between the relative (the human) and the absolute (the divine), a di-unity that characterizes each religion.[3] In itself, this

anthropological approach has a long history in Christianity. Speaking of the Christ-in-us is not strange to the New Testament nor to the history of doctrine. But the question that always arises sooner or later with respect to this third answer is that of the meaning of the "external" Jesus, the historical Jesus. Does the "internal" Jesus not always have the inclination to push aside the "external"?

Speaking of Jesus as "crucified people," as we encountered in Asian theology and in African theology,[4] can also be seen as a variant of this anthropological answer. Jesus is here primarily the suffering one, and the one who suffers can also see himself in Jesus. Here the historical cross of Jesus does certainly not disappear behind the horizon, but all kinds of questions do arise with respect to what is specific about Jesus' cross.

The most interesting answer will be an affirmative one to the question of Jesus' presence in Asia and Africa when as much as possible of the historical Jesus and of the proclamation of his cross and resurrection can be included in the Asian and African attribution of meaning, as suggested by the Filipino theologian Fabella.[5] Any image of Jesus that does not incorporate the historical Jesus and the heart of the sacraments of baptism and communion, i.e. the cross and resurrection, will fall outside the criteria we articulated in Chapter 1 under the heading "Who Decides?"

There we employed the criterion of the *catholicity of the church*. By that we meant the *historical and actual Christian community of transmission* in which the Bible, church history and liturgy form the soil and foundation for the meanings that can be attributed to Jesus. Concretely, this means that each attribution of meaning to Jesus presupposes a Bible that is open and read, is acquainted with the way in which it was attempted in the history of the church to keep the divine and human together and realizes that the church of all times and places has seen the heart of the Christian tradition in the feasts of Christmas, Easter and Pentecost and in the sacraments of baptism and communion.

Every contextual articulation of the faith always has to take account of this fact. If we apply that fact to the content of this book, we can state that the material offered contains a large number of points of contact for a responsible, renewed reflection on the meaning of Jesus in a non-Western context. So as not to repeat ourselves, we refer to the concrete examples found in Chapter 18. Including the critical questions mentioned there, they undoubtedly form the overture for a new, global reflection on the doctrine about Jesus (Christology).

Notes

Preface

1. For an English summary see M. E. Brinkman, "Shifts in the Interpretation of Christian History: Cases from the Middle-East, Africa and Asia Compared," *Exchange* 29 (2000): 97–116.

Chapter 1

1. R. E. Hood, *Must God Remain Greek? Afro Cultures and God-Talk* (Minneapolis: Fortress Press, 1990).

2. M. Lee, "Identifying an Asian Theology: A Methodological Quest," *Asia Journal of Theology* 13 (1999): 257–62.

3. David B. Barret et al., *World Christian Encyclopedia : A Comparative Survey of Churches and Religions in the Modern World*, 2nd ed. (Oxford: Oxford University Press, 2001).

4. P. Jenkins, *The Next Christendom: The Coming of Global Christianity* (Oxford: Oxford University Press, 2002), 1–14, 79–105; P. Jenkins, "After the Next Christendom," *International Bulletin of Missionary Research* 28 (2004): 20–22.

5. F. Eboussi-Boulaga, *Christianity without Fetishes: An African Critique and Recapture of Christianity* (Maryknoll: Orbis Books, 1984), 115.

6. R. Horton, "African Conversion," *Africa* 41.2 (1971): 50–71.

7. J. Dunn, *Jesus Remembered*, Christianity in the Making, vol. 1 (Grand Rapids/ Cambridge: Eerdmans, 2003), 130–32 and 881–93.

8. K.-H. Ohlig, *Fundamentalchristologie: Im Spannungsfeld von Christentum und Kultur* (Munich: Kösel-Verlag, 1986), 620–21.

9. Dunn, op. cit., 653–54.

10. A. Grillmeier, *From the Apostolic Age to Chalcedon (451)*, Christ in Christian Tradition, vol. 1 (London: Mowbray, 1975), 520–39 and 543–50; J. N. D. Kelly, *Early Christian Doctrines* (London: Black, 1980), 338–43.

11. Grillmeier, op. cit., 543–50.

12. A. Wessels, *Images of Jesus: How Jesus is Perceived and Portrayed in Non-European Cultures* (Grand Rapids: Eerdmans, 1990), 13–17.

13. Grillmeier, op. cit., 555–70.

14. E. Pagels, "Christology in Dialogue with Gnosticism," in R. F. Berkey and S. A. Edwards, eds, *Christology in Dialogue* (Cleveland: Pilgrim Press, 1993), 66–77.

15. A. Wessels, *Europe: Was It Ever Really Christian?* (London: SCM, 1994), 17–54; J. Pelikan, *Jesus through the Centuries: His Place in the History of Culture* (New Haven/

London: Yale University Press, 1999), 34–45; T. Schmeller, "The Greco-Roman Background of New Testament Christology," in Berkey and Edwards, op. cit., 54–65.

16. R. L. Fox, *Pagans and Christians in the Mediterranean World from the Second Century AD to the Conversion of Constantine* (London: Penguin Books, 1988), 34–35 and 260–61; Kelly, op. cit., 12–13.

17. A. Droogers, "Syncretism: The Problem of Definition, the Definition of the Problem," in J. D. Gort et al., eds, *Dialogue and Syncretism: An Interdisciplinary Approach*, Currents of Encounter 1 (Grand Rapids/Amsterdam: Eerdmans/Rodopi, 1989), 20–21.

18. J. H. de Wit et al., eds, *Through the Eyes of Another: Intercultural Reading of the Bible* (Elkhart: Institute of Mennonite Studies, 2004); P. Ricoeur, "The Task of Hermeneutics," in P. Ricoeur, *Hermeneutics and the Human Sciences: Essays on Language, Action, and Interpretation*, ed. and trans. John B. Thompson (Cambridge: Cambridge University Press, 1981), 43–62; idem, "The Hermeneutical Function of Distantiation," in Ricoeur, op. cit., 131–45; idem, "The Model of the Text: Meaningful Action Considered as a Text," in Ricoeur, op. cit., 197–221.

19. R. S. Sugirtharajah, ed., *Asian Faces of Jesus* (London: SCM, 1993), IX.

20. T. S. Maluleke, "Black Missiologist: Contradiction in Terms?" in R. Gerloff, ed., *Mission is Crossing Frontiers: Essays in Honour of Bongani A. Mazibuko, 1932–1997* (Pietermaritzburg: Cluster Publications, 2003); idem, "Will Jesus Ever Be the Same Again? What Are the Africans Doing to Him?" *Journal of Black Theology in South Africa* 11 (1997): 27; idem, "Christ in Africa: The Influence of Multi-Culturity on the Experience of Christ," *Journal of Black Theology in South Africa* 8 (1994): 54, 61–62.

Chapter 2

1. M. Weippert, "Synkretismus und Monotheismus: Religionsinterne Konfliktbewältigung im alten Israel," in M. Weippert, *Jahwe und die anderen Götte: Studien zur Religionsgeschichte des antiken Israel in ihrem syrisch-palästinischen Kontext*, Forschungen zum Alten Testament 18 (Tübingen: Mohr Siebeck, 1997), 1–24.

2. Weippert, op. cit., 24.

3. L. Jonker, "'Contextuality' in (South) African Exegesis: Reflections on the Communality of our Exegetical Methodologies," *Old Testament Essays* 18 (2005): 637–50, esp. 640.

4. L. Sanneh, *Translating the Message: The Missionary Impact on Culture* (New York: Orbis, 1989), 157–91.

5. C. S. Song, *Jesus, the Crucified People*, The Cross in the Lotus World, vol. 1 (Minneapolis: Augsburg, 1996), 24.

6. See the section on Minjung theology in Chapter 8.

7. D. K.-s. Suh, *The Korean Minjung in Christ* (Hongkong: Christian Conference of Asia, 1991), 112–13; K. J. Kim, *Christianity and the Encounter of Asian Religions: Method of Correlation, Fusion of Horizons, and Paradigm Shifts in the Korean Grafting Process*, Mission 10 (Zoetermeer: Meinema, 1994), 59–73 and 87–95.

8. Richard Niebuhr, *Christ and Culture* (New York: Harper Torch Books, 1951).

9. N. Sheth, "Hindu Avatara and Christian Incarnation: A Comparison II," *Vidyajyoti* 67.4 (2003): 285–302; for the quotation see p. 302.

10. Wolfhart Pannenberg, "The Appropriation of the Philosophical Concept of God as a Dogmatic Problem of Early Christian Theology," in Wolfhart Pannenberg, *Basic Questions in Theology*, vol. 2, trans. George H. Kehm (Philadelphia: Westminster Press, 1971), 119–83.

11. Pannenberg, op. cit., 140–83.

12. A. Droogers, "Meaning, Power, and the Sharing of Religious Experience: An Anthropology of Religion Point of View," in J. D. Gort et al., eds, *On Sharing Religious Experience: Possibilities of Interfaith Mutuality*, Currents of Encounter 4 (Grand Rapids/ Amsterdam: Eerdmans/Rodopi, 1992), 45–54.

13. A. Wessels, *Europe: Was It Ever Really Christian?* (London: SCM, 1994), 134–42.

14. H. M. Vroom, *Religions and the Truth: Philosophical Reflections and Perspectives*, trans. J. W. Rebel, Currents of Encounter 2 (Grand Rapids/Amsterdam: Eerdmans/ Rodopi), 361–70.

15. A. Houtepen, *God: An Open Question*, trans. John Bowden (London: Continuum, 2002), 97–106.

16. E. Przywara, *Analogia entis* (Munich: Kösel & Pustet, 1932), 97.

17. A. Houtepen, "Intercultural Theology: A Postmodern Ecumenical Mission," in M. Frederiks et al., eds, *Towards an Intercultural Theology: Essays in Honour of Jan B. Jongeneel*, IIMO Resarch Publication 61 (Zoetermeer: Meinema, 2003), 23–38; F. Wijsen, "Intercultural Theology and the Mission of the Church," *Exchange* 30.3 (2001): 218–28 and "New Wine in Old Wineskins? Intercultural Theology instead of Missiology," in Frederiks, op. cit., 39–54.

18. C. Yongtao, "Towards a *Tao* Christology: Rethinking Christology in the Chinese Context," *Chinese Theological Review* 17 (2003): 30–31.

19. http://www.spurgeon.org/~phil/history/ath-inc.htm.

20. D. Bonhoeffer, *Christology*, trans. John Bowden, The Fontana Library of Theology and Philosophy (London: Collins, 1966), 108.

21. D. Burrel, *Freedom and Creation in Three Traditions* (Notre Dame: University of Notre Dame Press, 1983), 171–84.

22. A. Pieris, "Speaking of the Son of God in Non-Christian Cultures, e.g. in Asia," *Concilium* 18.3 (1982): 67.

23. S. J. Samartha, *The Search for New Hermeneutics in Asian Christian Theology* (Bangalore: Board of Theological Education of the Senate of Serampore College, 1987), 30–32.

24. M. S. Mogoba, "Christianity in an African Context," *Journal of Theology for Southern Africa* 52 (1985): 11.

25. C. S. Song, *Jesus, the Crucified People*, The Cross in the Lotus World, vol. 1 (Minneapolis: Augsburg, 1996), 21.

26. *Epistle to Diognetus*, in *Early Christian Writings*, trans. Maxwell Stanforth (London: Penguin Classics, 1987), 145.

27. M. Heidegger, "Building, Dwelling, Thinking," in M. Heidegger, *Poetry, Language, Thought*, trans. Albert Hofstadter (New York: Harper Colophon Books, 1975), 143–61.

28. E. Levinas, "Heidegger, Gagarin and Us," in E. Levinas, *Difficult Freedom: Essays on Judaism*, trans. Seán Hand (Baltimore: John Hopkins University Press, 1990), 221–24.

29. Suh, op. cit.

30. T. A. Mofokeng, "The Crucified and Permanent Crossbearing: A Christology for Comprehensive Liberation," in N. Schreurs and H. van de Sandt, eds, *De ene Jezus en de*

vele culturen: Christologie en contextualiteit (Tilburg: Tilburg University Press, 1992), 37–49.

31. R. S. Sugirtharajah, ed., *Asian Faces of Jesus* (London: SCM, 1993), X.

32. H. Y. Kim, *Christ and the Tao* (Hong Kong: Christian Conference of Asia, 2003), 128.

33. M. M'nteba, "Inculturation in the 'Third Church': God's Pentecost or Cultural Revenge?" *Concilium* 28.1 (1992): 129–46.

34. L. Newbigen, *Foolishness to the Greeks: The Gospel and Western Culture* (Geneva: World Council of Churches, 1986), 1–41.

Chapter 3

1. S. J. Samartha, "Preface," in S. J. Samartha, *The Search for New Hermeneutics in Asian Christian Theology* (Bangalore: Board of Theological Education of the Senate of Serampore College, 1987).

2. Samartha, op. cit., 47–49.

3. Samartha, op. cit., 6–8, 27.

4. Samartha, op. cit., 50.

5. C. S. Song, "From Israel to Asia: A Theological Leap," *The Ecumenical Review* 28 (1976): 258.

6. Ibid., 258–61.

7. Ibid., 263 and 265; C. S. Song, *Third Eye Theology: Theology in Formation in Asian Settings* (Maryknoll: Orbis, 1979), 13.

8. C. S. Song, *Jesus, the Crucified People*, The Cross in the Lotus World, vol. 1 (Minneapolis: Augsburg, 1996), 12; P. C. Phan, "Jesus the Christ with an Asian Face," *Theological Studies* 57.3 (1996): 418–20.

9. C. S. Song, "The Decisiveness of Christ," in D. J. Elwood, ed., *What Asian Christians Are Thinking: A Theological Source Book* (Quezon City: New Day Publishers, 1976).

10. C. S. Song, *Tell us Our Names: Story Theology from an Asian Perspective* (Maryknoll: Orbis, 1984), 10 and 37.

11. John Calvin, *Institutes of the Christian Religion*, trans. Ford Lewis Battles, Library of Christian Classics (Philadelphia: Westminster, 1960), I.1.1.

12. C. S. Song, "Do This in Memory of Jesus: The Root of the Reformed Heritage," in H. S. Wilson, ed., *Gospel and Cultures: Reformed Perspectives*, Studies from the World Alliance of Reformed Churches 35 (Geneva: World Alliance of Reformed Churches, 1996), 20.

13. Song, "The Decisiveness," 244 and 247.

14. Ibid., 248–50.

15. Ibid., 261.

16. Song, *Tell us Our Names*, 15–16 and 139–41.

17. Song, *Jesus, the Crucified People*, 12.

18. Song, *Tell us Our Names*, 3–24.

19. Song, *Jesus, the Crucified People*, 39, 50–51; 127 and 132.

20. S. T. Chan, "Narrative, Story and Storytelling: A Study of C. S. Song's Theology of Story," *Asia Journal of Theology* 12 (1998): 34–35.

21. C. S. Song, "The Role of Christology in the Christian Encounter with Eastern Religions," in G. F. Vicedom, ed., *Christ and the Younger Churches: Theological Contributions from Asia, Africa and Latin America*, SPCK Theological Collections 15 (London: SPCK, 1972), 77–82.

22. K. P. Aleaz, "The Role of Asian Religions in Asian Christian Theology," *Asia Journal of Theology* 15 (2001): 279–85.

23. A. Pieris, "Does Christ Have a Place in Asia? A Panoramic View," *Concilium* 29.2 (1993): 34–35.

24. C. S. Song, *Theology from the Womb of Asia* (London: SCM, 1988), 18.

25. A. Pieris, *An Asian Theology of Liberation* (Maryknoll: Orbis, 1988), 41–42.

26. Aleaz, "The Role of Asian Religions," 281.

27. Pieris, *Asian Theology of Liberation*, 56–58; A. Pieris, *Love Meets Wisdom: A Christian Experience of Buddhism* (Maryknoll: Orbis, 1988), 61–79 and 89–96.

28. Phan, op. cit., 408–10.

29. Ibid., 426.

30. A. Pieris, "Western Christianity and Asian Buddhism: A Theological Reading of Historical Encounters," *Dialogue* 7 (1980): 275–76.

31. Pieris, "Does Christ Have a Place in Asia?" 43–44.

32. D. Tombs, "Liberating Christology: Images of Christ in the Work of Aloysius Pieris," in S. E. Porter et al., eds, *Images of Christ: Ancient and Modern* (Sheffield: Sheffield Academic Press, 1997), 186–87.

33. A. Pieris, "Speaking of the Son of God in Non-Christian Cultures, e.g. in Asia," *Concilium* 18 (1982): 69; Pieris, *Asian Theology of Liberation*, 45–50 and 62–63; Tombs, op. cit., 187.

34. Pieris, "Does Christ Have a Place in Asia?" 43–44.

35. A. A. Yewangoe, *Theologia Crucis in Asia: Asian Christian Views on Suffering in the Face of Overwhelming Poverty and Multifaceted Religiosity in Asia* (Amsterdam: Rodopi, 1987), 290–94.

36. Pieris, "Speaking of the Son of God," 77.

37. Phan, op. cit., 404.

38. Tombs, op. cit., 183–85.

Chapter 4

1. C. L. Yeow, "Theological Education in South East Asia, 1957–2002," *International Bulletin of Missiological Research* 28.1 (2004): 26–29.

2. E. P. Nacpil, "The Critical Asian Principle," in D. J. Elwood, ed., *Asian Christian Theology: Emerging Themes* (Philadelphia: Westminster, 1980), 56–59.

3. Yeow, op. cit., 24–25.

4. R. S. Sugirtharajah, ed., *Asian Faces of Jesus* (London: SCM, 1993), 127; P. C. Phan, "Jesus the Christ with an Asian Face," *Theological Studies* 57.3 (1996): 399ff.

5. Phan, op. cit., 402–403.

6. E. Tang, "East Asia," in J. Parratt, ed., *An Introduction to Third World Theologies* (Cambridge: Cambridge University Press, 2004), 82–90.

7. Phan, op. cit., 426–27.

8. N. B. Lewis, "An Overview of the Role of Women in Asia," *East Asia Journal of Theology* 3.2 (1985): 139–46.

9. Phan, op. cit., 405; H. K. Chung, *The Struggle to be the Sun Again: Introducing Asian Women's Theology* (Maryknoll: Orbis Books, 1990); *idem*, "Who is Jesus for Asian Women?" in Sugirtharajah, op. cit., 223–46; V. Fabella, "Christology from an Asian Woman's Perspective," in Sugirtharajah, op. cit., 211–22; A. Gnanadason, "Jesus and the Asian Women: A Post-Colonial Look at the Syro-Phoenician Woman/Canaanite Woman from an Indian Perspective," *Studies in World Christianity* 7.2 (2001): 162–77; P.-l. Kwok, "Christology," in P.-l. Kwok, *Introducing Asian Feminist Theology*, Introductions in Feminist Theology 1 (Cleveland: Pilgrim, 2000), 12–24.

10. B. Zhimin, "China's Nicodemuses," *Chinese Theological Review* 7 (1991): 112–16.

11. F. Wilfred, "Jesus-Interpretation in Asia: A Methodological Fragment," *Vaiharai* 7.4 (2002): 3–19.

12. Ibid., 18–19.

Chapter 5

1. S. H. Moffett, *A History of Christianity in Asia*, vol. I: *Beginnings to 1500* (San Francisco: Harper, 1992), 291–95; I. Gillman and H.-J. Klimkeit, *Christians in Asia before 1500* (Ann Arbor: University of Michigan Press, 1999), 267–82.

2. For the text see R. Malek, ed., *The Chinese Face of Jesus Christ*, vol. I, Monumenta Serica Monograph Series 50/1 (Nettetal: Steyler Verlag, 2002), 295–313.

3. Ibid., 19–53; S. Eskildsen, "Christology and Soteriology in the Chinese Nestorian Texts," in Malek, op. cit., 181–218.

4. H.-J. Klimkeit, "Jesus' Entry into Parinirvana: Manichaean Identity in Buddhist Central Asia," *Numen* 33 (1986): 225–40.

5. Moffett, *A History of Christianity in Asia*, vol. I, 302–14; Gillman and Klimkeit, op. cit., 282–85.

6. D. Scott, "Christian Responses to Buddhism in Pre-Medieval Times," *Numen* 32 (1985): 94–96.

7. P. Rule, "The Jesus of the 'Confucian Christians' of the Seventeenth Century," in R. Malek, ed., *The Chinese Face of Jesus Christ*, vol. II, Monumenta Serica Monograph Series 50/2 (Nettetal: Steyler Verlag, 2003), 499–516.

8. A. Camps, "The People's Republic of China: From Foreignness to Contextualization," in F. J. Verstraelen, ed., *Missiology: An Ecumenical Introduction. Texts and Contexts of Global Christianity* (Grand Rapids: Eerdmans, 1995), 52–54.

9. D. J. Adams, "Ancestors, Folk Religion and Korean Christianity," in M. R. Mullins and R. F. Young, eds, *Perspectives on Christianity in Korea and Japan: The Gospel and Culture in East Asia* (Lewiston/Queenston/Tokyo: Edwin Mellon, 1995), 96–97.

10. K. M. Panikkar, *Asia and Western Dominance* (London: George Allen & Unwin, 1953), 287–88; J. Ching, *Confucianism and Christianity: A Comparative Study* (Tokyo: Kodansha International, 1977), 19–24; M. Loewe, "Imperial China's Reactions to the Catholic Missions," *Numen* 35 (1988): 205–207 and G. Minamiki, *The Chinese Rites*

Controversy: From its Beginning to Modern Times (Chicago: Loyola University Press, 1985).

11. J. Ching, "The Ambiguous Character of Chinese Religions," *Studies in Interreligious Dialogue* 11.2 (2001): 215–16.

12. J. Ching, *Chinese Religions* (Maryknoll: Orbis, 1993), 2.

13. S. Liu, "Christianity in the Reflections of Chinese Religion," *Concilium* 22.1 (1986): 75–83.

14. X. Yao, "Confucian Christ: A Chinese Image of Christianity," in W. Usdorf and T. Murayama, eds, *Identity and Marginality: Rethinking Christianity in North East Asia*, Studies in the Intercultural History of Christianity 121 (Frankfurt: Peter Lang, 2000), 29; M. W. Izutsu, "Emulating their Good Qualities, Taking their Defects as a Warning: Confucian Attitudes toward Other Religions," in J. D. Gort et al., eds, *Religions View Religions: Explorations in Pursuit of Understanding*, Currents of Encounter 25 (Amsterdam/New York: Rodopi, 2006), 55–59; also D. Wingeier, "Leadership: The Confucian Paradigm," *Trinity Theological Journal* 12 (2004): 121–37.

15. J. Ching, "The Ambiguous Character of Chinese Religions," *Studies in Interreligious Dialogue* 11.2 (2001): 213–14.

16. Ching, *Chinese Religions*, 51–67.

17. Yao, op. cit., 37.

18. Ching, *Chinese Religions*, 60.

19. Ibid., 44–45, 75 and 79.

20. Ching-yuen Cheung, "The Problem of Evil in Confucianism," in J. D. Gort et al., eds, *Probing the Depths of Evil and Good: Multireligious Views and Case Studies*, Currents of Encounter 33 (Amsterdam/New York: Rodopi, 2007), 87–99, esp. 92.

21. Yao, op. cit., 38.

22. Ching, *Confucianism and Christianity*, 73–79.

23. Ching, *Chinese Religions*, 74–77 and also Yao, op. cit., 30.

24. Ching, *Chinese Religions*, 83–84.

25. Yao, op. cit., 31–33 and 36.

26. Cf. also J. H. Wong, "Tao – Logos – Jesus. Lao Tzu, Philo and John Compared," in Malek, *The Chinese Face of Jesus Christ*, vol. I, 109–10.

27. Cf. C. Yongtao, "Towards a *Tao* Christology: Rethinking Christology in the Chinese Context," *Chinese Theological Review* 17 (2003): 25.

28. Cf. also Wong, op. cit., 90–94.

29. Wong, op. cit., 89–95 and 108–109.

30. Ching, *Chinese Religions*, 104–108.

31. J. Ching, "The Challenge of the Chinese Religion," *Concilium* 22.1 (1986): 84–89; Ching, *Chinese Religions*, 113–14.

32. J. Lagerwey, "Evil and its Treatment in Early Taoism," in Gort et al., *Probing the Depths*, 73–86, esp. 77–79.

33. Ching, *Chinese Religions*, 113–16 and 117–18.

34. H. Y. Kim, "Toward a ChristoTao: Christ as the Theanthropocosmic Tao," *Studies in Interreligious Dialogue* 10.1 (2000): 16.

35. C. S. Song, *Third Eye Theology: Theology in Formation in Asian Settings* (Maryknoll: Orbis, 1979), 69.

36. See also E. Tang, "The Second Chinese Enlightenment: Intellectuals and Christianity Today," in W. Usdorf and T. Murayama, eds, *Identity and Marginality:*

Rethinking Christianity in North East Asia, Studies in the Intercultural History of Christianity 121 (Frankfurt: Peter Lang, 2000), 58.

37. Yongtao, op. cit., 47.

38. J. D. M. Derrett, "St-John's Jesus and the Buddha," in Malek, ed., *The Chinese Face of Jesus Christ*, vol. I, 127–40.

39. Ching, *Chinese Religions*, 136.

40. K. Takizawa, *Das Heil im Heute: Texte einer Japanischen Theologie*, Theologie der Ökumene 21 (Göttingen: Vandenhoeck und Ruprecht, 1987), 181–96; S. Takada, "Is 'Theology of Religions' Possible in (Pure Land/Shin) Buddhism? The 'Shock of Non-Being' and the 'Shock of Revelation'," in J. D. Gort *et al.*, *Religions View Religions*, 30–33.

41. H. Inagaki and J. Nelson Jennings, *Philosophical Theology and East-West Dialogue*, Currents of Encounter 15 (Amsterdam/Atlanta: Rodopi, 2000), 27.

42. Inagaki and Jennings, op. cit., 30 and 32; H. M. Vroom, *A Spectrum of Worldviews: An Introduction to Philosophy of Religion in a Pluralistic World*, trans. M. Greidanus and A. Greidanus, Currents of Encounter 29 (Amsterdam/New York: Rodopi, 2006), 140–43 and 158–60.

43. D. Bonhoeffer, *Letters and Papers from Prison* (London: SCM Press, 2001); letter of 16 July 1944.

44. Ching, *Chinese Religions*, 140.

45. Ibid., 138–43.

46. H. Küng and J. Ching, *Christianity and Chinese Religions* (London: Doubleday, 1993), 222.

47. Ching, *Chinese Religions*, 149–50.

48. Ching, "The Ambiguous Character of Chinese Religions," 222–23.

49. P.-l. Kwok, "Chinese Non-Christian Perceptions of Christ," *Concilium* 29.2 (1993): 24–32 and P.-l. Kwok, "Christology," in P.-l. Kwok. *Introducing Asian Feminist Theology*, Introductions in Feminist Theology 1 (Cleveland: Pilgrim Press, 2000), 90.

50. Kwok, "Chinese Non-Christian Perceptions of Christ," 30.

51. I. Kern, "Buddhist Perception of Jesus and Christianity in the Early Buddhist-Christian Controversies in China during the 17th Century," in P. Schmidt-Leukel *et al.*, eds, *Buddhist Perceptions of Jesus* (St. Ottilien: EOS-Verlag, 2001), 38–41; Loewe, op. cit., 179–211.

52. Loewe, op. cit., 196 and 203.

53. Malek, *The Chinese Face of Jesus Christ*, vol. II, 30–31 and 43–44.

54. See Malek, *The Chinese Face of Jesus Christ*, vol. II, 313 and Eskildsen, op. cit., 190–91.

55. Eskildsen, op. cit., 194–209.

56. Ching, *Chinese Religions*, 221 and 224–25.

57. Camps, op. cit., 59–64.

58. Tang, op. cit., 62–67.

59. Yao, op. cit., 34; Camps, op. cit.

60. Tang, op. cit., 68.

61. B. Whyte, "Three Self Revisited," in Usdorf and Murayama, op. cit., 99–112.

62. R. L. Whitehead, ed., *No Longer Strangers: Selected Writings of Bishop K.H. Ting* (Maryknoll: Orbis, 1989), 72–74.

63. Kwok, "Christology," 80; V. Küster, *The Many Faces of Jesus Christ: Intercultural Christology*, trans. John Bowden (London: SCM, 2001), 176.

64. K. H. Ting, *Love Never Ends: Papers by K.H. Ting* (Nanjing: Yilin Press, 2000), 408–18 and 433–40.

65. Yongtao, op. cit., 42–46; E. Tang, "East Asia," in J. Parratt, ed., *An Introduction to Third World Theologies* (Cambridge: Cambridge University Press, 2004), 82–90.

66. P. Wickeri, "Theological Reorientation in Chinese Protestantism, 1949–1984, II," *Ching Feng* 28.2-3 (1985): 121; also Tang, "The Second Chinese Enlightenment," 58–59.

67. Tang, "The Second Chinese Enlightenment," 68–70.

Chapter 6

1. D. Scott, "Christian Responses to Buddhism in Pre-Medieval Times," *Numen* 32 (1985): 92–93.

2. For Alopen's exegesis see R. Malek, ed., *The Chinese Face of Jesus Christ*, vol. I, Monumenta Serica Monograph Series 50/1 (Nettetal: Steyler Verlag, 2002), 315–35.

3. Scott, op. cit., 96.

4. Ibid., 97–98.

5. H.-S. Keel, "Jesus the Bodhisattva: Christology from a Buddhist Perspective," *Buddhist-Christian Studies* 16 (1996): 176–92.

6. John Calvin, *Institutes of the Christian Religion*, trans. Ford Lewis Battles, Library of Christian Classics (Philadelphia: Westminster, 1960), IV.17.7–20 and II.13.7–13.

7. K. Barth, *Church Dogmatics* IV/2, trans. G. T. Thompson and Harold Knight (Edinburgh: T. & T. Clark, 1970), 661.

8. A. Wayman, "Buddha as Savior," *Studia Missionalia* 29 (1980): 191–207.

9. L. A. de Silva, "Wisdom and Compassion of the Buddha and Jesus Christ in their Role as Religious Teachers," *Dialogue (New Series)* 17.1-3 (1990): 2 and 25.

10. A. Pieris, "The Buddha and the Christ: Mediators of Liberation," in R. S. Sugirtharajah, ed., *Asian Faces of Jesus* (London: SCM, 1993), 57.

11. J. Makransky, "Buddhist Analogues of Sin and Grace: A Dialogue with Augustine," *Studies in Interreligious Dialogue* 15.1 (2005): 12–13.

12. Pieris, op. cit., 56–57.

13. Makransky, op. cit., 8–11.

14. H. M. Vroom, *A Spectrum of Worldviews: An Introduction to Philosophy of Religion in a Pluralistic World*, trans. M. Greidanus and A. Greidanus, Currents of Encounter 29 (Amsterdam/New York: Rodopi, 2006), 117–51; E. Hanaoka-Kawamura, "Buddhism and Christianity from a Christian-Buddhist Perspective," in J. D. Gort et al., eds, *Religions View Religions: Explorations in Pursuit of Understanding*, Currents of Encounter 25 (Amsterdam/New York: Rodopi, 2006), 285–86 and 293.

15. L. Thunsberg, *Man and the Cosmos: The Vision of St Maximus the Confessor* (New York: St Vladimirs Seminary Press, 1985), 71–91.

16. S. Takada, "Is 'Theology of Religions' Possible in (Pure Land/Shin) Buddhism? The 'Shock of Non-Being' and the 'Shock of Revelation'," in J. D. Gort et al., *Religions View Religions*, 33.

17. Cf. M. E. Brinkman, *The Tragedy of Human Freedom: The Failure and Promise of the Christian Concept of Freedom in Western Culture*, Currents of Encounter 20 (Amsterdam/New York: Rodopi, 2003), 162–64.

18. Takada, op. cit., 22 and 26.

19. S. Yagi, "Christ and Buddha," in R. S. Sugirtharajah, ed., *Asian Faces of Jesus* (London: SCM, 1993), 26.

20. D. Bonhoeffer, *Ethics*, trans. Neville Horton Smith (New York: Touchstone, 1995), 120–85 ("The Last Things and the Things Before the Last").

21. M. Luther, *Epistola ad Romanos*, ed. J. Ficker *et al.*, D. Martin Luthers Werke: Kritische Gesamtausgabe, vol. 56 (Weimar: Böhlau, 1938), 356.

22. P. Schmidt-Leukel, "Buddhism and Christianity: Antagonistic or Complementary?" *Studies in World Christianity* 9.2 (2003): 272–75.

23. Brinkman, op. cit., 157.

24. Keel, op. cit., 188.

25. Pieris, op. cit., 47 and 50.

26. L. A. de Silva, "Buddhism and Christianity Relativised," *Dialogue* 9 (1982): 51 and 55.

27. Irenaeus, *Adversus Haereses*, IV.18. 4, 17/18.

28. L. A. de Silva, "The Problem of the Self in Buddhism and Christianity," in D. J. Elwood, ed., *What Asian Christians are Thinking: A Theological Source Book* (Quezon City: New Day Publishers, 1976), 108–10.

29. Cf. Brinkman, *The Tragedy of Human Freedom*, 21–24 and 38–40.

Chapter 7

1. P. S. Chung, "Martin Luther and Shinran: The Presence of Christ in Justification and Salvation in a Buddhist-Christian Context," *Asia Journal of Theology* 18.2 (2004): 295–309.

2. K. Barth, *Church Dogmatics* I/2, trans. G. W. Bromiley, 2nd ed. (Edinburgh: T. & T. Clark, 1975), 340–44.

3. H. Sakurai, "The Religion of Self-Awareness: The Co-Existence of Religions from the Perspective of Shinto," in J. D. Gort *et al.*, eds, *Religions View Religions: Explorations in Pursuit of Understanding*, Currents of Encounter 25 (Amsterdam/New York: Rodopi, 2006), 11–19; S. Takada, "Is 'Theology of Religions' Possible in (Pure Land/Shin) Buddhism? The 'Shock of Non-Being' and the 'Shock of Revelation'," in J. D. Gort *et al.*, *Religions View Religions*, 35.

4. W. M. Fridell, "The Establishment of Shrine Shinto in Meiji Japan," *Japanese Journal of Religious Studies* 2.2-3 (1975): 166–67.

5. E. Tang, "East Asia," in J. Parratt, ed., *An Introduction to Third World Theologies* (Cambridge: Cambridge University Press, 2004), 94–95.

6. M. R. Mullins, "Christianity Transplanted: Toward a Sociology of Success and Failure," in M. R. Mullins and R. F. Young, eds, *Perspectives on Christianity in Korea and Japan: The Gospel and Culture in East Asia* (Lewiston: Edwin Mellon, 1995), 73 and Y.-B. Kim, "A Re-reading of History of Asian Missiology from Below: A Korean Perspective," in W. Usdorf and T. Murayama, eds, *Identity and Marginality: Rethinking Christianity in*

North East Asia, Studies in the Intercultural History of Christianity 121 (Frankfurt: Peter Lang, 2000), 78–86.

7. S. H. Moffett, "Has Christianity Failed in Asia?" *The Princeton Seminary Bulletin* 26.2 (2005): 119–211.

8. Y. Furuya, ed., *A History of Japanese Theology* (Grand Rapids/Cambridge: Eerdmans, 1997), 143.

9. I. Shuntaro, "The Introduction of Western Cosmology in Seventeenth Century Japan: The Case of Christovao Ferreira (1580–1652)," *The Japan Foundation Newsletter* 14 (1986): 1–9.

10. M. Harrington, "The Kakure Kirishitan and their Place in Japan's Religious Tradition," *Japanese Journal of Religious Studies* 7.4 (1980): 334.

11. Ibid., 331–32.

12. M. R. Mullins, *Christianity Made in Japan: A Study of Indigenous Movements* (Honolulu: University of Hawai'i Press, 1998), 167–72.

13. Furuya, op. cit., 142–44.

14. Mullins, *Christianity Made in Japan*, 61. Mullins refers here to *The Complete Works of Uchimura Kanzô*, vol. 30, 192.

15. Ibid., 54–67.

16. Ibid., 68–128.

17. Ibid., 166; Mullins, "Christianity Transplanted," 66–68.

18. Sakurai, op. cit., 12.

19. M. Tsushima *et al.*, "The Vitalistic Conception of Salvation in Japanese New Religions: An Aspect of Modern Religious Consciousness," *Japanese Journal of Religious Studies* 6.1–2 (1979): 139–61.

20. R. F. Young, "The 'Christ' of the Japanese New Religions," in M. R. Mullins and R. F. Young, eds, *Perspectives on Christianity in Korea and Japan: The Gospel and Culture in East Asia* (Lewiston: Edwin Mellen, 1995), 115–31.

21. K. Kitamori, *Theology of the Pain of God* (Richmond: Knox, 1965), 134–36 and 148.

22. K. Kitamori, "The Problem of Pain in Christology," in G. F. Vicedom, ed., *Christ and the Younger Churches: Theological Contributions from Asia, Africa and Latin America*, SPCK Theological Collections 15 (London: SPCK, 1972), 85–88; Kitamori, *Theology of the Pain of God*, 15–16, 44–49 and 115.

23. Kitamori, *Theology of the Pain of God*, 138; Y. Terazono, *Die Christologie Karl Barths und Takizawas: Ein Vergleich* (Bonn: Rheinische Friedrich-Wilhelms-Universität, 1976), 43–46.

24. Kitamori, *Theology of the Pain of God*, 54–57.

25. Ibid., 12, 15–16 and 150.

26. H. Inagaki and J. Nelson Jennings, *Philosophical Theology and East-West Dialogue*, Currents of Encounter 15 (Amsterdam/Atlanta: Rodopi, 2000), 113–14.

27. Kitamori, *Theology of the Pain of God*, 8 and 151–67; cf. also A. A. Yewangoe, *Theologia Crucis in Asia: Asian Christian Views on Suffering in the Face of Overwhelming Poverty and Multifaceted Religiosity in Asia* (Amsterdam: Rodopi, 1987), 185–201.

28. K. Koyama, *Mount Fuji and Mount Sinai: A Pilgrimage in Theology* (London: SCM, 1984), 209–61.

29. Ibid., 3–56.

30. K. Koyama, *Water Buffalo Theology*, rev. ed. (Maryknoll: Orbis, 1999), 82–89.

31. Koyama, *Mount Fuji and Mount Sinai*, 256–61.

32. Furuya, op. cit., 146; with critique Tang, op. cit., 95.

33. Yewangoe, op. cit., 174.

34. V. Küster, *The Many Faces of Jesus Christ: Intercultural Christology* (London: SCM, 2001), 173–77; K. Tanimoto, "Mission from the *Buraku*," in Usdorf and Murayama, op. cit., 141–53; R. G. Stieber, "*Buraku* Stories," in Usdorf and Murayama, op. cit., 155–67; A. M. Suggate, "Theology from Below in Japan as a Challenge to the West: Professor Kuribayashi's Theology of the Crown of Thorns," in Usdorf and Murayama, op. cit., 229–42.

35. T. Kuribayashi, *A Theology of the Crown of Thorns: Towards the Liberation of the Asian Outcasts* (New York, 1987), 168 and 206.

36. S. Endo, *Silence*, trans. W. Johnston (Tokyo: Monumenta Nipponico, 1969), 259.

37. S. Endo, *Deep River*, trans. Van C. Gessel (London/Chester Springs: Peter Owen, 1994), 42.

38. S. Endo, *Scandal*, trans. Van C. Gessel (London/Chester Springs: Peter Owen, 1988), 151–54.

39. A. G. Hoekema, "The 'Christology' of the Japanese Novelist Shusaku Endo," *Exchange* 29 (2000): 230–48.

40. Endo, *Deep River*, 44–45, 62 and 209.

41. Ibid., 215.

42. Ibid., 193.

43. Ibid., 191.

44. Ibid., 119.

45. Endo, *Scandal*, 133, 136 and 228–31.

46. Endo, *Deep River*, 140.

47. Ibid., 65.

48. Ibid., 120.

49. Endo, *Scandal*, 13.

50. Ibid., 221.

51. Ibid., 96.

52. Ibid., 135.

53. Ibid., 97.

54. S. Machida, "Jesus, Man of Sin towards a New Christology in the Global Era," *Buddhist-Christian Studies* 19.1 (1999): 81–91.

55. Endo, *Scandal*, 192 and 222.

56. Endo, *Deep River*, 62.

57. Endo, *Scandal*, 209.

58. Ibid., 235.

59. Endo, *Deep River*, 66.

60. T. Kuribayashi, "Recovering Jesus for Outcasts in Japan: From a Theology of the Crown of Thorns," *Japan Christian Review* 58 (1992): 19–32; S. Kuwahara, "Images of Women as 'the Other': An Illustration from the Novels of Shusaku Endo," *God's Image* 18.4 (1999): 35–36.

61. T. Sundermeier, "Das Kreuz in Japanischer Interpretation," *Evangelische Theologie* 44 (1984): 439.

62. A. van Heijst, *Longing for the Fall*, trans. H. Jansen (Kampen: Kok Pharos, 1992), esp. 160–61, 179–81, 189–92, 282–83.

63. Tang, op. cit., 93; K. Takizawa, *Das Heil im Heute: Texte einer Japanischen Theologie*, Theologie der Ökumene 21 (Göttingen: Vandenhoeck und Ruprecht, 1987), 128–80.

64. K. Takizawa, *Reflexionen über die universale Grundlage von Buddhismus und Christentum*, Studien zur interkulturellen Geschichte des Christentums 24 (Frankfurt: Peter Lang, 1980), 127–71; Takizawa, *Das Heil im Heute*, 33–40.

65. Takizawa, *Reflexionen*, 21 and 113; *Das Heil im Heute*, 200–202.

66. Takizawa, *Reflexionen*, 160.

67. Takizawa, *Das Heil im Heute*, 18.

68. Takizawa, *Reflexionen*, 9–12 and 144–48; T. Sundermeier, "Präsentische Theologie: Der Beitrag K. Takizawas im interkulturellen theologischen Gespräch," in Takizawa, *Das Heil im Heute*, 12–13.

69. Inagaki and Jennings, op. cit., 49 and 58; H. M. Vroom, *A Spectrum of Worldviews: An Introduction to Philosophy of Religion in a Pluralistic World*, trans. M. Greidanus and A. Greidanus, Currents of Encounter 29 (Amsterdam/New York: Rodopi, 2006), 162–63.

70. Takizawa, *Reflexionen*, 161; Terazono, op. cit., 24–42.

71. S. Yagi and L. Schwidler, *A Bridge to Buddhist-Christian Dialogue* (New York: Paulist Press, 1990), 139–44; Küster, op. cit., 104–14.

72. Küster, op. cit., 115–16.

73. S. Yagi, "The Third Generation, 1945–1970," in Y. Furuya, ed., *A History of Japanese Theology* (Grand Rapids/Cambridge: Eerdmans, 1997), 93–101; M. Odagaki, "Theology after 1970," in Y. Furuya, ed., *A History of Japanese Theology* (Grand Rapids/ Cambridge: Eerdmans, 1997), 117–24.

74. S. C. Fritsch-Opperman, "Christian Existence in a Buddhist Context," *Studies in Interreligious Dialogue* 13.2 (2003): 227–30.

75. K. Barth, *Church Dogmatics* IV/1, trans. G. W. Bromiley (Edinburgh: T. & T. Clark, 1980), 480; Iganaki and Jennings, op. cit., 72 and 92.

76. K. Barth, *Church Dogmatics* III/1, trans. J. W. Edwards et al. (Edinburgh: T. & T. Clark, 1982), 184.

77. H. Inagaki, "Comparative Study of the Kuperian Palingenesis: The Transcendent and Human Ego in Japanese Thought," in C. van der Kooi and J. de Bruijn, eds, *Kuyper Reconsidered: Aspects of his Life and Work*, VU Studies on Protestant History 3 (Amsterdam: VU Uitgeverij, 1999), 172.

78. S. Yagi, "'I' in the Words of Jesus," in J. Hick and P. F. Knitter, eds, *The Myth of Christian Uniqueness: Towards a Pluralistic Theology of Religions* (Maryknoll: Orbis, 1987), 118–34.

79. Inagaki, op. cit., 173.

80. Yagi, op. cit., 128; Küster, op. cit., 108–10.

81. B. Nagel, "Beyond a Personal God? Shizuteru Ueda's Zen Buddhist Interpretation of Meister Eckhart," *Studies in Interreligious Dialogue* 8.1 (1998): 74–98; H.-S. Keel, "Meister Eckhart's Asian Christianity: Mysticism as a Bridge between Christianity and Zen Buddhism," *Studies in Interreligious Dialogue* 14.1 (2004): 75–94.

82. Fritsch-Opperman, op. cit., 232; Inagaki and Jennings, op. cit., 52–54 and 124.

83. S. Ueda, "Jesus in Contemporary Japanese Zen: With Special Regards to Keiji Nishitani," in P. Schmidt-Leukel et al., eds, *Buddhist Perceptions of Jesus* (St. Ottilien: EOS-Verlag, 2001), 42–58.

84. Inagaki and Jennings, op. cit., 32 and 131.

Chapter 8

1. D. J. Adams, "Ancestors, Folk Religion and Korean Christianity," in M. R. Mullins and R. F. Young, eds, *Perspectives on Christianity in Korea and Japan: The Gospel and Culture in East Asia* (Lewiston: Edwin Mellon, 1995), 95–113.

2. M. E. Brinkman, *The Tragedy of Human Freedom: The Failure and Promise of the Christian Concept of Freedom in Western Culture* (Amsterdam/New York: Rodopi, 2003).

3. John Calvin, *Institutes of the Christian Religion*, trans. Ford Lewis Battles, Library of Christian Classics (Philadelphia: Westminster, 1960), II.16.8–12.

4. C. S. Song, *Jesus in the Power of the Spirit*, The Cross in the Lotus World, vol. 3 (Minneapolis: Augsburg, 1994), 176–79; M. R. Mullins, "What About the Ancestors? Some Japanese Christian Responses to Protestant Individualism," *Studies in World Christianity* 4.1 (1998): 58–60.

5. See Parts VII and VIII of this volume.

6. A. G. Honig, "The Search for Identity as a Source of Renewal," in F. J. Verstraelen, ed., *Missiology: An Ecumenical Introduction. Texts and Contexts of Global Christianity* (Grand Rapids: Eerdmans, 1995), 323–32.

7. M. R. Mullins, *Christianity Made in Japan: A Study of Indigenous Movements* (Honolulu: University of Hawai'i Press, 1998), 129–55.

8. H. Y. Kim, *Christ and the Tao* (Hong Kong: Christian Conference of Asia, 2003), V–VI and 128–30.

9. S. M. Park, *The Unity of the Church: The Implications of Karl Barth's Ecclesiology for the Korean Context*, diss. VU University (Amsterdam, 2005), 150–52 and 164–66.

10. P. C. Phan, "The Christ of Asia: An Essay on Jesus as the Eldest Son and Ancestor," *Studia Missionalia* 45 (1996): 40–47.

11. P.-l. Kwok, *Introducing Asian Feminist Theology*, Introductions in Feminist Theology 1 (Cleveland: Pilgrim, 2000), 90.

12. Phan, op. cit., 40.

13. Adams, op. cit., 95–113.

14. J. Y. Lee, "Relationship between Christianity and Shamanism in Korea: A Historical Perspective," *Asia Journal of Theology* 10.2 (1996): 333–38.

15. S.-D. Oak, "Shamanistic Tan'gun and Christian Hananim: Protestant Missionaries' Interpretation of the Korean Founding Myth, 1985–1934," *Studies in World Christianity* 7.1 (2001): 42–57.

16. See also the reference to this example in the first section of Chapter 2.

17. D. K-s. Suh, *The Korean Minjung in Christ* (Hongkong: Christian Conference of Asia, 1991), 107.

18. Ibid., 89–107.

19. M. Kalsky, *Christaphanien: Die Re-Vision der Christologie aus der Sicht von Frauen in unterschiedlichen Kulturen* (Gütersloh: Kaiser, 2000), 262–63.

20. D. K-s. Suh, op. cit., 114–17.

21. H. K. Chung, "Who is Jesus for Asian Women?" in R. S. Sugirtharajah, ed., *Asian Faces of Jesus* (London: SCM, 1993), 236.

22. H. K. Chung, "'Han-pu-ri': Doing Theology from Korean Women's Perspective," *The Ecumenical Review* 40.1 (1988): 34–35; Kalsky, op. cit., 249–50 and 255–58.

23. H. Y. Kim, "Toward a ChristoTao: Christ as the Theanthropocosmic Tao," *Studies in Interreligious Dialogue* 10.1 (2000): 12; H. Y. Kim, *Christ and the Tao*, 141–44.

24. H. K. Chung, "Come, Holy Spirit – Renew the Whole Creation," in M. Kinnamon, ed., *Signs of the Spirit: Official Reports of the Seventh Assembly* (Geneva/Grand Rapids: WCC/Eerdmans, 1991), 46.

25. D. K-s. Suh, op. cit., 153–56; Y.-B. Kim, "A Re-reading of History of Asian Missiology from Below: A Korean Perspective," in W. Usdorf and T. Murayama, eds, *Identity and Marginality: Rethinking Christianity in North East Asia*, Studies in the Intercultural History of Christianity 121 (Frankfurt: Peter Lang, 2000), 76–77.

26. N. D. Suh, "Historical References for a Theology of Minjung," in Y. B. Kim, ed., *Minjung Theology: People as the Subjects of History* (London: Zed, 1981), 176–78.

27. Y. B. Kim, "Korean Christianity as a Messianic Movement of the People," in Y. B. Kim, op. cit., 77–116; Y. B. Kim, "Messiah and Minjung: Discerning Messianic Politics over against Political Messianism," in Y. B. Kim, op. cit., 185–96; Honig, op. cit., 324–26.

28. B.-M. Ahn, "Jesus and People (Minjung)," in R. S. Sugirtharajah, ed., *Asian Faces of Jesus* (London: SCM, 1993), 167–72; N. D. Suh, op. cit., 158–61; A. A. Yewangoe, *Theologia Crucis in Asia: Asian Christian Views on Suffering in the Face of Overwhelming Poverty and Multifaceted Religiosity in Asia* (Amsterdam: Rodopi, 1987), 136–43.

29. Y. B. Kim, op. cit., 96–102.

30. N. D. Suh, op. cit., 172–73.

31. J. H. Lee, "I am at the Mercy of the Rats: Christological Images in Korean Folklore," in W. Usdorf and T. Murayama, eds, *Identity and Marginality: Rethinking Christianity in North East Asia*, Studies in the Intercultural History of Christianity 121 (Frankfurt: Peter Lang, 2000), 44–46.

32. N. D. Suh, "Towards a Theology of Han," in Y. B. Kim, ed., *Minjung Theology: People as the Subjects of History* (Singapore: Commission on Theological Concerns, 1981), 54 and 65.

33. See the last two sections of Chapter 3.

34. J. H. Kim, "Christianity and Korean Culture: The Reasons for the Success of Christianity in Korea," *Exchange* 33 (2004): 151; Lee, op. cit., 41–44; H. E. Hwang, "The Legacy of the Minjung Congregation Movement in South Korea 1983–1997," in W. Usdorf and T. Murayama, eds, *Identity and Marginality: Rethinking Christianity in North East Asia*, Studies in the Intercultural History of Christianity 121 (Frankfurt: Peter Lang, 2000), 113–19.

35. H. Y. Kim, "Toward a ChristoTao," 5–29; H. Y. Kim, *Christ and the Tao*, 135–54.

36. Chung, *The Struggle to be the Sun Again*.

37. H. Y. Kim, "Toward a ChristoTao," 10–14; H. Y. Kim, *Christ and the Tao*, 138–48.

38. V. Turner, *On the Edge of the Bush: Anthropology as Experience* (Tucson: University of Arizona Press, 1985), 158–61.

39. J. Y. Lee, *Marginality: The Key to Multicultural Theology* (Minneapolis: Fortress Press, 1995), 29–76.

40. J. Y. Lee, "The Perfect Realization of Change: Jesus Christ," in R. S. Sugirtharajah, ed., *Asian Faces of Jesus* (London: SCM, 1993), 71–72.

41. K. Barth, *Church Dogmatics* IV/1, trans. G. W. Bromiley (Edinburgh: T. & T. Clark, 1980), 157–642 and IV/2, trans. G. W. Bromiley (Edinburgh: T. & T. Clark, 1970), 1–840.

42. J. Y. Lee, *The Theology of Change: A Christian Concept of God in an Eastern Perspective* (Maryknoll: Orbis, 1979), 98–99.

43. H. Y. Kim, *Christ and the Tao*, 16–40; 41–88 on Barth and 165–66, 168 and 173–76 on *yin* and *yang*.

44. A. G. Hoekema, "Barth and Asia: .No Boring Theology," *Exchange* 33 (2004): 102–31.

45. L. Pan-chiu, "Barth's Doctrines of Sin and Humanity in Buddhist Perspective," *Studies in Interreligious Dialogue* 16.1 (2006): 41–58; K. Takizawa, *Reflexionen über die universale Grundlage von Buddhismus und Christentum*, Studien zur interkulturellen Geschichte des Christentums 24 (Frankfurt: Peter Lang, 1980), 161–64; Y. Terazono, *Die Christologie Karl Barths und Takizawas: Ein Vergleich* (Bonn: Rheinische Friedrich-Wilhelms-Universität, 1976), 137–62.

Chapter 9

1. K. Kim, "India," in J. Parratt, ed., *An Introduction to Third World Theologies* (Cambridge: Cambridge University Press, 2004), 58; R. C. Heredia, "Hindu Aversion for Dalit Conversion: No Entry, No Exit," *Vidyajyoti* 67.6 (2003): 401–26.

2. M. E. Prabhakar, "Christology in Dalit Perspective," in V. Devasahayam, ed., *Frontiers of Dalit Theology* (New Delhi: Indian Society for Promoting Christian Knowledge, 1997), 402–32.

3. J. B. Carman, "When Hindus Become Christian: Religious Conversion and Spiritual Ambiguity," in J. D. Gort *et al.*, *Religions View Religions: Explorations in Pursuit of Understanding*, Currents of Encounter 25 (Amsterdam/New York: Rodopi, 2006), 255–57.

4. S. H. Moffet, *A History of Christianity in Asia*, vol. I: *Beginnings to 1500* (San Francisco: Harper, 1992), 22–44; I. Gillman and H.-J. Klimkeit, *Christians in Asia before 1500* (Ann Arbor: University of Michigan Press, 1999), 159–66.

5. X. Koodapuzha, *Oriental Churches: An Introduction* (Kottayam: Oriental Institute of Religious Studies India, 1996), 110–11 and 115–17.

6. Ibid., 42–59.

7. X. Kochuparampil, "The St. Thomas Christians of India: Ecumenical and Missiological Challenges," *Exchange* 25.3 (1996): 243–60.

8. G. Thumpanirappel, *Christ in the East Syriac Tradition: A Study of the Christology of the Assyrian Church of the East and the Common Christological Declaration of 1994* (Satna: Ephrems Publications, 2003), 56–57.

9. E. J. Sharpe, "Neo-Hindu Images of Christianity," in A. Sharma, ed., *Neo-Hindu Views of Christianity* (Leiden: Brill, 1988), 1–15.

10. S. J. Samartha, *The Hindu Response to the Unbound Christ*, Interreligious Dialogue Series 6 (Madras: Christian Literature Society, 1974), 19–41; C. Crawford, "Raja Ram Mohan Roy's Attitude toward Christians and Christianity," in Sharma, op. cit., 16–65.

11. D. Kopf, "Neo-Hindu Views of Unitarian and Trinitarian Christianity in Nineteenth Century Bengal: The Case of Keshub Chandra Sen," in Sharma, op. cit., 106–19.

12. Sharpe, op. cit., 8–10.

13. S. Rayan, "Hindu Perceptions of Christ in the Nineteenth Century," *Concilium* 29 (1993): 13–23.

14. E. Klootwijk, *Commitment and Openness: The Interreligious Dialogue and Theology of Religions in the Work of Stanley J. Samartha* (Zoetermeer: Boekencentrum, 1992), 172–75; F. Wilfred, *Beyond Settled Foundations: The Journey of Indian Theology* (Madras: Dept. of Christian Studies, University of Madras, 1993), 26; J. Dupuis, *Jesus Christ at the Encounter of World Religions* (Maryknoll: Orbis, 1991), 37–42.

15. Rayan, op. cit., 19.

16. S. Clarke, *Dalits and Christianity: Subaltern Religion and Liberation in India* (New Delhi: Oxford University Press, 1998), 40–44.

17. Samartha, op. cit., 73–97; K. L. S. Rao, "Mahatma Gandhi and Christianity," in Sharma, op. cit., 143–55.

18. H. W. French, "Swami Vivekananda's Experiences and Interpretations of Christianity," in Sharma, op. cit., 82–105; J. P. Schouten, "Jesus in Hindu Garb: Images of Jesus Christ in the Ramakrisna Movement," *Studies in Interreligious Dialogue* 11.1 (2001): 37–63.

19. Samartha, op. cit., 44–61; Rayan, op. cit.

20. G. Robinson, "Jesus Christ, the Open Way and the Fellow-Struggler: A Look into the Christologies in India," *Asia Journal of Theology* 3.2 (1989): 407–408.

21. V. Ramachandra, *The Recovery of Mission: Beyond the Pluralist Paradigm* (Grand Rapids: Eerdmans, 1996), 16; Carman, op. cit., 256.

22. Dupuis, op. cit., 81–86.

23. A. J. Appasamy, *Christianity as Bhakti Marga: A Study in the Mysticism of the Johannine Writings* (London: Macmillan, 1927).

24. M. Amaladoss, "Images of Jesus in India," in N. Schreurs and H. van de Sandt, eds, *De ene Jezus en de vele culturen: Christologie en contextualiteit* (Tilburg: Tilburg University Press, 1992), 27–28; M. Dhavamony, *Hindu-Christian Dialogue: Theological Soundings and Perspectives*, Currents of Encounter 18 (Amsterdam/New York: Rodopi, 2002), 58–63.

25. Schouten, "Jesus in Hindu Garb," 56.

Chapter 10

1. See Chapter 3, last section.

2. R. Panikkar, *The Trinity and the Religious Experience of Man* (Maryknoll: Orbis, 1973), 42.

3. R. Panikkar, *The Trinity and World Religions: Icon-Person-Mystery*, Inter-Religious Dialogue Series 4 (Madras: Christian Literature Society, 1970), 42.

4. Ibid., 44–50.

5. R. Panikkar, *The Silence of God: The Answer of the Buddha* (Maryknoll: Orbis, 1990), 101–47.

6. Panikkar, *The Trinity and World Religions*, 50–67, and *The Trinity and the Religious Experience of Man*, 51–58 and 64.

7. R. Panikkar, *The Unknown Christ of Hinduism: Towards an Ecumenical Christophany* (Maryknoll: Orbis, 1981), 152–54.

8. Ibid., 164.

9. Panikkar, *The Trinity and World Religions*, 69–75 and *The Trinity and the Religious Experience of Man*, 71–82.

10. Panikkar, *The Trinity and the Religious Experience of Man*, 71.

11. R. Panikkar, *The Cosmotheandric Experience: Emerging Religious Consciousness* (Maryknoll: Orbis, 1993), 72–77.

12. Panikkar, *The Unknown Christ*, 130.

13. Ibid., 19–20 and 25–26.

14. Ibid., 92.

15. Panikkar, *The Trinity and the Religious Experience of Man*, 54 and 68; R. Panikkar, "The Jordan, the Tiber, and the Ganges: Three Kairological Moments of Christic Self-Consciousness," in J. Hick and P. F. Knitter, eds, *The Myth of Christian Uniqueness: Towards a Pluralistic Theology of Religions* (Maryknoll: Orbis, 1987), 114; J. Komulainen, *An Emerging Cosmotheandric Religion? Raimon Panikkar's Pluralistic Theology of Religions*, Studies in Christian Mission 30 (Leiden: Brill, 2005), 116–49.

16. Panikkar, *The Trinity and the Religious Experience of Man*, 53–55.

17. See the second last section of Chapter 7.

18. W. Strolz, "Panikkar's Encounter with Hinduism," in J. D. Gort et al., eds, *Dialogue and Syncretism: An Interdisciplinary Approach*, Currents of Encounter 1 (Amsterdam/Grand Rapids: Rodopi/Eerdmans, 1989), 151; V. Ramachandra, *The Recovery of Mission: Beyond the Pluralist Paradigm* (Grand Rapids: Eerdmans, 1996), 87; A. Karokaran, "Raymond Panikkar's Theology of Religions: A Critique," *Vidyajyoti* 58 (1994): 670.

19. Ramachandra, op. cit., 90.

20. M. E. Prabhakar, "Christology in Dalit Perspective," in V. Devasahayam, ed., *Frontiers of Dalit Theology* (New Delhi: Indian Society for Promoting Christian Knowledge, 1997), 414–17.

21. G. Robinson, "Jesus Christ, the Open Way and the Fellow-Struggler: A Look into the Christologies in India," *Asia Journal of Theology* 3.2 (1989): 411–13.

22. S. J. Samartha, *The Hindu Response to the Unbound Christ*, Interreligious Dialogue Series 6 (Madras: Christian Literature Society, 1974), 139–42.

23. Samartha, *The Hindu Response*, 10; S. J. Samartha, "The Cross and the Rainbow: Christ in a Multireligious Culture," in R. S. Sugirtharajah, ed., *Asian Faces of Jesus* (London: SCM, 1993), 119.

24. Samartha, "The Cross and the Rainbow," 118.

25. Samartha, *The Hindu Response*, 163.

26. Samartha, *The Hindu Response*, 143.

27. S. J. Samartha, *One Christ, Many Religions: Towards a Revised Christology* (Maryknoll: Orbis, 1991), 131.

28. E. Klootwijk, *Commitment and Openness: The Interreligious Dialogue and Theology of Religions in the Work of Stanley J. Samartha* (Zoetermeer: Boekencentrum, 1992), 188–95.

29. Samartha, *The Hindu Response*, 164–66, 171 and 191–200, and Samartha, *One Christ, Many Religions*, 140.

30. Samartha, *One Christ, Many Religions*, 138.

31. K. P. Aleaz, *An Indian Jesus from Sankara's Thought* (Calcutta: Punthi Pustak, 1997), 226–31; K. P. Aleaz, "An Indian Understanding of Jesus – Findings of a Research," *Asia Journal of Theology* 12.1 (1998): 128–30 and 134.

32. Samartha, *One Christ, Many Religions*, 119 and 139–40; Ramachandra, op. cit., 9–11.

33. Samartha, *One Christ, Many Religions*, 115–16.

34. Samartha, *One Christ, Many Religions*, 133–35.

35. Samartha, "The Cross and the Rainbow," 114.

36. Samartha, *One Christ, Many Religions*, 116–19.

37. Samartha, "The Cross and the Rainbow," 116–17.

38. Samartha, *One Christ, Many Religions*, 124–31; Klootwijk, op. cit., 262–69.

Chapter 11

1. M. Alphonse, "Christianity as Bhakti Religion," *Dharma Deepika* 1.1 (1995): 5–32.

2. The Bhagavad Gita, trans. from the Sanskrit by Juan Mascaró, with an introduction by Simon Brodbeck (London: Penguin Classics, 2003), 22–23.

3. F. X. D'Sa, "Christian Incarnation and Hindu Avatara," *Concilium* 29.2 (1993): 81–82; N. Sheth, "Hindu Avatara and Christian Incarnation: A Comparison I," *Vidyajyoti* 67.3 (2003): 182–83.

4. Sheth, op. cit., 192.

5. N. Sheth, "Hindu Avatara and Christian Incarnation: A Comparison II," *Vidyajyoti* 67.4 (2003): 296.

6. Ibid., 299.

7. D'Sa, op. cit., 82–84.

8. M. Dhavamony, "Hindu 'Incarnations'," *Studia Missionalia* 21 (1972): 142–52.

9. Ibid., 152 and 164–65.

10. N. Sheth, "Hindu Avatara I," 186–87.

11. D. Alphonse, "Jesus, the Avatar," *Vaiharai* 7.4 (2002): 33–34.

12. J. Dupuis, *Jesus Christ at the Encounter of World Religions* (Maryknoll: Orbis, 1991), 47.

13. S. J. Samartha, "The Cross and the Rainbow: Christ in a Multireligious Culture," in R. S. Sugirtharajah, ed., *Asian Faces of Jesus* (London: SCM, 1993), 121.

14. M. Dhavamony, *Hindu-Christian Dialogue: Theological Soundings and Perspectives*, Currents of Encounter 18 (Amsterdam/New York: Rodopi, 2002), 85–90.

15. O. N. Mohammed, "Jesus and Krishna," in R. S. Sugirtharajah, ed., *Asian Faces of Jesus* (London: SCM, 1993), 14.

16. Wendy Doniger, "Reincarnation in Hinduism," *Concilium* 29 (1993): 6.

17. S. J. Samartha, "The Unbound Christ: Toward a Christology in India Today," in D. J. Elwood, ed., *Asian Christian Theology: Emerging Themes* (Philadelphia: Westminster, 1980), 152–57.

18. Doniger, op. cit., 3–15.

19. R. De Smet, "Jesus and the Avatara," in J. D. Gort et al., eds, *Dialogue and Syncretism: An Interdisciplinary Approach*, Currents of Encounter 1 (Amsterdam/Grand Rapids: Eerdmans, 1989), 161–62; M. Alphonse, op. cit., 28; V. Ramachandra, *The Recovery of Mission: Beyond the Pluralist Paradigm* (Grand Rapids: Eerdmans, 1996), 240–43.

20. A. Pragasam, "Jesus the Guru," *Vaiharai* 7.4 (2002): 38.

21. C. Cornille, *The Guru in Indian Catholicism: Ambiguity or Opportunity of Inculturation?* Louvain Theological & Pastoral Monographs 6 (Louvain: Peeters, s.a.), 39–40.

22. X. Irudayaraj, "The Guru in Hinduism and Christianity," *Vidyajyoti* 39 (1975): 339–40.

23. Ibid., 341–45.

24. M. T. Thangaraj, *The Crucified Guru: An Experiment in Crosscultural Christology* (Nashville: Abingdon, 1994), 114.

25. A. Wayman, "The Guru in Buddhism," *Studia Missionalia* 36 (1987): 195–213.

26. Thangaraj, op. cit., 91–105; M. T. Thangaraj, "The Word Made Flesh: The Crucified Guru," in M. A. Oduyoye and H. M. Vroom, eds, *One Gospel – Many Cultures: Case Studies and Reflections on Cross-Cultural Theology* (Amsterdam/New York: Rodopi, 2003), 112–19.

27. Thangaraj, *The Crucified Guru*, 112–15 and "The Word Made Flesh," 121–22.

28. S. Kappen, "Jesus and Transculturation," in Sugirtharajah, op. cit., 177–87.

29. Cf. J. P. Schouten, *Revolution of the Mystics: On the Social Aspects of Virasiavism* (Kampen: Kok Pharos, 1991).

Chapter 12

1. K. Steenbrink, *Dutch Colonialism and Indonesian Islam: Contacts and Conflicts 1596–1950*, Currents of Encounter 7 (Amsterdam/Atlanta: Rodopi, 1993), 142.

2. J. A. Titaley, "The Pancasila of Indonesia: A Lost Ideal?" in E. A. J. G. van der Borght et al., eds, *Faith and Ethnicity I*, Studies in Reformed Theology 6 (Zoetermeer: Meinema, 2002), 37–102; G. Singgih, "Indonesian Churches and the Problem of Nationality and Ethnicity," in van der Borght, op. cit., 103–23; K. Steenbrink, "Indonesia: A Christian Minority in a Strong Position," in F. J. Verstraelen, ed., *Missiology: An Ecumenical Introduction. Texts and Contexts of Global Christianity* (Grand Rapids: Eerdmans, 1995), 88–98.

3. J. Aritonang, "Faith and Ethnic Conflicts in Indonesia: A Brief Historical Survey and Theological Reflection," in Van der Borght et al., op. cit., 124–37; K. Steenbrink, "Christianity and Islam: Civilizations or Religions? Contemporary Indonesian Discussions," *Exchange* 33.3 (2004): 223–43.

4. A. Yewangoe, "The Trinity in the Context of Tribal Religion," *Studies in Interreligious Dialogue* 13.1 (2003): 86–87.

5. J. B. Banawiratma, "Contextual Christology and Christian Praxis: An Indonesian Reflection," *East Asian Pastoral Review* 37 (2000): 174–76.

6. S. Rambitan, "Jesus in Islamic Context of Indonesia," *REC Focus* 3 (2003): 42.

7. K. Steenbrink, "Indonesian Churches 1978–1984: Main Trends, Issues and Problems," *Exchange* 13 (1984): 10–12; Steenbrink, *Dutch Colonialism and Indonesian Islam*, 145–48.

8. S. Ririhena, "Pela as Inclusive Socio-Cosmic System in the Central Moluccas," in M. E. Brinkman and D. van Keulen, eds, *Christian Identity in Cross-Cultural Perspective*, Studies in Reformed Theology 8 (Zoetermeer: Meinema, 2003), 26–29.

9. S. Ririhena, "Ethnicity as the Reshaping Force of Christian Belief Systems: Moluccan Ethnicity in the Netherlands Reshaping Reformed Theology," in van der Borght, op. cit., 168.

10. E. S. Patty, "Liminality and Worship in the Korean American Context," in Brinkman and van Keulen, op. cit., 91–95.

11. E. S. Patty, "Ethnicity: A Means of Grace?" in van der Borght, op. cit., 158–61.

12. Ririhena, "Pela as Inclusive Socio-Cosmic System," 23–25 and 33–40; *idem*, "Ethnicity as the Reshaping Force of Christian Belief Systems," 170–77.

13. Ririhena, "Pela as Inclusive Socio-Cosmic System," 38–39.

14. Ibid., 18–40.

15. Ibid., 38–39.

16. E. T. Maspaitella, "Jesus and the Gunman: Why Agnes Might Be Shot. A Theological Reflection from Ambon, Based on Local Ientities of Jesus," in van der Borght, op. cit., 279–81.

17. T. Sumartana, *Mission at the Crossroads: Indigenous Churches, European Missionaries, Islamic Association and Socio-Religious Change in Java 1812–1936* (Leiderdorp: De Zijl, 1991), 33–37 and 47–48; A. A. Yewangoe, *Theologia Crucis in Asia: Asian Christian Views on Suffering in the Face of Overwhelming Poverty and Multifaceted Religiosity in Asia* (Amsterdam: Rodopi, 1987), 221–26.

18. M. de Jonge, *Christology in Context: The Earliest Christian Response to Jesus* (Philadelphia: Westminster, 1988), 144–49.

19. D. A. Kerr, "Christology in Christian–Muslim Dialogue," in R. F. Berkey and S. A. Edwards, eds, *Christology in Dialogue* (Cleveland: Pilgrim Press, 1993), 209.

20. J. Dunn, *Jesus Remembered*, Christianity in the Making, vol. 1 (Grand Rapids/ Cambridge: Eerdmans, 2003), 709–11.

21. Ibid., 708–24; de Jonge, op. cit., 167–69.

Chapter 13

1. K. Steenbrink, "Indonesian Churches 1978–1984: Main Trends, Issues and Problems," *Exchange* 13 (1984): 27–28.

2. S. Rambitan, "Jesus in Islamic Context of Indonesia," *REC Focus* 3 (2003): 38–48.

3. Ibid., 40–46.

4. J. B. Banawiratma, "Contextual Christology and Christian Praxis: An Indonesian Reflection," *East Asian Pastoral Review* 37 (2000): 173.

5. Ibid., 173 and 176.

6. Ibid., 177.

7. Ibid., 179–80.

8. P. O. Tobing, *The Structure of Batak-Toba Belief in the High God* (Amsterdam: South and South-East Celebes Institute for Culture, 1956).

9. A. Yewangoe, "The Trinity in the Context of Tribal Religion," *Studies in Interreligious Dialogue* 13.1 (2003): 95–97 and 104.

10. Ibid., 99–100 and 104.

11. N. K. Tebay, "Jesus as *Iniuwai Ibo* (The Great Elder Brother) – Christology Expressed in the Hymns of Mee Christians of West Papua," *Exchange* 29.4 (2000): 311–30.

12. M. T. Mawene, "Christ and Theology of Liberation in Papua," *Exchange* 33.2 (2004): 153–79.

13. J. Dunn, *Jesus Remembered*, Christianity in the Making, vol. 1 (Grand Rapids/ Cambridge: Eerdmans, 2003), 655–67; M. de Jonge, *Christology in Context: The Earliest Christian Response to Jesus* (Philadelphia: Westminster, 1988), 155–73.

14. De Jonge, op. cit., 105–6.

Chapter 14

1. A. A. Yewangoe, *Theologia Crucis in Asia: Asian Christian Views on Suffering in the Face of Overwhelming Poverty and Multifaceted Religiosity in Asia* (Amsterdam: Rodopi, 1987), 221–26.

2. Ibid., 226–33.

3. Ibid., 233–39.

4. A. G. Honig, "The Search for Identity as a Source of Renewal," in F. J. Verstraelen, ed., *Missiology: An Ecumenical Introduction. Texts and Contexts of Global Christianity* (Grand Rapids: Eerdmans, 1995), 324–26; H.-R. Weber, *Kreuz und Kultur: Deutungen der Kreuzigung Jesu im neutestamentlichen Kulturraum und in Kulturen der Gegenwart* (Lausanne-Genf: Institut des Sciences Bibliques, Université de Lausanne, 1975), 177; idem, *On a Friday Noon: Meditations under the Cross* (Geneva: World Council of Churches, 1979), 53 and 81–82.

5. P. G. van Hooijdonk, "Jesus as Guru: A Christology in the Context of Java (Indonesia)," *Exchange* 13 (1984): 35–45.

6. Ibid., 47–48.

7. K. Steenbrink, "Jesus as a Javanese Prophet," in M. Frederiks *et al.*, eds, *Towards an Intercultural Theology: Essays in Honour of Jan B. Jongeneel*, IIMO Research Publication 61 (Zoetermeer: Meinema, 2003), 137–52.

8. Ibid., 148–50.

9. Yewangoe, op. cit., 321–22.

10. O. Leirvik, *Images of Jesus Christ in Islam: Introduction, Survey of Research, Issues of Dialogue*, Studia Missionalia Upsaliensia LXXVI (Uppsala: Swedish Institute of Missionary Research, 1999), 245–48.

11. Leirvik, op. cit., 78–79 and 232; D. A. Kerr, "Christology in Christian–Muslim Dialogue," in R. F. Berkey and S. A. Edwards, eds, *Christology in Dialogue* (Cleveland: Pilgrim Press, 1993), 209; M. Borrmans, "Muslims and the Mystery of the Cross," *Vidyajyoti* 42 (1978): 125.

12. A. A. Roest Crollius, "Salvation in the Qur'an," *Studia Missionalia* 29 (1980): 129–31.

13. Kerr, op. cit., 209; Borrmans, op. cit., 121.

14. A. J. Malik, "Confessing Christ in the Islamic Context," in R. S. Sugirtharajah, ed., *Asian Faces of Jesus* (London: SCM, 1993), 83.

15. Willibrodus Surendra Rendra, *Ballads and Blues: Poems*, trans. (from Indonesian) by Burton Raffel, Harry Aveling, Derwent May, Oxford in Asia Modern Authors (Oxford:

Oxford University Press, 1974), 26–28 ("Ballad of the Crucifixion") and 78–79 ("After Confession"). In addition to the "Ballad of the Crucifixion," "Litany for the Holy Lamb" is included in a Dutch translation as Appendix IV in the contribution by A. Teeuw on "Ontmoetingen met Christus in de moderne Indonesische poëzie" in the book *Indonesia* by the Nederlandse Studenten Zendingscommissie (Amsterdam, 1966).

Chapter 15

1. A. G. Nnamani, *The Paradox of a Suffering God: On the Classical, Modern-Western and Third World Struggles to Harmonise the Incompatible Attributes of the Trinitarian God*, Studies in the Intercultural History of Christianity 95 (Frankfurt: Peter Lang, 1994), 316–17; L. R. Holme, *The Extinction of the Christian Churches in North Africa* (New York: Burt Franklin, 1969).

2. E. Isichei, *A History of Christianity in Africa: From Antiquity to the Present* (Grand Rapids/Lawrenceville: Eerdmans/Africa World Press, 1995), 13–44.

3. J. U. Young, *African Theology: A Critical Analysis and Annotated Bibliography* (Westport: Greenwood Press, 1993), 13–20.

4. U. A. Ezeh, *Jesus Christ the Ancestor: An African Contextual Christology in the Light of the Major Dogmatic Christological Definitions of the Church from the Council of Nicea (325) to Chalcedon (451)*, Studies in the Intercultural History of Christianity 130 (Bern: Peter Lang, 2003), 95–98.

5. P. Mwaura, "African Independent Churches: Their Role and Contribution to African Christianity," in K. Bediako *et al.*, eds, *A New Day Dawning: African Christians Living the Gospel. Essays in Honour of Dr. J. J. (Hans) Visser* (Zoetermeer: Boekencentrum, 2004), 96–115.

6. A. Anderson, "Exorcism and Conversion to African Pentecostalism," *Exchange* 35.1 (2006): 116–33.

7. Mwaura, op. cit., 111–12; P. Mwaura, "Gender and Power in African Christianity: African Instituted Churches and Pentecostal Churches," in O. U. Kalu, ed., *African Christianity: An African Story* (Pretoria: Department of Church History, University of Pretoria, 2005), 410–45.

8. J. Parratt, ed., *A Reader in African Christian Theology*, new ed. (London: SPCK, 1997), 2–3.

9. Cf. P. Gregorios *et al.*, eds, *Does Chalcedon Divide or Unite? Towards Convergence in Orthodox Christology* (Geneva: World Council of Churches, 1981).

10. T. Witvliet, *A Place in the Sun: Liberation Theology in the Third World* (Maryknoll: Orbis, 1985), 111–17.

11. A. Grillmeier, *From the Apostolic Age to Chalcedon (451)*, *Christ in Christian Tradition*, vol. 1 (London: Mowbray, 1975), 301–86; F. A. Oborji, *Towards a Christian Theology of African Religion: Issues of Interpretation and Mission* (Limuru: AMECEA Gaba Publications, 2005), 152; K. Bediako, "'Ethiopia Shall Soon Stretch out Her Hands to God' (Ps. 68, 31): African Christians Living the Faith. A Turning Point in Christian History?" in K. Bediako *et al.*, eds, *A New Day Dawning: African Christians Living the Gospel. Essays in Honour of Dr. J. J. (Hans) Visser* (Zoetermeer: Boekencentrum, 2004), 32–36.

12. Mwaura, "African Independent Churches," 98–99; J. Persoon, "New Perspectives on Ethiopian and African Christianity: Communalities and Contrasts in Twentieth Century Religious Experience," *Exchange* 34.4 (2005): 306–36.

13. E. J. Pénoukou, "Christology in the Village," in J. Schreiter, ed., *Faces of Jesus in Africa* (Maryknoll: Orbis, 2000), 29.

14. K. Wiredu, "Are there Cultural Universals?" in P. H. Coetzee and A. P. J. Roux, eds, *The African Philosophy Reader* (London/New York: Routledge, 1998), 31–40.

15. K. Bediako, *Theology and Identity: The Impact of Culture upon Christian Thought in the Second Century and Modern Africa*, Regnum Studies in Mission (Oxford: Regnum Books, in association with Lynx Communications, 1992), 4; K. Bediako, *Christianity in Africa: The Renewal of a Non-Western Religion* (Edinburgh: Edinburgh University Press, 1995), 258; K. Cragg, "Conversion and Convertibility, with Special Reference to Muslims," in J. R. W. Stott and R. T. Coote, eds, *Gospel and Culture: The Papers of a Consultation on the Gospel and Culture, Convened by the Lausanne Committee's Theology and Education Group*, The William Carey Library Series on Applied Cultural Anthropology, 263–82 (Pasadena: William Carey Library, 1979).

16. D. B. Stinton, *Jesus of Africa: Voices of Contemporary African Christology*, Faith and Cultures Series (Maryknoll: Orbis, 2004), 43–44.

17. J. S. Mbiti, *African Religions and Philosophy* (Oxford: Heineman, 1990), xiii.

18. E. B. Idowu, *African Traditional Religion: A Definition* (London: SCM, 1973), 104.

19. G. van 't Spijker, "Man's Kinship with Nature: African Reflection on Creation," *Exchange* 23.2 (1994): 119–22.

20. K. Wiredu, "On Decolonising African Religions," in Coetzee and Roux, op. cit., 186–204.

21. K. A. Appiah, "Old Gods, New Worlds," in Coetzee and Roux, op. cit., 245–74.

22. O. p'Bitek, *African Religions in Western Scholarship* (Kampala: East African Literature Bureau, 1971), 47.

23. Ibid., 62.

24. Ezeh, op. cit., 49–50.

25. Oborji, op. cit., 59–68.

26. Nnamani, op. cit., 330–32.

27. Oborji, op. cit., 45–46.

28. Ibid., 64.

29. F. Kabasélé, "Christ as Ancestor and Elder Brother," in Schreiter, op. cit., 117.

30. Nnamani, op. cit., 326–29.

31. E. B. Idowu, *Olódùmarè: God in Yoruba Belief* (London: Longman, 1966), 204; Idowu, *African Traditional Religion*, 135.

32. K. Gyekye, "The Problem of Evil: An Akan Perspective," in E. C. Eze, ed., *African Philosophy: An Anthology* (Malden/Oxford: Blackwell, 1998), 468–71; G. Brand, *Speaking of a Fabulous Ghost: In Search of Theological Criteria, with Special Reference to the Debate on Salvation in African Christian Theology*, Contributions to Philosophical Theology 7 (Frankfurt: Peter Lang, 2002), 73–102.

33. E. G. Parrinder, *African Traditional Religion* (London: Hutchinson's Univ. Libr., 1974), 38–39.

34. Van 't Spijker, op. cit., 113.

35. Nnamani, op. cit., 330–32.

36. J. S. Pobee, *Towards an African Theology* (Nashville: Abingdon, 1979), 99–119.

37. J. S. Mbiti, *Concepts of God in Africa* (London: SPCK, 1970), 166–77; Mbiti, *African Religions and Philosophy*, 90–97; Oborji, op. cit., 16–19.

38. J. M. Lupande et al. "The Sukuma Sacrificial Goat: A Basis for Inculturation in Africa," *African Ecclesial Review (AFER)* 40 (1998): 244–54; J. O. Ubrurhe, "The African Concept of Sacrifice: A Starting Point for Inculturation," *African Ecclesial Review (AFER)* 40 (1998): 203–15.

39. E. Dovlo, "Ancestors and Soteriology in African and Japanese Religions," *Studies in Interreligious Dialogue* 3 (1993): 48–57.

40. B. Bujo, *African Theology in its Social Context* (Maryknoll: Orbis, 1992), 79.

41. Stinton, op. cit., 113–14.

42. J.-M. Ela, *My Faith as an African* (Maryknoll: Orbis, 1990), 18–26.

43. Mbiti, *African Religions and Philosophy*, 81–89.

44. Parrinder, *African Traditional Religion*, 63–66.

45. C. Nyamiti, *Christ as our Ancestor: Christology from an African Perspective* (Gweru: Mambo, 1984), 15–16.

46. Pobee, op. cit., 94.

47. Z. Kurewa, "Who Do You Say That I Am?" *International Review of Mission* 69.274 (1980): 184–85.

48. G. Abe, "Redemption, Reconciliation, Propitiation," *Journal of Theology for Southern Africa* 95 (1996): 7–8; Obrurhe, op. cit., 210–13.

49. Oborji, op. cit., 21–22 and 26; T. Adeyemo, *Salvation in African Tradition* (Nairobi: Evangel Publishing House, 1997), 60–62.

50. Oborji, op. cit., 71–74.

51. K. Bediako, "Types of African Theology," in C. Fyfe and A. Walls, eds, *Christianity in Africa in the 1990s* (Edinburgh: Centre of African Studies, University of Edinburgh, 1996), 62.

52. Parratt, op. cit., 4–6.

53. Ela, op. cit., 3–12.

54. Bujo, op. cit., 17–37; B. Bujoand and J. I. Muya, eds, *African Theology in the 21st Century: The Contribution of the Pioneers*, I (Nairobi: Paulines Publications Africa, 2003), 179–82.

55. J. N. K. Mugambi, *From Liberation to Reconstruction: African Christian Theology after the Cold War* (Nairobi: East African Educational Publishers, 1995), 5.

56. J. S. Mbiti, *African Religions and Philosophy* (Oxford: Heineman, 1969), 108–109.

57. Pobee, *Towards an African Theology*, 49.

58. J. S. Mbiti, "Some African Concepts of Christology," in G. F. Vicedom, ed., *Christ and the Younger Churches: Theological Contributions from Asia, Africa and Latin America*, SPCK Theological Collections 15 (London: SPCK, 1972), 51.

59. Stinton, op. cit., 7–9 and 31–34.

60. Y. A. Obaje, "Theocentric Christology," in J. S. Pobee, ed., *Exploring Afro-Christology*, Studies in the Intercultural History of Christianity 79 (Frankfurt: Peter Lang, 1992), 43–53.

61. E. Udoh, "Guest Christology: An Interpretative View of the Christological Problem in Africa," unpublished Ph.D. diss. (Princeton: Princeton Theological Seminary, 1993), 80–83.

62. C. Villa-Vicencio, *A Theology of Reconstruction: Nation Building and Human Rights* (Cambridge: Cambridge University Press, 1992).

63. T. A. Mofokeng, *The Crucified among the Crossbearers: Towards a Black Christology* (Kampen: Kok, 1983).

64. Y. Tesfai ed., *The Scandal of a Crucified World: Perspectives on the Cross and Suffering* (Maryknoll: Orbis, 1994).

65. J.-M. Ela, "The Memory of the African People and the Cross of Christ," in Tesfai, op. cit., 19; Ela, *My Faith as an African*, 108–11.

66. A. Wessels, *Images of Jesus: How Jesus is Perceived and Portrayed in Non-European Cultures* (Grand Rapids: Eerdmans, 1990), 62–65.

67. A. A. Yewangoe, "An Asian Perspective on the Cross and Suffering," in Tesfai, op. cit., 62.

68. W. Altmann, "A Latin American Perspective on the Cross and Suffering," in Tesfai, op. cit., 75–78; for the quote see p. 77.

69. T. A. Mofokeng, "The Crucified and Permanent Crossbearing: A Christology for Comprehensive Liberation," in N. Schreurs and H. van de Sandt, eds, *De ene Jezus en de vele culturen: Christologie en contextualiteit* (Tilburg: Tilburg University Press, 1992), 40–48; G. I. Akper, "Contemporary African Perspectives on Jesus' Cross and Human Suffering: A Critical Comparison of African Christologies," unpublished doctoral diss. (Stellenbosch: University of Stellenbosch, 2004), 53–96.

70. Nelson Mandela, "Religious Diversity," in Nelson Mandela, *In His Own Words: From Freedom to the Future: Tributes and Speeches*, Kader Asmal et al., eds (London: Abacus, 2004), 320.

71. Cf. J. M. Waliggo, "African Chrstology in a Situation of Suffering," in Schreiter, op. cit., 164–80.

72. S. Maimela, "The Suffering of Human Divisions and the Cross," in Tesfai, op. cit., 36–47.

73. S. Maimela, "Jesus Christ: The Liberator and Hope of Oppressed Africa," in Pobee, *Exploring Afro-Christology*, 31–41.

74. J.-M. Ela, *African Cry*, trans. Robert R. Barr (Maryknoll: Orbis, 1986).

75. G. van 't Spijker, "Credal Hymns as Summa Theologiae: New Credal Hymns in Rwanda after the 1994 War and Genocide," *Exchange* 30.3 (2001): 256–75.

76. K. A. Dickson, *Theology in Africa* (London/Maryknoll: Dartman, Longman and Todd, 1984), 192–95; K. A. Dickson, "The Theology of the Cross," in Parratt, op. cit., 80–82, Ezeh, op. cit., 71–88 and G. van 't Spijker, "The Role of Social Anthropology in the Debate on Funeral Rites in Africa," *Exchange* 34.3 (2005): 156–76.

77. Dickson, *Theology in Africa*, 196–99; Dickson, "The Theology of the Cross," 83–84.

78. Bujo, *African Theology in its Social Context*, 78; Brand, op. cit., 123 and 144.

Chapter 16

1. K. Appiah-Kubi, "Jesus Christ – Some Christological Aspects from African Perspectives," *Voices from the Third World* 16.2 (1993): 7–29; K. Appiah-Kubi, "Christology," in J. Parratt, ed., *A Reader in African Christian Theology*, new ed.

(London: SPCK, 1997), 65–74; J. Schreiter, ed., *Faces of Jesus in Africa* (Maryknoll: Orbis, 2000).

2. D. B. Stinton, *Jesus of Africa: Voices of Contemporary African Christology*, Faith and Cultures Series (Maryknoll: Orbis, 2004), 54–61; B. Bujo, *African Theology in its Social Context* (Maryknoll: Orbis, 1992), 17–23.

3. Bujo, op. cit., 17.

4. G. Brand, "*Salvation* in African Christian Theology: A Typology of Existing Approaches," *Exchange* 28.3 (1999): 220.

5. C. Nyamiti, "African Christologies Today," in Schreiter, op. cit., 15.

6. Bujo, op. cit., 25–26; U. A. Ezeh, *Jesus Christ the Ancestor: An African Contextual Christology in the Light of the Major Dogmatic Christological Definitions of the Church from the Council of Nicea (325) to Chalcedon (451)*, Studies in the Intercultural History of Christianity 130 (Bern: Peter Lang, 2003), 285.

7. J.-M. Ela, *My Faith as an African* (Maryknoll: Orbis, 1990), 14–18.

8. C. Nyamiti, *Christ as our Ancestor: Christology from an African Perspective* (Gweru: Mambo, 1984), 15–16.

9. Ibid., 16–17 and 71.

10. F. Kabasélé, "Christ as Ancestor and Elder Brother," in Schreiter, op. cit., 121–23; A. O. Nkwoka, "Jesus as Eldest Brother, (Okpara): An Igbo Paradigm for Christology in the African Context," *Asia Journal of Theology* 5.1 (1991): 87–103.

11. See Chapter 2.

12. Nyamiti, *Christ as our Ancestor*, 131 and 136.

13. Ibid., 19–24.

14. B. Bujo, "A Christocentric Ethic for Black Africa," *Theology Digest* 30.2 (1982): 143–46; J. I. Muya, "Bénézet Bujo: The Awakening of a Systematic and Authentically African Thought," in B. Bujo and J. I. Muya, eds, *African Theology in the 21st Century: The Contribution of the Pioneers*, I (Limuru: Paulines Publications Africa, 2003), 132–37.

15. B. Bujo, *Christmas: God becomes Man in Black Africa* (Nairobi: Paulines Publications, 1995), 127–36; K. Bediako, *Jesus in African Culture: A Ghanaian Perspective* (Accra: Asempa, 1990), 41–42; K. Bediako, "How is Jesus Christ Lord? Aspects of an Evangelical Christian Apologetics in the Context of African Religious Pluralism," *Exchange* 25.1 (1996): 39–40; Nyamiti, *Christ as our Ancestor*, 145.

16. A. Akrong, "Christology from an African Perspective," in J. S. Pobee, ed., *Exploring Afro-Christology*, Studies in the Intercultural History of Christianity 79 (Frankfurt: Peter Lang, 1992), 125.

17. Ibid., 127.

18. Nyamiti, *Christ as our Ancestor*, 140.

19. Ibid., 74–76.

20. Akrong, op. cit., 128.

21. Ezeh, op. cit., 310.

22. F. Eboussi-Boulaga, *Christianity without Fetishes: An African Critique and Recapture of Christianity* (Maryknoll: Orbis Books, 1984), 134–37.

23. A. G. Nnamani, *The Paradox of a Suffering God: On the Classical, Modern-Western and Third World Struggles to Harmonise the Incompatible Attributes of the Trinitarian God*, Studies in the Intercultural History of Christianity 95 (Frankfurt: Peter Lang, 1994), 335; J. S. Mbiti, "Is Jesus Christ in African Religion?" in Pobee, op. cit., 21

and 28; A. Walls, *The Cross-Cultural Process in Christian History: Studies in the Transition and Appropriation of Faith* (Maryknoll: Orbis, 2002), 4–5.

24. Bujo, *African Theology in its Social Context*, 18; K. Bediako, "Types of African Theology," in C. Fyfe and A. Walls, eds, *Christianity in Africa in the 1990s* (Edinburgh: Centre of African Studies, University of Edinburgh, 1996), 63.

25. See Chapter 2.

26. J. O. Kombo, "The Doctrine of God in African Christian Thought: An Assessment of African Inculturation Theology from a Trintarian Perspective," unpublished doctoral diss. (Stellenbosch: University of Stellenbosch, 2000).

27. Ibid., 217–23.

28. Ibid., 223–30.

29. A. Walls, "African Christianity in the History of Religions," in Fyfe and Walls, op. cit., 5.

30. K. A. Dickson and P. Ellingworth, eds, *Biblical Revelation and African Beliefs* (London: Lutterworth, 1972), 16.

31. G. van 't Spijker, "Man's Kinship with Nature – African Reflection on Creation," *Exchange* 23.2 (1994): 105–106.

32. A. Vanneste, "D'abord une vraie théologie," *Revue du Clergé Africain* 15 (1960): 346–52.

33. Van 't Spijker, op. cit., 102–105.

34. Vanneste, op. cit., 346–52.

35. T. Tshibangu, "Vers une théologie de couleur africaine?" *Revue du Clergé Africain* 15 (1960): 333–46; T. Tshibangu, "The Task and Method of Theology in Africa," in Parratt, op. cit., 29–35; J. P. Heijke, "Africa: Between Cultural Rootedness and Liberation," in F. J. Verstraelen, ed., *Missiology: An Ecumenical Introduction. Texts and Contexts of Global Christianity* (Grand Rapids: Eerdmans, 1995), 267–69.

36. Bujo, "A Christocentric Ethic for Black Africa," 143–46; Bujo, *African Theology in its Social Context*, 84; Nyamiti, *Christ as our Ancestor*, 77–84.

37. Nnamani, op. cit., 337–46.

38. J. S. Pobee, *Towards an African Theology* (Nashville: Abingdon, 1979), 83; J. S. Pobee, "In Search of Christology in Africa: Some Considerations for Today," in Pobee, *Exploring Afro-Christology*, 17.

39. Nyamiti, *Christ as our Ancestor*, 81.

40. For a short historical anthology, ending in contemporary African positions see *La Descente du Christ aux enfers*, Cahiers Supplément Evangile 128, June (Paris: Service Biblique Catholique Évangile et Vie, 2004).

41. Nnamani, op. cit., 353–62.

42. Walls, "African Christianity in the History of Religions," 6–14.

43. Stinton, op. cit., 123–26.

44. Ibid., 142.

45. Ibid., 140–41 and 244–46.

46. Kabasélé, op. cit., 118.

47. Ibid., 130–35 and 139; also Ezeh, op. cit., 312–13.

48. Ela, op. cit., 28–29.

49. C. Nyamiti, "Contemporary African Christologies: An Assessment and Practical Suggestions," in R. Gibellini, ed., *Paths of African Theology* (Maryknoll: Orbis Books, 1994), 128, 132, 141; G. Brand, *Speaking of a Fabulous Ghost: In Search of Theological*

Criteria, with Special Reference to the Debate on Salvation in African Christian Theology, Contributions to Philosophical Theology 7 (Frankfurt: Peter Lang, 2002), 140–43.

50. Bujo, *African Theology in its Social Context*, 83; J. S. Mbiti, "Some African Concepts of Christology," in G. F. Vicedom, ed., *Christ and the Younger Churches: Theological Contributions from Asia, Africa and Latin America*, SPCK Theological Collections 15 (London: SPCK, 1972), 58.

51. R. Luneau, "Einleitung: Und ihr, was sagt ihr von Jesus Christus?" in F. Kabasélé, ed., *Der Schwarze Christus. Wege afrikanischer Christologie*, Theologie der dritten Welt 12 (Freiburg: Herder, 1986), 13–14.

52. C. Kolié, "Christ as Healer?" in Schreiter, op. cit., 128–50, esp. 128.

53. Ibid., 149.

54. Ela, op. cit., 50–52.

55. Brand, *Speaking of a Fabulous Ghost*, 103–106.

56. Kolié, op. cit., 141–42; Bujo, *African Theology in its Social Context*, 31; R. Luneau, "Afrikanische Frauen sprechen von Jesus: Réné Luneau im Gespräch mit Bibiana Tshibola und Yvette Aklé," in Kabasélé, *Der Schwarze Christus*, 203.

57. G. ter Haar, *Spirit of Africa: The Healing Ministry of Archbishop Milingo of Zambia* (London: Hurst, 1992).

58. Stinton, op. cit., 64–71.

59. Luneau, "Einleitung," 9.

60. Ela, op. cit., 76–80.

61. F. A. Oborji, "Healing in the African Independent Churches: An Encounter between Traditional Religiosity and Christianity?" *Studies in Interreligious Dialogue* 15.2 (2005): 182–210.

62. Stinton, op. cit., 80–97.

63. For a similar comment see the last section of Chapter 11.

64. M. A. Oduyoye, "An African Women's Christ," *Voices from the Third World* 11 (1988): 119–24.

65. Stinton, op. cit., 101.

66. Ibid., 102.

67. Kolié, op. cit., 142.

68. M. Schoffeleers, "Christ in African Folk Theology: The Nganga Paradigm," in T. D. Blakely et al., eds, *Religion in Africa: Experience and Expression* (London/Portmouth: James Currey/Heinemann, 1994), 73–88.

69. Luneau, "Afrikanische Frauen sprechen von Jesus," 205.

70. E. J. Pénoukou, "Christology in the Village," in Schreiter, op. cit., 41–48.

71. Brand, *"Salvation" in African Christian Theology*, 220.

72. Luneau, "Afrikanische Frauen sprechen von Jesus," 198–205; A. Nasimiyu-Wasike, "Christology and an African Woman's Experience," in Schreiter, op. cit., 70–81.

73. P. Mwaura, "Gender and Power in African Christianity: African Instituted Churches and Pentecostal Churches," in O. U. Kalu, ed., *African Christianity: An African Story* (Pretoria: Department of Church History, University of Pretoria, 2005), 433–34.

74. Nasimiyu-Wasike, op. cit., 70–81; J. H. de Wit, "Door het oog van een ander: Achtergronden," in H. de Wit et al., eds, *Putten uit de Bron: Een bijbelverhaal intercultureel gelezen* (Zoetermeer: Meinema, 2004), 67–88.

75. Eboussi-Boulaga, op. cit., 85–227.

76. K. Bediako, "African Theology as a Challenge for Western Theology," in M. E. Brinkman and D. van Keulen, eds, *Christian Identity in Cross-Cultural Perspective*, Studies in Reformed Theology 8 (Zoetermeer: Meinema, 2003), 65–66.

77. See Chapter 2.

78. O. U. Kalu, *Power, Poverty and Prayer: The Challenges of Poverty and Pluralism in African Christianity, 1960–1996*, Studies in the Intercultural History of Christianity 122 (Frankfurt: Peter Lang, 2000), 103–32.

Chapter 17

1. P. Jenkins, "After the Next Christendom," *International Bulletin of Missionary Research* 28.1 (2004): 22.

2. See the first section of Chapter 8.

3. Cf. last section of Chapter 3.

4. See the third section of Chapter 1: "Who Decides?"

5. See the first section of Chapter 2.

6. K. Bediako, *Theology and Identity: The Impact of Culture upon Christian Thought in the Second Century and Modern Africa*, Regnum Studies in Mission (Oxford: Regnum Books, in association with Lynx Communications, 1992), 4; K. Bediako, *Christianity in Africa: The Renewal of a Non-Western Religion* (Edinburgh: Edinburgh University Press, 1995), 258.

7. J. G. D. Dunn, *The Theology of Paul the Apostle* (Grand Rapids: Eerdmans, 1997), 390–412.

8. J. Meyerdorff and P. Robias, eds, *Salvation in Christ: A Lutheran-Orthodox Dialogue* (Minneapolis: Augsburg, 1992), 67–83.

9. http://www.spurgeon.org/~phil/history/ath-inc.htm.

10. J. Leemans, "'God Became Human in Order that Humans Might Become God': A Reflection on the Soteriological Doctrine of Divinization," in T. Merrigan and J. Haers, eds, *The Myrad Christ: Plurality and the Quest for Unity in Contemporary Christology* (Louvain: Louvain University Press, 2000), 215–16.

11. N. K. K. Ng, "A Reconsideration of the Use of the Term 'Deification' in Athanasius," *Coptic Church Review* 22.1 (2001): 34–42.

12. J. Y. Lee, *The Theology of Change: A Christian Concept of God in an Eastern Perspective* (Maryknoll: Orbis, 1979), 94.

13. J. Y. Lee, "The Perfect Realization of Change: Jesus Christ," in R. S. Sugirtharajah, ed., *Asian Faces of Jesus* (London: SCM, 1993), 71–72; A. Wessels, *Images of Jesus: How Jesus is Perceived and Portrayed in Non-European Cultures* (Grand Rapids: Eerdmans, 1990), 148–57.

14. D. Bonhoeffer, *Christology*, trans. John Bowden, The Fontana Library of Theology and Philosophy (London: Collins, 1966), 108.

15. D. Bonhoeffer, *Ethics*, trans. Neville Horton Smith (New York: Touchstone, 1995), 84.

16. C. S. Song, "The Role of Christology in the Christian Encounter with Eastern Religions," in G. F. Vicedom, ed., *Christ and the Younger Churches: Theological*

Contributions from Asia, Africa and Latin America, SPCK Theological Collections 15 (London: SPCK, 1972), 80.

17. V. Fabella, "Christology from an Asian Woman's Perspective," in R. S. Sugirtharajah, op. cit., 211–22, esp. 215–16; V. Fabella, "Keynote Address: Christology and Popular Religions," *Voices of the Third World* 18.2 (1995): 22–37.

18. T. Kuribayashi, *A Theology of the Crown of Thorns: Towards the Liberation of the Asian Outcasts* (New York, 1987), 94.

19. H. E. Hwang, "The Legacy of the Minjung Congregation Movement in South Korea 1983-1997," in W. Usdorf and T. Murayama, eds, *Identity and Marginality: Rethinking Christianity in North East Asia*, Studies in the Intercultural History of Christianity 121 (Frankfurt: Peter Lang, 2000), 118.

20. A. A. Yewangoe, *Theologia Crucis in Asia: Asian Christian Views on Suffering in the Face of Overwhelming Poverty and Multifaceted Religiosity in Asia* (Amsterdam: Rodopi, 1987), 302.

21. Hwang, op. cit., 118.

22. Yewangoe, op. cit., 312.

23. K. Barth, *Church Dogmatics* IV/1, trans. G. W. Bromiley (Edinburgh: T. & T. Clark, 1980), 157–642 and IV/2, trans. G. W. Bromiley (Edinburgh: T. & T. Clark, 1970), 1–840.

Chapter 19

1. See Chapter 2.

2. See Chapters 5, 6, 9 and 15.

3. Cf. Chapter 10.

4. Cf. Chapters 3 and 15.

5. V. Fabella, "Keynote Address: Christology and Popular Religions," *Voices of the Third World* 18.2 (1995): 32.

Bibliography

General

Barth, K. *Church Dogmatics* I/2. Trans. G. W. Bromiley. 2nd ed. Edinburgh: T. & T. Clark, 1975.
——*Church Dogmatics* III/1. Trans. J. W. Edwards *et al.* Edinburgh: T. & T. Clark, 1982.
——*Church Dogmatics* IV/1. Trans. G. W. Bromiley. Edinburgh: T. & T. Clark, 1980.
——*Church Dogmatics* IV/2. Trans. G. T. Thompson and Harold Knight. Edinburgh: T. & T. Clark, 1970.
The Bhagavad Gita. Trans. from the Sanskrit by Juan Mascaró, with an Introduction by Simon Brodbeck. London: Penguin Classics, 2003.
Bonhoeffer, D. *Christology*. Trans. John Bowden. The Fontana Library Theology and Philosophy. London: Collins, 1966.
——*Ethics*. Trans. Neville Horton Smith. New York: Touchstone, 1995.
——*Letters and Papers from Prison*. London: SCM Press, 2001.
Brinkman, M. E. "Shifts in the Interpretation of Christian History: Cases from the Middle-East, Africa and Asia Compared." *Exchange* 29 (2000): 97–116.
——*The Tragedy of Human Freedom: The Failure and Promise of the Christian Concept of Freedom in Western Culture*. Currents of Encounter 20. Amsterdam/New York: Rodopi, 2003.
Burrel, D. *Freedom and Creation in Three Traditions*. Notre Dame: University of Notre Dame Press, 1983.
Calvin, John. *Institutes of the Christian Religion*. Trans. Ford Lewis Battles. Library of Christian Classics. Philadelphia: Westminster, 1960.
Cragg, K. "Conversion and Convertibility, with Special Reference to Muslims." In J. R. W. Stott and R. T. Coote, eds, *Gospel and Culture: The Papers of a Consultation on the Gospel and Culture, Convened by the Lausanne Committee's Theology and Education Group*. The William Carey Library Series on Applied Cultural Anthropology, 263–82. Pasadena: William Carey Library, 1979.
Dunn, J. G. D. *The Theology of Paul the Apostle*. Grand Rapids: Eerdmans, 1997.
Epistle to Diognetus. In *Early Christian Writings*. Trans. Maxwell Stanforth. London: Penguin Classics, 1987.
Heidegger, M. "Building, Dwelling, Thinking." In M. Heidegger, *Poetry, Language, Thought*. Trans. Albert Hofstadter, 143–61. New York: Harper Colophon Books, 1975.
Houtepen, A. *God: An Open Question*. Trans. John Bowden. London: Continuum, 2002.
La Descente du Christ aux enfers. Cahiers Supplément Evangile 128 (June). Paris: Service Biblique Catholique Évangile et Vie, 2004.
Levinas, E. "Heidegger, Gagarin and Us." In E. Levinas, *Difficult Freedom: Essays on Judaism*, 221–24. Trans. Seán Hand. Baltimore: John Hopkins University, 1990.

Luther, M. *Epistola ad Romanos*. Ed. J. Ficker *et al*. D. Martin Luthers Werke: Kritische Gesamtausgabe, 56. Weimar: Böhlau, 1938.

Meyerdorff, J., and P. Robias, eds. *Salvation in Christ: A Lutheran-Orthodox Dialogue*. Minneapolis: Augsburg, 1992.

Ng, N. K. K. "A Reconsideration of the Use of the Term 'Deification' in Athanasius." *Coptic Church Review* 22.1 (2001): 34–42.

Rendra, Willibrodus Surendra. *Ballads and Blues: Poems*. Trans. [from Indonesian] by Burton Raffel, Harry Aveling and Derwent May. Oxford in Asia Modern Authors. Oxford: Oxford University Press, 1974.

Song, C. S. *Theology from the Womb of Asia*. London: SCM, 1988.

Thunsberg, L. *Man and the Cosmos: The Vision of St Maximus the Confessor*. New York: St Vladimirs Seminary Press, 1985.

Turner, V. *On the Edge of the Bush: Anthropology as Experience*. Tucson: University of Arizona Press, 1985.

van Heijst, A. *Longing for the Fall*. Trans. H. Jansen. Kampen: Kok Pharos, 1992.

The "Remembered" Jesus in the Bible and Church (History)

Dunn, J. D. G. *Jesus Remembered*. *Christianity in the Making*. Vol. 1. Grand Rapids/ Cambridge: Eerdmans, 2003.

Du Toit, C. W. *Images of Jesus*. Pretoria: University of South Africa, 1997.

Glasswell, M. E., and E. W. Fasholé-Luke, eds. *New Testament Christianity for Africa and the World: Essays in Honour of Harry Sawyerr*. London: SPCK, 1974.

Gregorios, P., et al., eds. *Does Chalcedon Divide or Unite? Towards Convergence in Orthodox Christology*. Geneva: World Council of Churches, 1981.

Grillmeier, A. *From the Apostolic Age to Chalcedon (451)*. *Christ in Christian Tradition*. Vol. 1. London: Mowbray, 1975.

Jonge, M. de. *Christology in Context: The Earliest Christian Response to Jesus*. Philadelphia: Westminster, 1988.

Kalsky, M. *Christaphanien: Die Re-Vision der Christologie aus der Sicht von Frauen in unterschiedlichen Kulturen*. Gütersloh: Kaiser, 2000.

Kelly, J. N. D. *Early Christian Doctrines*. London: Black, 1980.

Küster, V. *The Many Faces of Jesus Christ: Intercultural Christology*. London: SCM, 2001.

Leemans, J. "'God Became Human in Order that Humans Might Become God': A Reflection on the Soteriological Doctrine of Divinization." In T. Merrigan and J. Haer, eds, *The Myriad Christ: Plurality and the Quest for Unity in Contemporary Christology*, 207–16. Louvain: Louvain University Press, 2000.

Merrigan, T., and J. Haers, eds. *The Myriad Christ: Plurality and the Quest for Unity in Contemporary Christology*. Louvain: Louvain University Press, 2000.

Ohlig, K.-H. *Fundamentalchristologie: Im Spannungsfeld von Christentum und Kultur*. Munich: Kösel-Verlag, 1986.

Pagels, E. "Christology in Dialogue with Gnosticism." In R. F. Berkey and S. A. Edwards, eds, *Christology in Dialogue*, 66–77. Cleveland: Pilgrim Press, 1993.

Pelikan, J. *Jesus through the Centuries: His Place in the History of Culture*. New Haven/London: Yale University Press, 1985.

Ricoeur, P. "The Hermeneutical Function of Distantiation." In P. Ricoeur, *Hermeneutics and the Human Sciences: Essays on Language, Action and Interpretation*, 131–45. Ed. and trans. John B. Thompson. Cambridge: Cambridge University Press, 1981.

——*Hermeneutics and the Human Sciences: Essays on Language, Action and Interpretation*. Ed. and trans. John B. Thompson. Cambridge: Cambridge University Press, 1981.

——"The Model of the Text: Meaningful Action Considered as a Text." In P. Ricoeur, *Hermeneutics and the Human Sciences: Essays on Language, Action and Interpretation*, 197–221. Ed. and trans. John B. Thompson. Cambridge: Cambridge University Press, 1981.

——"The Task of Hermeneutics." In P. Ricoeur, *Hermeneutics and the Human Sciences: Essays on Language, Action and Interpretation*, 43–62. Ed. and trans. John B. Thompson. Cambridge: Cambridge University Press, 1981.

Samuel, V., and C. Sugden, eds. *Sharing Jesus in the Two Thirds World: Evangelical Christologies from the Contexts of Poverty, Powerlessness and Religious Pluralism*. Bangalore: Partnership in Mission-Asia, 1983.

Schmeller, T. "The Greco-Roman Background of New Testament Christology." In R. F. Berkey and S. A. Edwards, eds, *Christology in Dialogue*, 54–65. Cleveland: Pilgrim Press, 1993.

Slusser, M. "Primitive Christian Soteriological Themes." *Theological Studies* 44 (1983): 555–69.

Wanamaker, C. "The Historical Jesus Today." *Journal of Theology for Southern Africa* 94 (1996): 3–17.

Weber, H.-R. *Kreuz und Kultur: Deutungen der Kreuzigung Jesu im neutestamentlichen Kulturraum und in Kulturen der Gegenwart*. Lausanne-Genf: Institut des Sciences Bibliques, Université de Lausanne, 1975.

——*On a Friday Noon: Meditations under the Cross*. Geneva: World Council of Churches, 1979.

Wessels, A. *Images of Jesus: How Jesus is Perceived and Portrayed in Non-European Cultures*. Grand Rapids: Eerdmans, 1990.

Williams, R. "A History of Faith in Jesus." In M. Bockmuehl, ed., *The Cambridge Companion to Jesus*, 220–36. Cambridge: Cambridge University Press, 2001.

Studies on Inculturation

Ariarajah, S. W. *Gospel and Culture: An Ongoing Discussion within the Ecumenical Movement*. Geneva: WCC Publications, 1994.

——"Intercultural Hermeneutics – A Promise for the Future?" *Exchange* 34.2 (2005): 89–101.

Bediako, K. *Theology and Identity: The Impact of Culture upon Christian Thought in the Second Century and Modern Africa*. Regnum Studies in Mission. Oxford: Regnum Books, in association with Lynx Communications, 1992.

Bowie, F. "The Inculturation Debate in Africa." *Studies in World Christianity* 5.1 (1999): 67–92.

Brand, G. "African and Western Theologies between Church, University and Society: A Philosophical Inquiry into the Contextuality of Theological Criteria." In M. E. Brinkman et al., eds, *Theology between Church, University and Society*, 175–93. Assen: Royal Van Gorcum, 2003.

——*Speaking of a Fabulous Ghost: In Search of Theological Criteria, with Special Reference to the Debate on Salvation in African Christian Theology*. Contributions to Philosophical Theology 7. Frankfurt: Peter Lang, 2002.

Brinkman, M. E. "The Theological Basis for the Local-Universal Debate." In L. Koffeman and H. Witte, eds, *Of All Times and of All Places: Protestants and Catholics on the Church Local and Universal*, 171–85. IIMO Research Publication 56. Zoetermeer: Meinema, 2001.

Brinkman, M. E., and D. van Keulen, eds. *Christian Identity in Cross-Cultural Perspective*. Studies in Reformed Theology 8. Zoetermeer: Meinema, 2003.

Cornille, C. *The Guru in Indian Catholicism: Ambiguity or Opportunity of Inculturation?* Louvain Theological & Pastoral Monographs 6. Louvain: Peeters, 1991.

de Wit, J. H. et al., eds. *Through the Eyes of Another: Intercultural Reading of the Bible*. Elkhart: Institute of Mennonite Studies, 2004.

Droogers, A. "Meaning, Power, and the Sharing of Religious Experience: An Anthropology of Religion Point of View." In J. D. Gort et al., eds, *On Sharing Religious Experience: Possibilities of Interfaith Mutuality*, 45–54. Currents of Encounter 4. Grand Rapids/ Amsterdam: Eerdmans/Rodopi, 1992.

——"Syncretism: The Problem of Definition, the Definition of the Problem." In J. D. Gort et al., eds, *Dialogue and Syncretism: An Interdisciplinary Approach*, 7–25. Currents of Encounter 1. Grand Rapids/Amsterdam: Eerdmans/Rodopi, 1989.

Fox, R. L. *Pagans and Christians in the Mediterranean World from the Second Century AD to the Conversion of Constantine*. London: Penguin Books, 1988.

Frederiks, M. et al., eds. *Towards an Intercultural Theology: Essays in Honour of Jan B. Jongeneel*. IIMO Research Publication 61. Zoetermeer: Meinema, 2003.

Gort, J. D. et al., eds. *Dialogue and Syncretism: An Interdisciplinary Approach*. Currents of Encounter 1. Grand Rapids/Amsterdam: Eerdmans/Rodopi, 1989.

——*On Sharing Religious Experience: Possibilities of Interfaith Mutuality*. Currents of Encounter 4. Grand Rapids/Amsterdam: Eerdmans/Rodopi, 1992.

Hood, R. E. *Must God Remain Greek? Afro Cultures and God-Talk*. Minneapolis: Fortress Press, 1990.

Horton, R. "African Conversion." *Africa* 41.2 (1971): 50–57.

Houtepen, A. "Intercultural Theology: A Postmodern Ecumenical Mission." In M. Frederiks et al., eds, *Towards an Intercultural Theology: Essays in Honour of Jan B. Jongeneel*, 23–38. IIMO Resarch Publication 61. Zoetermeer: Meinema, 2003.

Jansen, M. M. "African Theology as a Challenge for Western Theology: Comments on Kwame Bediako's Paper." In M. E. Brinkman and D. van Keulen, eds, *Christian Identity in Cross-Cultural Perspective*, 68–72. Studies in Reformed Theology 8. Zoetermeer: Meinema, 2003.

Jenkins, P. "After the Next Christendom." *International Bulletin of Missionary Research* 28.1 (2004): 20–22.

——*The Next Christendom: The Coming of Global Christianity.* Oxford: Oxford University Press, 2002.

Jonker, L. "'Contextuality' in (South) African Exegesis: Reflections on the Communality of our Exegetical Methodologies." *Old Testament Essays* 18.3 (2005): 637–50.

Lee, J. Y. *Marginality: The Key to Multicultural Theology.* Minneapolis: Fortress Press, 1995.

Lienemann-Perrin, C. *et al.*, eds. *Contextuality in Reformed Europe: The Mission of the Church in the Transformation of European Culture.* Currents of Encounter 23. Amsterdam: Rodopi, 2004.

Maluleke, S. T. and S. Nadar. "Alien Fraudsters in the White Academy: Agency in Gendered Colour." *Journal of Theology for Southern Africa* 120 (2004): 5–17.

Maluleke, T. S. "Black and African Theologies in a New World Order: A Time to Drink from our own Wells." *Journal of Theology for Southern Africa* 112 (1996): 3–19.

——"Black Missiologist: Contradiction in Terms?" In R. Gerloff, ed., *Mission is Crossing Frontiers: Essays in Honour of Bongani A. Mazibuko, 1932–1997,* 280–303. Pietermaritzburg: Cluster Publications, 2003.

——"In Search of 'the True Character of African Christian Identity': A Review of the Theology of Kwame Bediako." *Missionalia* 25.2 (1997): 210–19.

M'nteba, M. "Inculturation in the 'Third Church': God's Pentecost or Cultural Revenge?" *Concilium* 28.1 (1992): 129–46.

Moffett, S. H. "Has Christianity Failed in Asia?" *The Princeton Seminary Bulletin* 26 (2005): 199–211.

Mulder, D. C. "Dialogue and Syncretism: Some Concluding Observations." In J. D. Gort *et al.*, eds, *Dialogue and Syncretism: An Interdisciplinary Approach,* 203–11. Currents of Encounter 1. Grand Rapids/Amsterdam: Eerdmans/Rodopi, 1989.

Mullins, M. R. "Christianity Transplanted: Toward a Sociology of Success and Failure." In M. R. Mullins and R. F. Young, eds, *Perspectives on Christianity in Korea and Japan: The Gospel and Culture in East Asia,* 61–77. Lewiston: Edwin Mellon, 1995.

Mullins, M. R., and R. F. Young, eds. *Perspectives on Christianity in Korea and Japan: The Gospel and Culture in East Asia.* Lewiston: Edwin Mellon, 1995.

Murphy, G. R. *The Heliand: The Saxon Gospel.* Oxford: Oxford University Press, 1992.

Nacpil, E. P. "The Critical Asian Principle." In D. J. Elwood, ed., *Asian Christian Theology: Emerging Themes,* 56–59. Philadelphia: Westminster, 1980.

Newbigin, L. *Foolishness to the Greeks: The Gospel and Western Culture.* Geneva: World Council of Churches, 1986.

Oduyoye, M. A., and H. M. Vroom, eds. *One Gospel – Many Cultures: Case Studies and Reflections on Cross-Cultural Theology.* Currents of Encounter 21. Amsterdam/New York: Rodopi, 2003.

Panikkar, K. M. *Asia and Western Dominance.* London: George Allen & Unwin, 1953.

Pannenberg, W. "The Appropriation of the Philosophical Concept of God as a Dogmatic Problem of Early Christian Theology." In W. Pannenberg, *Basic Questions in Theology,* vol. II, 119–83. Trans. George H. Kehm. Philadelphia: Westminster Press, 1971.

Parratt, J., ed. *An Introduction to Third World Theologies.* Cambridge: Cambridge University Press, 2004.

Pieris, A. "Is the Church too Asian? A Response to Norman Tanner's *Is the Church too Asian? Reflections on the Ecumenical Councils.*" *Vidyajyoti* 67 (2003): 782–92.

Przywara, E. *Analogia entis.* Munich: Kösel & Pustet, 1932.

Ramachandra, V. *The Recovery of Mission: Beyond the Pluralist Paradigm.* Carlisle: Paternoster, 1996.

Samartha, S. J. *The Search for New Hermeneutics in Asian Christian Theology.* Bangalore: Board of Theological Education of the Senate of Serampore College, 1987.

Schreiter, R. J. *Constructing Local Theologies.* London: SCM Press, 1985.

——*The New Catholicity: Theology between the Global and the Local.* Maryknoll: Orbis Books, 1997.

Tanner, N. "Asian Influences Revisited." *Vidyajyoti* 67.11 (2003): 948–53.

——*Is the Church too Asian? Reflections on the Ecumenical Councils.* Rome/Bangalore: Chavara Institute of Indian and Inter-religious Studies/Dharmaram Publications, 2002.

Vassiliadis, P. "The Universal Claims of Orthodoxy and the Particularity of its Witness in a Pluralistic World." In E. Clapsis, ed., *The Orthodox Churches in a Pluralistic World: An Ecumenical Conversation*, 192–206. Geneva/Brookline: WCC Publications/Holy Cross Orthodox Press, 2004.

Vicedom, G. F., ed. *Christ and the Younger Churches: Theological Contributions from Asia, Africa and Latin America.* SPCK Theological Collections 15. London: SPCK, 1972.

Vroom, H. M. "Can Religious Experience Be Shared? Introduction to the Theme 'Sharing religious Experience'." In J. D. Gort et al., eds, *On Sharing Religious Experience: Possibilities of Interfaith Mutuality*, 3–12. Currents of Encounter 4. Grand Rapids/Amsterdam: Eerdmans/Rodopi, 1992.

——*Religions and the Truth: Philosophical Reflections and Perspectives.* Trans. J. W. Rebel. Currents of Encounter 2. Grand Rapids/Amsterdam: Eerdmans/Rodopi, 1989.

——"Syncretism and Dialogue: A Philosophical Analysis." In J. D. Gort et al., eds, *Dialogue and Syncretism: An Interdisciplinary Approach*, 26–35. Currents of Encounter 1. Grand Rapids/Amsterdam: Eerdmans/Rodopi, 1989.

——"Understanding the Gospel Contextually: Legitimate and Suspect?" In C. Lienemann-Perrin et al., eds, *Contextuality in Reformed Europe: The Mission of the Church in the Transformation of European Culture*, 35–54. Currents of Encounter 23. Amsterdam/New York: Rodopi, 2004.

Waliggo, J. M., ed. *Inculturation: Its Meaning and Urgency.* Kampala: St. Paul Publ., 1986.

Walls, A. *The Cross-Cultural Process in Christian History: Studies in the Transition and Appropriation of Faith.* Maryknoll: Orbis, 2002.

Weippert, M. "Synkretismus und Monotheismus. Religionsinterne Konfliktbewältigung im alten Israel." In M. Weippert, *Jahwe und die anderen Götter: Studien zur Religionsgeschichte des antiken Israel in ihrem syrisch-palästinischen Kontext*, 1–24. Forschungen zum Alten Testament 18. Tübingen: Mohr Siebeck, 1997.

Welte, P. H. "Does Jesus Need a Facelift? A Critical Voice to the Project 'The Chinese Face of Jesus.' Remarks on Some Problems of Inculturation." In R. Malek, ed., *The Chinese Face of Jesus Christ*, vol. II, 55–61. Monumenta Serica Monograph Series 50/1. Nettetal: Steyler Verlag, 2002.

Wessels, A. "Biblical Presuppositions for and against Syncretism." In J. D. Gort et al., eds, *Dialogue and Syncretism: An Interdisciplinary Approach*, 52–65. Currents of Encounter 1. Grand Rapids/Amsterdam: Eerdmans/Rodopi, 1989.

——*Europe: Was It Ever Really Christian?* London: SCM, 1994.

Wiredu, K. "Are there Cultural Universals?" In P. H. Coetzee and A. P. J. Roux, eds, *The African Philosophy Reader*, 31–40. London/New York: Routledge, 1998.

Witvliet, T. "Mercy Amba Oduyoye en het probleem van een vitale en coherente theologie." In M. Kalsky and T. Witvliet, eds, *De gewonde genezer: Christologie vanuit het perspectief van vrouwen in verschillende culturen*, 26–50. Baarn: Ten Have, 1991.

Wijsen, F. "Intercultural Theology and the Mission of the Church." *Exchange* 30.3 (2001): 218–28.

——"Popular Christianity in East-Africa: Inculturation or Syncretism?" *Exchange* 29 (2000): 37–60.

——"New Wine in Old Wineskins? Intercultural Theology instead of Missiology." In M. Frederiks *et al.*, eds, *Towards an Intercultural Theology: Essays in Honour of Jan B. Jongeneel*, 39–54. IIMO Research Publication 61. Zoetermeer: Meinema, 2003.

Wilson, H. S., ed. *Gospel and Cultures: Reformed Perspectives*. Studies of the WARC 35. Geneva: World Alliance of Reformed Churches, 1996.

Witvliet, T. *A Place in the Sun: Liberation Theology in the Third World*. Maryknoll: Orbis, 1985.

Yeow, C. L. "Christianity in a South-East-Asian Metropolis: Cross-Cultural Hermeneutics." In M. A. Oduyoye and H. M. Vroom, eds, *One Gospel – Many Cultures: Case Studies and Reflections on Cross-Cultural Theology*, 13–37. Amsterdam/New York: Rodopi, 2003.

Asian Studies on Jesus

Background Studies

Elwood, D. J., ed. *Asian Christian Theology: Emerging Themes* (revised version of *What Asian Christians Are Thinking*). Philadelphia: Westminster Press, 1980.

England, J. C., ed. *Living Theology in Asia*. London: SCM Press, 1981.

England, J. C. *et al.*, eds. *Asian Christian Theologies: A Research Guide to Authors, Movements, Sources I*, vol. I–III. Maryknoll: Orbis, 2002–2004.

Gillman, I., and H.-J. Klimkeit. *Christians in Asia before 1500*. Ann Arbor: University of Michigan Press, 1999.

Hoekema, A. G. "Barth and Asia: 'No Boring Theology'." *Exchange* 33 (2004): 102–31.

Honig, A. G. "The Search for Identity as a Source of Renewal." In F. J. Verstraelen, ed., *Missiology: An Ecumenical Introduction. Texts and Contexts of Global Christianity*, 306–32. Grand Rapids: Eerdmans, 1995.

——"Trends in Present Asian Theology." *Exchange* 11 (1982): 1–67.

Koodapuzha, X. *Oriental Churches: An Introduction*. Kottayam: Oriental Institute of Religious Studies India, 1996.

Koshy, N., ed. *History of the Ecumenical Movement in Asia*, vol. 1–2. Hong Kong: World Student Christian Federation, Asia-Pacific Region, 2004.

Kwok, P.-l. *Introducing Asian Feminist Theology*. Introductions in Feminist Theology. Cleveland: Pilgrim, 2000.

Lewis, N. B. "An Overview of the Role of Women in Asia." *East Asia Journal of Theology* 3.2 (1985): 139–46.

Moffett, S. H. *A History of Christianity in Asia*. Vol. I: *Beginnings to 1500*. San Francisco: Harper, 1992.

——*A History of Christianity in Asia*. Vol. II: *1500–1900*. Maryknoll: Orbis, 2005.

Song, C. S. "From Israel to Asia: A Theological Leap." *The Ecumenical Review* 28 (1976): 252–65.

——*Tell us Our Names: Story Theology from an Asian Perspective*. Maryknoll: Orbis, 1984.

——*Third Eye Theology: Theology in Formation in Asian Settings*. Maryknoll: Orbis, 1979.

Sugirtharajah, R. S., ed. *Asian Faces of Jesus*. London: SCM, 1993.

Suh, N. D. "Historical References for a Theology of Minjung." In Y. B. Kim, ed., *Minjung Theology: People as the Subjects of History*, 155–82. Singapore: Commission on Theological Concerns, 1981.

——"Towards a Theology of Han." In Y. B. Kim, ed., *Minjung Theology: People as the Subjects of History*, 55–69. Singapore: Commission on Theological Concerns, 1981.

Thumpanirappel, G. *Christ in the East Syriac Tradition: A Study of the Christology of the Assyrian Church of the East and the Common Christological Declaration of 1994*. Satna: Ephrems Publications, 2003.

Thumpeparampil, T. *Towards an Eastern Christology: Byzantine Christological Tradition and John Meyendorff*. New Delhi: Intercultural Publications, 1996.

Wessels, A. "The Middle East: Cradle and Crucible." In F. J. Verstraelen, ed., *Missiology: An Ecumenical Introduction. Texts and Contexts of Global Christianity*, 11–30. Grand Rapids: Eerdmans, 1995.

Wingeier, D. "Leadership: The Confucian Paradigm." *Trinity Theological Journal* 12 (2004): 121–37.

Yeow, C. L. "Theological Education in South East Asia, 1957–2002." *International Bulletin of Missiological Research* 28.1 (2004): 26–29.

Background Studies from a Buddhist Context

Adams, D. J. "Ancestors, Folk Religion and Korean Christianity." In M. R. Mullins and R. F. Young, eds, *Perspectives on Christianity in Korea and Japan: The Gospel and Culture in East Asia*, 95–113. Lewiston: Edwin Mellon, 1995.

Camps, A., "The People's Republic of China: From Foreignness to Contextualization." In F. J. Verstraelen, ed., *Missiology: An Ecumenical Introduction. Texts and Contexts of Global Christianity*, 49–64. Grand Rapids: Eerdmans, 1995.

Chan, S. T. "Narrative, Story and Storytelling: A Study of C.S. Song's Theology of Story." *Asia Journal of Theology* 12 (1998): 14–45.

Chang, J. S. "A Post-Colonial Discourse on Minjung Theology." In W. Usdorf and T. Murayama, eds, *Identity and Marginality: Rethinking Christianity in North East Asia*, 181–89. Studies in the Intercultural History of Christianity 121. Frankfurt: Peter Lang, 2000.

Cheung, Ching-yuen. "The Problem of Evil in Confucianism." In J. D. Gort *et al.*, eds, *Probing the Depths of Evil and Good: Multireligious Views and Case Studies*, 87–99. Currents of Encounter 33. Amsterdam/New York: Rodopi, 2007.

Ching, J. "The Ambiguous Character of Chinese Religions." *Studies in Interreligious Dialogue* 11.2 (2001): 213–23.

——"The Challenge of the Chinese Religion." *Concilium* 22.1 (1986): 84–89.

——*Chinese Religions*. Maryknoll: Orbis, 1993.

——*Confucianism and Christianity: A Comparative Study*. Tokyo: Kodansha International, 1977.

Chung, H. K. "'Han-pu-ri': Doing Theology from Korean Women's Perspective." *The Ecumenical Review* 40.1 (1988): 27–36.

Fridell, W. M. "The Establishment of Shrine Shinto in Meiji Japan." *Japanese Journal of Religious Studies* 2.2-3 (1975): 137–67.

Fritsch-Opperman, S. C. "Christian Existence in a Buddhist Context." *Studies in Interreligious Dialogue* 13.2 (2003): 215–39.

Furuya, Y., ed. *A History of Japanese Theology*. Grand Rapids/Cambridge: Eerdmans, 1997.

Harrington, M. "The Kakure Kirishitan and their Place in Japan's Religious Tradition." *Japanese Journal of Religious Studies* 7.4 (1980): 318–36.

Hwang, H. E. "The Legacy of the Minjung Congregation Movement in South Korea 1983–1997." In W. Usdorf and T. Murayama, eds, *Identity and Marginality: Rethinking Christianity in North East Asia*, 113–19. Studies in the Intercultural History of Christianity 121. Frankfurt: Peter Lang, 2000.

Inagaki, H. "Comparative Study of the Kuperian Palingenesis: The Transcendent and Human Ego in Japanese Thought." In C. van der Kooi and J. de Bruijn, eds, *Kuyper Reconsidered: Aspects of his Life and Work*, 166–76. VU Studies on Protestant History 3. Amsterdam: VU Uitgeverij, 1999.

Inagaki, H., and J. Nelson Jennings. *Philosophical Theology and East-West Dialogue*. Currents of Encounter 15. Amsterdam/Atlanta: Rodopi, 2000.

Izutsu, M. W. "Emulating their Good Qualities, Taking their Defects as a Warning: Confucian Attitudes toward Other Religions." In J. D. Gort et al., eds, *Religions View Religions: Explorations in Pursuit of Understanding*, 45–61. Currents of Encounter 25. Amsterdam/New York: Rodopi, 2006.

Kamstra, J. H. "Kakure Kirishitan: The Hidden or Secret Christians of Nagasaki." *Nederlands Theologisch Tijdschrift* 47 (1993): 139–50.

Keel, H.-S. "Meister Eckhart's Asian Christianity: Mysticism as a Bridge between Christianity and Zen Buddhism." *Studies in Interreligious Dialogue* 14.1 (2004): 75–94.

Kim, I.-J. *History and Theology of Korean Pentecostalism: Sunbogeum (Pure Gospel) Pentecostalism*. Mission 35. Zoetermeer: Boekencentrum, 2004.

Kim, J. H. "Christianity and Korean Culture: The Reasons for the Success of Christianity in Korea." *Exchange* 33.2 (2004): 132–52.

Kim, K. J. *Christianity and the Encounter of Asian Religions: Method of Correlation, Fusion of Horizons, and Paradigm Shifts in the Korean Grafting Process*. Mission 10. Zoetermeer: Boekencentrum, 1994.

Kim, Y. B. "A Re-reading of History of Asian Missiology from Below: A Korean Perspective." In W. Usdorf and T. Murayama, eds, *Identity and Marginality: Rethinking Christianity in North East Asia*, 73–88. Studies in the Intercultural History of Christianity 121. Frankfurt: Peter Lang, 2000.

Koyama, K. *Mount Fuji and Mount Sinai: A Pilgrimage in Theology*. London: SCM, 1984.

——*Water Buffalo Theology*. Rev. ed. Maryknoll: Orbis, 1999.

Küng, H., and J. Ching. *Christianity and Chinese Religions*. London: Doubleday, 1993.

Kuribayashi, T. *A Theology of the Crown of Thorns: Towards the Liberation of the Asian Outcasts*. New York, 1987.

Kuwahara, S. "Images of Women as 'the Other': An Illustration from the Novels of Shusaku Endo." *God's Image* 18.4 (1999): 35–36.

Lagerwey, J. "Evil and its Treatment in Early Taoism." In J. D. Gort et al., eds, *Probing the Depths of Evil and Good: Multireligious Views and Case Studies*, 73–86. Currents of Encounter 33. Amsterdam/New York: Rodopi, 2007.

Lee, J. Y. "Relationship between Christianity and Shamanism in Korea: A Historical Perspective." *Asia Journal of Theology* 10.2 (1996): 333–47.

——*The Theology of Change: A Christian Concept of God in an Eastern Perspective*. Maryknoll: Orbis, 1979.

Lee, M. "Identifying an Asian Theology: A Methodological Quest." *Asia Journal of Theology* 13.2 (1999): 256–75.

Lee, P. K. H. "Breaking New Grounds in Confucian-Christian Dialogue." *Current Dialogue* 21 (1991): 12–15.

Liu, S. "Christianity in the Reflections of Chinese Religion." *Concilium* 22.1 (1986): 75–83.

Loewe, M. "Imperial China's Reactions to the Catholic Missions." *Numen* 35 (1988): 179–212.

Malek, R., ed. *The Chinese Face of Jesus Christ*, vol. I. Monumenta Serica Monograph Series 50/1. Nettetal: Steyler Verlag, 2002.

——*The Chinese Face of Jesus Christ*, vol. II. Monumenta Serica Monograph Series 50/2. Nettetal: Steyler Verlag, 2003.

Minamiki, G. *The Chinese Rites Controversy: From its Beginning to Modern Times*. Chicago: Loyola University Press, 1985.

Mullins, M. R., *Christianity Made in Japan: A Study of Indigenous Movements*. Honolulu: University of Hawai'i Press, 1998.

——"What About the Ancestors? Some Japanese Christian Responses to Protestant Individualism." *Studies in World Christianity* 4.1 (1998): 41–64.

Nagel, B. "Beyond a Personal God? Shizuteru Ueda's Zen Buddhist Interpretation of Meister Eckhart." *Studies in Interreligious Dialogue* 8.1 (1998): 74–98.

Oak, S.-D. "Shamanistic Tan'gun and Christian Hananim: Protestant Missionaries' Interpretation of the Korean Founding Myth, 1985–1934." *Studies in World Christianity* 7.1 (2001): 42–57.

Odagaki, M. "Theology after 1970." In Y. Furuya, ed., *A History of Japanese Theology*, 113–40. Grand Rapids/Cambridge: Eerdmans, 1997.

Pan-chiu, L. "Barth's Doctrines of Sin and Humanity in Buddhist Perpsective." *Studies in Interreligious Dialogue* 16.1 (2006): 41–58.

Park, S. M. *The Unity of the Church: The Implications of Karl Barth's Ecclesiology for the Korean Context*. Diss. VU University, Amsterdam, 2005.

Sakurai, H. "The Religion of Self-Awareness: The Co-Existence of Religions from the Perspective of Shinto." In J. D. Gort et al., eds, *Religions View Religions: Explorations in Pursuit of Understanding*, 11–19. Currents of Encounter 25. Amsterdam/New York: Rodopi, 2006.

Shuntaro, I. "The Introduction of Western Cosmology in Seventeenth Century Japan: The Case of Christovao Ferreira (1580–1652)." *The Japan Foundation Newsletter* 14 (1986): 1–9.

304   *The Non-Western Jesus*

Stieber, R. G. "*Buraku* Stories." In W. Usdorf and T. Murayama, eds, *Identity and Marginality: Rethinking Christianity in North East Asia*, 155–67. Studies in the Intercultural History of Christianity 121. Frankfurt: Peter Lang, 2000.

Suggate, A. M. "Theology from Below in Japan as a Challenge to the West: Professor Kuribayashi's Theology of the Crown of Thorns." In W. Usdorf and T. Murayama, eds, *Identity and Marginality: Rethinking Christianity in North East Asia*, 229–42. Studies in the Intercultural History of Christianity 121. Frankfurt: Peter Lang, 2000.

Sundermeier, T. "Präsentische Theologie: Der Beitrag K. Takizawas im interkulturellen theologischen Gespräch." In K. Takizawa, *Das Heil im Heute: Texte einer japanischen Theologie*, 11–24. Theologie der Ökumene 21. Göttingen: Vandenhoeck und Ruprecht, 1987.

Takada, S. "Is 'Theology of Religions' Possible in (Pure Land/Shin) Buddhism? The 'Shock of Non-Being' and the 'Shock of Revelation'." In J. D. Gort *et al.*, eds, *Religions View Religions: Explorations in Pursuit of Understanding*, 21–44. Currents of Encounter 25. Amsterdam/New York: Rodopi, 2006.

Takanaka, M. *God is Rice: Asian Culture and Christian Faith*. Geneva: World Council of Churches, 1986.

Takizawa, K. *Das Heil im Heute: Texte einer Japanischen Theologie*. Theologie der Ökumene 21. Göttingen: Vandenhoeck und Ruprecht, 1987.

Tang, E. "East Asia." In J. Parratt, ed., *An Introduction to Third World Theologies*, 74–104. Cambridge: Cambridge University Press, 2004.

——"The Second Chinese Enlightenment: Intellectuals and Christianity Today." In W. Usdorf and T. Murayama, eds, *Identity and Marginality: Rethinking Christianity in North East Asia*, 55–70. Studies in the Intercultural History of Christianity 121. Frankfurt: Peter Lang, 2000.

Tanimoto, K. "Mission from the *Buraku*." In W. Usdorf and T. Murayama, eds, *Identity and Marginality: Rethinking Christianity in North East Asia*, 141–53. Studies in the Intercultural History of Christianity 121. Frankfurt: Peter Lang, 2000.

Terazono, Y. *Die Christologie Karl Barths und Takizawas: Ein Vergleich*. Bonn: Rheinische Friedrich-Wilhelms-Universität, 1976.

Ting, K. H. *Love Never Ends: Papers by K.H. Ting*. Nanjing: Yilin Press, 2000.

Tsushima, M. *et al.* "The Vitalistic Conception of Salvation in Japanese New Religions: An Aspect of Modern Religious Consciousness." *Japanese Journal of Religious Studies* 6.1-2 (1979): 139–61.

Usdorf, W., and T. Murayama, eds. *Identity and Marginality: Rethinking Christianity in North East Asia*. Studies in the Intercultural History of Christianity 121. Frankfurt: Peter Lang, 2000.

Wayman, A. "Buddha as Savior." *Studia Missionalia* 29 (1980): 191–207.

——"The Guru in Buddhism." *Studia Missionalia* 36 (1987): 195–213.

Wells, H., "Korean Syncretism and Theologies of Interreligious Encounter: The Contribution of Kyoung Jae Kim." *Asia Journal of Theology* 12.1 (1998): 56–76.

Whelan, C. *The Beginning of Heaven and Earth: The Sacred Book of Japan's Hidden Christians*. Honolulu: University of Hawai'i Press, 1996.

Whitehead, R. L., ed. *No Longer Strangers: Selected Writings of Bishop K.H. Ting*. Maryknoll: Orbis, 1989.

Whyte, B. "Three Self Revisited." In W. Usdorf and T. Murayama, eds, *Identity and Marginality: Rethinking Christianity in North East Asia*, 99–112. Studies in the Intercultural History of Christianity 121. Frankfurt: Peter Lang, 2000.

Wickeri, P. "Theological Reorientation in Chinese Protestantism, 1949–1984, II." *Ching Feng* 28.2-3 (1985): 105–29.

Yagi, S. "The Third Generation, 1945–1970." In Y. Furuya, ed., *A History of Japanese Theology*, 83–111. Grand Rapids/Cambridge: Eerdmans, 1997.

Yongtao, C. "Towards a *Tao* Christology: Rethinking Christology in the Chinese Context." *Chinese Theological Review* 17 (2003): 23–49.

Young, R. F. "The 'Christ' of the Japanese New Religions." In M. R. Mullins and R. F. Young, eds, *Perspectives on Christianity in Korea and Japan: The Gospel and Culture in East Asia*, 115–31. Lewiston: Edwin Mellon, 1995.

Zhimin, B. "China's Nicodemuses." *Chinese Theological Review* 7 (1991): 112–16.

Images of Jesus from a Buddhist Context

Ahn, B.-M. "Jesus and the Minjung in the Gospel of Mark." In Y. B. Kim, ed., *Minjung Theology: People as the Subjects of History*, 136–51. Singapore: Commission on Theological Concerns, 1981.

——"Jesus and People (Minjung)." In R. S. Sugirtharajah, ed., *Asian Faces of Jesus*, 163–72. London: SCM, 1993.

——"The Korean Church's Understanding of Jesus." *Voices from the Third World* 8.3 (1985): 49–59.

Chung, H. K. *The Struggle to be the Sun Again: Introducing Asian Women's Theology*. Maryknoll: Orbis Books, 1990.

——"Who is Jesus for Asian Women?" In R. S. Sugirtharajah, ed., *Asian Faces of Jesus*, 223–46. London: SCM, 1993.

de Silva, L. "Wisdom and Compassion of the Buddha and Jesus Christ in their Role as Religious Teachers." *Dialogue (New Series)* 17.1-3 (1990): 1–28.

Endo, S. *Deep River*. Trans. Van C. Gessel. London/Chester Springs: Peter Owen, 1994.

——*A Life of Jesus*. Tokyo: Tuttle Company, 1979.

——*Scandal*. Trans. Van C. Gessel. London/Chester Springs: Peter Owen, 1988.

——*Silence*. Trans. W. Johnston. Tokyo: Monumenta Nipponico, 1969.

"Endo and Johnston Talk of Buddhism and Christianity." *The Japan Mission Journal* 49.2 (1995): 122–26.

Eskildsen, S. "Christology and Soteriology in the Chinese Nestorian Texts." In R. Malek, ed., *The Chinese Face of Jesus Christ*, vol. I, 181–218. Monumenta Serica Monograph Series 50/1. Nettetal: Steyler Verlag, 2002.

Fabella, V. "Christology from an Asian Woman's Perspective." In R. S. Sugirtharajah, ed., *Asian Faces of Jesus*, 211–22. London: SCM, 1993.

——"Keynote Address: Christology and Popular Religions." *Voices of the Third World* 18.2 (1995): 22–37.

Gnanadason, A. "Jesus and the Asian Women: A Post-Colonial Look at the Syro-Phoenician Woman/Canaanite Woman from an Indian Perspective." *Studies in World Christianity* 7.2 (2001): 162–77.

Hoekema, A. G. "The 'Christology' of the Japanese Novelist Shusaku Endo." *Exchange* 29 (2000): 230–48.

Keel, H.-S. "Jesus the Bodhisattva: Christology from a Buddhist Perspective." *Buddhist-Christian Studies* 16 (1996): 176–92.

Kern, I. "Buddhist Perception of Jesus and Christianity in the Early Buddhist-Christian Controversies in China during the 17th Century." In P. Schmidt-Leukel *et al.*, eds, *Buddhist Perceptions of Jesus*, 32–41. St. Ottilien: EOS-Verlag, 2001.

Kim, H. Y. *Christ and the Tao*. Hong Kong: Christian Conference of Asia, 2003.

——"Toward a ChristoTao: Christ as the Theanthropocosmic Tao." *Studies in Interreligious Dialogue* 10.1 (2000): 5–29; also in H. Y. Kim, *Christ and the Tao*, 155–76. Hong Kong: Christian Conference of Asia, 2003.

——"The Word Made Flesh: A Korean Perspective on Rye Young-mo's Christotao." In M. A. Oduyoye and H. M. Vroom, eds, *One Gospel – Many Cultures: Case Studies and Reflections on Cross-Cultural Theology*, 129–49. Amsterdam/New York: Rodopi, 2003.

Kim, Y. B., "Korean Christianity as a Messianic Movement of the People." In Y. B. Kim, ed., *Minjung Theology: People as the Subjects of History*, 77–116. Singapore: Commission on Theological Concerns, 1981.

——"Messiah and Minjung: Discerning Messianic Politics over against Political Messianism." In Y. B. Kim, ed., *Minjung Theology: People as the Subjects of History*, 185–96. Singapore: Commission on Theological Concerns, 1981.

——*Messiah and Minjung: Christ's Solidarity with the People for New Life*. Hong Kong: Christian Conference of Asia, 1992.

——"Messianic Buddhism and Christianity in Korea." In M. R. Mullins and R. F. Young, eds, *Perspectives on Christianity in Korea and Japan: The Gospel and Culture in East Asia*, 81–94. Lewiston: Edwin Mellon, 1995.

Kitamori, K. "The Problem of Pain in Christology." In G. F. Vicedom, ed., *Christ and the Younger Churches: Theological Contributions from Asia, Africa and Latin America*, 83–90. SPCK Theological Collections 15. London: SPCK, 1972.

——*Theology of the Pain of God*. Richmond: Knox, 1965 (based on the 5th Japanese edition of 1958).

Klimkeit, H.-J. "Jesus' Entry into Parinirvana: Manichaean Identity in Buddhist Central Asia." *Numen* 33 (1986): 225–40 (also in R. Malek, ed., *The Chinese Face of Jesus Christ*, vol. I, 243–57. Monumenta Serica Monograph Series 50/1. Nettetal: Steyler Verlag, 2002).

Koyama, K. "The Crucified Christ Challenges Human Power." In R. S. Sugirtharajah, ed., *Asian Faces of Jesus*, 149–62. London: SCM, 1993.

Kuribayashi, T. "Recovering Jesus for Outcasts in Japan: From a Theology of the Crown of Thorns." *Japan Christian Review* 58 (1992): 19–32.

Kwok, P.-l. "Chinese Non-Christian Perceptions of Christ." *Concilium* 29.2 (1993): 24–32.

—— "Christology." In P.-l. Kwok, *Introducing Asian Feminist Theology*, 79–97. Introductions in Feminist Theology. Cleveland: Pilgrim Press, 2000.

Lee, J. H. "I am at the Mercy of the Rats: Christological Images in Korean Folklore." In W. Usdorf and T. Murayama, eds, *Identity and Marginality: Rethinking Christianity in North East Asia*, 41–53. Studies in the Intercultural History of Christianity 121. Frankfurt: Peter Lang, 2000.

Lee, J. Y. "The Perfect Realization of Change: Jesus Christ." In R. S. Sugirtharajah, ed., *Asian Faces of Jesus*, 62–74. London: SCM, 1993.

Machida, S. "Jesus, Man of Sin: Towards a New Christology in the Global Era." *Buddhist-Christian Studies* 19.1 (1999): 81–91.

Malek, R. "Faces and Images of Jesus Christ in Chinese Context. Introduction." In R. Malek, ed., *The Chinese Face of Jesus Christ*, vol. I, 19–53. Monumenta Serica Monograph Series 50/1. Nettetal: Steyler Verlag, 2002.

Malek, R., ed. *The Chinese Face of Jesus Christ*, vol. I. Monumenta Serica Monograph Series 50/1. Nettetal: Steyler Verlag, 2002.

——*The Chinese Face of Jesus Christ*, vol. II. Monumenta Serica Monograph Series 50/2. Nettetal: Steyler Verlag, 2003.

Phan, P. C. "The Christ of Asia: An Essay on Jesus as the Eldest Son and Ancestor." *Studia Missionalia* 45 (1996): 25–55.

——"Jesus the Christ with an Asian Face." *Theological Studies* 57.3 (1996): 399–431.

Pieris, A. *An Asian Theology of Liberation*. Maryknoll: Orbis, 1988.

——"The Buddha and the Christ: Mediators of Liberation." In R. S. Sugirtharajah, ed., *Asian Faces of Jesus*, 46–61. London: SCM, 1993.

——"Does Christ Have a Place in Asia? A Panoramic View." *Concilium* 29.2 (1993): 33–47.

——"Speaking of the Son of God in Non-Christian Cultures, e.g. in Asia." *Concilium* 18.3 (1982): 65–70.

Rule, P. "The Jesus of the 'Confucian Christians' of the Seventeenth Century." In R. Malek, ed., *The Chinese Face of Jesus Christ*, vol. II, 499–516. Monumenta Serica Monograph Series 50/2. Nettetal: Steyler Verlag, 2003.

Scott, D. "Christian Responses to Buddhism in Pre-Medieval Times." *Numen* 32 (1985): 88–100.

Song, C. S. "The Decisiveness of Christ." In D. J. Elwood, ed., *What Asian Christians Are Thinking: A Theological Source Book*, 240–64. Quezon City: New Day Publishers, 1976.

——"Do This In Memory of Jesus: The Root of the Reformed Heritage." In H. S. Wilson, ed., *Gospel and Cultures: Reformed Perspectives*, 17–36. Studies from the World Alliance of Reformed Churches 35. Geneva: World Alliance of Reformed Churches, 1996.

——*Jesus, the Crucified People*. The Cross in the Lotus World 1. Minneapolis: Fortress Press, 1996.

——*Jesus and the Reign of God*. The Cross in the Lotus World 2. Minneapolis: Fortress Press, 1993.

——*Jesus in the Power of the Spirit*. The Cross in the Lotus World 3. Minneapolis: Fortress Press, 1994.

——"The Role of Christology in the Christian Encounter with Eastern Religions." In G. F. Vicedom, ed., *Christ and the Younger Churches: Theological Contributions from Asia, Africa and Latin America*, 63–82. SPCK Theological Collections 15. London: SPCK, 1972.

Suh, D. K.-s. *The Korean Minjung in Christ*. Hong Kong: Christian Conference of Asia, 1991.

Sundermeier, T. "Das Kreuz in Japanischer Interpretation." *Evangelische Theologie* 44 (1984): 417–40.

Takenaka, M. *Cross and Circle*. Hong Kong: Christian Conference of Asia, 1990.

Tombs, D. "Liberating Christology: Images of Christ in the Work of Aloysius Pieris." In S.
    E. Porter *et al.*, eds, *Images of Christ: Ancient and Modern*, 173–88. Sheffield:
    Sheffield Academic Press, 1997.
Ueda, S. "Jesus in Contemporary Japanese Zen: With Special Regards to Keiji Nishitani."
    In P. Schmidt-Leukel *et al.*, eds, *Buddhist Perceptions of Jesus*, 42–58. St. Ottilien:
    EOS-Verlag, 2001.
Wong, J. H. "Tao – Logos – Jesus: Lao Tzu, Philo and John Compared." In R. Malek, ed.,
    The Chinese Face of Jesus Christ, vol. I, 87–125. Monumenta Serica Monograph
    Series 50/1. Nettetal: Steyler Verlag, 2002.
Yagi, S. "Christ and Buddha." In R. S. Sugirtharajah, ed., *Asian Faces of Jesus*, 25–45.
    London: SCM, 1993.
——"'I' in the Words of Jesus." In J. Hick and P. F. Knitter, eds, *The Myth of Christian
    Uniqueness: Towards a Pluralistic Theology of Religions*, 117–34. Maryknoll: Orbis,
    1987.
Yao, X. "Confucian Christ: A Chinese Image of Christianity." In W. Usdorf and T. Murayama,
    eds, *Identity and Marginality: Rethinking Christianity in North East Asia*, 27–39. Studies
    in the Intercultural History of Christianity 121. Frankfurt: Peter Lang, 2000.

Background Studies from a Hindu Context

Alphonse, M. "Christianity as Bhakti Religion." *Dharma Deepika* 1.1 (1995): 5–32.
Amaladoss, M. "Asians Encountering Jesus: Cultural and Philosophical Perspectives."
    Quest 3.2 (2004): 1–11.
Appasamy A. J. *Christianity as Bhakti Marga: A Study in the Mysticism of the Johannine
    Writings*. London: Macmillan, 1927.
Ariarajah, S. W. "Christianity and People of Other Religious Traditions." In N. Koshy,
    ed., *A History of the Ecumenical Movement in Asia*, vol. II, 139–65. Hong Kong:
    World Student Christian Federation, Asia-Pacific Region, 2004.
——*Hindus and Christians: A Century of Protestant Ecumenical Thought*. Currents of
    Encounter 5. Amsterdam/Grand Rapids: Rodopi, 1991.
Carman, J. B. "When Hindus Become Christian: Religious Conversion and Spiritual
    Ambiguity." In J. D. Gort *et al.*, eds, *Religions View Religions: Explorations in Pursuit
    of Understanding*, 241–63. Currents of Encounter 25. Amsterdam/New York: Rodopi,
    2006.
Chandran, R., ed. *Third World Theologies in Dialogue: Essays in Memory of D.S.
    Amalorpavadass*. Bangalore: Ecumenical Association of Third World Theologians,
    1991.
Clarke, S. *Dalits and Christianity: Subaltern Religion and Liberation in India*. New Delhi:
    Oxford University Press, 1998.
Heredia, R. C. "Hindu Aversion for Dalit Conversion: No Entry, No Exit." *Vidyajyoti* 67.6
    (2003): 401–26.
Hoynacki, G. J. "'And The Word Made Flesh' – Incarnations in Religious Traditions." *Asia
    Journal of Theology* 7.1 (1993): 12–34.
Kim, K. "India." In J. Parratt, ed., *An Introduction to Third World Theologies*, 44–73.
    Cambridge: Cambridge University Press, 2004.
Kochuparampil, X. "The St. Thomas Christians of India: Ecumenical and Missiological
    Challenges." *Exchange* 25.3 (1996): 243–60.

Komulainen, J. *An Emerging Cosmotheandric Religion? Raimon Panikkar's Pluralistic Theology of Religions*. Studies in Christian Mission 30. Leiden/Boston: Brill, 2005.

Koodapuzha, X. *Oriental Churches: An Introduction*. Kottayam: Oriental Institute of Religious Studies India, 1996.

Mangatt, G. "The Thomas Christians and the Persian Church." *Vidyajyoti* 52 (1988): 437–46.

Massey, J., ed. *Indigenous People: Dalits. Dalits Issues in Today's Theological Debate*. New Delhi: ISPCK, 1994.

Nirmal, A. R., ed. *A Reader in Dalit Theology*. Madras: Gurukul Lutheran Theological College & Research Institute for the Department of Dalit Theology, 1990.

Panikkar, R. "The Jordan, the Tiber, and the Ganges: Three Kairological Moments of Christic Self-Consciousness." In J. Hick and P. F. Knitter, eds, *The Myth of Christian Uniqueness: Towards a Pluralistic Theology of Religions*, 89–116. Maryknoll: Orbis, 1987.

Samartha, S. J. *The Search for New Hermeneutics in Asian Christian Theology*. Bangalore: Board of Theological Education of the Senate of Serampore College, 1987.

Schouten, J. P. *Revolution of the Mystics: On the Social Aspects of Virasiavism*. Kampen: Kok Pharos, 1991.

Wilfred, F. *Beyond Settled Foundations: The Journey of Indian Theology*. Madras: Dept. of Christian Studies, University of Madras, 1993.

——"Jesus-Interpretation in Asia: A Methodological Fragment." *Vaiharai* 7.4 (2002): 3–19.

Images of Jesus from a Hindu Context

Aleaz, K. P. *An Indian Jesus from Sankara's Thought*. Calcutta: Punthi Pustak, 1997.

——"An Indian Understanding of Jesus: Findings of a Research." *Asia Journal of Theology* 12.1 (1998): 118–38.

——"The Role of Asian Religions in Asian Christian Theology." *Asia Journal of Theology* 15 (2001): 268–87.

Alphonse, D. "Jesus, the Avatar." *Vaiharai* 7.4 (2002): 20–35.

Amaladoss, M. "Images of Jesus in India." In N. Schreurs and H. van de Sandt, eds, *De ene Jezus en de vele culturen: Christologie en contextualiteit*, 23–35. Tilburg: Tilburg University Press, 1992.

——"Jesus Christ in the Midst of Religions: An Indian Perspective." In T. Merrigan and J. Haers, eds, *The Myriad Christ: Plurality and the Quest for Unity in Contemporary Christology*, 219–33. Louvain: Louvain University Press, 2000.

Ariarajah, S. W. "Christology in Asia: Perspectives from Hindu-Christian Dialogue." *CTC Bulletin* 7.3 (1987): 32–36.

Clarke, S. "The Jesus of Nineteenth Century Indian Christian Theology: An Indian Inculturation with Continuing Problems and Prospects." *Studies in World Christianity* 5.1 (1999): 32–46.

Crawford, C. "Raja Ram Mohan Roy's Attitude toward Christians and Christianity." In A. Sharma, ed., *Neo-Hindu Views of Christianity*, 16–65. Leiden: Brill, 1988.

David, A. M. "An Indian Quest for a Relevant Christology." *Vaiharai* 7.4 (2002): 51–64.

De Smet, R. "Jesus and the Avatara." In J. D. Gort et al., eds, *Dialogue and Syncretism: An Interdisciplinary Approach*, 153–62. Currents of Encounter 1. Amsterdam/Grand Rapids: Rodopi/Eerdmans, 1989.

Dhavamony, M. "Hindu 'Incarnations'." *Studia Missionalia* 21 (1972): 127–69.
Doniger, Wendy. "Reincarnation in Hinduism." *Concilium* 29 (1993): 3–15.
D'Sa, F. X. "Christian Incarnation and Hindu Avatara." *Concilium* 29.2 (1993): 77–85.
French, H. W. "Reverence to Christ through Mystical Experience and Incarnational
    Identity: Sri Ramakrishna." In A. Sharma, ed., *Neo-Hindu Views of Christianity*,
    66–81. Leiden: Brill, 1988.
——"Swami Vivekananda's Experiences and Interpretations of Christianity." In A. Sharma,
    ed., *Neo-Hindu Views of Christianity*, 82–105. Leiden: Brill, 1988.
Irudayaraj, X. "The Guru in Hinduism and Christianity." *Vidyajyoti* 39 (1975): 338–51.
Kappen, S. *Jesus and Freedom*. Maryknoll: Orbis, 1977.
——*Jesus Today*. Madras: AICUF, 1985.
——"Jesus and Transculturation." In R. S. Sugirtharajah, ed., *Asian Faces of Jesus*,
    173–88. London: SCM, 1993.
Karokaran, A. "Raymond Panikkar's Theology of Religions: A Critique." *Vidyajyoti* 58
    (1994): 663–72.
Kopf, D. "Neo-Hindu Views of Unitarian and Trinitarian Christianity in Nineteenth
    Century Bengal: The Case of Keshub Chandra Sen." In A. Sharma, ed., *Neo-Hindu
    Views of Christianity*, 106–19. Leiden: Brill, 1988.
Livermore, C. W., M.-R. Yoon, and N. S. Sanders. "Christology of Response: Neo-Hindu
    Interpretations of Jesus." *Studies in Interreligious Dialogue* 4.1 (1994): 5–31.
Mohammed, O. N. "Jesus and Krishna." In R. S. Sugirtharajah, ed., *Asian Faces of Jesus*,
    9–24. London: SCM, 1993.
Panikkar, R. *The Cosmotheandric Experience: Emerging Religious Consciousness*.
    Maryknoll: Orbis, 1993.
——*The Trinity and the Religious Experience of Man*. Maryknoll: Orbis, 1973.
——*The Trinity and World Religions: Icon–Person–Mystery*. Inter-Religious Dialogue
    Series 4. Madras: Christian Literature Society, 1970.
——*The Unknown Christ of Hinduism: Towards an Ecumenical Christophany*. Maryknoll:
    Orbis, 1981.
Parapally, J. *Emerging Trends in Indian Christology*. Bangalore: SFS Publications, 1995.
Prabhakar, M. E. "Christology in Dalit Perspective." In V. Devasahayam, ed., *Frontiers of
    Dalit Theology*, 402–32. New Delhi: Indian Society for Promoting Christian
    Knowledge, 1997.
Pragasam, A. "Jesus the Guru." *Vaiharai* 7.4 (2002): 36–50.
Prasannabhai, C. M. I. "Sadguru." *Vidyajyoti* 40 (1976): 315–19.
Rao, K. L. S. "Mahatma Gandhi and Christianity." In A. Sharma, ed., *Neo-Hindu Views of
    Christianity*, 143–55. Leiden: Brill, 1988.
Rao, M. S. "Ananyatva: The Realization of Christian Non-Duality." In G. F. Vicedom, ed.,
    *Christ and the Younger Churches: Theological Contributions from Asia, Africa and
    Latin America*, 91–105. SPCK Theological Collections 15. London: SPCK, 1972.
Rayan, S. "Hindu Perceptions of Christ in the Nineteenth Century." *Concilium* 29
    (1993): 13–23.
Robinson, G. "Jesus Christ, the Open Way and the Fellow-Struggler: A Look into the
    Christologies in India." *Asia Journal of Theology* 3.2 (1989): 403–15.
Samartha, S. J. "The Cross and the Rainbow: Christ in a Multireligious Culture." In R. S.
    Sugirtharajah, ed., *Asian Faces of Jesus*, 104–23. London: SCM, 1993.

——*The Hindu Response to the Unbound Christ*. Interreligious Dialogue Series 6. Madras: Christian Literature Society, 1974.

——*One Christ, Many Religions: Towards a Revised Christology*. Maryknoll: Orbis, 1991.

——"The Unbound Christ: Toward a Christology in India Today." In D. J. Elwood, ed. *Asian Christian Theology: Emerging Themes*, 145–60. Philadelphia: Westminster, 1980.

Schouten, J. P. "Jesus in Hindu Garb: Images of Jesus Christ in the Ramakrisna Movement." *Studies in Interreligious Dialogue* 11.1 (2001): 37–63.

Sharma, A., ed. *Neo-Hindu Views of Christianity*. Leiden: Brill, 1988.

Sharpe, E. J. "Neo-Hindu Images of Christianity." In A. Sharma, ed., *Neo-Hindu Views of Christianity*, 1–15. Leiden: Brill, 1988.

Sheth, N. "Hindu Avatara and Christian Incarnation: A Comparison I." *Vidyajyoti* 67.3 (2003): 181–93.

——"Hindu Avatara and Christian Incarnation: A Comparison II." *Vidyajyoti* 67.4 (2003): 285–302.

Strolz, W. "Panikkar's Encounter with Hinduism." In J. D. Gort et al., eds, *Dialogue and Syncretism: An Interdisciplinary Approach*, 146–52. Currents of Encounter 1. Amsterdam/Grand Rapids: Rodopi/Eerdmans, 1989.

Sugirtharajah, R. S. "The Magi from Bengal and their Jesus: Indian Construals of Christ during Colonial Times." In W. Usdorf and T. Murayama, eds, *Identity and Marginality: Rethinking Christianity in North East Asia*, 15–26. Studies in the Intercultural History of Christianity 121. Frankfurt: Peter Lang, 2000.

Sugirtharajah, R. S., ed. *The Asian Faces of Jesus*. London: SCM, 1993.

Thangaraj, M. T. *The Crucified Guru: An Experiment in Crosscultural Christology*. Nashville: Abingdon, 1994.

——"The Word Made Flesh: The Crucified Guru." In M. A. Oduyoye and H. M. Vroom, eds. *One Gospel – Many Cultures: Case Studies and Reflections on Cross-Cultural Theology*, 107–27. Currents of Encounter 21. Amsterdam/New York: Rodopi, 2003.

Thomas, M. M. *The Acknowledged Christ of the Indian Renaissance*. London: SCM Press, 1969.

Vandana, S. "The Guru as Present Reality." *Vidyajyoti* 39 (1975): 352–57.

Background Studies on Jesus from an Islamic (Indonesian) Context

Aritonang, J. "Faith and Ethnic Conflicts in Indonesia: A Brief Historical Survey and Theological Reflection." In E. A. J. G. van der Borght et al., eds, *Faith and Ethnicity I*, 124–37. Studies in Reformed Theology 6. Zoetermeer: Meinema, 2002.

Maspaitella, E. T. "Jesus and the Gunman: Why Agnes Might Be Shot. A Theological Reflection from Ambon, Based on Local Identities of Jesus." In E. A. J. G. van der Borght et al., eds, *Faith and Ethnicity I*, 277–81. Studies in Reformed Theology 6. Zoetermeer: Meinema, 2002.

Patty, E. S. "Ethnicity: a Means of Grace?" In E. A. J. G. van der Borght et al., eds, *Faith and Ethnicity I*, 146–62.. Studies in Reformed Theology 6. Zoetermeer: Meinema, 2002.

———"Liminality and Worship in the Korean American Context." In M. E. Brinkman and D. van Keulen, eds, *Christian Identity in Cross-Cultural Perspective*, 73–96. Studies in Reformed Theology 8. Zoetermeer: Meinema, 2003.

Ririhena, S. "Ethnicity as the Reshaping Force of Christian Belief Systems: Moluccan Ethnicity in the Netherlands Reshaping Reformed Theology." In E. A. J. G. van der Borght *et al.*, eds, *Faith and Ethnicity I*, 163–79. Studies in Reformed Theology 6. Zoetermeer: Meinema, 2002.

———"Pela as Inclusive Socio-Cosmic System in the Central Moluccas." In M. E. Brinkman and D. van Keulen, eds, *Christian Identity in Cross-Cultural Perspective*, 18–40. Studies in Reformed Theology 8. Zoetermeer: Meinema, 2003.

Singgih, G. "Indonesian Churches and the Problem of Nationality and Ethnicity." In E. A. J. G. van der Borght *et al.*, eds. *Faith and Ethnicity I*, 103–23. Studies in Reformed Theology 6. Zoetermeer: Meinema, 2002.

Steenbrink, K. "Christianity and Islam: Civilizations or Religions? Contemporary Indonesian Discussions." *Exchange* 33.3 (2004): 223–43.

———*Dutch Colonialism and Indonesian Islam: Contacts and Conflicts 1596–1950*. Currents of Encounter 7. Amsterdam/Atlanta: Rodopi, 1993.

———"Indonesia: A Christian Minority in a Strong Position." In F. J. Verstraelen, ed., *Missiology: An Ecumenical Introduction. Texts and Contexts of Global Christianity*, 88–98. Grand Rapids: Eerdmans, 1995.

———"Indonesian Churches 1978–1984: Main Trends, Issues and Problems." *Exchange* 13.39 (1984): 1–31.

Sumartana, T. *Mission at the Crossroads: Indigenous Churches, European Missionaries, Islamic Association and Socio-Religious Change in Java 1812–1936*. Leiderdorp: De Zijl, 1991.

Titaley, J. A. "The Pancasila of Indonesia: A Lost Ideal?" In E. A. J. G. van der Borght *et al.*, eds, *Faith and Ethnicity I*, 37–102. Studies in Reformed Theology 6. Zoetermeer: Meinema, 2002.

Tobing, P. O. *The Structure of Batak-Toba Belief in the High God*. Amsterdam: South and South-East Celebes Institute for Culture, 1956.

Van Hooijdonk, P. G. "Jesus as Guru: A Christology in the Context of Java (Indonesia)." *Exchange* 13.39 (1984): 32–57.

Yewangoe, A. "The Trinity in the Context of Tribal Religion." *Studies in Interreligious Dialogue* 13.1 (2003): 86–105.

Images of Jesus from an Islamic (Indonesian) Context

Banawiratma, J. B. "Contextual Christology and Christian Praxis: An Indonesian Reflection." *East Asian Pastoral Review* 37 (2000): 173–83.

Mawene, M. T. "Christ and Theology of Liberation in Papua." *Exchange* 33.2 (2004): 153–79.

Rambitan, S. "Jesus in Islamic Context of Indonesia." *REC Focus* 3 (2003): 38–48.

Steenbrink, K., "Jesus as a Javanese Prophet." In M. Frederiks *et al.*, eds, *Towards an Intercultural Theology: Essays in Honour of Jan B. Jongeneel*, 137–52. IIMO Resarch Publication 61. Zoetermeer: Meinema, 2003.

Tebay, N. K. "Jesus as *Iniuwai Ibo* (The Great Elder Brother) – Christology Expressed in the Hymns of Mee Christians of West Papua." *Exchange* 29.4 (2000): 311–30.

Yewangoe, A. A. "An Asian Perspective on the Cross and Suffering." In Y. Tesfai, ed., *The Scandal of a Crucified World: Perspectives on the Cross and Suffering*, 61–74. Maryknoll: Orbis, 1994.

——*Theologia Crucis in Asia: Asian Christian Views on Suffering in the Face of Overwhelming Poverty and Multifaceted Religiosity in Asia*. Amsterdam: Rodopi, 1987.

African Studies on Jesus

Background Studies

Abble, A. *et al. Les Prêtres Noirs S'Interrogent*. Rencontres 47. Paris: Les Editions du Cerf, 1956.

Abe, G. "Redemption, Reconciliation, Propitiation." *Journal of Theology for Southern Africa* 95 (1996): 3–12.

Adeyemo, T. *Salvation in African Tradition*. Nairobi: Evangel Publishing House, 1997.

Anderson, A. "Exorcism and Conversion to African Pentecostalism." *Exchange* 35 (2006): 116–33.

Appiah, K. A. "Old Gods, New Worlds." In P. H. Coetzee and A. P. J. Roux, eds, *The African Philosophy Reader*, 245–74. London/New York: Routledge, 1998.

Appiah-Kubi, K., and S. Torres, eds. *African Theology en Route*. Maryknoll: Orbis, 1979.

Balcomb, A. "Faith or Suspicion? Theological dialogue north and south of the Limpopo with special reference to the theologies of Kwame Bediako and Andrew Walls." *Journal of Theology for Southern Africa* 100 (1998): 3–19.

Bediako, K. "African Theology as a Challenge for Western Theology." In M. E. Brinkman and D. van Keulen, eds, *Christian Identity in Cross-Cultural Perspective*, 52–67. Studies in Reformed Theology 8. Zoetermeer: Meinema, 2003.

——*Christianity in Africa: The Renewal of a Non-Western Religion*. Edinburgh: Edinburgh University Press, 1995.

——"'Ethiopia Shall Soon Stretch out Her Hands to God' (Ps. 68, 31). African Christians Living the Faith: A Turning Point in Christian History?" In K. Bediako *et al.*, eds, *A New Day Dawning: African Christians Living the Gospel: Essays in Honour of Dr. J. J. (Hans) Visser*, 30–40. Zoetermeer: Boekencentrum, 2004.

——"Types of African Theology." In C. Fyfe and A. Walls, eds, *Christianity in Africa in the 1990s*, 56–69. Edinburgh: Centre of African Studies, University of Edinburgh, 1996.

Brand, G. "Salvation in African Christian Theology: A Typology of Existing Approaches." *Exchange* 28.3 (1999): 193–223.

Bujo, B. *African Theology in its Social Context*. Maryknoll: Orbis, 1992.

——"A Christocentric Ethic for Black Africa." *Theology Digest* 30.2 (1982): 143–46.

Bujo, B., and J. I. Muya, eds. *African Theology in the 21ˢᵗ Century: The Contribution of the Pioneers*, vol. I. Nairobi: Paulines Publications Africa, 2003.

Dickson, K. A. *Theology in Africa*. London/Maryknoll: Dartman, Longman and Todd/Orbis, 1984.

Dickson, K. A., and P. Ellingworth, eds. *Biblical Revelation and African Beliefs*. London: Lutterworth, 1972.

Dovlo, E. "Ancestors and Soteriology in African and Japanese Religions." *Studies in Interreligious Dialogue* 3 (1993): 48–57.

Ela, J.-M. *African Cry.* Trans. Robert R. Barr. Maryknoll: Orbis, 1986.

——*My Faith as an African.* Maryknoll: Orbis, 1990.

Greene, S. E. "Religion, History and the Supreme Gods of Africa: A Contribution to the Debate." *Journal of Religion in Africa* 26.2 (1996): 122–38.

Gyekye, K. "The Problem of Evil: An Akan Perspective." In E. C. Eze, *African Philosophy: An Anthology,* 468–71. Malden/Oxford: Blackwell, 1998.

Heijke, J. P. "Africa: Between Cultural Rootedness and Liberation." In F. J. Verstraelen, ed., *Missiology: An Ecumenical Introduction. Texts and Contexts of Global Christianity,* 265–80. Grand Rapids: Eerdmans, 1995.

Holme, L. R. *The Extinction of the Christian Churches in North Africa.* New York/London: Burt Franklin, [1898] 1969.

Horton, R. *Patterns of Thought in Africa and the West: Essays on Magic, Religion and Science.* Cambridge: Cambridge University Press, 1993.

Idowu, E. B. *African Traditional Religion: A Definition.* London: SCM, 1973.

——*Olódùmarè: God in Yoruba Belief.* London: Longman, 1966.

Isichei, E. *A History of Christianity in Africa: From Antiquity to the Present.* Grand Rapids/Lawrenceville: Eerdmans/Africa World Press, 1995.

Kalu, O. U. *Power, Poverty and Prayer: The Challenges of Poverty and Pluralism in African Christianity, 1960–1996.* Studies in the Intercultural History of Christianity 122. Frankfurt: Peter Lang, 2000.

Kalu, O. U., ed. *African Christianity: An African Story.* Pretoria: Department of Church History, University of Pretoria, 2005.

Kombo, J. O. *The Doctrine of God in African Christian Thought: An Assessment of African Inculturation Theology from a Trintarian Perspective.* Unpublished Doctoral diss. Stellenbosch: University of Stellenbosch, 2000.

Lupande, J. M. et al. "The Sukuma Sacrificial Goat: A Basis for Inculturation in Africa." *African Ecclesial Review (AFER)* 40 (1998): 244–54.

Magesa, L. *African Religion: The Moral Traditions of Abundant Life.* Maryknoll: Orbis, 1997.

Masalo, D. A. *African Philosophy in Search of Identity.* Edinburgh: Edinburgh University Press, 1994.

Mbiti, J. S. *African Religions and Philosophy.* Oxford: Heineman, 1990 [1969].

——*Concepts of God in Africa.* London: SPCK, 1970.

Mogoba, M. S. "Christianity in an African Context." *Journal of Theology for Southern Africa* 52 (1985): 5–16.

Mugambi, J. N. K. *African Christian Theology: An Introduction.* Nairobi: Heinemann Kenya, 1989.

——*From Liberation to Reconstruction: African Christian Theology after the Cold War.* Nairobi: East African Educational Publishers, 1995.

Munga, S.I. *Beyond the Controversy: A Study of African Theologies of Inculturation and Liberation.* Lund: Lund University Press, 1998.

Muya, J. I. "Bénézet Bujo: The Awakening of a Systematic and Authentically African Thought." In B. Bujo and J. I. Muya, eds, *African Theology in the 21ˢᵗ Century: The Contribution of the Pioneers,* vol. I, 107–49. Limuru: Paulines Publications Africa, 2003.

Mwaura, P. "African Independent Churches: Their Role and Contribution to African Christianity." In K. Bediako et al., eds, *A New Day Dawning: African Christians Living the Gospel: Essays in Honour of Dr. J. J. (Hans) Visser*, 96–115. Zoetermeer: Boekencentrum, 2004.

——"Gender and Power in African Christianity: African Instituted Churches and Pentecostal Churches." In O. U. Kalu, ed., *African Christianity: An African Story*, 410–45. Pretoria: Department of Church History, University of Pretoria, 2005.

Nnamani, A. G. *The Paradox of a Suffering God: On the Classical, Modern-Western and Third World Struggles to Harmonise the Incompatible Attributes of the Trinitarian God*. Studies in the Intercultural History of Christianity 95. Frankfurt: Peter Lang, 1994.

Nyamiti, C. "Uganda Martyrs: Ancestors of All Mankind." *African Christian Studies* 1–2 (1985–1986): 41–66.

Oborji, F. A. "Healing in the African Independent Churches: An Encounter between Traditional Religiosity and Christianity?" *Studies in Interreligious Dialogue* 15.2 (2005): 182–210.

——*Towards a Christian Theology of African Religion: Issues of Interpretation and Mission*. Limuru: AMECEA Gaba Publications, 2005.

Parrat, J. *Reinventing Christianity: African Theology Today*. Grand Rapids: Eerdmans, 1995.

Parratt , J., ed. *A Reader in African Christian Theology*. New ed. London: SPCK, 1997.

Parrinder, E. G. *African Traditional Religion*. London: Hutchinson's Univ. Libr., 1974.

P'Bitek, O. *African Religions in Western Scholarship*. Kampala: East African Literature Bureau, 1971.

Persoon, J. "New Perspectives on Ethiopian and African Christianity: Communalities and Contrasts in Twentieth Century Religious Experience." *Exchange* 34.4 (2005): 306–36.

Pobee, J. S. "Health, Healing and Religion: An African View." *International Review of Mission* 90.356/7 (2001): 55–64.

——"The Sources of African Theology." In J. Parratt, ed., *A Reader in African Christian Theology*, 23–28. New ed. London: SPCK, 1997.

——*Towards an African Theology*. Nashville: Abingdon, 1979.

Sanneh, L. *Translating the Message: The Missionary Impact on Culture*. New York: Orbis Books, 1989.

Sawyer, H. "What is African Theology?" In J. Parratt, ed., *A Reader in African Christian Theology*, 9–22. New ed. London: SPCK, 1997.

ter Haar, G. *Spirit of Africa: The Healing Ministry of Archbishop Milingo of Zambia*. London: Hurst, 1992.

Tshibangu, T. "The Task and Method of Theology in Africa." In J. Parratt, ed., *A Reader in African Christian Theology*, 29–35. New ed. London: SPCK, 1997.

——"Vers une théologie de couleur africaine?" *Revue du Clergé Africain* 15 (1960): 333–46.

Ubrurhe, J. O. "The African Concept of Sacrifice: A Starting Point for Inculturation." *African Ecclesial Review (AFER)* 40 (1998): 203–15.

Vanneste, A. "D'abord une vraie théologie." *Revue du Clergé Africain* 15 (1960): 346–52.

van 't Spijker, G. "Credal Hymns as Summa Theologiae: New Credal Hymns in Rwanda after the 1994 War and Genocide." *Exchange* 30.3 (2001): 256–75.

van 't Spijker, G. "Man's Kinship with Nature: African Reflection on Creation." *Exchange* 23.2 (1994): 89–148.

van 't Spijker, G. "The Role of Social Anthropology in the Debate on Funeral Rites in Africa." *Exchange* 34.3 (2005): 156–76.

Villa-Vicencio, C. *A Theology of Reconstruction: Nation Building and Human Rights*. Cambridge: Cambridge University Press, 1992.

Walls, A. "African Christianity in the History of Religions." In C. Fyfe and A. Walls, eds, *Christianity in Africa in the 1990s*, 56–69. Edinburgh: Centre of African Studies, University of Edinburgh, 1996.

Wiredu, K. "On Decolonising African Religions." In P. H. Coetzee and A. P. J. Roux, eds, *The African Philosophy Reader*, 186–204. London/New York: Routledge, 1998.

Young, J. U. *African Theology: A Critical Analysis and Annotated Bibliography*. Westport: Greenwood Press, 1993.

African Images of Jesus

Akper, G. I. *Contemporary African Perspectives on Jesus' Cross and Human Suffering: A Critical Comparison of African Christologies*. Unpublished Doctoral diss. Stellenbosch: University of Stellenbosch, 2004.

Akrong, A. "Christology from an African Perspective." In J. S. Pobee, ed., *Exploring Afro-Christology*, 119–31. Studies in the Intercultural History of Christianity 79. Frankfurt: Peter Lang, 1992.

Appiah-Kubi, K. "Christology." In J. Parratt, ed., *A Reader in African Christian Theology*, 65–74. New ed. London: SPCK, 1997.

——"Jesus Christ: Some Christological Aspects from African Perspectives." *Voices from the Third World* 16.2 (1993): 7–29.

Bahemuka, J. "The Hidden Christ in African Traditional Religion." In J. N. K. Mugambi and L. Magesa, eds, *Jesus in African Christianity: Experimentation and Diversity in African Christianity*, 1–6. Nairobi: Initiatives, 1989.

Bediako, K. "How is Jesus Christ Lord? Aspects of an Evangelical Christian Apologetics in the Context of African Religious Pluralism." *Exchange* 25.1 (1996): 27–42.

——*Jesus in African Culture: A Ghanaian Perspective*. Accra: Asempa, 1990.

Bourdillon, M. F. C. *Where are the Ancestors? Changing Culture in Zimbabwe*. Harare: University of Zimbabwe Publications, 1993.

Bujo, B. *Christmas: God becomes Man in Black Africa*. Nairobi: Paulines Publications, 1995.

Chikane, F. "The Incarnation in the Life of the People in Southern Africa." *Journal of Theology for Southern Africa* 51 (1985): 37–50.

Dickson, K. "The Theology of the Cross." In J. Parratt, ed., *A Reader in African Christian Theology*. New ed. London: SPCK, 1997.

Eboussi-Boulaga, F. *Christianity without Fetishes: An African Critique and Recapture of Christianity*. Maryknoll: Orbis Books, 1984.

Ela, J.-M. "The Memory of the African People and the Cross of Christ." In Y. Tesfai, ed., *The Scandal of a Crucified World: Perspectives on the Cross and Suffering*, 17–35. Maryknoll: Orbis, 1994.

Ezeh, U. A. *Jesus Christ the Ancestor: An African Contextual Christology in the Light of the Major Dogmatic Christological Definitions of the Church from the Council of Nicea (325) to Chalcedon (451)*. Studies in the Intercultural History of Christianity 130. Bern: Peter Lang, 2003.

Heijke, J. "Fabien Eboussi Boulaga's Fight against Fetishism." *Exchange* 30.4 (2001): 300–27.

Kabasélé, F. "Christ as Ancestor and Elder Brother." In J. Schreiter, ed., *Faces of Jesus in Africa*, 116–27. Maryknoll: Orbis, 2000.

——"Christ as Chief." In J. Schreiter, ed., *Faces of Jesus in Africa*, 103–15. Maryknoll: Orbis, 2000.

——"Jenseits der Modelle." In F. Kabasélé, ed., *Der Schwarze Christus: Wege afrikanischer Christologie*, 198–205. Theologie der dritten Welt 12. Freiburg: Herder, 1986. (Trans. of *Chemins de la christologie africaine*, 138–61. Paris: Desclée, 1986).

Kolié, C. "Christ as Healer?" In J. Schreiter, ed., *Faces of Jesus in Africa*, 128–50. Maryknoll: Orbis, 2000.

Kurewa, J. W. Z. "Who Do You Say That I Am?" *International Review of Mission* 69.274 (1980): 182–88.

Luneau, R. "Afrikanische Frauen sprechen von Jesus: Réné Luneau im Gespräch mit Bibiana Tshibola und Yvette Aklé." In F. Kabasélé, ed., *Der Schwarze Christus: Wege afrikanischer Christologie*, 198–205. Theologie der dritten Welt 12. Freiburg: Herder, 1986.

——"Einleitung: Und ihr, was sagt ihr von Jesus Christus?" In F. Kabasélé, ed., *Der Schwarze Christus: Wege afrikanischer Christologie*, 7–20. Theologie der dritten Welt 12. Freiburg: Herder, 1986.

Maimela, S. "Jesus Christ: The Liberator and Hope of Oppressed Africa." In J. S. Pobee, ed., *Exploring Afro-Christology*, 31–41. Studies in the Intercultural History of Christianity 79. Frankfurt: Peter Lang, 1992.

——"The Suffering of Human Divisions and the Cross." In Y. Tesfai, ed., *The Scandal of a Crucified World: Perspectives on the Cross and Suffering*, 36–47. Maryknoll: Orbis, 1994.

Magesa, L. "Christ the Liberator and Africa Today." In J. Schreiter, ed., *Faces of Jesus in Africa*, 151–63. Maryknoll: Orbis, 2000.

Maluleke, T. S. "Christ in Africa: The Influence of Multi-Culturity on the Experience of Christ." *Journal of Black Theology in South Africa* 8.1 (1994): 49–64.

——"Will Jesus ever be the Same Again: What are the Africans doing to Him?" *Journal of Black Theology in South Africa* 11.1 (1997): 13–30.

Manus, U. C. "African Christologies: The Centre-Piece of African Christian Theology." *Zeitschrift für Missionswissenschaft und Religionswissenschaft* 82 (1998): 3–23.

——*Christ, the African King: New Testament Christology*. Studies in the Intercultural History of Christianity 82. Frankfurt: Peter Lang, 1993.

——"Jesu Kristi Oba: A Christology of 'Christ the King' among the Indigenous Christian Churches in Yorubaland, Nigeria." *Asia Journal of Theology* 5.2 (1991): 311–30.

Mbiti, J. S. "Is Jesus Christ in African Religion?" In J. S. Pobee, ed., *Exploring Afro-Christology*, 21–29. Studies in the Intercultural History of Christianity 79. Frankfurt: Peter Lang, 1992.

——"Some African Concepts of Christology." In G. F. Vicedom, ed., *Christ and the Younger Churches: Theological Contributions from Asia, Africa and Latin America*, 51–62. SPCK Theological Collections 15. London: SPCK, 1972.

Mofokeng, T. A. *The Crucified among the Crossbearers: Towards a Black Christology.* Kampen: Kok, 1983.

——"The Crucified and Permanent Crossbearing: A Christology for Comprehensive Liberation." In N. Schreurs and H. van de Sandt, eds, *De ene Jezus en de vele culturen: Christologie en contextualiteit*, 37–49. Tilburg: Tilburg University Press, 1992.

——"Hermeneutical Explorations for Black Christology." In J. S. Pobee, ed., *Exploring Afro-Christology*, 85–94. Studies in the Intercultural History of Christianity 79. Frankfurt: Peter Lang, 1992.

Mugambi, J. N. K. "Christological Paradigms in African Christianity." In J. N. K. Mugambi and L. Magesa, eds, *Jesus in African Christianity: Experimentation and Diversity in African Christianity*, 136–61. Nairobi: Initiatives, 1989.

Mwaura, P. N. "Gender and Power in African Christianity: African Instituted Churches and Pentecostal Churches." In O. U. Kalu, ed., *African Christianity: An African Story*, 410–45. Pretoria: Department of Church History, University of Pretoria, 2005.

Nasimiyu-Wasike, A. "Christology and an African Woman's Experience." In J. Schreiter, ed., *Faces of Jesus in Africa*, 70–81. Maryknoll: Orbis, 2000.

Njoroge, N. J. "Confessing Christ in Africa Today." In J. S. Pobee, ed., *Exploring Afro-Christology*, 131–36. Studies in the Intercultural History of Christianity 79. Frankfurt: Peter Lang, 1992.

Nkwoka, A. O. "Jesus as Eldest Brother (Okpara): An Igbo Paradigm for Christology in the African Context." *Asia Journal of Theology* 5.1 (1991): 87–103.

Nthamburi, Z. "Christ as Seen by an African: A Christological Quest." In J. Schreiter, ed., *Faces of Jesus in Africa*, 65–69. Maryknoll: Orbis, 2000.

Nyamiti, C. "African Christologies Today." In J. Schreiter, ed., *Faces of Jesus in Africa*, 3–23. Maryknoll: Orbis, 2000.

——*Christ as our Ancestor: Christology from an African Perspective.* Gweru: Mambo, 1984.

——"Comparison between African Brother-Ancestorship and Christ's Relationship to Men." *Voices from the Third World* 8 (1985): 16–19.

——"Contemporary African Christologies: An Assessment and Practical Suggestions." In R. Gibellini, ed., *Paths of African Theology*, 62–77. Maryknoll: Orbis Books, 1994.

——"Uganda Martyrs: Ancestors of all Mankind." *African Christian Studies* 2 (1986): 41–66.

Obaje, Y. A. "Theocentric Christology." In J. S. Pobee, ed., *Exploring Afro-Christology*, 43–53. Studies in the Intercultural History of Christianity 79. Frankfurt: Peter Lang, 1992.

Oduyoye, M. A. "An African Woman's Christ." *Voices from the Third World* 11.2 (1988): 119–24.

Oduyoye, M. A., and E. Amoah. "The Christ for African Women." In V. Fabella and M. A. Oduyoye, eds, *With Passion and Compassion: Third World Women Doing Theology*, 35–46. Maryknoll: Orbis, 1988.

Pénoukou, E. J. "Christology in the Village." In J. Schreiter, ed., *Faces of Jesus in Africa*, 24–51. Maryknoll: Orbis, 2000.

Pobee, J. S. "Confessing Christ à la African Instituted Churches." In J. S. Pobee, ed. *Exploring Afro-Christology*, 145–51. Studies in the Intercultural History of Christianity 79. Frankfurt: Peter Lang, 1992.

——"In Search of Christology in Africa: Some Considerations for Today." In J. S. Pobee, ed., *Exploring Afro-Christology*, 9–20. Studies in the Intercultural History of Christianity 79. Frankfurt: Peter Lang, 1992.

——"Nog éénmaal Christus onze voorvader." *Wereld en Zending* 25.3 (1996): 34–40.

——*West Africa: Christ would be an African Too.* Gospel and Culture Studies 9. Geneva: WCC Publications, 1996.

Pobee, J. S., ed. *Exploring Afro-Christology.* Studies in the Intercultural History of Christianity 79. Frankfurt: Peter Lang, 1992.

Sanon, A. T. "Jesus, Master of Initiation." In J. Schreiter, ed., *Faces of Jesus in Africa*, 85–102. Maryknoll: Orbis, 2000.

Sawyer, H. *God. Ancestor or Creator? Aspects of Traditional Belief in Ghana, Nigeria and Sierra Leone.* London: Longman, 1970.

Schoffeleers, M. "Christ in African Folk Theology: The Nganga Paradigm." In T. D. Blakely *et al.*, eds, *Religion in Africa: Experience and Expression*, 73–88. London/Portmouth: James Currey/Heinemann, 1994.

Schreiter, R. J. "Introduction: Jesus Christ in Africa Today." In J. Schreiter, ed., *Faces of Jesus in Africa*, vii–xiii. Maryknoll: Orbis, 2000.

Setiloane, G. "Confessing Christ Today from an African Perspective: Man and Community." *Journal of Theology for Southern Africa* 12 (1975): 29–38.

Shorter, A. *Jesus and the Witchdoctor: An Approach to Healing and Wholeness.* Maryknoll: Orbis, 1985.

Stinton, D. B. "Africa, East and West." In J. Parratt, ed., *An Introduction to Third World Theologies*, 105–36. Cambridge: Cambridge University Press, 2004.

——*Jesus of Africa: Voices of Contemporary African Christology.* Faith and Cultures Series. Maryknoll: Orbis, 2004.

——"Jesus of Africa: Voices of Contemporary African Theology." In T. Merrigan and J. Haers, eds, *The Myriad Christ: Plurality and the Quest for Unity in Contemporary Christology*, 287–313. Louvain: Louvain University Press, 2000.

Tesfai, Y., ed. *The Scandal of a Crucified World: Perspectives on the Cross and Suffering.* Maryknoll: Orbis, 1994.

Udoh, E. *Guest Christology: An Interpretative View of the Christological Problem in Africa.* PhD dissertation. Princeton: Princeton Theological Seminary, 1993 (microfilm); also published as vol. 59 in the series Studies in the Intercultural History of Christianity. Frankfurt: Peter Lang, 1988.

Upkong, J. S. "Christology and Inculturation: A New Testament Perspective." In R. Gibellini, ed., *Paths of African Theology*, 40–61. Maryknoll: Orbis, 1994.

Waliggo, J. M. "African Christology in a Situation of Suffering." In J. Schreiter, ed., *Faces of Jesus in Africa*, 164–80. Maryknoll: Orbis, 2000.

Waruta, D. W. "Who is Jesus Christ for Africans Today? Prophet, Priest, Potentate." In J. Schreiter, ed., *Faces of Jesus in Africa*, 52–64. Maryknoll: Orbis, 2000.

Literature on Dialogue

The Christian–Buddhist Dialogue on Jesus

Chung, P. S. "Martin Luther and Shinran: The Presence of Christ in Justification and Salvation in a Buddhist-Christian Context." *Asia Journal of Theology* 18.2 (2004): 295–309.

Cobb, J. *Beyond Dialogue: Towards a Mutual Transformation of Christianity and Buddhism*. Philadelphia: Fortress Press, 1982.

Cornille, C. "Buddhist Views of Christ and the Question of Uniqueness." In T. Merrigan and J. Haers, eds, *The Myriad Christ: Plurality and the Quest for Unity in Contemporary Christology*, 249–62. Louvain: Louvain University Press, 2000.

Derrett, J. D. M. "St-John's Jesus and the Buddha." In R. Malek, ed., *The Chinese Face of Jesus Christ*, vol. I, 127–40. Monumenta Serica Monograph Series 50/1. Nettetal: Steyler Verlag, 2002.

de Silva, L. A. "Buddhism and Christianity Relativised." *Dialogue* 9 (1982): 43–72.

——"Emergent Theology in the Context of Buddhism." In D. J. Elwood, ed., *Asian Christian Theology: Emerging Themes*, 220–38. Philadelphia: Westminster, 1980.

——"The Problem of the Self in Buddhism and Christianity." In D. J. Elwood, ed., *What Asian Christians Are Thinking: A Theological Source Book*, 105–18. Quezon City: New Day Publishers, 1976.

Drummond, R. H. "A Broader Vision: Perspectives on the Buddha and the Christ." *Studies in Interreligious Dialogue* 6 (1996): 181–97.

Dykstra Eusden, J. "Christology: The Dialogue of East and West." In R. F. Berkey and S. A. Edwards, eds, *Christology in Dialogue*, 258–66. Cleveland: Pilgrim Press, 1993.

Fernhout, R. "Kevalam Khitthassa punnena mutti (Salvation through the Merit of Christ Alone): An Attempt to Translate the Central Theme of Protestant Christianity into the Language of Theravada Buddhism." In I. Daneel et al., eds, *Fullness of Life for All: Challenges for Mission in Early 21st Century*, 279–91. Currents of Encounter 22. Amsterdam/New York: Rodopi, 2003.

Gross, R. M. "This Buddhist's View of Jesus." *Buddhist-Christian Studies* 19.1 (1999): 62–75.

Hanaoka-Kawamura, E. "Buddhism and Christianity from a Christian-Buddhist Perspective." In J. D. Gort et al., eds, *Religions View Religions: Explorations in Pursuit of Understanding*, 283–94. Currents of Encounter 25. Amsterdam/New York: Rodopi, 2006.

Keel, H.-S. "Meister Eckhart's Asian Christianity: Mysticism as a Bridge between Christianity and Zen Buddhism." *Studies in Interreligious Dialogue* 14.1 (2004): 75–94.

Keenan, J. *The Meaning of Christ: A Mahayana Theology*. Maryknoll: Orbis, 1989.

Makransky, J. "Buddhist Analogues of Sin and Grace: A Dialogue with Augustine." *Studies in Interreligious Dialogue* 15.1 (2005): 5–15.

Pieris, A. *Love Meets Wisdom: A Christian Experience of Buddhism*. Maryknoll: Orbis, 1988.

——"Western Christianity and Asian Buddhism: A Theological Reading of Historical Encounters." *Dialogue* 7.2 (1980): 49–85.

Schmidt-Leukel, P. "Buddhism and Christianity: Antagonistic or Complementary?" *Studies in World Christianity* 9.2 (2003): 265–79.

Takizawa, K. *Reflexionen über die universale Grundlage von Buddhismus und Christentum*. Studien zur interkulturellen Geschichte des Christentums 24. Frankfurt: Peter Lang, 1980.

Vetter, T. "John B. Cobb, Jr. and the Encounter with Buddhism." In J. D. Gort et al., eds, *Dialogue and Syncretism: An Interdisciplinary Approach*, 122–33. Currents of Encounter 1. Grand Rapids/Amsterdam: Eerdmans/Rodopi, 1989.

Von Brück, M. "What do I Expect Buddhists to Discover in Jesus? 'Christ and the Buddha embracing each other'." In P. Schmidt-Leukel et al., eds, *Buddhist Perceptions of Jesus*, 158–75. St. Ottilien: EOS-Verlag, 2001.

Vroom, H. M. "No-Self, Emptiness, and God." In H. M.Vroom, *No Other Gods: Christian Belief in Dialogue with Buddhism, Hinduism, and Islam*, 9–42. Trans. Lucy Jansen. Grand Rapids: Eerdmans, 1996.

——*A Spectrum of Worldviews: An Introduction to Philosophy of Religion in a Pluralistic World*. Trans. Maurice and Alice Greidanus. Currents of Encounter 29. Amsterdam/New York: Rodopi, 2006.

Wayman, A. " Buddha as Savior." *Studia Missionalia* 29 (1980): 191–207.

——"The Guru in Buddhism." *Studia Missionalia* 36 (1987): 195–213.

Yagi, S., and L. Schwidler. *A Bridge to Buddhist-Christian Dialogue*. New York: Paulist Press, 1990.

The Christian–Hindu Dialogue on Jesus

Ariarajah, S. W. *Hindus and Christians: A Century of Protestant Ecumenical Thought*. Amsterdam: Rodopi/Eerdmans, 1991.

Dhavamony, M. *Hindu-Christian Dialogue: Theological Soundings and Perspectives*. Currents of Encounter 18. Amsterdam/New York: Rodopi, 2002.

Dupuis, J. *Jesus Christ at the Encounter of World Religions*. Maryknoll: Orbis, 1991.

Klootwijk, E. *Commitment and Openness: The Interreligious Dialogue and Theology of Religions in the Work of Stanley J. Samartha*. Zoetermeer: Boekencentrum, 1992.

Krieger, D. J. "Salvation in the World: A Hindu-Christian Dialogue on Hope and Liberation." In J. D. Gort et al., eds, *Dialogue and Syncretism: An Interdisciplinary Approach*, 163–73. Currents of Encounter 1. Grand Rapids/Amsterdam: Eerdmans/Rodopi, 1989.

Panikkar, R. *The Silence of God: The Answer of the Buddha*. Maryknoll: Orbis, 1990.

Samartha, S. *Courage for Dialogue: Ecumenical Issues in Inter-religious Relationships*. Geneva: World Council of Churches, 1981.

Vroom, H. M. "God has an Inexhaustible Number of Names." In H. M. Vroom, *No Other Gods: Christian Belief in Dialogue with Buddhism, Hinduism, and Islam*, 45–78. Trans. Lucy Jansen. Grand Rapids: Eerdmans, 1993.

Ward, K. "Christian Vedanta: An Absurdity or an Opportunity?" In T. Merrigan and J. Haers, eds, *The Myriad Christ: Plurality and the Quest for Unity in Contemporary Christology*, 235–47. Louvain: Louvain University Press, 2000.

The Christian–Muslim Dialogue on Jesus

Borrmans, M. "Muslims and the Mystery of the Cross." *Vidyajyoti* 42 (1978): 115–26.

Goddard, H. *Muslim Perceptions of Christianity*. London: Grey Seal, 1996.

Kerr, D. A. "Christology in Christian-Muslim Dialogue." In R. F. Berkey and S. A. Edwards, eds, *Christology in Dialogue*, 201–20. Cleveland: Pilgrim Press, 1993.

Leirvik, O. *Images of Jesus Christ in Islam: Introduction, Survey of Research, Issues of Dialogue*. Studia Missionalia Upsaliensia LXXVI. Uppsala: Swedish Institute of Missionary Research, 1999.

Logister, W. "The Challenge of Mohammed about the Place of Jesus Christ." In T. Merrigan and J. Haers, eds, *The Myriad Christ: Plurality and the Quest for Unity in Contemporary Christology*, 263–72. Louvain: Louvain University Press, 2000.

Malik, A. J. "Confessing Christ in the Islamic Context." In R. S. Sugirtharajah, ed., *Asian Faces of Jesus*, 75–84. London: SCM, 1993 (also in *CTC Bulletin* 7.3 [1987]: 37–43).

Nasr, S. H. "De islamitische visie op het christendom." *Concilium* 22.1 (1986): 12–20.

Parrinder, G. *Jesus in the Qur'an*. Oxford: Oneworld Publications, 1995.

Ridgeon, L., ed. *Islamic Interpretations of Christianity*. Richmond: Curzon, 2001.

Roest Crollius, A. A. "Salvation in the Qu'an." *Studia Missionalia* 29 (1980): 125–39.

Vroom, H. M. "The One God, the Prophet and the Cross." In H. M. Vroom, *No Other Gods: Christian Belief in Dialogue with Buddhism, Hinduism, and Islam*, 79–115. Trans. Lucy Jansen. Grand Rapids: Eerdmans, 1996.

Waardenburg, J. "Classical Attitudes in Islam towards Other Religions." In J. D. Gort et al., eds, *Religions View Religions: Explorations in Pursuit of Understanding*, 127–48. Currents of Encounter 25. Amsterdam/New York: Rodopi, 2006.

Index of Names

Index of Subjects